THIS
SCEPTRED ISLE:
THE DYNASTIES

THIS SCEPTRED ISLE: THE DYNASTIES

CHRISTOPHER LEE

This book accompanies the series
This Sceptred Isle – The Dynasties
written by Christopher Lee and produced by Pete Atkin
as a Martin Weitz Associates production for BBC Radio 4
and first broadcast in 2002.

First published in 2002
© Christopher Lee 2002
The moral right of the author has been asserted.

ISBN 0 563 53748 5

Published by BBC Worldwide Limited
Woodlands, 80 Wood Lane, London W12 0TT

Commissioning editor: Sally Potter
Project editor: Christopher Tinker
Copy-editor: Esther Jagger
Proofreader: Margaret Cornell
Additional checking: David Appleby
Picture researcher: Deirdre O'Day

Set in Bembo by BBC Worldwide Limited
Printed and bound in Great Britain by
Butler & Tanner Limited, Frome, Somerset
Colour separations by Radstock Reproductions Limited
Jacket and plate sections printed by
Lawrence-Allen Limited

CONTENTS

For Bertie
Incomparable breeding, incomparable company.

INTRODUCTION

British history written as a saga may easily trivialize and glamorize what is a serious subject. Yet it can be presented as a general story rather than an academic discipline.

Many histories of the ways and means of the people of these islands of Britain have tended to be colourful and not always accurate accounts. It is no surprise, then, that revisionists are scornful of many earlier histories than their own. This scepticism is healthy, although the smugness which too often tags along is less agreeable. A colleague coined the phrase, 'a spite of historians' – an exaggeration, of course, but only an exaggeration.

It is important that historians should not treat their readers with arrogance. We may all be foolish, but not all will be fools. So we look for a balance between, on the one hand, telling the story of Britain to a wide audience without a background knowledge of dates and issues, and, on the other hand, sufficient analysis and explanation to satisfy the zealots. Neither approach is wrong. However, the two ways rarely meet unless a specific moment of history is the subject of the story. Here we have the dilemma for the historian or history writer: for whom is the history written?

When I wrote *This Sceptred Isle*, I had in mind the large group of people who wanted to know something without first needing a good grounding in history. Typically, the audience turned out to include those who wanted to know more than they had learned years ago (in some case many years, in others very few) but had had little time to catch up on the history of these islands. Since it covered such a huge period – from 55BC to AD1999 – *This Sceptred Isle* caused me enormous frustration, for there were subjects, and most of all people, to which and to whom I wanted to give more space but could not do so. The purpose of *The Dynasties* is to start, but only start, to fulfil that wish.

This is the story of powerful families. Here are the men and women who, through ten centuries of British history, have held influence and therefore often power over those who were nominally the most powerful in the land.

Once there were separate regions called Mercia, Wessex, Northumbria and so on, their people led by powerful princes. Here were the Saxon origins of kingship.

In return for allegiance a king would promise to protect his people from their enemies. But who would protect the king? The king's enemies were not all Frenchmen and invaders from what we now call Scandinavia. Most of those who would usurp his authority, take his throne and therefore probably his life were about him. So perhaps we think too much of the power of monarchs. Should we not think more about the powerful families who kept the throne intact? Further, those same families could bring about a monarch's downfall and, of course, suffer the consequences of their own failures.

Within these families lay the real power of the throne and the longer and sometimes bloodier story of these islands. Take, for example, the eleventh- and twelfth-century families who commanded the English–Welsh border – the marches, from the Old French word *marchir*. The so-called marcher lords were there to protect the kingdom from invasion; in return they had rights over the territory granted by the monarch, and even their own jurisdiction. By the beginning of the twelfth century the marches of the Welsh border were well established; here were Lincoln, Warren, Poole, Corbet, Mortimer, Clare, Lancaster, Bohun and Gifford. Long after the conquest, Edward I advanced and overpowered thirteenth-century Wales; more marcher lords were created. These royal political gamekeepers protected the monarch and the kingdom as best they could – and, of course, opposed the monarch when it suited their general interest. They and their families were the dynasties that often proved longer-lasting than the monarchies.

Some families became loyal servants of the crown and its estate; some changed sides; others wasted away. Many would survive and be powerful figures for centuries, even to the present day. The obvious example is the Cecil family, who by the sixteenth century wielded a commanding influence over the Tudors. When the first Stuart arrived on the throne in 1603, a Cecil was at his elbow. The line continued, usually in high office, into the twenty-first century through Lord Salisbury and, more recently, Viscount Cranborne. Robert Cranborne's title is a courtesy title granted in 1604. His barony was created a year earlier, the year Elizabeth I died. He is (at the time of writing) the heir to the 6th Marquess of Salisbury. Yet the Cecils are but one example of the great British dynasties.

Furthermore, legacies and monuments to those families did not die with the personalities. As I sit writing, I can look across the lane to the village school here in Queen Camel in Somerset; it is the school named after Countess Gytha whose most famous son, Harold, perished at the Battle of Hastings. Across the way hangs the coat of arms of the Mildmay family, signifying land given in return for loyalty – in this case, by Elizabeth I to Sir Walter Mildmay. Sir Walter was Queen Elizabeth's Chancellor of the Exchequer and the founder in 1584 of Emmanuel College, Cambridge.

Most of us are closer than we may realize to the origins and traces of great and influential families, past and some still present. It is easy to touch our history through those families and their homes – we do not have to be good at dates and battles and the greater contexts of historical periods. That is why this book is about the families of these islands. The great families survived because they were prosperous, their loyalties were tested and rewarded, and they knew when to jump from sinking political ships and on which side was the firm beach.

Our story begins with the Godwines, towards the end of Saxon England. We continue with the Despensers, the ancestors, some say, of the family of the late Diana, Princess of Wales; the Mortimers, famous marcher lords; a group of often warring Irish families; the Cecils, who seemingly counselled monarchs from Elizabeth I to Elizabeth II; the Churchills, but not so much Winston; the Percys, who kept the northern hordes from the monarchy sometimes quietly, yet sometimes, as in Hotspur's case, not so quietly; the Berkeleys, who once boasted they could ride from Bristol to London without leaving their land; the Cavendishes, who were and are the Devonshires; the Comptons, one of whom was the only Bishop of London to crown a monarch; the Dalrymples and the stain of the Glencoe massacre; the Norfolks, who are, but have not always been, prominent Roman Catholics; the Russells, whose dukes were of Bedford, whose nineteenth-century scion was a Prime Minister and whose twentieth-century one was a world-famous philosopher; the Waldegraves, who provided one of the earliest Speakers of the House of Commons; and the Carringtons, who got their title because it was more easily supplied than a permit to cross a privileged piece of ground, and became favourites of the monarchs of two centuries.

We end with the present day, when the concept of the dynasty is hard to pin down. For once the monarchy lost its power, what need for dynasties? Yet there were newspaper barons handing on their mastheads and convinced that they were the new power brokers. If so, could they be for long?

The Dynasties, therefore, is about the use of power and its failures as well as its successes. Some of the families, say the Percys and Cecils, exercised enormous influence over monarchy, both at court and on the battlefields, for centuries. Consequently, these families are more interesting than those of monarchs, because so often monarchs relied on them to stay in power. Members of these families were therefore, individually, as vulnerable as the monarch, but the family was often more likely to survive. This is the key to the dynasties: ability to survive while committed to scheming at the highest level.

Who will be the modern dynasties? About whom do the powerful whisper? The answer, perhaps, lies somewhere in the radical changes in commercial and political power during the past fifty years. Where once the marcher lords protected the monarchy and its lands, their modern equivalents are those who protect not the monarchy but the institutions through which the state breathes: the financial institutions, the threads of surviving democracy. The modern marcher lords are therefore, like their twelfth-century predecessors, those who are able to preserve power and to manipulate and even remove it.

However, the way in which our society is structured and the speed at which its influences change means that the power behind the state is now short-lived.

As Britain divests itself of its own responsibilities of government and becomes part of the new empire with its capital in Brussels, so the importance of the dynasties quickly disappears.

I set out with some twenty families in mind but I might easily have selected as many others. Some, like the Cecils, may be obvious selections. All have been chosen because they interest me, not because I feel a burning determination to record their rightful places in British history.

The first story, in Chapter 2, is about the Godwines, the first 'powerful' family in British history in the sense that we now understand the phrase. They were confidants of royalty at a time when the monarch ruled above all others. They ruled on behalf of the monarch and of course one, Harold, eventually became king. Each chapter then covers a single family, with the exception of the final chapter, on the modern media barons, and the chapter on the early Irish, whom I have included because I wanted to show the importance of the Celtic clans. Most importantly, these chapters are not meant to be biographies. They are sketches of people who particularly interest me, and they allow us to spy on areas of our history that otherwise we might overlook. For example, the Godwines allow us to see how the Conquest might have been avoided; the Despensers remind us why Simon de Montfort and his barons were so appalled by Henry III and why de Montfort, and not the young Prince Edward, perished at the Battle of Evesham.

As was my intention with the original *This Sceptred Isle*, I hope that some readers may be encouraged to delve more deeply into those personalities or subjects that appeal to them most. I have therefore included some book titles at the end of each chapter. Inevitably, some of these works are out of print, but all are available in some publicly accessible library.

To start our story I offer in Chapter 1 some thoughts on the Saxon period, which after all is the basis of modern British history. In an attempt to make it easier to see why people who otherwise might have settled for a quiet and comfortable life did not, I have posed (and tried to answer) five questions that set the time line of British history:

How did we get kings?

When did we start dating our period of history from the birth of Jesus Christ (and why)?

Why do we start each year on 1 January?

Who were the Saxons, and which ones were important?

How do we really know what went on?

Obvious questions, but worth asking. The story of our dynasties deserves that.

CHAPTER ONE

IN THE BEGINNING

Alfred the Great died in 899. Apart from an incident with cakes (a story for which we are thankful to the twelfth-century *Chronicle of St. Neots*), Alfred is best remembered for defending the English against the Danes and as being the father of the Royal Navy.

We should remember him also as an inspiration for the *Anglo-Saxon Chronicle*, which was started in about 891. This work is enormously important to our understanding of the times because this period, which included the Godwines, was the start of modern British history. Perhaps that is a sweeping statement, yet it is more true than doubtful. For the time of Alfred, Aethelstan, Edgar, Cnut (sometimes known as Canute), the Godwines and Edward the Confessor was the time of the ideas that would lead to institutions recognizable even in the twenty-first century.

Furthermore, this was the period when what we now call England began to be ruled as a state rather than as a collection of tribal allegiances; thus the ruler would be a king instead of regional princes. Importantly, all this would be recorded. More specifically, the writing would be in a form that we understand today and it would have each year a starting point and an ending point.

If that seems unremarkable, we must first understand that in these times many people simply did not know, or agree, when one year finished and another started. There were seasons, of course, but these were relatively imprecise. Today, when we write in our diaries that such-and-such an event happened in, say, March, we know that this means it happened in the third month of the year. That is because everyone knows when New Year's Day is. But it has not always been so: the year has not always started on 1 January, and so there has not always been an agreed point from which to date anything. The importance of this is obvious: when we try to track centuries-old events, our game of historical detectives may easily be confused because the diarist of the time was thinking in different time frames from our own. What is more, the early chroniclers often recorded events without defining them in time spans as we understand them. We have only to look at the complications of understanding biblical stories to grasp the uncertainties of reading sagas as history.

So what did writers do for dates? It was common to describe something as having happened a year after the death of a leader, perhaps an emperor. But the matter is further complicated. Even if we could agree on a date for New Year's Day, what would we do about counting the numbers of years? How, for example, would you know how old you were? How would you know when something happened? We might say that a battle took place in 1342. But one thousand, three hundred and forty-two years after what? We are so used to dating everything BC or AD that we sometimes fail to ask when we started doing this.

It is not an idle question. After all, if events, however insignificant, are not put in some date form that can relate to another period (one year compared with another) it is very difficult to say that we are reading history. We are simply reading about events which may interest as facts but do not satisfy us. How often we are told some mundane thing and then ask when it was. Once we are told, its significance falls into place. This thought extends from the date a Tudor monarch was crowned to the cancellation of a bus or train. On a small scale, the time of day is as significant as is the year in which a major event took place.

In this Saxon period, we find only a gradual use of chronology. It is impossible to date hardly any of the surviving documents from a common point such as the birth of Christ; therefore, they can rarely be seen as more than a statement of facts. A chronicler might mention that something happened when a particular king was on the throne, or, more specifically, in the year that he died. A writer might well have made notes of facts and events in the margins of the dates for feast days and especially Easter, which, being a movable feast, would not always show a common cycle of twelve months. Nor was there always a common starting point.

For example, by the third century AD throughout their empire the Romans had not an annual budget but a fifteen year tax cycle. A date would be a moment within that cycle. This would be called the Indiction number of that period. From our modern viewpoint we could say that something happened in, say, 425; but they could not.

Certainly long after the departure of the Romans, even in the tenth century – which is where our story of the Godwines starts and therefore our evidence for them – some chroniclers were still calculating the calendar with the year beginning at the start of the tax period, that is, September. Other chroniclers dated the year as starting with the Feast of the Annunciation in March. Yet even here there were two possibilities: the 25 March preceding 1 January, and the 25 March following 1 January. Thus records might suggest one year, when the event had actually occurred in the previous year.

Even when there was a primitive but recognizable dating system, such as everything dated from the death of a particular Saxon king, the result remained complicated. Imagine the later confusion when a group of leaders gathered. Each would have a different tribal background, so each would have his own idea of time dated from his particular king.

Gradually, the idea emerged of dating from the birth of Jesus Christ. Yet this too presents confusion since the custom of celebrating 25 December as the Mass of Christ was not generally accepted until the second century. The Nativity was normally celebrated with Epiphany (in modern times, 6 January); at another time, it was celebrated in May.

The next clue to dating was given by a Syrian monk named Dionysius Exiguus, who determined that Easter Sunday should be the Sunday after the Spring Equinox when the moon was fifteen days old. Thus came the habit of recording events in the Easter calendar. From this period came the concept that time could be calibrated before and after the Christian period.

But it is not until the writings of the Venerable Bede (*c.*673–735) in Saxon England that we start to understand the importance of chronology; then we can say that we are discovering history writing. It was Bede who adopted the notion of Dionysius and started to date events as happening in relation to the Incarnation – the birth of Christ. Thus, for some centuries, the year started not on 1 January but on 25 December, the winter festival – later Christmas Day. There seems to have been a period in the eighth century when 25 December was abandoned as the start of the year and the Roman Civil Calendar, starting on 1 January, was adopted.

We can now see the importance of the *Anglo-Saxon Chronicle*. More than a source of our story about the Godwines, it really marks the beginning of the use of chronologically identified events and so is the first long comprehensive record of life in these islands. Probably the most significant source of history in the English language prior to 1066, it offers an almost almost unique view of such a wide period. It starts before the birth of Christ: 'Sixty years before the Incarnation of Christ, the emperor Julius Caesar was the first of the Romans to come to Britain, and hard pressed the Britons in battle and overcame them, but could not gain a kingdom there....' And here is a description of Britain in those times: 'The island of Britain is eight hundred miles long and two hundred miles broad; and here in this island are five languages: English, British or Welsh, Irish, Pictish and Latin. The first inhabitants of this land were the Britons, who came from Armenia [Armorica, that is, Brittany] and took possession at first of the southern part of Britain....'[1]

The *Anglo-Saxon Chronicle* is a collection of historical accounts written in five monasteries – Abingdon, Canterbury, Peterborough, Winchester and Worcester. The books describe events from the dawning of Christianity until 1154. Since they were started during the reign of Alfred the Great it is often thought that he encouraged the monks to write this history and that his glorification in the text is some reward. This is quite possible, but no more than that.

Of greater significance is the fact that the *Anglo-Saxon Chronicle* was written in English. Certainly the earlier sources for chroniclers would have been in Latin. Moreover, if this is the first long history in the nation's own language, then it stands alongside the earliest recorded Northern histories (of the Irish and Russians) as the story of a people in their own language.

Of course, an account must not be based entirely on one chronicle, however admired. This period is nearly one thousand years ago; the historical references are very limited and, as with much detective work, often confusing. So we turn also to other documents such as the *Gesta Regum* of William of Malmesbury, the *Codex, Vita Eadwardi* (the life of Edward the Confessor) and the Norman scribes William of Poitiers and William of Jumièges. But it is to the *Anglo-Saxon Chronicle* that we turn for our general reading.

This apparently lengthy detour was worth making because it gives us a clearer insight into the importance of our characters at the times in which they lived. It is, too, the beginning of our collection of sagas. To set the times in context, we should start by looking at the character of these islands during, say, the five hundred or so years that led to the Conquest and the deaths of the Godwines.

Our starting point might be the fact that the racial split and geography in these islands has not much changed from, say, the sixth century to the present day. That cannot be said by many states in continental Europe. The three languages, Gaelic, Welsh and English, were established. The latter has changed during the thousand years since the Conquest. However, those changes do not appear to be as marked as they were during the half millennium before the invasion. The first Christian church was built in the second century – at Glastonbury. The Celtic Church appears to have existed in the second century and certainly in the third century. However, the relationship between the Celtic Christians and Rome was not to last because Rome insisted on its authority being paramount. The Celtic Christians resisted, but, even though some sort of doctrinal and liturgical truce was recognized at the Synod of Whitby in 664, inevitably Rome would win. During the sixth and seventh centuries the Church of Rome exerted a religious, cultural and even military influence over the people.[2]

Just as the shape of the islands remained consistent, so too has the demography and local geography. In, say, the sixth century, Scotland, Wales and England had more or less their present borders. A large number of modern place names were established before the Conquest. (Going one step further, it is rare to find a rural community in the twenty-first century that did not exist by, say, the thirteenth century.)

So established was Saxon England that it has been well argued that, when the Normans arrived in 1066, they became English rather than the English becoming Norman.[3] And, of course, the Saxons already had kings. But what sort of kings? Indeed, what was a king?

We tend to think of England, even in Saxon times, as a kingdom. But we have to ask ourselves who, if it were a kingdom, kept it that way? In other words, who defended it from its enemies and how, in a time of foot soldiers, primitive weaponry and no navy to speak of, could anyone have defended something like the British Isles? The answer is that it was an almost impossible task, and therefore a kingdom did not exist as a safe and secure entity.

The simplest way to defend anything is to make it known that you are so powerful that an invader will be vanquished in the most terrifying manner. (In the twentieth century, this was known as deterrence.) The second way is to have loyal and powerful people throughout the kingdom who will unite to defend the whole. The third way is to be on friendly terms with everyone who can reach you. In Saxon times, this latter option was perhaps never considered seriously until Cnut, the Danish king, threatened at the beginning of the eleventh century. So, in the earliest Saxon times, there was no kingdom. The origins of a realm are to be found in the smallest communities. They were called marks and were groups of dwellings about a manor – a sort of parish. Marks were reasonably self-governing although, because of continuous military threats, particularly from Norse and Teutonic raiders, not necessarily independent of other marks. Because the land was sparsely populated, the next size of governable area was the shire. The shire became a collection of marks, just as the kingdom eventually became a collection of shires. It happened that way rather than the other way round – a kingdom being split into smaller entities.

By the end of the sixth century there were seven major kingdoms in what we call England. The most important of them was that of the West Saxons. These people were originally identified within a small group of communities on the south coast of what is now Hampshire. Gradually they had extended until Wessex covered an area relating to modern Hampshire, Somerset, Berkshire, Dorset and Wiltshire, and possibly parts of Avon, up into Gloucestershire and even Worcestershire. The western boundary was the River Axe. Devon and Cornwall were West Wales – these were the Britons.

North of the Wessex line, effectively north of the Thames, were the three kingdoms of the Angles, including the Germanic East Anglia. This was the kingdom of Offa (not the dyke builder), who started his reign in 571. North of the Humber was, as the name suggests, the great kingdom of Northumbria. The other kingdom was the mid-lands of the Mercians.

The powerful West Saxons had several kings at one time, because each section of the territory was led by a minor king, or earldorman. Even then, there were anomalies and at least one still survives. East Kent and West Kent had separate rulers, each king with his own bishop. Today, only Kent has two diocesan bishops, those of Canterbury and Rochester.

The obvious conclusion from this brief explanation of the structure of Saxon England is that it was a tapestry of independent states. Until the tenth century, no one had the ways and means to unite the kingdom and claim its allegiance. But let us see what we mean by 'king'.

The earliest groups of Saxons had not a king but a military chief known as a heretoga. Their 'magistrate' or civil lord was an earldorman. Certainly in Saxon England until quite late into the seventh century a region might have several earldormen. As the regions appeared, then to unite the different – and often differing – groups a figure above the earldormen emerged. A good example is Egbert (sometimes spelt Ecgberht). In 802, he was elected king of Wessex and eventually ruled that 'kingdom' and the smaller kingdoms that depended upon it, Essex, Kent, Surrey and Sussex.

Although the earldorman retained authority over his people he had effectively become a viceroy, ruling in the name of the king. The word 'king' comes from the Saxon *cyning*. This in turn is connected to the word *cyn*, as in 'kith and kin'. Here, then, is a clue to the origins of the nature of an early king. The king is leader of the people, not the owner of the land. This is not an unreasonable notion. After all, on continental Europe a nation might move about. Wherever they settled, its people remained for the moment at least the same in origin, language and custom. The king was still their king, even when they were in someone else's land. So being the king of the English did not mean he was king of England. It was a distinction that survived among the Scottish clans and Irish families.

How did the king become king? Clearly, he would probably have the broadest sword. For here was the concept of kingship – the allegiance of the people in return for his promise to protect them and his ability to implement that promise. This obvious qualification carried a codicil: in Saxon times, a king was elected. The twenty-first century debate on the possibility of an elected monarchy is less than new thinking.

This sketch of the origins of Saxon power allows us to see why the emergence of the Godwines in the tenth century was so remarkable. The 1st Earl Godwine, someone who became more powerful than the monarch and, in all but title, was ruler of the whole kingdom, was a relatively recent phenomenon. Moreover, we can see now why the events which led to a Norman duke becoming *cyning* of England are so important to the whole history of these islands.

We could pick a Saxon date at random and start our story with that reign. There is, however, a good argument to trace the origins of power through intrigue in these islands from the time of the monarch who began the peaceful settlement of the kingdoms, Alfred the Great. Alfred was king of Wessex, the most important kingdom in what we can call England. After his death in AD899 his son, Edward the Elder, became king. It was Edward who eventually gained control of the Danish territory south of the Wash and much of Wales. Yet although he managed to take Mercia in 918 he was still not king of England. Only the kings of York, Scotia and Strathclyde accepted Edward the Elder. This is why the king who followed him is so important in British history. He was Aethelstan, the grandson of Alfred the Great.

Aethelstan came to his throne in 924 as king of Wessex and Mercia. He then conquered Northumbria, the territories of the northern princes, before decisively defeating the Scots and the minor kings who had made alliance with the Danes. This last encounter took place in 937, when Aethelstan's army of Mercians and men of Wessex met the Britons, Scots, Picts and Celtic Norsemen led, apparently not brilliantly, by the Scottish kings at the Battle of Brunanburgh. The battle was recorded in verse, probably the first epic poem in British history.[4] Thus Aethelstan had conquered England and, with the allegiance – however dubious – of all the regional monarchs and princelings, became its first king. His powerbase was Wessex, the birthplace of Britain's monarchy which, except for eleven years during the seventeenth century, was to survive for more than a thousand years.

Yet there was no peace. By 1016 Cnut, the king of Denmark, had overcome the English. His enormous task was made easier by the death of Aethelred's son, Edmund Ironside, who had fallen not in battle but perhaps in exhaustion. Just thirty-five when he died in 1016, this Saxon king was the only leader who could rally enough troops and inspire them to warfare on the bloodiest of scales against Cnut's forces. In 1016 he fought and harried the Danes in six terrible battles. He did so in spite of the treachery of his brother-in-law Eadric, who time and again betrayed him to the invaders. Then, when all seemed possible for him, Edmund died. The *Chronicle* simply tells us, 'then on St Andrew's Day, king Edmund passed away, and is buried with his grandfather Edgar at Glastonbury….'[5] Perhaps it was the strain of fighting in six battles that year, of gathering and rallying troops, of travelling enormous distances to once more unsheathe his sword against the Danes, or perhaps some terrible illness. Obviously he could not have fought so hard and in so many battles that year without being wounded; maybe he simply died of those wounds. Some have wondered if he might have been murdered; probably not, for the chroniclers would have spoken of some treachery. Whatever the reason, this young and apparently strong prince's passing left all England for Cnut, who reigned from 1016 to 1035.

Thanks to the *Historia Anglorum* of Henry, a twelfth-century archdeacon of Huntingdon, Cnut is popularly remembered for sitting on the beach trying to stem the tide. This surely apocryphal image obscures his importance and the ways in which he gained victory over the English and was eventually elected king. Cnut settled England into two decades of relative peace, partly because he became very English. He married the widow of Aethelred II, the dowager queen Emma, a remarkable woman who was the wife of two kings of England and mother of two more.

This brief explanation of the evolving power of monarchy has also demonstrated the way in which strong families were established over huge tracts of the kingdom – not simply restricted to the influences about their manors. It is at this point that we start our story of the dynasties, because the Godwine family was deeply involved with the intrigues and dangers of kingmaking surrounding at least two monarchs and the wrath and indignation of more than one court. It is shortly before the coming of King Cnut that our story of the Godwines and the great – though not always likeable – families of these islands begins.

NOTES

1 *Anglo-Saxon Chronicle*, Parker Chronicle, Everyman Library, 1953.
2 563 Columba founds the Iona community; 597 Augustine arrives in Kent and converts King Aethelbert; 607 the first St Paul's is built in London; 625 Paulinus arrives in Northumbria; 635 Aidan founds Lindisfarne monastery; 657 Hild founds Whitby; 681 Benedict Biscop founds Jarrow; *c.*685 work starts on Winchester Cathedral.
3 See Edward A. Freeman, *The History of the Norman Conquest of England*, Clarendon Press, 1867.
4 The poem has no name, but it is generally known as 'The Battle of Brunanburgh'.
5 Freeman, *The History of the Norman Conquest of England*.

CHAPTER TWO

THE GODWINES

The king who was killed at the Battle of Hastings on 14 October 1066 was Harold Godwineson – Harold, son of Godwine. He was Harold II of England. With him died his brothers, the Earl Gyrth (sometimes, Gurth) and Leofwine (sometimes known as Alwy), Abbot of Newminster. These were scions of the family that came very close to preventing the Norman invasion. Had it succeeded, British history would have taken a quite different direction, for the arrival of William the Bastard's army at Pevensey Bay on Michaelmas Eve that year was more than a prelude to a change of monarchy. This was the end of Saxon England. Had Harold triumphed, then the strength of the Godwine family suggests that they would have ruled for at least another generation. There probably would not have been an Angevin throne in England and therefore no Plantagenets. Imagine the consequences of deleting all those characters from the royal tree of British history.

The Norman Conquest may be seen as the most important event in the saga of the British Isles. It is more significant than, say, the Roman invasion, the defeat of the Armada, the Battle of Trafalgar or even the arrival of Christianity. What would have followed had Harold Godwine survived that October day on Senlac Hill is a fascinating 'what if?' question of British history. So who was this family, and how did it gather so much power that at one time, during the reign of Edward the Confessor, it virtually over-ruled the monarch?

The Godwines first appeared in British history in the late 900s, and perhaps the cleverest of them all was not King Harold, of Hastings fame, but his father, Earl Godwine. It was he, usually known simply as Godwine, who married Gytha, the sister-in-law of King Cnut.

Godwine was the son of a man called Wulfnoth – not an uncommon name in those times, so trying to pin down which Wulfnoth is not an easy task. In the eleventh-century Saxon *Knytlinga Saga* Godwine's father was said to be a rich farmer in what is today north Wiltshire, probably near the village of Sherstone. Yet there is not much evidence to support this version. The *Anglo-Saxon Chronicle* is probably the best source for identifying Wulfnoth and determining his importance; yet in the year 1007 the *Chronicle*[1] introduces Wulfnoth without any explanation of his background. This is not, however, unusual for the *Chronicle* rarely elaborated on any of its characters. An important person would appear without any warning and, unless he or she figured in following events, would then disappear. Even influential people, for example a new archbishop of Canterbury, might be accorded nothing more than '...in that year so-and-so became archbishop' despite the fact that the manoeuvrings and politics of the appointment would have been particularly important to the kingdom.

More likely, the Wulfnoth in question was the one called Cild of the South Saxons – modern Sussex. In Saxon times a cild (pronounced 'child') was someone of 'good' birth, although this did not suggest the son of, for example, an earl. One thousand years ago there was no aristocracy in the way we think of dukes, earls, viscounts, marquesses and baronets today. This Wulfnoth was a thegn; this meant literally a server, but not a menial – more accurately, a noble or, slightly below that, a gentleman.

An earl would have thegns, as would the king. Clearly, the standing of a thegn was measured by the one to whom he owed allegiance, the king's thegns being the most senior. Their authority lay not so much in the importance of their family, but in their office. Consequently, the bureaucracy that accompanies great offices of state developed not so much from the landed earls but from the thegns. The title could be hereditary, although various commitments had to be executed before a thegn could inherit. For example, Cnut's thegns had to give him four horses, two swords, four spears, various pieces of armour and a certain quantity of gold before they could come into their inheritance. As thegns to the monarch their influence could be substantial and the opportunities for profit great.[2]

It was one of this breed, then, Cild Wulfnoth (or Wulfnoth Cild), who appears as candidate for the first Godwine. However, Wulfnoth was no comfortable courtier. Under Aethelred II, more popularly known as Aethelred the Unready (c.968–1016), there was rarely a time when earls and thegns simply wandered leafy glades to the twitter of calling birds and the idle chuckles of musing friars. Aethelred's England was frequently threatened by brutal raiders from without and crude and equally brutal ambitions from within. In the year 1009, Wulfnoth appeared as a treacherous practitioner of both these threats.

Aethelred ruled England for nearly four awesomely bloody decades. His very coming to the throne resulted from an act of terror. His brother, Edward the Martyr, had been king for three years when, in 978, Aelfthryth, his step-mother, had him murdered at Corfe Castle in Dorset in order that her natural son Aethelred should have his throne. Two years on, the Danish raids began once more. A decade later, the English were heavily defeated at the Battle of Maldon; London was put under siege and the Isle of Wight was invaded. Then, in 1002, Aethelred ordered the massacre of all Danes living in England – most of whom had lived peacefully enough for many years. The Danish onslaughts resumed, this time in search of revenge. Aethelred bought off the invaders with tens of thousands of pounds in silver – the infamous Danegeld. It was against this setting that Wulfnoth committed his treachery.

Since the summer of 1006 the Danish fleet had been raiding the south-east coast of England, and confident warriors had driven inland across southern England. Aethelred called on one of his thegns, Eadric Streona, to whom he had given the earldom of Mercia,[3] to build an army and navy that would resist and eventually deter the Danish raiders. Eadric was an example of a thegn who had no noble birthright to authority; what he did possess was the brains to understand the strategic as well as the tactical tapestry of the defence of southern and central England. In 1008 he started to build the fleet on a national scale: the country was considered to have more than three hundred districts, and each hide, as these districts were called, had to produce a warship. In those days warships were measured not in tonnage but in banks of oars: these warships were each sixty oars 'big'. The armour for the marines was also to be provided by the hides. The fleet was assembled in 1009 off the Kentish port of Sandwich, ready for the defence of the homelands. One of the flotilla commanders in that fleet was Wulfnoth.

Here the *Chronicle* takes up the story and introduces both Earl Godwine's father and his future father-in-law.

About this same time or a little before it, it happened that Beorhtric, the brother of the earldorman Eadric, made an accusation to the king against Wulfnoth, a nobleman of Sussex, and he then fled the country and succeeded in winning over as many as twenty ships, and went harrying everywhere along the south coast, and did all manner of evil.... Then the aforesaid Beorhtric procured eighty ships, and thought to win great fame for himself by taking Wulfnoth dead or alive. But when his ships were on their way, he was met by a storm worse than anyone could remember: the ships were all battered and knocked to pieces and cast ashore. Then that Wulfnoth came and straightway burned the ships....[4]

What was behind this story? While the ships were waiting for the Danes to arrive, Wulfnoth was accused of treason – that is, a threat against the throne. It is not known whether the accusation was well founded, or whether it was nothing more than intrigue because Eadric wanted rid of Wulfnoth (note that Wulfnoth's accuser, Beorhtric, was Eadric's brother). Whatever the truth, before Wulfnoth could be brought to trial he escaped. Furthermore, he managed to persuade the crews of twenty ships in the Sandwich fleet (perhaps his own flotilla) that they too should desert the king's fleet. Possibly with the promise of riches rather than facing the Danish hordes, they sailed with Wulfnoth as crude privateers and began doing exactly what the Danes had done – raiding the largely defenceless south coast.

Beorhtric, his ships outnumbering Wulfnoth's by four to one, not unreasonably felt that he could take Wulfnoth and, by so doing, win great favour with the king. But these were crude vessels enormously vulnerable to weather conditions and almost always relying on fortune rather than seamanship. The fortune (and perhaps seamanship) was not with Beorhtric. The great storm and Wulfnoth's torchings did for the ships, for Beorhtric's reputation and for the whole fleet still at Sandwich. When the king and his councillors heard that Beorhtric's flotilla had been destroyed and that Wulfnoth was still at large, they were in great confusion: 'the king, the earldormen and the chief councillors went home, abandoning the ships thus irresponsibly'. Irresponsibly? Ill-counselled? Not necessarily; after all, the king had just lost a hundred of his ships. Whatever the reason, the remaining ships were withdrawn to London, leaving Sandwich Bay undefended. The Danes invaded Kent, which led to more killing and more Danegeld.

What happened to Wulfnoth is not clear except that he was never reconciled with the court and in 1009 his considerable lands were confiscated and put under royal stewardship. In 1014 King Aethelred's eldest son, Aethelstan, died and in his will left Godwine his father's confiscated estate in Sussex. This offers three pointers to Godwine's position at this important time, just two years before the start of Cnut's reign. First, his father, Wulfnoth, was either still a fugitive or dead. Second, although in the king's eyes Godwine was stained with his father's treason, he was not without very high friends at court – particularly the monarch's first son, the aetheling (prince) Aethelstan. Third, this bequest must have betokened more than friendship.

The politics of eleventh-century Anglo-Saxon England were as complex and cruel as anything since, and court allegiances were truly matters of life and death. King Aethelred had six sons. Four of them, Aethelstan, Edmund (Ironside), Edward the Exile and Edgar the Aetheling, were from his first marriage, to Ælfgifu. Edward and Alfred were by his second wife, Emma of Normandy[5] (also known sometimes as Ælfgifu).

So here, then, is another clue to the Anglo-Saxon whodunit that is the story of the Godwines. The two 'families' of brothers were manoeuvring for the throne of their father, Aethelred: on one side, Aethelstan and Edmund; on the other, Edward and Alfred. Godwine was encouraged to be in Aethelstan's camp. If Godwine was indeed held in suspicion as his father's son by Aethelred, then he was not alone. Alongside him stood three other thegns very much out of favour with the king and his closest henchmen – the brothers Morcar and Siferth, and Thurbrand.[6] Godwine's importance as a thegn was enough for Aethelstan to want him with them rather than as an uncertain ally. Considering that no one else was offering protection (and in Anglo-Saxon England, there seems to have been no such thing as neutrality), Godwine perhaps needed little encouragement. The restoration of his father's lands five years after their confiscation was more than payment for his services. With estates came the right to raise forces for his patron, and after Aethelstan's death Godwine's patron became the young Edmund – just twenty-one years of age. It was a political marriage of some importance and not a little danger.

In 1015, fearful of the alliance against him and of the increasing loyalties shown to the Danish invader, Cnut, Aethelred encouraged his thegn Eadric Streona to murder the brothers Morcar and Siferth. Edmund and his allies had been tested, and he was now irrevocably opposed to his father. Worse for both of them, Cnut had invaded England and, because Edmund and his father were divided and the unspeakably opportunistic Eadric in charge of the army, opposition to the Danes was weak. Eadric, in fact, swapped sides and joined Cnut. Godwine had no choice but to remain with Edmund; he had considerable estates in Wessex (Sussex was a dependent territory within Wessex) but that great region was now under Eadric and Cnut. Aethelred, who had been ill for some months, died on 23 April 1016. Edmund, quite likely with Godwine at his side, claimed the throne.

As we have seen, 1016 was the year of the six great battles for control of Saxon England. Eadric had once more changed sides and claimed to be for Edmund, about which Godwine was probably sceptical. Once more, it was Eadric who left Edmund vulnerable and virtually defeated. On 30 November that year, Edmund died. So where did this leave Godwine? By the laws of Saxon political averages, he should have been executed: he had fought against Cnut, and Eadric was his enemy. Yet such was Cnut's wrath that not even the latter survived. Within a year of Cnut taking the English throne, Eadric Streona of Mercia was executed along with almost all those who had held power under Aethelred and his son Edmund.

Then why should Godwine survive? There are two possible explanations. Either Godwine had not fought against Cnut, or Cnut must have found something about Godwine that appealed or was to the king's advantage. There are no mentions of Godwine in the six battles of 1016; equally, there is no convincing evidence that he avoided them. It is difficult to see how he could have remained neutral. What then might have appealed to Cnut? Unlike Eadric, Godwine is not mentioned as having changing sides, and Godwine's loyalty to Edmund may have been something which Cnut admired. Now, when Godwine submitted to Cnut, the king took him into his court – on probation.

Cnut now had his trusted Scandinavians in key positions of power. His brothers-in-law Erik and Haakon, Hrani and Thorkell were the four powerful earls in England, although the latter would lose favour and be sent into exile. They were loyal to Cnut and, most importantly, had no following in England and so were beholden to him. It would have been a shrewd move by Cnut to place certain former enemies in powerful positions, just as he was shrewd enough immediately to marry Aethelred's widow, Emma of Normandy. Godwine fitted this plan, especially as someone had to gather payment for the battles that year. Many of Cnut's troops had been mercenaries: they had to be paid off, and his standing army needed to be paid too. The money had to come from Cnut's new subjects. 'In this year the following tribute was paid over all England: it amounted to seventy-two thousand pounds, in addition to that which the citizens of London paid, which was eleven thousand pounds.'[7]

Godwine is very likely to have been one of the tax-gatherers; not to have been would have meant that he was on the king's blacklist. As we shall see in successive centuries, he (rarely she) who raised taxes for the monarch was likely to be very much in favour. Having Godwine raising revenue, especially in Wessex, showed the people that this was not a total Danish take-over – it was, of course, but Godwine's participation eased matters for Cnut. His reward was the earldom of middle Wessex.

In this period, the start of the eleventh century, the definition of 'earl' was changing. The title comes from the Norse, and it is a corruption of 'Jarl' or 'eorl'. An eorl was once a prince, and an earldorman was at the very least a very senior official and in some cases a member of the royal line, thus wielding enormous power, though never as much as a monarch. By Cnut's time, an earl had assumed the role with which it is more commonly associated – that of a nobleman appointed by the king to rule, in his name, over a shire or group of shires. Here is the origin of the more modern lord lieutenant of a county – but then, of course, with real power. So the fact that Godwine is described as an earl[8] reveals that he is now important and very close to the monarch.

It is tempting to look for new tests of Godwine's loyalty to Cnut. But was it really in doubt? There were those such as Thorkell who muttered and, in Denmark, plotted against Cnut; but Godwine was hardly in a position to join any faction against the Danish-born monarch. He was amassing land, but had no power base other than that of his patron – the king. Moreover, there is nothing to suggest that Godwine was inclined to plot against Cnut, for by this time he was earl of Kent – a sort of minor-county earldom: there were six earldoms at this time and Kent was number six. Furthermore, Godwine was trusted in title and in marriage.

In about 1018, Godwine married the daughter of a man called Beorhtric. Although little is known about him, it is very likely that he was the Beorhtric who had accused Godwine's father of raiding the coastal villages of Kent and Sussex and, unlike his brother Eadric, had survived the purge of Cnut's court. Furthermore, the king attended the marriage. Here, then, are three more pieces of the Godwine family jigsaw and further evidence that, by this date, Godwine was a person of sufficient importance for his marriage to be probably a political one.

A year later, Godwine was at the very side of his king – this time in battle. During the winter of 1019–20 Cnut took Godwine with him to Denmark to campaign against uprisings and impose his military authority on the land. The Danish adventure was a grand expedition of nine ships and many soldiers. It was no brief visit. The previous year a truce had been made between the Danes and the English; but it was only a truce, not a permanent peace. The expedition was well planned and it was fully expected to be a hard one and very possibly a long one. The skills of navigation and seamanship were by no means crude even in the eleventh century, but each man who went knew that, once the winter had set in, return from Denmark would be delayed until the weather allowed the fleet to put to sea. So it was of some significance that Cnut took Godwine with him as his close counsel. And it was Godwine who took command of a small English army on behalf of his king and fought alongside him against the Wends, Slavonic tribespeople from northern Germany. It could be argued that it was better to take Godwine rather than leave him at home to plot. But, again, there is no recorded evidence that Godwine was under suspicion or a member of any emerging faction. In fact Cnut was gradually bringing considerable stability to his lands. (Eventually, in 1023 even the recalcitrant Thorkell would be reconciled with his monarch.) Cnut's most problematic enemies were in Sweden and Norway. But by the end of the decade even the great warrior Olaf of Norway had been overcome.

Shortly after their return to England, at Easter 1020, Cnut's confidant, the Archbishop Lyfing, died. Now Godwine became Cnut's closest adviser and the most powerful man in England after the king. Cnut had made him what nowadays we should probably call his chief of staff. More was to come. Godwine now married for the second time (it is not known what happened to his first wife) and soon his second son, Harold, was born. The bloodline to the throne was far from dotted.

The king's brother-in-law was Danish, earl Ulf, who had a sister called Gytha. Following the apparently successful Danish campaign, Godwine was given Gytha as his bride and became Earl of all Wessex – which was effectively most of England south of the Thames and as far west as the River Axe. Clearly, Godwine's position and importance were considerable. Remember, he was English and held arguably the most influential earldom in terms of territory. The king did not hand out estates simply as amusements. Giving title over land created power, and that power was to be used in the king's interest: the king had to make a judgement as to the likelihood of that power being turned against him. His judgement was that this Englishman was perhaps even more loyal than his own Danish countrymen. The chronicles place Godwine in precedence over others and his signature appears at the head of the columns witnessing to royal diplomas.[9] Godwine had taken the place of the still exiled Thorkell and the late Earl Erik.

When, in 1025, some of Cnut's supposed loyal followers at his court rebelled, Godwine remained steadfast. One of those who went against the monarch was the brother-in-law of Cnut and Godwine, Earl Ulf, and in 1026 Cnut had him murdered. The dreadful battles described by the *Chronicle* that took place between 1025 and 1028 involved many English soldiers and fleets of 'English thegns'. It is not known if Godwine fought alongside Cnut. There is no mention of his name in this connection in the *Chronicle*, which suggests that Godwine may have risen even higher in the king's confidence than is often imagined. When a monarch went abroad to wage war, someone had to be left in charge of the kingdom. That person had to be more than a faithful administrator: he must watch his monarch's back and protect him from the intrigues and worse that might so easily arise in his absence. Only the most trusted and militarily supreme could be left to rule in the king's stead and be relied on to hand back the land in good order in due course. It was likely that it was Earl Godwine who ruled as regent.

Godwine was now established as premier earl of England. His marriage was happy and his children reflected his close relationship with the monarch:

Godwine and Gytha named their first son Swein in memory of Cnut's father; Harold – their second son[10] – was the name of Cnut's revered grandfather; one of their daughters was named after Cnut's own child, Gunnhild. Good friends with good Danish names – only Leofwine and Wulfnoth (after Godwine's father) were English names. This harmony was first distorted, then ruptured in November 1035.

> ...in this year king Cnut passed away on 12 November at Shaftesbury; and he was conveyed thence to Winchester and there buried. And Ælfgifu Emma, the Lady [the queen, Emma of Normandy] was then residing there. Harold [Harefoot, Cnut's illegitimate son who eventually became King Harold I], who claimed to be Cnut's son by the other Ælfgifu [Cnut's first wife Ælfgifu of Northampton] – although it was quite untrue – sent thither and had all king Cnut's best valuables that she could not keep back taken from her; she remained however, in residence there as long as she could...[11]

This was the second greatest test of Godwine's life thus far. The first had been his loyalty to Aethelred and his submission to Cnut. Now he had to decide what he should do about the succession to his patron, Cnut. There was no way in which Godwine could avoid, or indeed wished to avoid, the conflict that would surely follow. He was too powerful a figure to step aside. Apart from his position and lands, his very life could depend on the outcome.

Cnut had two sons: Harthacnut, son of his second wife Emma of Normandy, who at the time of his father's death was Cnut's regent in Denmark; and Harold Harefoot, son of Cnut's other wife Ælfgifu of Northampton (d.1040). Both men claimed the empty throne, and both mothers supported their son's claim. Harold Harefoot claimed it by right of birth; but Harthacnut asserted that he himself was more than rightful heir and that it was the wish of his late father that he should succeed. Godwine, his loyalty to the late king never in doubt, appears to have believed this to be true although hindsight suggests that his judgement must have been tempered by his sense of survival. Harthacnut was more likely to be his patron than Harold Harefoot. Whatever his reasoning – and there is no record of it – Godwine supported Harthacnut's claim and formed an alliance with Emma of Normandy, who, as the *Chronicle* tells us, remained in Winchester.

Powerful as Godwine was, given his control of all Wessex, he could not deliver the kingdom for Harthacnut. England was divided by loyalties and thus by geography. Harthacnut's powerbase through Godwine was in the south. Harold Harefoot was supported by those in the midlands and north: the Earl of Mercia, Leofric, and the Earl of Northumbria, Siward. Godwine's strength lay in the territory he commanded and therefore the armies he could call upon, plus his wealth and reputation and a considerable group of allies, together with his determination to remain loyal to what he believed were the wishes of the late king and obviously those of Emma of Normandy. The obvious weakness was Harthacnut's own position. He was, remember, King of Denmark and had to stay there because the Norwegians were about to invade. For all Godwine's resources, how could he fight without the would-be king in the van of his mother's campaign to hold the throne for him? Answer: he could not. Harold Harefoot, already established in the midlands and the north, gradually moved south. Cnut's gold was in Winchester, the home of Emma and within the earldom of Godwine. Harold Harefoot had enough power to move on Winchester and take that treasure – which, after all, he regarded as his inheritance. It is at this point that many would have to abandon their belief in Godwine's unswerving loyalty to Cnut's memory. He began the battle for succession true to that memory. But this second great test was governed by quite different rules within months of Cnut's death.

First, Harthacnut had failed to arrive in England and so his cause was all but collapsed. Second, watching Harold Harefoot's seemingly unstoppable march to the throne, Emma of Normandy decided to abandon her son Harthacnut and call on her other sons. Third, Godwine's own position and that of his not inconsiderable extended family was perilous. When he had relied on the largesse of Cnut after the death of Edmund Ironside in 1016, he was an important figure, but by no means territorially and politically grand. On the death of Cnut, the Godwine family was perhaps the biggest threat to Harold Harefoot. Wessex was the home of the British monarchy; Godwine ruled Wessex.

Here, then, were three reasons for Godwine to change sides: his own survival and that of his family; Harold Harefoot's growing, and Harthacnut's falling, support; and, perhaps most of all, Emma of Normandy's decision to desert her son by Cnut and turn to her older sons (the aethelings, Princes Edward and Alfred) by the earlier king Aethelred. What could the Godwines do? For the moment, nothing. Emma's decision to call for Harold Harefoot's half-brothers, Alfred and Edward, took away any initiative from Godwine, and what followed was to affect the Godwines for the rest of their lives.

In theory, Edward and Alfred might have drawn their support from Normandy. They did not. The Normans at that stage had no direct ambitions for England and, in any case, the then Duke of Normandy had his own military concerns at home. Consequently neither brother mustered much of an army.

Edward landed with a small force on the south coast, but turned back to Normandy even though the force that faced him in Hampshire was not very powerful. His mother waited in vain for his arrival at Winchester. Alfred landed at Dover and headed for London, where Harold Harefoot was in control. He did not get there, because at this point Godwine had decided that his own security could not rely on Emma of Normandy. Clearly Harthacnut was not in a position to seize his father's throne; Harold Harefoot was, and more or less had done so. Godwine now deserted Emma's crusade for Edward and Alfred.

When Alfred reached Guildford, he may have thought he was safe. This was part of Wessex and Godwine, hitherto Emma's loyal subject, was Earl of Wessex. But Alfred was far from safe, and here was an opportunity for Godwine to look to his own future. He arrested the young aetheling, slaughtered his followers, then handed over Alfred to Harold Harefoot. Alfred was taken to Ely, where he was cruelly blinded and died. Godwine had, without question, switched sides. He most certainly needed the patronage of Harold Harefoot. Yet it should not be forgotten how powerful was the Godwine family. Harold needed Godwine's support perhaps as much as Godwine needed his monarch's protection – and most certainly Harold Harefoot was now monarch. He was Harold I of England.

This one act of Godwine's may not have changed the course of the conflict between the dowager Queen Emma's sons, but it did put beyond question the futility of her hopes that anyone other than Harold would be king. Harold had no loyalty and no blood ties to Emma, and she was now forced to flee to the continent, where she would bide her time in Bruges. Of her remaining sons, Harthacnut was still in Norway fending off Magnus while the very unwarlike Edward was for the moment in Normandy.

Godwine's action was welcomed by Harold. Yet for the rest of England, this must have been the new and less acceptable face of the hitherto trustworthy earl. 'Needs must' might well have been the Godwine family motto from that moment. History is full of stories which seem to end tidily but rarely do. Here we have the tale of the powerful magnate who supports one claimant against another for the throne of England, then changes sides – apparently successfully when the second contender has all but won. The turncoat Godwine kept his vast estates, and the king accepted him at his court. All very neat but for two factors: the original pretender, Harthacnut, had not given up, and the victor, Harold Harefoot, was not long for this earth.

In 1036 Harold tidied up the opposition, and by the following year had been accepted by the whole country as monarch. Three years later, at Oxford on 17 March 1040, he died.

> ...in this year, died king Harold. Then with the best intentions, they sent to Bruges for Harthacnut [who by this time had entered into a truce with Magnus of Norway and so was with his mother, Emma] and he came then to this country with sixty ships before midsummer, and then imposed a severe tax which was borne with difficulty...and all who had been zealous on his behalf now became disloyal to him. He never did anything worthy of a king while he reigned. He had the body of the dead Harold disinterred and cast into a marsh...[12]

Godwine, presumably on the direct order of Harthacnut, was one of those who took Harold's body from his tomb. Moreover, Godwine and the Bishop of Worcester and Gloucester, Lyfing, were accused of complicity in the death of Alfred. Godwine was in a serious fix, for he had no allies. Emma would not have befriended him; nor would her son Edward, Alfred 's brother and Harthacnut's half-brother, who was now called to England and received by the new king with great civility and friendship. So Godwine swore a solemn oath that the blinding and consequent death of the young Prince Alfred were all Harold Harefoot's doing, and as a mark of 'respect' Godwine made doubly sure of his neck by giving Harthacnut a ship. This was an expensive and practical gift, reflecting Godwine's own power should he be allowed to continue to exercise it. He was so allowed, as long as he did the king's bidding – although he would never totally clear his name.

The Godwine family remained powerful overlords of Wessex, then still the most important territory in the kingdom. Yet their power must have been exercised with some stress, for Godwine was now frequently associated with intrigue and plots whereas in Cnut's time he seemed above such doings. Harthacnut may have been a spiteful and bad monarch, but he seemed justified in his suspicions of Godwine and, when the king died in 1042 during a feast at Lambeth, the Earl of Wessex's difficulties were hardly relieved.

The new king was the late Alfred's brother Edward, now thirty-seven years old, who would become known as the Confessor, the builder of Westminster Abbey, and until the crusades, patron saint of the English. The albino Edward was no mighty warrior – nor was he foolish. He appears never to have rid his mind of the notion that Godwine was responsible for his brother's blinding and death. His suspicions were correct inasmuch as Godwine's only defence was that he had done nothing more than arrest Alfred. His exact part in the death of the aetheling can never be explained, but there can be no doubt that he played some role – it is only the billing that is doubted. Whatever Edward's suspicions, he could ill afford to act upon them at the start of his reign. He was a foreigner in England. Indeed, he needed the support of the three great surviving earls, Godwine, Leofric and Siward, whatever their previous allegiances. Leofric could deliver Mercia and Siward Northumbria. But the Godwine family were the kingmakers.

Just as Godwine had to safeguard his position, so the new king and his supporters had to consolidate their grip on the throne. One of Edward's actions, for which he needed Godwine's active complicity, was to rid himself of his mother, Emma of Normandy. In 1043, the king, with Harold at his side, went to Winchester – Emma's home. He ordered her lands to be confiscated and she was banished. The reasons for this seemingly cruel act remain uncertain. One theory is that Emma favoured Magnus of Norway as king. This Queen Mother remains one of the most remarkable women in British history. Wife of two kings, mother of two further kings, Emma, the daughter of Richard, Duke of Normandy, was the archetypal scheming matriarch. Now Emma was no longer a power at court and an influence on her son. Godwine, by contrast, strengthened his hold on Edward, because the king increasingly needed Harold's advice and the strength of his influence throughout much of England. This became even more the case because Edward gave Harold even more estates and therefore power through the offices that came with those lands. Moreover, the king now bestowed earldoms on the two eldest Godwine sons, Swein and Harold, and on a nephew called Beorn. There was an even greater prize for the family to come.

On 23 January 1045 King Edward married Edith, Godwine's eldest daughter. The richest earl in all England was now truly the most powerful. Was he not the king's father-in-law? Were his sons not brothers-in-law to the monarch? The dotted line to the Godwine claim on the throne was clearly drawn.

Godwine's second son had become Earl of East Anglia. This was no sinecure: with the title came the obligation to defend the region's long coastline and vulnerable hinterland, particularly from the Norwegians who still believed they could overthrow the English monarch. But Harold Godwineson could not simply appear in East Anglia and declare that he was the people's appointed leader and that they must do his, and therefore the king's, bidding. True, his name appeared on important documents without which nothing could be exchanged, nothing could become law and no cause could be advanced or countered, and these documents usually carried the ultimate authority, that of the monarch. But Harold still needed the implicit good will of the region, which had to come not only from the ordinary people but from the great families. Just as the Godwines ruled Wessex in the south of England through the extended family and the support of lesser but still influential houses, so the new earl had to consolidate his own strength through the eastern manors and their halls. It is not surprising, then, that he chose to marry a 'local' girl.

Perhaps shortly after 1045 Harold took as his wife a Cambridgeshire heiress, Edith 'Swan-neck',[13] whose family held estates in five counties, Buckinghamshire, Cambridgeshire, Essex, Hertfordshire and Suffolk. This was a dowry of more than land: it represented influence. Then, something happened that gave the young Earl of East Anglia even more power: he acquired some of his elder brother's lands, though not in the happiest of circumstances either for their father or for the family name.

The black sheep of the family was Earl Godwines's eldest son, Swein. Most honourably named after the father of King Cnut, Swein behaved most dishonourably. One of the marcher lords, he was returning from a punitive expedition in south Wales when he stopped at Leominster, where he repeatedly raped the abbess of the convent. It is written in the *Chronicle*: '…in this year earl Swein marched into Wales and Gruffydd, the northern king [of Wales] together with him, and hostages were given to him. When he was on his homeward way, he had the abbess of Leominster fetched to him, and kept her as long as he pleased, and then let her go home…'.

But Swein did not let her go for a whole year. Godwine attempted to protect his son from the charge of *nithing* – that is, of being without honour. But he was unsuccessful, and Swein was sent into exile first in Flanders and later in Denmark. Godwine's failure to protect his son posed a personal dilemma for the family. Harold, Godwine's second son, and his cousin, Cnut's nephew Beorn, wasted little time in dividing the spoils of Swein's earldom. However, of deeper consequence for the family was its relationship with the king. Earl Godwine's politicking had damaged the trust he had rebuilt with Edward and, more importantly perhaps, here was an opportunity to exploit for the many enemies of the Godwine family. The Earl of Wessex may have been the monarch's father-in-law, but he was continually vulnerable to plotting by enemies at court who resented the family's power and to Edward's fickle nature. Not even his daughter's marriage to the king could help much, for the union was childless and this in itself was a political conundrum for Godwine. The king wanted an heir. Godwine wanted his daughter to provide one, thereby making him grandfather to the future monarch, with all the political power that offered.

Perhaps another sign of Godwine's faltering influence was a relatively ignored incident in Denmark. In 1047, by which time Swein Godwineson was in exile, Earl Godwine's nephew by his marriage to Gytha, the brother of *jarl* Ulf, was King Swein of Denmark. His kingdom was, as ever, threatened by the Norwegians under Magnus. Godwine asked Edward to send help to defend Denmark. Edward, either for his own reasons or on the advice of those about him, refused. In the event Godwine's exiled son, Swein, took a force to help the Danish king, his cousin, though his intervention failed.

Edward's refusal to support the Danish expedition was far from the last of the reverses endured by the Godwine family. In 1049 Swein Godwineson landed in England, hoping that his sentence of exile could be lifted and his estates restored. What followed was hardly a picture of a happy family pulling together. Earl Harold and his cousin Earl Beorn refused to hand back Swein's lands which had been given them by authority of the king himself. Edward was not inclined to pardon Swein, especially when he saw that the Godwine majority view was against the wayward earl. It seems that Earl Godwine himself spoke for his son, but his voice was unheeded. By this time Earl Harold was in his late twenties and established as one of the most powerful men in England; here he was, not only opposing his brother but, more importantly, going against his father's wishes. The old order was changing.

The king, turning away Swein, gave him a few days' grace to clear England's shores. Now the terrible nature of Swein Godwineson and the stark cruelty possible in these times were demonstrated. The king had been told that enemy ships were in the English Channel, and Earl Godwine was ordered to put to sea to fend off the marauders. He commanded a fleet of some forty vessels, one of them commanded by Earl Harold and the other by his cousin, Earl Beorn.

> ...while earl Godwine and earl Beorn lay at Pevensey [they were sheltering from a storm] then came earl Swein [who had not sailed, as ordered, from England but was anchored at Bosham further along the Sussex coast] and deceitfully begged earl Beorn who was his uncle's son to accompany him to the king at Sandwich and improve his relations with him. Because of his kinship Beorn went with him with three followers, and he [Swein] led him then towards Bosham where his ships lay, and then he [Beorn] was bound and led on board ship. Thence he [Swein] sailed with him to Dartmouth and had him slain there and buried deep...[14]

Why would Swein Godwineson do such a thing to his own cousin? Perhaps his very nature had much to do with it. Perhaps Beorn had refused to help. Perhaps news may have reached Swein, shortly before he and Beorn arrived at Dartmouth, of the capturing of half his fleet and the slaughter of all their crews by men of Hastings. The reason is uncertain, though the consequences are clearer. Swein once more fled into exile in Flanders. Harold Godwineson had the king's favour, since his objection to a pardon for his brother Swein was justified and he was thereby, tacitly at least, supporting Edward.

We might assume that Earl Godwine's standing was now weakened. He had failed to get help for Denmark, and he had failed to get royal absolution for his eldest son. However, Godwine still had power in Wessex – he virtually ruled southern England. It may have been part of Edward's kingdom, but the true power was Godwine's. Some indication of this power might be seen in the way, apparently against the odds, that Godwine continued his determined efforts to restore his eldest son to his estates until he was successful.

In 1050, Swein returned. This was a political triumph for Godwine, for he must have been set against both the king's real wishes and his own family, particularly his nephew Ralf who had some of Swein's land. The objections of Swein's brother Harold were less likely to matter, for after the death of Earl Beorn Harold had managed to acquire some of his dead cousin's estates.

The king was increasingly frustrated by the Godwine family's influence. Moreover, he was still without an heir. Many writers have suggested that Edith's failure to produce a child had everything to do with Edward's saintly celibacy. We should not, however, ignore the hypothesis of others, among them Ian W. Walker, who suggest that Edward did not want children by Edith because this would cement the Godwine hold on the throne for decades to come.[15] Whatever the reason, it was a good indication of Edward's sense that it was the Godwines and not he who ruled England. In 1050, relations between the Godwine family (probably including Queen Edith) and the king reached an extremely low point. The catalyst for the schism that was to follow within twelve months was the appointment of a new archbishop of Canterbury.

In October 1050, the present incumbent died. Aethelric, one of the monks of Christ Church, Canterbury,[16] was related to Godwine and his fellow friars wanted him to be the new prelate, so they asked Godwine to speak for him. But the king found Godwine's intervention presumptuous, to say the least. The appointment of bishops was in the royal gift, not Godwine's. Edward tossed aside Godwine's candidate and appointed one of his own people, the Norman bishop of London, Robert of Jumièges. He then installed another of his supporters, Spearhafoc, in the see of London. Edward's action was a political defeat for Godwine. However, the king soon regretted giving Canterbury to his supposed friend Robert when the latter refused to consecrate Spearhafoc as bishop of London. The reason is uncertain except that there was suspicion that Spearhafoc had paid the king in gold for the bishopric. Robert of Jumièges, a zealot who had the support of the Pope, next turned his attention to Godwine's estates in the south-east of England. He claimed that some of Godwine's land was in fact owned by the archbishopric and, determined to do down the Earl of Wessex, began to speak against him to Edward, who was hardly unreceptive. It would appear that by the summer of 1051 the campaign against Godwine was in full flow. Yet even the combined forces of king and archbishop could not dislodge Godwine's grip on the virtual running of England. There had to be something else that could be done to discredit the earl.

In July 1051 Count Eustace of Boulogne, who had once been Edward's brother-in-law,[17] arrived in England to solicit the king's support against William, Duke of Normandy and Count Baldwin, the ruler of Flanders; a planned union of Normandy and Flanders threatened Eustace. A plot was hatched. While Eustace was at Dover there was a skirmish with the local people and some of his entourage were killed. What had this to do with Godwine? Godwine was also Earl of Kent, so the king ordered him to send his troops into Dover and plunder in retaliation. Godwine refused.

The coincidence of the marriage of Godwine's son Tostig to the sister of the Count of Flanders only gave Edward more cause for alarm and increased his determination to banish the Godwines from his court and therefore from England. Little wonder that the Godwine family, father and sons, rallied their troops. In September, the king summoned his royal council to Gloucester. At the same time Godwine and his armies arrived at Beverstone, not far away. What had or had not happened at Dover, and even the apparent alliance with Flanders, were not insurmountable difficulties. The deeper charge against Earl Godwine was an older one – his part in the arrest, blinding and then death of Prince Alfred, Edward's brother.

In times not long past, Godwine's allies had been the two other powerful earls of Edward's kingdom, Siward and Leofric. They now, most sensibly, moved for the king. Together with minor magnates, the archbishop's men and probably Eustace, they stood their armies against the Godwines'. In other centuries, there might have been an enormous battle to settle the issue; but instead of a battle there was a truce. Why that should have been is not certain. It is perhaps true that Godwine, for all his great power, would have judged that, although he could have overcome Edward's forces at Gloucester, he might not have survived the subsequent com-bined forces of all the earls and estates. Equally, Edward did not yet have those forces in place. A third possibility is that each side had lived through the dreadful months of the fight for the succession after Cnut's death and so found the idea of civil war unacceptable. Furthermore, if the country did go to war with itself, outsiders would raid and the whole kingdom might fall. Therefore every effort had to be made to maintain peace while there was a chance that the status quo ante could be restored – although, of course, it could never be in the prevailing circumstances.

Edward was determined to banish Godwine from his court; so to do would loosen the grip Godwine had over the king. The two groups of armies were facing each other around London. In theory, the Godwine family should have been stronger – in the past, the fact that Godwine 'owned' such a huge tract of southern England had told for him. But now it told against him. When the confrontation was with the monarch and there was no certain outcome, the Godwines could not prevent desertions. Moreover, Harold had never managed to gain the complete loyalty of his East Anglian earldom in spite of his good local marriage. Faced with the men loyal to the king in the south and news of a weakening Wessex, Harold too was deserted.

Realizing that he was outnumbered, that the matter of Alfred's death was still at his feet and that his eldest son Swein had been outlawed by the king, Godwine and his family made haste to escape England and the lands of Wessex. Earl Godwine, his wife Gytha and their sons Tostig, Swein and Gyrth were at the family estate at Bosham in Sussex. It was from here that they sailed, with as many men and as much treasure as their ships could carry, to Flanders, the home of Judith, Tostig's new wife and the sister of the Count of Flanders, Baldwin. Harold and his other brother, Leofwine, sailed from Bristol to Ireland and the patronage of the king of Leinster, Diarmait. It was to Diarmait that the sons of Harold would flee for refuge after the Battle of Hastings in 1066.

Although Edward now started to take those parts of Wessex he wanted for himself and split the rest of the Godwine spoils among his followers, the family was far from destitute and certainly not without hope. Both in Flanders and in Ireland, there was enough treasure and sufficient sympathy from their hosts to begin raising an army to invade England. The one matter they could not control was the fate of Earl Godwine's daughter Edith. It is more than likely that Edward had long since decided that he wished to rid himself of his Godwine wife, but never could because the earl would have opposed the divorce. Now, free of the Godwines, he sent his wife to the charge of the abbess of Wherwell in Hampshire. The generally accepted theory is that Edward got rid of Edith either because she was barren and could not provide an heir or because he did not want his heir to be a Godwine. However, if Edith was discarded so that he could take another queen, who might that be? Looking through family trees of the time, including that of William of Normandy, it is hard to spot a would-be queen of England.

Moreover, it seems incredible that Edward really thought he had rid himself of the Godwines. He knew exactly where alliances started and ended. He understood perfectly that Earl Godwine was at Bruges and that Count Baldwin would encourage him to raise a mercenary army to support his return. He knew that Earl Harold was in a similarly strong position in Ireland. He must also have known that, should a much reinforced Godwine choose to return, he, Edward, would have considerable difficulty in repelling him for two simple reasons: the only skilled and reliable naval commanders he had ever had who were capable of fending off marauding fleets were the Godwines; and he could no longer rely on the northern earls for their support. Siward and Leofric had no great stomach for a pitched battle that would lead to a civil war, and were possibly none too happy with the way in which Edward had taken chunks of Wessex for himself and settled the rest of the Godwine estates among his immediate friends.

In June 1052, Godwine sailed for south-east England. This was not an invasion – more a reconnaissance. He went ashore at Dungeness and picked up crews from Kent (his stock was high in Dover, where he had defended the people from trumped up charges of attacking Eustace) and East Sussex. Edward's fleet, commanded without distinction by the earls Odda and Ralf and hampered by rough weather, failed to stop Godwine who sailed westwards to keep out of harm's way. He sent raiding parties ashore along the south coast like some Norse plunderer, perhaps because the people of these parts had deserted him the previous year. On the Bristol Channel coast, Earl Harold was carrying out similar punitive raids. Within weeks, the raiding had given way to an advance on the south-east and London. By the autumn of 1052 all roads, including the Thames, would lead to Southwark, the great estate of the Godwines on the banks of the Thames. Edward had little chance of stopping them; there had to be compromise. Compromise meant victory for the Godwines and that Edward would once more be in the power of this resilient Saxon dynasty.

On 15 September 1052, Godwine's formal oath denying all charges against him was accepted. His position and therefore his estates were almost fully restored. The family's position and Edward's face-saving were made easier by the death of the outlawed eldest son of Earl Godwine, Swein. He had, by way of penance, been sent by his father on pilgrimage to Jerusalem, and that autumn died on his way home.

The above account concerns the fortune of the Godwines and the misfortune of Edward's ambitions. There was, too, a casualty who is sometimes overlooked and whose own misfortune resulted in an action that changed the course of British history and would result in the death of King Harold at the Battle of Hastings. This unfortunate was Robert, the archbishop of Canterbury. The story of what happened to him during 1051–2 is necessarily complicated because of the way loss and fortune swapped sides between Edward and the Godwines. The short version is that Robert had been appointed archbishop by Edward in preference to a relation of Earl Godwine and had, not surprisingly, taken the king's side in the dispute that led to the exile of the Godwines. Now the family was back, Robert believed it very likely that he would not have the king's protection, only the Godwines' wrath. Not much interested in finding out what that wrath might mean for him, he fled from his see of Canterbury.

Robert of Jumièges was to be replaced by one of the fascinating survivors of late Saxon England, Stigand. He first appeared in chronicles during the reign of Cnut and continued into the time of William of Normandy. For our story, Stigand is not so important as the man who was by now a political exile, Robert. For it may well be that it was this disgruntled cleric, himself a Norman, who carried the notion to Duke William that, in the absence of a natural heir to Edward, he, William of Normandy, was to consider himself the successor to the English throne. The blood was thin – Emma of Normandy was his great-aunt. Furthermore, he had no English connection and surely Earl Ralf, Edward's nephew – or, better still, the little-known Edward, son of Edmund Ironside – were closer to the natural line of succession. Primogeniture was not an exclusive right to the English throne during these times, but anyone with such a link would surely have enough support and self-interest to insist upon its authority.

All this happened in 1052, fourteen years before the invasion. William of Normandy was then not a powerful leader; indeed, his own position in Normandy was constantly threatened and far from established. So we might reasonably discount any suggestion that Edward had sent Robert to William with the promise of his kingdom in return for help in defeating the Godwines. It is far more likely that the suggestion to William came from Robert of Jumièges himself. Why should he have said this? Perhaps he recognized what terrible mischief would come about through some future claim by William, and so it was something of a reflection of his bitterness. We shall never be certain, but it does seem likely that the confrontation between Edward and the Godwines, king and kingmakers, in 1051–2 led to Hastings in October 1066.

Whatever the interpretation of the events of the late autumn of 1052, the Godwine family, after the death of Swein and the restoration of their estates, seemed in good and authoritative fettle. But Earl Godwine would not long see the fruits of that autumn. It is not known how old Godwine was on his return, but he was very likely in his sixties. It had been an arduous time and he could well have succumbed to the exertions of exile and recovery. He fell seriously ill during a royal feast at Winchester and died three days later. One version has it that Godwine died because of the matter which most vexed the king, the death of his brother Alfred. At the banquet, according to the chronicler in the *Gesta Regum* and to Henry of Huntingdon, the king once more probed Godwine about the blinding and death of Alfred. Godwine again pleaded his innocence and called God as his witness that if he were so guilty he would choke on the next piece of food. That version says that he did indeed choke, and died. More likely is the story given in the entry for 1053 in the *Parker Chronicle*.

> In this year the king was at Winchester at Easter, and with him earl Godwine and earl Harold, his son, and Tostig. When on the second day of Easter he sat at table with the king, he suddenly sank down against the footstool, speechless and helpless: he was carried into the king's chamber and it was thought it would pass off, but it was not to be; yet he lingered on like this, unable to speak and helpless, until the Thursday, and then gave up his life. He is buried in the Old Minster [Winchester] and his son Harold succeeded to his earldom…

So at Easter 1053 the most important, although not the most famous, member of the Godwine dynasty was dead. He had steered his family from the often violent days of Aethelred the Unready, through the six great battles of Edmund Ironside, through the equally tumultuous early days and then the relative prosperity and stability of Cnut, through the revolution and treachery that followed that king's death, and finally he had consolidated, lost and retrieved his family's fortunes and power under Edward the Confessor. In all ways, Earl Godwine should be listed as a truly remarkable head of a family that for decades was more powerful than the monarch. Little wonder that Edward failed to grieve for him.

The king was now rid of Godwine and Swein, but not of the Godwines as a family – whom presumably he now felt were loyal subjects and good allies. Harold Godwineson was now Earl of Wessex, though it was not a matter of course but a matter for the monarch. This was no natural inheritance, as such titles would become in future centuries. Edward gave Harold the title Earl of Wessex and, according to the chronicles, did so without hesitation. Seemingly, then, Harold suffered none of the suspicions of the old order. Just as Earl Godwine had been free of his father Wulfnoth's sins against the crown, so Harold was not held responsible for his father's part in the death of the king's brother Alfred. Moreover, Harold had been against the return from exile of his outlawed brother Swein, a position which would have pleased King Edward. Therefore, with the Wessex succession settled Harold would become even more powerful than his late father. Thus the relationship between King Edward and the Godwines would be an important link in the transition from Saxon to Norman England.

The succession in Wessex was done, but what to do about the throne of England once Edward was dead remained a conundrum for the king. He had wanted to be rid of Edith, but now had his queen back from care. The truth or otherwise of the banished archbishop Robert's promise (if that indeed is what it was) of Edward's crown for William of Normandy did not figure in the calculations of those charged with thinking about who should succeed the king. In 1053, the year of Godwine's death, Edward was almost fifty years old – therefore not yet in old age[18] – yet it was past time to decide who should follow him. The natural successor was Prince Edward, son of the then fondly remembered Edmund Ironside; he would be a popular as well as a blood-line choice. However, at that date he was far from England in Hungary, having been banished for being his father's son by Cnut, whom Edmund Ironside had so nearly defeated in 1016. Now he was established in the Hungarian court, having married Agatha, a sister of the king.

Sending an emissary from England to Hungary was not an easy task. Apart from the physical perils of the journey, various permissions had to be gained and diplomatic overtures made *en route* as well as at the destination before anyone could travel in the Hungarian kingdom in safety, and be above suspicion of infiltration – perhaps even to incite rebellion. Nothing in eleventh-century continental Europe was simple. The trusted clerics and minor lords who might have succeeded in an easier task failed. It is very likely, from evidence of his other continental journeys around this time, that Harold Godwineson was the person who eventually arranged for the prince to leave Hungary and return to England to meet his cousin the king and for the two of them to arrange the former's accession. In 1057, probably during the early autumn, Edward the aetheling arrived in England but died shortly afterwards. Here, the *Anglo-Saxon Chronicle* eulogizes the memory of Edmund Ironside and insists that his son's death was a tragedy for the throne and the peoples of England:

Now came prince Edward to England,
Son of the brother of king Edward,
Son of king Edmund, known as Ironside
For his valour.
This prince king Cnut had banished
Into Hungary to be put out of the way,
But he there grew up to be a good man
As God granted and as became him well,
So that he won the emperor's kinswoman for his wife
(And by her begat a noble family)
Whose name was Agatha.
We do not know for what reason
It was so arranged that he could not see his kinsman, king Edward.
Alas! His was a cruel fate, and disastrous
To all this nation:
That he ended his life so soon
After he came to England
To the misfortune of this wretched people…

The misfortune of wretched England was widespread, and now came the schism in the Godwine family that would not be resolved until the terrible Battle of Stamford Bridge. There, Godwine would fight Godwine to the death and by so doing would divert Harold Godwineson from his task of defending the kingdom against William, Duke of Normandy.

There had been three great earls in Cnut's time and they had survived, indeed influenced, the troublesome changes of power. Consequently, and in their different ways, these three men had governed Edward's England. Earl Siward of Northumbria had protected the enormous and vulnerable northern swathe of the kingdom, Earl Leofric of Mercia had done the same in the often troubled midlands and north-west, and Earl Godwine had controlled the southern counties from the Thames to the Atlantic, while for some eight years his son had protected the lowlands of East Anglia. In 1053 Godwine died, followed in 1055 by Siward. In 1057 came the death of the last of Cnut's powerful earls, Leofric. The consequence of this changed order is of importance to the story of the Godwine dynasty.

Harold's position had been strengthened by his father's death. He appeared very close to Edward, even though he did not have his father's long and hard-won experience. This, then, was the plus side of the Godwine ledger. When Siward died his only heir was a child, Waltheof, but Northumbria in 1055 was no estate for a child or his regents to govern. The people needed an established and proven leader, and the king needed these vulnerable shires to be protected and to remain loyal. He turned to the Godwines (or perhaps they turned to him) and created Tostig, Harold Godwineson's brother, Earl of Northumbria. The appointment was the beginning of a decade of cruelty that would end with out-and-out rebellion and much slaughter.

Leofric's death in 1057 resulted in the king appointing his son Aelfgar – who already had his father's considerable Mercian estates – to succeed him. Aelfgar had been earl of East Anglia. Who became the new earl in his place? Almost inevitably, it was a Godwine: Harold's and Tostig's brother Gyrth. The seemingly unstoppable and powerful rise of the Godwines had not ended. In the same year the king's nephew, Earl Ralf, died. He had been earl of a number of shires which included Herefordshire and Gloucestershire, therefore an important marcher lord charged with defending the English from the Welsh. Harold Godwineson, now Earl Harold, took over the western part of the late Ralf's earldom, while Harold's other brother, Leofwine, received the eastern end of the earldom.

By the following year, 1058, every earl in England apart from Aelfgar was a Godwine. It was justifiable to some extent: the Godwinesons were strapping sons of the old Godwine, whereas the other descendants of the Cnut earldoms had either died or were in no position to take on the task of defending the kingdom on Edward's behalf. But it is an understatement to suspect that Earl Aelfgar of Mercia was put out. He most certainly would have felt vulnerable to the power – both politically and militarily – of the Godwines. He made an alliance with the Welsh king Gruffydd, a scourge of the English, and gave his daughter Alditha to him in marriage as a seal of the alliance. We can only imagine that in Edward's eyes Aelfgar now supped with a Welsh demon, and so the king banished the earl – who naturally took refuge in Wales. The matter was eventually settled and Aelfgar returned to Mercia. What happened to the earl after that is hard to establish. The traditional sources, such as the *Anglo-Saxon Chronicle*, say very little about the kingdom. It may be that the land was in relative peace, and diaries are not much kept in such times. It is possible that he died in 1062 and was then replaced by his son, Edwin.

In 1062, Earl Harold raided Wales in an attempt to capture and presumably kill Gruffydd; Gruffydd's ally Aelfgar must have been dead by then. Gruffydd escaped, but as so often happened with the Welsh, he was turned upon by his own people. Judging that the English earl would never give up his bloody onslaught and leave them alone, in August 1063 they decided they had had enough, killed their leader – the only king of all Wales the nation ever had – and gave Harold his head. Whatever the reason for the Welsh treachery among themselves, and whatever the ambition of Harold, he had proved himself a forceful and thoughtful commander and had rid the English of the western enemy. He was the most powerful man in

England. Edward the Confessor could not rule without this brother-in-law and his siblings. So why did Harold almost immediately commit such a grievous mistake? It was an error that would lead to his death.

It was probably in 1064 that he visited Normandy. In later years, the Normans claimed he went to confirm that, on Edward's death, Duke William would be offered the English throne.[19] This is a popular view, but by 1064 it was generally accepted in England that the king's nephew, the aetheling Edgar, was the most suitable blood-line successor. If Harold did not go for that reason, why travel to Normandy at all? When a man of his importance travelled it was for a purpose other than pleasure: usually to do battle or to conduct political business. As there was no war in progress (other than William's minor conflict with the province of Maine) it would seem that Harold went to test or propose some form of alliance. The most likely reason would be to arrange a marriage – perhaps between his sister Aelfgyfa and one of William's sons, or even with someone from another region. And then, of course, the trip might just have been a mistake. One chronicler suggests that Harold was at sea when a storm blew up and he was forced on to the Normandy coast where he was captured by Guy, the Count of Ponthieu, who sold him on to William.[20]

There is yet another possibility. Some of the Godwines had been held in Normandy as hostage for more than a decade since the fleeing archbishop Robert had taken them as his warrant for safe passage to William. Why it had taken Harold so long to attempt their release is not clear, although, as already explained, he had been occupied with building the family's position in England and doing down the Welsh king. Moreover, Duke William was no local warlord to bow to Harold's wish; in fact, William was quite possibly unimpressed with Harold's position in England. Should Harold have been particularly wary of William? In retrospect, perhaps he should, but at the time the Normans were not considered a military threat. Raids on British shores had mostly come from northern lands, from the Swedes, Norwegians and Danes – few had been perpetrated by the French of any region.

Whatever else happened that year, we know from the Bayeux Tapestry that the English earl was indeed handed over to the Norman duke, and we know also that Harold was there for some considerable time, even taking part in military skirmishes against the Bretons on William's behalf. There must have come a time when Harold wanted to be done with his Norman escapade and return to England. As far as we understand, William then suggested that he, William, was the rightful heir to Edward and that Harold should pledge his support of that claim – in one version William had been promised the throne by Edward. Certainly, he had some family entitlement because he and Edward were cousins.

It is not hard to guess Harold's feelings. If he refused William's demands that he should swear an oath to support his claim, then the corridor from guest chamber to dungeon steps was short and steep. It seems that Harold did swear an oath, and would have done so over the bones of a saint – a relic. In Saxon times the swearing of an oath on a holy relic was a deeply solemn act, in no way a gesture to be abandoned when England's shores were reached. Harold was allowed to go, and returned with one of the Godwine hostages, his nephew, Haakon. But William refused to free Harold's brother Wulfnoth, who remained in Rouen. So Harold returned to England, probably wondering whether the oath he had sworn was valid since it had not been freely given. More positively, he now knew the intentions of the Duke of Normandy: to claim the throne of England on the death of Edward. William was not one to pursue his claims through diplomatic and legal channels.

We are now within a year of the death of Edward the Confessor and the Battle of Hastings. For a decade Northumbria had been ruled by Harold's brother, Earl Tostig, as ruthless as any Saxon earl and an alien to his people. He was not of Northumbria, an Anglo-Danish earldom: his mother was Danish, but he had been brought up an Anglo-Saxon. It is possible that, in spite of the length of time he had ruled the region, Tostig was seen as 'unconnected' since he had no family there and was a totally hard ruler who was never described in any account as a fair or favoured man.

Northumbria, as the name suggests, was that region north of the River Humber up to the Scottish borders. The further north it went, the wilder and the more vulnerable to invasion it became. For some time Tostig appears to have been a successful earl, being on good terms with his regional lieutenants, with the Church (including the all-important see of Durham) and, perhaps most important for him, with Malcolm king of the Scots. It was never good to have a belligerent neighbour, and it was particularly bad to have one in Scotland where ambitions and alliances dogged English politics for a millennium.

In or about 1064, Tostig Godwineson apparently ordered a series of assassinations of potential rivals in his earldom. There was little new in this form of Saxon diplomacy. Why would Tostig do this? Either because he felt vulnerable, or perhaps because he was settling old scores and displacing lordships in order to give authority and land to his new-found lieutenant Gospatric – who a few years later, under William the Conqueror, became Earl of Northumbria.

There followed, in 1065, a rebellion, ostensibly in protest at these murders. This may be partly correct, although it is likely that the huge taxes Tostig was demanding from his earldom were equally responsible. Very simply, many of his people did not like Tostig and wanted him replaced by Earl Aelfgar's son Morcar. Only the king could remove and appoint earls. There was but one person who had sufficient authority to put their case to the monarch – ironically, Earl Harold, Tostig's brother. The *Anglo-Saxon Chronicle* for that year explains how Tostig was removed:

> ...all the thanes of Yorkshire and Northumberland came together and out-lawed their earl Tostig, slew all his retainers whom they could catch, whether English or Dane, and seized his stock of weapons in York, his gold and his silver and all his treasures which they came to hear of anywhere there. They

sent for Morcar, son of earl Aelfgar, and chose him to be their earl. He marched south with all the men of the shire, together with men from the shires of Nottingham, Derby and Lincoln until he came to Northampton, where he was joined by his brother Edwin and men from his earldom with whom were many Welshmen. There came Harold to meet them, and they charged him with a mission to King Edward, and sent messengers to accompany him to request that they may have Morcar as their earl. This the king granted, and sent Harold back to them at Northampton, on the eve of the festival of St Simon and St Jude to announce this same decision to them, giving them pledges and re-enacted there the laws of Cnut.... Earl Tostig and his wife and all his supporters sailed south over sea with him to count Baldwin [Count of Flanders and Tostig's brother-in-law] and he gave them all shelter and they were there the whole winter...

This account makes two factors plain: the ferocity of the rebellion and the fact that Harold had no power to restore his brother Tostig to his earldom. The alternative would have been a full-scale civil war, and we have already seen the reluctance of Saxon England to test itself in this way at times of great schism. And if there were to be a civil war, William of Normandy would be in an excellent position to invade along the south coast of England.

Now, in late 1065, a further twist occurred in the saga of the Godwines. There is no evidence that Earl Harold used the rebellion as part of any plan to succeed Edward. Moreover, there is no evidence that the king's health at this time suggested an urgent need to revive the debate about his succession. But in November the situation changed. Just a couple of weeks after the rebellion was calmed, Edward became ill and Earl Harold took command of the day-to-day running of the kingdom, for the young Prince Edgar was in no position to assume authority over the realm from his great-uncle. The Northumbrian lords lived in a state of uneasy truce and could not be relied upon to defend the throne. The Welsh looked for reason to attack. The Scots, as ever, delighted in making mischief. Tostig gathered mercenaries in Flanders to invade and reclaim his earldom. In Normandy, William was preparing his forces to claim what he believed was rightfully his: the throne of England. Harold Godwineson, perhaps more reluctantly than might be imagined, decided that he was the best person to become king and thus manage the country and its increasingly dangerous factions. He could rely on his two brothers in England, Gyrth and Leofwine, but upon who else? The queen, his sister, would not wish to take his side. Her favourite brother was Tostig, and it seems likely that she had not forgiven Harold for abandoning him to the wishes of the northern earls. What of those earls? Would they elect him king?

The court would meet at Christmas and all the powerful figures in the land would attend the king who by then was so ill that the Christian festival took on the appearance of a conclave, even a convocation, of kingmakers. We cannot know what went on at that gathering, but there are two possibilities to consider. First,

Edwin and Morcar could not have thought harshly of Harold; whether or not he had had any realistic alternative option at the time, he had made their case for Tostig's removal and, more importantly, had shown no sign of going back on that decision. Secondly, Harold might have agreed at this gathering to marry Alditha, the sister of the two men – thus linking their families.

There was another aspect that must not be ignored in the making of Harold as king. Who would crown him? Only the archbishops could perform this role, so he needed their support. Archbishop Stigand, he who had been Cnut's priest, was a pragmatist who must have known it was nonsense to hope that the aetheling Edgar would succeed the dying Edward. This leads us to the most important vote of all, the king's. On 5 January 1066, Edward the Confessor lay on his deathbed and appointed Harold Godwineson, whom once he had banished, as his successor: '…in this year was Harold consecrated king, but was not to enjoy a tranquil reign while he ruled the kingdom…'[21]

Harold, the second son of Earl Godwine of Wessex, was the first king of England not descended from Alfred the Great. He was crowned immediately following Edward's funeral in Westminster Abbey, founded by the Confessor and consecrated a few days before his death. Harold Godwineson was probably crowned not by Stigand, the Archbishop of Canterbury (who had no canonical authority and therefore wore no bishop's shoulder stole or pallium, the sign of papal blessing on a senior cleric), but by Ealdred, the Archbishop of York. This is no insignificant observation. Stigand had no authority to crown the monarch; the Normans claimed that it was he who had performed the task and declared that Harold was not a properly consecrated monarch. It mattered not a fig how Harold or the Church might have replied. William of Normandy made plans to invade England to claim the crown, while King Harold II made plans to defend as well as manage his kingdom.

William was the obvious threat, but not the only one, for Tostig had not given up hope of returning to England. Harold, who now needed the reassurances of the northern earls more than ever, had to promise that Tostig would not be allowed back. It was probably at this point that he married Alditha, the sister of Morcar and Edwin. Later that year she bore him a son, also named Harold.

King Harold quickly established his reign. By now he had considerable experience of government, particularly as he had virtually ruled the country as regent before Edward's death. None could doubt his authority as a governor of England. Equally, none could doubt the chance of calamity striking English shores. The first threat materialized in the form of Tostig and his mercenaries, who did exactly as his father and family had done fourteen years earlier when he too attempted to regain his earldom: during the late spring of 1066 Tostig raided the southern coastal communities. Apart from his concern about his brother's actions, Harold would have understood that, if Tostig's fleet were able to cross the Channel easily and pick and choose landings, then the weather conditions and sea state were easy enough for William of Normandy too. But the duke did not come, and in the meantime Harold 'gathered together greater naval and land hosts [forces] than any king had ever done in this country, because he was informed that William the Bastard was about to invade this land....'[22]

Yet there was no idle time, for Tostig now sailed east along the south coast, gave the royal fleet at its traditional anchorage at Sandwich a wide berth and then headed up the east coast. He plundered and killed in Norfolk before sailing round into the Humber with sixty ships. Morcar and Edwin were committed to repelling Tostig at all costs. The *Chronicle* tells us that Earl Edwin drove them back with such effect that Tostig's men deserted and he escaped to the safety of Scotland and his ally King Malcolm to lick his wounds. His brother Harold could rely on the northern earls to watch his military back, and set up his own headquarters on the Isle of Wight where he could face the threat he knew would come from across the channel.

The summer of 1066 was something of a Saxon phoney war. Tostig, defeated only temporarily, planned but did not move. William remained in Normandy. There were excursions in the Channel and naval skirmishes which effectively laid low William's immediate plans to land in England. Moreover, by September the weather had changed and the risk of a large Norman invasion by sea appeared to have diminished. Harold's forces – the biggest ever gathered by an English monarch – must have been restless. The logistical problems involved in bringing together, paying, feeding and keeping a sense of urgency among so many thegns and thousands of their men were enormous. So that month the army and navy were stood down from their war footing. Into this lull stepped Harald Hardrada, King of Norway. His appearance was a major factor in bringing to a close the Godwine dynasty and truly changing the course of the history of these islands.

Harald had been driven from Norway in the wars that for our story began with Cnut. Harald and his nephew Magnus Olafsson were banished when Cnut conquered Norway in 1030. When Cnut died in 1035, Magnus returned; Harald did not, and became one of the most famous mercenaries in Europe. In 1047 Magnus died and Harald succeeded him on the throne of Norway. He also wanted to be king of Denmark, but failed: the long series of battles to overcome that country cost Harald dearly in terms of men, prestige and exchequer. His instinct to fight and his almost empty coffers made timely allies for Tostig; perhaps with promises of England's riches, in late 1066 Harald joined him. A huge force aboard hundreds of ships sailed down the English east coast, landed and headed for York. The armies of Harald and Tostig met those of Morcar and Edwin at the Battle of Fulford on 20 September. Harald Hardrada was a fine general who had learnt much from his years as a mercenary and his campaigns in Denmark; Edwin and Morcar and their troops had no such battle temper. There was much slaughter of the English, and the earls were probably fortunate to escape the field.

King Harold would have been told of the Norwegian invasion long before it reached York, but could not have been expected to come immediately to the aid of Edwin and Morcar. Having released his watch for William, he now had to travel north with what forces he could muster from his own guard, together with those of the younger Godwine, Earl Gyrth, the *fyrd* (a sort of Saxon conscript) and the forces of the abbots of the monasteries – ever an important source for a warrior king. Harold left the south on 16 September, four days before the dreadful defeat at Fulford. His northern advance was made with remarkable haste: on the 25th his armies marched through York towards Stamford Bridge, just 8 miles away, where his brother Tostig and Harald Hardrada were encamped. The ensuing fight was by all accounts a fearsome affair, with great slaughter on both sides, and when the battle was stilled the invaders were comprehensively vanquished.

The Battle of Stamford Bridge is sometimes overlooked in the rush to read about Hastings. It should not be. This was the greatest victory of any of the Godwines. How poignant it was therefore, that Tostig should have been killed alongside Harald Hardrada. If it had not been for a change of wind direction, Stamford Bridge might have marked the opening of a long, powerful and peaceful reign for King Harold II, the most famous of the Godwines. His victory might well have persuaded William that his foe was too powerful a figure to take on that year. The Duke of Normandy was weather-bound in France because the north wind that had blown the Norwegian fleet south had kept his own ships – perhaps as many as 350 – in port.[23] But before the news of Stamford Bridge reached him, the weather changed. A new wind, a southerly, enabled the Norman fleet to set sail for Pevensey.

A Channel crossing with such a force in the eleventh century was a considerable task. Here was no beach landing sweeping inland to its objective. Instead, William's first decision was to regroup and think about the news from Stamford Bridge, which most likely did not reach him until he arrived ashore in England. News of William's landing did not reach Harold until as late as 30 September, while he was still at York. Most of his forces were exhausted. The followers of Morcar and Edwin had been slashed to pieces at Fulford and their remnants further decimated at Stamford Bridge. Harold had to march south with those troops he could muster and hope that others would join in on the way.

By the end of the first week of October he had reached London. There he rested and gathered what few reinforcements he could, then pressed on into Sussex. The details of what happened are well known and need no reiteration here. Harold gave William an order to quit the English shores, an order which both knew William could not accept. The two sides met at Hastings on 14 October 1066, when Harold and his brothers Gyrth and Leofwine were slain.

Harold's mother, the Countess Gytha, offered the Conqueror Harold's weight in gold for her son's body. William refused and ordered it instead to be buried on the Sussex seashore. He had no intention of allowing Harold's remains to become a rallying point for an uprising against him. The Godwines now retreated to the far West Country, the stronghold of the West Saxons, where they held lands in Somerset, Devon and Cornwall. From their headquarters at Exeter the Countess ruled the family while her grandchildren, Harold's sons Godwine, Edmund and

Magnus, planned a campaign to harry the Conqueror and regain their dead father's throne. We know, of course, that it was never to be. Yet at the time William did not underestimate the memory of Harold, which was a more popular cause that that of the aetheling Edgar to whom many had turned on hearing of Harold's death.

For more than a year after the Battle of Hastings, William had little control over England. Only in the south-east could he rest easily. In 1068, needing to conduct a new campaign to gain authority over all his people, he first attempted to subdue the West Country and attacked the Godwine lands in that region. True, the city of Exeter fell after a cruel siege lasting nearly three weeks. But the strength of opposition was surely found in the local loyalty to the Godwines rather than an opposition to an invader.

The surviving Godwines escaped. Gytha took refuge on the Bristol Channel island of Flatholm. The sons went, as had their father a decade and more earlier during his exile, to Ireland where King Diarmait still ruled. Within months they had rallied mercenaries to augment their loyal followers, landed in England from the River Avon and attempted to take Bristol. Repelled, they went south and fought for the Taunton mint, but were not welcomed by old friends of their father. Back they went to Dublin to rally more mercenaries and ships.

In 1069, three years after their father's defeat, two of the brothers (one, his identity uncertain, may have been killed during the previous expedition) returned to the south-west and began raiding the coastal towns. They killed and burned their way through the West Country until, faced with a superior Norman army, they were lucky to escape back to Ireland. The Conqueror was at last rid of the Godwines.

Countess Gytha went to live in exile in Flanders, which suggests that the family had no further ambitions in England because the Count of Flanders was the brother-in-law of Duke William, by now William I of England. The sons lived with their mother until they moved to Denmark and their cousin King Swein. With them went Harold's daughter named after his mother, Gytha. The young Gytha is said to have become the wife of Vladimir, Prince of Smolensk. It was through this marriage that a dotted line can be traced through to the present day.

Gytha's son Msistislav had a daughter called Inga or Ingibiorg, whose son became King Vlademar I of Denmark, to whom Queen Elizabeth II traces her ancestry. Indirectly, then, the royal line of Godwineson survives.

NOTES
1 *Anglo-Saxon Chronicle*, Laud Chronicle.
2 See Sir Frank Stenton, *Anglo-Saxon England*, OUP, 1943.
3 One of the seven kingdoms that made up the heptarchy, and for a long time, with Wessex and Northumbria, one of the three most powerful. Mercia was, roughly, the north midlands of England.

4 *Anglo-Saxon Chronicle*, Everyman, 1953.

5 Daughter of Richard II, Duke of Normandy, thus one of the later claims to the English throne by William the Conqueror.

6 The *Anglo-Saxon Chronicle* refers to Morcar and Siferth as the chief thegns of the Seven Boroughs (Lincoln, Stamford, Leicester, Nottingham, Derby and possibly York and Torksey).

7 *Anglo-Saxon Chronicle*, Laud Chronicle, 1018.

8 *Codex Diplomaticus Aevi Saxonici* (*Codex Dipl.*)

9 A sign of seniority at the royal court.

10 Swein (1043–52); Harold (1045–66).

11 *Anglo-Saxon Chronicle*, Parker Chronicle.

12 *Anglo-Saxon Chronicle*.

13 Sometimes called Edith the Fair, but we do not have a family name for her.

14 *Anglo-Saxon Chronicle*.

15 Ian W. Walker, *Harold – The Last Anglo-Saxon King*, Sutton Publishing, 1997.

16 This Christ Church burned down on 6 December 1067.

17 Married Godifa, Edward's late sister.

18 Of those who died of natural causes, Aethelred was forty-eight when he died; Godwine was probably in his sixties; William the Conqueror nearly sixty; Stigand also was probably in his sixties; Cnut was only forty-one.

19 *Chronicle of William of Poitiers*.

20 William of Malmesbury (1095–1143), precentor of Malmesbury Abbey who wrote *Gesta Regum Anglorum* and *Historia Novella*.

21 *Anglo-Saxon Chronicle*, Laud Chronicle, 1066.

22 *Anglo-Saxon Chronicle*, Laud Chronicle.

23 The precise size of William's fleet is not known. The figure of 350 is based on a rough estimate of the number needed to carry 10,000 men and perhaps 2500–3000 horses.

FURTHER READING

The *Anglo-Saxon Chronicle*, almost any edition.

FREEMAN, Edward A., *History of the Norman Conquest*, Oxford, 1868.

STENTON, Sir Frank, *Anglo-Saxon England*, OUP, 1943.

WALKER, Ian W., *Harold – The Last Anglo-Saxon King*, Sutton Publishing, 1997.

CHAPTER THREE

THE DESPENSERS

There were three Despensers[1] each called Hugh: grandfather, father and son. They lived in the thirteenth and fourteenth centuries and none died peacefully. The first Hugh Despenser was killed in 1265 at the Battle of Evesham. The second, known as Hugh Despenser the Elder, was hanged at Bristol in 1326 and his head sent for public display at Winchester. The third, Hugh Despenser the Younger, was executed the same year at Hereford, after which his head was stuck on a pike and displayed on London Bridge.

The Despensers had many enemies, partly because of their insatiable greed for land, treasure and the associated power. In some cases, the barons hated them. As for Hugh Despenser the Younger, the fact that Edward II was in love with him hardly won him friends – most of the nobility despised that particular king.

The time of these three Despensers spanned three monarchs, the hapless Henry III, the magnificent Edward I and the sad Edward II. Henry III was the first of the undisputed Plantagenet kings of England. His predecessors Henry II, Richard I and John were also Plantagenets but are usually called Angevins, meaning natives of Anjou. The Plantagenets were descended from Geoffrey, Count of Anjou; the name comes from his botanical symbol, *plante genêt* or broom.[2] Henry III was the son of Isabella of Angoulême and her husband King John, he of Magna Carta and known as John Lackland because he had no estates. (It was this king who had been careless enough to 'lose' Normandy, Anjou and most of Poitou.) Henry was only nine years old when he succeeded his father, and therefore England was at first ruled by a regent. For the first three years after Henry's accession, the regent was the 1st Earl of Pembroke, William Marshal, the man who had acted as moderator to King John during the matter of the barons' demands which led to Magna Carta. After William Marshal's death in 1219, a new regent was appointed: Hubert de Burgh, another supporter of King John at Runnymede and from 1215 chief justiciar of England. This position was the medieval equivalent of the monarch's chief executive officer and its holder therefore ran the country whenever the king was absent. With the Angevin preoccupation with hanging on to English possessions in France, the post of justiciar was no sinecure. This, the most powerful office of state, was vital to the monarch's peace of mind while he was away fighting, and at the same time its holder was often much hated by jealous barons. But as the English retreated and the Angevin empire withered, the monarch took a more direct interest in his kingdom and so the office of justiciar declined in importance. The last justiciar of England was the first of our Despensers, the one who fell at Evesham. There is a strong connection between Henry III, that Hugh Despenser and that battle in August 1265.

In 1227, the twenty-year-old Henry III decided that he was old enough to make his own decisions and declared himself to be now full sovereign of England. At this time the exchequer was poorly managed and the degree of influence on government from continental favourites bred a vigorous opposition to his style of rule. For example, the old Bishop of Winchester, Peter des Roches, and the king's Treasurer, Peter des Rivaux (known from their backgrounds as Poitevins – from Poitou) were influential enough and displayed so little regard for baronial ways as to arouse violent opposition to their supposed influence on the king. Yet the latter may have gathered power, but if the financial resources of the land were to be understood and made profitable, then, as successive chancellors right to the twenty-first century have understood, it was better done without the conflicting opinions and interests of economists. As ever, the barons had only their own (hardly the nation's) interests at heart and perhaps exaggerated the importance of the Poitevins in the running of the realm. Whatever the truth, the terrible outcome of Henry's reliance on the two Peters and the baronial opposition to them was the Marshal Rebellion of 1233–4. It was named after its leader, Richard Marshal the 3rd Earl of Pembroke and Struguil, a direct descendant of Henry III's first regent. As chief protagonist in a revolt against French influence, Richard was in a curious position, for he had spent much of his life in Normandy until his somewhat unexpected recent appointment to the post of Earl Marshal.[3]

Henry III had followed his father King John to the throne as the First Barons' War was coming to a head. This war consisted of a series of battles between John and the barons because he had failed to implement all the reforms he had agreed to in the articles of Magna Carta. The ultimate treason of the barons was to offer John's throne to Louis VIII of France. It was probably only the death of John in October 1216, just five months after Louis' landing in Kent, and the reissuing of Magna Carta by the new king's supporters, that turned the war in the throne's favour. By the following year the barons were vanquished, Louis had been expelled and the crown, for the moment anyway, was safe. The man behind the defeat of the barons and Louis in 1217 was the chief justiciar, William Marshal, whose grandson was now, some fifteen years later, leading a new barons' rebellion.

This affair was about who governed England – the Poitevins or the monarch (or, for monarch, read barons). The Anglo-Irish lords joined the rebellion and so did the marcher lords along the Welsh borders. The fighting was not widespread and took place mainly between royalist and baronial factions in Wales and Ireland. A settlement might easily have been achieved through the counsel of the bishops if it had not been for a grisly assassination in Ireland. Richard Marshal had gone over there to defend his estates from Henry's supporters, but at a meeting with the royalists he was murdered. However, Henry's supporters had done no service to their king, who was forced to bow to the barons and to send both the Poitevin advisers packing.

The rebellion was over, but there was no ease in the king's rule. In 1236 Henry had married Eleanor of Provence, and suspicions were aroused by the favours he granted at the English court to his uncles by marriage. The effective end of Henry III's reign came when he tried to raise money to pay for a war being conducted by the pope in Sicily; in return for financial support Henry had been promised the crown of Sicily for his second son, Edmund. At a convention at Oxford in 1258 the barons and, so some thought, the king agreed on a number of reforms in government. These Provisions of Oxford, as they became known, included an agreement that Parliament would meet three times a year with an elected commission of twelve men. Hitherto the king alone had been able to call parliament to meet, and had usually done so only when he wanted money – as now, for the financing of the papal war. To allow a provision that specified when Parliament would meet took away his power over the barons, so he reneged on what they had thought was a solemn agreement. Once more the barons felt that their patience had been tested enough. The Second Barons' War started in 1264 and its leader, Simon de Montfort, was to rule England for fifteen months until his death at the Battle of Evesham. With him on that fateful day was Hugh Despenser.

This first Hugh Despenser rose from untraceable beginnings. It is not even known who his parents were, although there is some obvious circumstantial evidence to suggest that his paternal grandfather, Hugh le Despenser, was a sheriff. But our Hugh does not really show up until the mid-1250s, not much more than a decade before he was killed. We know that he was the custodian of Harestan Castle in Derbyshire in 1256. His name was mentioned as a functionary and then he became quite prominent in the famous Parliament of 1258 – the one in which Henry III asked for money for the Sicilian Adventure and the barons reduced the monarch's powers under the Provisions of Oxford. It was at this Parliament that Hugh Despenser became one of the twelve commissioners appointed by the barons to look after their interests. So, in the years immediately before the Second Barons' War, Despenser clearly sided with the barons.

But he should not be seen as some raging anti-monarchist, even though in 1260 he was appointed justiciar to the barons in succession to Hugh Bigod. Bigod was the brother of the Earl of Norfolk and therefore, through their mother, the grandson of William Marshal and the nephew of Richard Marshal, who had led the rebellion named after him and had been murdered in Dublin. Through another uncle, William, he was distantly related to the king. The purpose of this brief Who's Who of thirteenth-century society is to demonstrate the close relationships between the key protagonists in the conflict between Henry III and the barons.

For example, it was about this time that Despenser married Aliva, the daughter of Sir Philip Basset (another of the twelve commissioners of the barons), who would shortly become co-justiciar with his new son-in-law because the king's fortunes had gathered strength after Oxford. Hugh and Aliva's son, later known as Hugh Despenser the Elder, was born in 1262.

The first Hugh Despenser's father-in-law was an important figure in the group that would eventually bring Prince Edward to the throne of his father, Henry III, and Despenser to his death. By the spring of 1259, Edward's cabal of gentlemen knights who would fight for him was more or less established. This group understood the frail substance of Henry's rule and the very real possibility that the barons' self-interest was stronger than their constitutional indignation.

Prince Edward had drawn close to Simon de Montfort, the Earl of Leicester, who had arrived in England from France in 1230 to claim his title (through his mother's side of the family) as the 6th Earl – to which he succeeded in 1231. De Montfort was not a quiet politician. One of his first acts as Earl of Leicester was to rid the city of all its Jews. It should be no surprise that this forceful personality became such a leading member of the group set on political reform in 1258 and therefore against Henry III. In return for the Provisions of Oxford which limited the monarch's powers the barons agreed to fund Henry's holy war as well as his excursions into Wales and France. At first Henry accepted the Provisions. De Montfort believed this contriteness would be short-lived and he would have no business with those who accepted the new strengths of Henry III after 1260 (which led among other things to Despenser's father-in-law becoming justiciar) and so returned to France to await the dissatisfaction with the king which he felt was inevitable. De Montfort was right. Henry could not tolerate the restriction of his power, so the Provisions were sent to the king of France for his opinion. When the French ruler said that he could not see any legitimacy in the conditions drawn up by the barons, Henry was delighted. He declared the recalcitrant nobles to be in rebellion. Came the uprising, came de Montfort – its obvious leader.

The fact that Hugh Despenser took de Montfort's side meant he opposed his father-in-law, Sir Philip Basset, who was for the king. In the spring of 1263, the events that led to Henry's downfall gathered pace. By July of that year the king's influence was so weakened that Basset was reduced to the justiciary ranks and Despenser, who had shared the chief justiciar's office with him, assumed it on his own. He also became Constable of the Tower of London, an office that was far more than symbolic. Moreover, Despenser was no idle office holder leaning this way and that according to the mood of the rebellion. He was firmly seated with those barons who were lined up against the king[4] and physically joined in the sackings and burnings of royalist property. For example, Despenser was in the van of the mob which raided and burned the Isleworth palace of the king's younger brother Richard, Earl of Cornwall.

There was no way to end the conflict between the supporters of Henry III and those of Simon de Montfort without a huge confrontation at which one side or the other would either have to sue for peace or be comprehensively defeated. The king, and more effectively his son Edward, had fought successfully across the midlands. De Montfort's barons were meeting in Northampton; on 3 April 1264 the young Edward broke into the town and, with considerable slaughter, took it. The attackers also captured de Montfort's son and removed him and other important prisoners to the Welsh borders where they were placed in the care of the marcher lords who were royalists. Edward omitted to press his advantage against de Montfort, whose forces were in the southern shires; instead, he and his father went north. This allowed de Montfort's troops to capture Rochester on the River Medway. By holding so much of the south-east, including the Kentish Weald and major ports such as Rochester and Dover, de Montfort was effectively cutting off Henry's means of obtaining any French help. The king and his son now marched south.

On 14 May 1264 the two sides moved towards Lewes, close to where the River Ouse flows into the English Channel from Sussex. At de Montfort's side was Hugh Despenser. The fight was not long that day. Prince Edward got some of the barons' forces on the run and chased them to the Lewes levels, the flat lands between the town and the sea. When he returned, it was to find that his father had lost the battle. Though short, it had been a bloody affair: Englishmen had killed six hundred of their compatriots. Some had been friends, some relatives. Despenser captured his much-wounded father-in-law Sir Philip Basset, along with the king's northern reinforcements. Despenser, highly trusted by de Montfort, was among those who prepared the peace treaty and negotiated its terms. The fact that the agreement[5] (known as the Mise of Lewes) allowed for the release of many of those captured, was to cause the downfall of de Montfort and the death of Despenser.

For the moment, Despenser was satisfied. The king had been virtually removed from his throne and he himself had been richly rewarded, his prizes including the rights, dues and governorships of six castles including Nottingham. Although some have thought otherwise, it seems difficult to believe that Hugh Despenser, or Hugo le Despenc Justic Angliæ as he was styled at Simon de Montfort's parliament, did not become even more powerful. In the capacity of de Montfort's constitutional attorney he travelled to France as mediator and witness about the country. De Montfort himself was ruling England in Henry's stead. But neither de Montfort nor Despenser was to enjoy either their power or their hopes for reform for very long.

Fourteen months or so after the Battle of Lewes, Henry's son Edward had regrouped. He first attacked and defeated the soldiers of de Montfort's son at Kenilworth, then marched through the night to surprise de Montfort and his barons and knights, including Despenser, at Evesham on 4 August 1265. De Montfort, seeing that the fight was a bloody and vicious one which would be lost, pleaded with Despenser to flee the field – he was, after all, justiciar and not a knight. He could have got away to Ireland or France, but Despenser chose to stay. No quarter was given, no mise written and discussed as at Lewes. De Montfort and Despenser were slaughtered.[6]

The widowed Aliva Despenser had found herself gaoler to royalist prisoners, now a somewhat precarious position given the recent events at Evesham. She immediately released her prisoners, took young Hugh, her three-year-old son, and fled to the custody of her father, Sir Philip Basset – who was loyal to the monarch. The Despensers were changing sides, but then so would everyone. Aliva subsequently married Roger, the son of Hugh Bigod whom her late husband had succeeded as justiciar in October 1260; Roger Bigod became Earl of Norfolk and Marshal of England.[7] The Bigods had come from Normandy with the Conqueror, although at the time they had had no great fortune. Seventy years after the Conquest, in 1136, King Stephen granted the Bigods the earldom of Norfolk; a later Bigod was one of the barons who persuaded King John to sign Magna Carta.

Although de Montfort was dead, not all the barons gave in. A truce was called in September that year but it was not to last. The rebels maintained their pockets of resistance to Edward's knights, particularly in the Kentish Cinque Ports and parts of the eastern counties. It took Edward until 1267 to turn the unsatisfactory truce into a genuine peace. The Barons' War was ended. The Despenser family, of course, continued.

Unlike his late father, the 'new' Hugh Despenser (to be known as Hugh Despenser the Elder, to distinguish him from his own son, known as Hugh Despenser the Younger) would grow up as a royalist. By 1272, when Hugh (the Elder) was just ten years old, that meant being loyal to the new monarch. Henry III was dead. Long live Edward I. As with the Godwines in Chapter 2, so Hugh Despenser was not, in the eyes of King Edward, tainted with the sin of his father. It was probably the fact that he was barely a child when the rebellious first Hugh was killed at Evesham by Edward's troops, together with the fact that his mother was clearly considered an innocent and very much her loyalist father's daughter, that caused no stigma to be attached to the name of Despenser.

In fact, Hugh the Elder seems to have done much to endear himself to the king through brave actions on his behalf. Before reaching his majority, he rode with Edward in the wars against the Welsh leader Llywelyn ap Gruffudd. In 1267 Edward's father, Henry III, had recognized Llywelyn as Prince of Wales, but ten years on the Welsh and the English were once more strapping on their swords. In 1282, Llywelyn was killed in battle. Two years later, the Statute of Rhuddlan carved the principality into counties and boroughs into which English adminis-trators were sent – thus Wales became subdued into a form that remained recognizable well into the twentieth century.

Perhaps it was respite from war that made Hugh Despenser think of taking a wife. It may have been a marriage made in heaven; it was certainly not made in Edward's court. Hugh married Isabel, the widow of one Patrick of Chaworth. Isabel Despenser, as she now was, was also the daughter of the Earl of Warwick. The law was very clear: such arrangements – her station in life and the possible political and military consequences of joining the two households – had to have a royal licence. Not only that – the monarch had a direct interest in who married whom at this level of society, and alliances were always scrutinized. The marriage was allowed to stand, but Despenser was made to pay a heavy fine of some 2000 marks. It was not an overbearing matter for his conscience, especially as the king needed him at his side. Despenser continued to travel with Edward at home and abroad, and in 1295 his authority could not have been questioned as he received the royal summons to attend the king's Parliament.

Soon after that, Despenser was once again in battle alongside his king. John Balliol, King of the Scots, had withdrawn his allegiance to King Edward; this was not to be tolerated. On 27 April 1296, Edward, with Despenser commanding troops in his army, defeated Balliol at the first Battle of Dunbar.[8] Balliol gave up his kingdom, but the rebel Scots were not vanquished. Moreover, the fierce rivalries within their own leadership made sure that they would be for ever fighting the English and even arguing over their own perceptions of independence. So Edward was back in 1298. This time, with the aid of his archers, he decisively defeated William Wallace's spearmen.[9]

Although he was evidently a fine soldier, we should not see Hugh Despenser the Elder as simply a strong knight in his king's service. Edward favoured Despenser greatly as an adviser and emissary – hence the animosities that grew about his personality. This did not matter as long as he had a strong patron. Edward I, unlike the son who would succeed him as Edward II, proved a good protector and Despenser proved a good servant. Edward I's war with, for example, Philip the Fair of France, who had invaded English possessions in Gascony, was a five-year test of steel both militarily and diplomatically; Despenser proved able in both spheres.

When King Edward thought it prudent to negotiate with Pope Boniface VIII, who was trying to reassert Rome's influence, it was Hugh Despenser whom he sent as his ambassador. The pope was concerned about two main topics: the Anglo-French war of 1294–8 and England's wars with the Scots, and his authority over the English clergy.

In 1296 Boniface had issued a papal bull entitled *Clericis Laicos*, whose main theme was the matter of who had the right to tax the clergy. Both Edward of England and Philip IV (the Fair) of France were strongly opposed to any interference. This conflict was more than a bureaucratic dispute and it was the direct cause of the seat of the papacy moving to Avignon at the start of the fourteenth century. Philip resisted all attempts to impose papal influence; Edward was in a more delicate position.

The intricacies of European politics during the late thirteenth century are not for this book; it is sufficient to know that England had never been isolated from what was going on in continental Europe. For example, Henry III's brother Richard, the Earl of Cornwall, had been King of the Romans, a title given to the ruler of Germany within the Holy Roman Empire. He was expected to become emperor, and would have done so had he not died prematurely in 1272. Edward I was a cousin of Philip III of France (father of Philip the Fair). Pope Gregory, in office from 1271 to 1276, was a friend of Edward's. The new king of Sicily was

Charles of Anjou, no friend of England's or the pope's. The election of the Swabian Rudolf of Habsburg as Holy Roman Emperor to end the interregnum following Richard's death only added to the political uncertainties of Europe at this time. Also, Edward was not of Saxon or even Norman stock. He was no Englishman in the sense that we might think a king would naturally be. Stories of him storming about England in defence of his father's throne, battling in everyday places with everyday names – Kenilworth, Northampton, Evesham, Dover – hide a far wider horizon across which this monarch roamed. Edward's background gives a further idea of the complexities of European kingship. He came from the southern slopes of France – he was Duke of Aquitaine. His mother was Eleanor of Provence, his grandmother had been Isabella of Angoulême and his wife was a Spaniard, Eleanor of Castile.

In short, late thirteenth- and fourteenth-century Europe was a web of family ties, treaties, obligations and promises, all subject to continental influences and threats to sovereignty just as disturbing as those of six hundred years later. Kings had the right of independent authority, yet the pope believed he too had a right: to cajole, warn and if necessary interfere; hence the need for high diplomacy. The story of what was going on between the pope, the European leaders and Edward is more complicated than outlined here, but it is clear that the English king's role was not simply to beat the local opposition and then settle back to a quiet life of minstrels and peacocks on the lawn. Hence Edward's reliance on Hugh Despenser, who appeared to be the perfect go-between and was now sent 'on an embassy' to Pope Boniface. At stake were the immediate future of relations with France; war in Scotland; war in Europe. Despenser, along with another envoy, Henry Lacy, had much to explain and much to negotiate. Pope Boniface did indeed broker an alliance between France and England, although few held out any hope that it would last.

In 1307, Edward I died on his way to campaign against the Scots. Hugh Despenser was a royalist, and his patron therefore the king. Indeed, Despenser carried Edward II's regalia during his coronation. Where his father had lined up with the barons against the excesses of Henry III, Hugh Despenser stood by the king in one of the more wretched if colourful periods in British history.

Edward II came to the throne at the age of twenty-three. He had been born at Caernarfon, and six years before his coronation had become the first heir to the English throne to be installed as Prince of Wales. He was already a friend of Hugh Despenser the Elder's son, also Hugh, known as Hugh Despenser the Younger. Hugh the Younger had been made a knight by Edward in 1306, the year before he came to the throne.

Many, perhaps most, of the barons despised Edward II. They found him weak, grasping, against their interests and excessively devoted to a Gascon, Piers de Gaveston. Edward's infatuation would bring about the end of both men. Gaveston had been a courtier to Edward I, and the young Prince Edward had been so taken with him that he asked his father the great favour of creating him Count of

Ponthieu. But the affair had gone too far and Gaveston was banished – for the first time. As soon as his father was dead, Edward recalled Gaveston to his side in his new court in England.

At the age of five Edward had been betrothed to the six-year-old Margaret, Queen of Scots, known as the Maid of Norway because her father was king of that country. Sadly, she died en route to Scotland. By the time of his accession, Edward, even though besotted by Gaveston, knew he had to take a wife. The following year, 1308, he married Isabella, sister of Charles IV of France, but this convenient arrangement did nothing to lessen his open passion for the Gascon. He created Gaveston Earl of Cornwall, and when he went to France to greet his betrothed he appointed Gaveston as his regent. It was inevitable that such an action, coming on top of the continual humiliation of their authority by Edward and his lover, would cause the barons once more to revolt against their monarch. Hugh Despenser the Elder would have found it good politics to join with the barons. After all, he could see as well as they could how risky the affair was for the country. He did not join them, and was probably the one courtier who sided with the king even when the barons successfully demanded that Gaveston be banished from the kingdom for the second time. In the same year as his regency, then, Gaveston was forced to exile himself to Ireland. That Edward accompanied him to his ship in tears suggested that his departure would not be for long and that the marriage to Isabella was more than farcical – it was dangerous. Isabella felt her humiliation even more than the barons. Still Despenser the Elder stuck by his patron and thus earned the everlasting animosity of the queen, which would cost him dearly.

When the Parliament met at Northampton in the same year, it dismissed Hugh the Elder from the council. It was a token victory for the barons, who were proving their strength elsewhere – for example they controlled London, which was really the king's demesne. Meanwhile Gaveston had returned, but was banished again and of course returned again; the king could not be without him. The barons had long since concluded that there was but one way to break Gaveston's grip on the king.

In 1310, the barons forced the king to agree to the appointment of a body known as the Ordainers. Its members comprised eight earls – including the king's own cousin, the powerful Thomas, Earl of Lancaster – six barons and seven bishops, among them the Archbishop of Canterbury. Clearly this was the most influential group of high-ranking men in England. Their role was to reform the royal household, and the way in which it governed the kingdom, through a series of Ordinances. They laid down laws to change the way the king's treasury was used, stating, for example, that the king could not make gifts until his considerable debts had been paid off. Edward was no longer allowed to enter into any war or even to travel abroad without the consent of the barons. They used their power to banish Gaveston yet again; by Christmas 1311 the king had brought him back. The Ordainers were supposed to have their authority for just one year, but continued beyond Michaelmas 1311 and then, using their self-approved (and lapsed) authority, set themselves against the king and particularly his favourite. Gaveston was captured, tried for treason (by the Ordainers) and executed in 1312. Although Hugh Despenser the Elder had supported Gaveston, he had no power against the baronial cabal.

With Gaveston dead, Edward felt bereft of trustworthy advice, for he neither accepted the Ordainers' authority nor forgave what they had done. He turned to Hugh Despenser the Elder and made him his most senior and trusted adviser. Whether it was simply a matter of telling the king what he wanted to hear, or whether he thought it the right thing to do, Despenser now encouraged the king to plan his revenge. Thomas of Lancaster knew this, despised Despenser as much as he had Gaveston, and when a sort of truce was agreed between the barons and the king Lancaster made it clear that Despenser was not included. However, the king did not abandon his new adviser. In 1314 Despenser may have wished otherwise, for he had to go north with Edward to relieve the besieged castle at Stirling in Scotland. The outcome, on 24 June 1314, was the Battle of Bannockburn, at which Robert the Bruce famously and with enormous blood-shed beat the English. There followed uprisings in Wales and Ireland. Edward's position was miserable, and it was impossible to sustain any authority that he thought he might still possess. Lancaster virtually ruled England:

> The earls said that the Ordinances had not been observed and therefore events had turned out badly for the king: both because the king had sworn to stand by the Ordinances and because the archbishop had excommunicated all those contravening them: so that no good could come unless the Ordinances were fully observed...in accordance with the Ordinances, the chancellor, treasurer, sheriffs, and other officers were removed...the earls also willed that Hugh Despenser, Henry Beaumont, and certain others should leave the king's court.... Hugh Despenser was compelled...to retire....[10]

Once more Hugh the Elder was forced to leave the court, and his career seemed to be finished. Edward had descended into deep gloom as he grieved for his lost love. In 1315 he took the body of Piers de Gaveston to the Dominican church at King's Langley, where the last rites were read by Archbishop Reynolds and the remains of the king's lover were interred. Perhaps cheered by this rite of passage, the king hoped for the return of his authority, but this was not to be. The unremit-ting rains that criss-crossed Europe in 1315 devastated the harvests. In the face of terrible famine, gruesome crimes were committed by normally easy-going folk now desperate to feed their aching bellies. There was no sign that social or political matters would improve. Lancaster and the earls had gained the reforms they had demanded under the Ordinances. The Ordainers had their own men in almost every office that mattered. Lancaster, that most arrogant of reformers, was now so firmly entrenched as ruler of England that, when his cousin the king offered at the Lincoln Parliament of 1316 to make him his chief adviser he felt no need to show any conciliation and merely said he would think about it.

Lancaster was unscrupulous, but no more so than the Despensers; and it was about this time that father and son, Despenser the Elder and Despenser the Younger, together became prominent opponents of the Lancaster party. But though the Despensers were ostensibly for the king, mostly the Despensers were for the Despensers. The relationship between them and Edward II strengthened in such a way that Lancaster and the other recalcitrant barons all but declared war on them. The father was now Earl of Winchester, whilst the son regarded himself as owner of anything he surveyed should he wish it. They became as much a target as was the king.

Hugh Despenser the Younger had replaced Gaveston in Edward's personal affections. The king laid gift upon gift, honour upon honour on both father and son. Yet, whereas Hugh the Elder had always been a royalist, for whatever his reasoning, his son had not always found favour with Edward II. True, he had received his knighthood from the then Prince Edward, but in the time immediately after the death of Edward I, Hugh the Younger seems to have been inclined more to the barons and in particular Lancaster. In fact, when the king needed a new chamberlain after Gaveston's execution, the barons 'gave' Edward the young Hugh. Imagine, at this stage, the king's suspicions of anyone nominated by the barons.

Among those killed at Bannockburn, in 1314 was the Earl of Gloucester. Five years earlier, Hugh Despenser the Younger had married the earl's sister Eleanor. After the Earl's death he shared the inheritance with the husbands of the earl's other two sisters. There was much jealousy at his inheritance and once more a Despenser found himself the object of intrigue and plotting because of his own fortune.

It would be easy to despise the Despensers for their blatant self-aggrandizement. But Hugh the Elder had for many years taken the king's side and stood defiantly at his side against the barons. This was no back-room courtier quietly feathering a considerable nest: the Despensers had risked far more than their positions in the name of the king and would soon pay with more than their wealth.

The greed and success of the Despensers, together with their blatant and often unquestioning support of the king, inevitably stirred the already potent bitterness against both father and son. Hugh the Younger may not quite have been a new Gaveston, but he was not far off and for many of the barons the difference could hardly be measured. It is likely that the baronial party saw the Despensers' power-base strengthening to such a degree that they feared the heights it might achieve, whereas their loathing of Gaveston was based on the fact that he was a foreigner, openly contemptuous and usurping the authority of the monarchy. The barons had high regard for the monarchy, if low esteem for its present incumbent. The Despensers, therefore, were a different case to be dealt with by the barons, many of whom were now related to them by virtue of Hugh the Younger's marriage to Eleanor of Gloucester. Moreover, much of the tragedy that followed was surely more to do with Hugh the Younger's quarrels within the aristocracy than with jealousies surrounding his position at court, even within Edward's private chambers.

By 1321 it seemed there could be no future compromise between barons and Despensers. When Hugh Despenser the Younger took his share of his inheritance from his wife's brother he gained control of a large part of Glamorgan. But he wanted much more. One of his brothers-in-law (yet another Hugh) held the estates at Audley in the midlands; Despenser acquired those lands for himself. He then turned his attention to the northern borders of Wales and England, the northern marches – the feudal fiefdoms of the Mortimers, with whom the story of the Despensers is from this point inextricably linked. Despenser used his friendship with the king to suggest that many of the Mortimer lands should revert to the sovereign – and ultimately to the Despensers. He did the same with John Mowbray's inheritance in the Gower peninsula of South Wales (see p. 63). Using a legal point about the king's licensing of land, Despenser tried again to get the king to take the land and then hand it on to him.

The marcher lords could easily see the influence that both Despensers brought to bear on the monarch and decided they had had enough of this avaricious and obscenely ambitious pair. The Earl of Hereford, Humphrey Bohun, set out to stop the Despensers and found it easy to establish a group of like-minded marcher lords including Roger de Mortimer, Hugh the Younger's brothers-in-law Audley and D'Amory and inevitably the Earl of Lancaster. There was nothing new in fourteenth-century factionalism, and the intensity of the hatred for the Despensers lived up to anything seen before. The fact that the barons were taking on the king's closest friends and advisers strengthened the animosities on both sides. Edward certainly had no illusions about his own weak position; he could plead for moderation like some unworldly cleric, but there was little more he could do. The Despensers must have understood this. Considering what had gone before, it is not clear why they believed they could overcome the barons. Perhaps the answer is simple arrogance. Arrogance was not enough.

So the marcher lords went to war against the Despensers and attacked and plundered their West Country lands. This was not a war against Edward. In Parliament, the Despensers were castigated. Hugh the Younger was accused of being against Edward by suggesting that his allegiance was to the concept of the monarchy rather than to the individual. Here, perhaps, the barons were not simply being devious in their charges against Despenser. There must have been much evidence for their view of his attitude towards the constitutional issues of kingship. Whether they were relevant at the time or were being used as an excuse for his indictment is another matter. There were other charges, including fraud. The barons could make any of their charges valid because the Despensers, especially Hugh the Younger, were self- seeking, greedy, corrupt bullies. Edward, whatever his personal feelings, was no more successful in protecting Hugh the Younger than he had been in saving Gaveston from exile. The two Despensers were banished from the kingdom. But it was, as had been Gaveston's, a short-lived banishment, and they were brought back by Edward in the following year, 1322, to join him in his war against Lancaster. The king's forces were successful, after a fashion.

The discussion of constitutional law pertaining to the monarch continued and clearly the Despensers, especially the son, had a great deal of interest in the outcome. They had few regards for civil and criminal law. They forced their way into new estates, including by legal means the constableship of Bristol Castle and by illegal means the manorial holdings of baronial widows.

The fragility of the Despenser authority was evident when the king proposed the idea of taking an army against the French. The queen, who held her husband in even greater contempt than had the barons (she had, after all, been rejected in favour of first Gaveston and then Hugh Despenser the Younger), had gone to France ostensibly to act as negotiator with her brother, Charles IV. Isabella was in no hurry to return. By 1325 she had become the mistress of Roger de Mortimer, Baron Wigmore, who had been imprisoned in the Tower of London in 1322 but had escaped to France in 1324. Their alliance was as ruthless as any in England. It was probably Mortimer who arranged the particularly sadistic murder of Edward II at Berkeley Castle in 1327.[11]

There was more talk of war between France and England, and Edward's notion that he might lead an expedition against the French was both tactically naïve and, for the Despensers, politically risky. They knew that if Edward stepped beyond England's shores their only means of protection would be gone.

At this point, Edward ordered his queen to return. She said she would not as long as the Despensers held his offices and the Younger his blatant affection. Hugh the Elder was forced to go to Parliament and declare his loyalty to the queen's interests. The bishops acted as go-betweens and dispatches containing the Despensers' protestations of innocence were sent to France. Here we can see clearly the power of the Despensers over the monarch. They told Edward to declare his queen and her son (the future Edward III), who was with her and Roger de Mortimer in France, outlaws. The king did the Despensers' bidding; another war was to come.

In September 1326, Isabella and Mortimer landed at Harwich. They had crossed the North Sea from the Low Countries where they had gone after Charles IV of France had become embarrassed by their love affair and plotting. They had brought their supporters in good number and were reinforced by many of the barons, including Henry of Leicester, so had a force strong enough to defeat Edward and the Despensers.

Hugh Despenser the Elder had been given the custody of Bristol Castle. Edward II now ordered him to the West Country to defend Bristol, but on 26 October 1326 he was obliged to surrender to Isabella and Mortimer. The following day he was hanged outside the city, after which his head was cut off and taken to Winchester (his earldom) and displayed for all to see. His son was to fare no better.

King Edward, predictably enough, had kept Hugh Despenser the Younger by his side. Now the two fled to Gloucester and then, on the day of the execution of

Hugh Despenser the Elder, Edward and the young Hugh escaped to Cardiff. They were intending to find refuge on the Isle of Lundy, which Despenser had taken for himself a couple of years earlier, but their escape route was blocked by troops and bad weather and so they pressed on to two other castles that the Despensers had taken, Neath and Caerphilly. The battlements offered little protection. The queen's forces, led by William de la Zouche, followed then and they surrendered on 16 November.

Hugh the Younger was taken to Hereford, where Isabella and Mortimer had made camp. The trial was predictably short – there was not one person at that court who did not hate the defendant. After his execution Hugh the Younger's head was taken to London and stuck on a pike on London Bridge for all to see and know that the rule of the Despensers was over. But the dynasty was not cut down at Bristol and Hereford.

Hugh the Younger's eldest son was a loyal if unremarkable parliamentarian just twelve years on from his father's execution. Yet another son, Edward, had a son, also Edward, who became a distinguished soldier respected for his campaigns in Italy and France, including fighting alongside the Black Prince at the Battle of Poitiers in 1356 during the Hundred Years' War between England and France. He became a knight of the most noble of all the monarch's orders, the Garter. Clearly there was no disgrace in this Despenser. His son, Thomas Despenser (1373–1400), had a more chequered and certainly short career.

Thomas was two when his celebrated father died a year after the Battle of Poitiers. His guardian was the Earl of Cambridge, Edmund Langley, who was one of Edward III's sons. This Despenser was even more 'connected' by family than the earlier Despensers: he married his guardian's daughter, Constance, thus becoming related by marriage to the king. Thomas Despenser was a firm loyalist and strongly countered the accusations of treason against Richard II. As a reward for this loyalty Richard made him Earl of Gloucester, an earldom to which he had some claim through the marriage of Hugh Despenser the Younger.

Thomas then went with Richard II on his Irish campaign, commanding a major part of his army. That was a sorry affair. Firstly, Henry Bolingbroke, son of John of Gaunt, had begun moves from his exile abroad to depose the king. When John of Gaunt died in 1399, Richard II seized his estates. That same year, while Richard was in Ireland, Bolingbroke invaded to reclaim his father's estates and acquire more. In August that year, Richard was forced to surrender. As part of his agreement to step aside, he wanted safety for Thomas Despenser, but it is here that we come to the second sad aspect of the Irish campaign. When Despenser left Ireland he took with him the son of the late Duke of Gloucester, Humphrey. Soon after reaching England, Humphrey died, and a rumour started that Despenser had had him murdered. This may have been one of the reasons for requesting Despenser's pardon, but the king need not have bothered. Thomas Despenser had too much family history not to understand the folly of supporting a falling, if not yet fallen, monarch. He deserted Richard – to be fair, as did most others.

His disgrace, and the suspicion that he had played a part in Humphrey Gloucester's death, persisted and Despenser lost his earldom. Again he was not alone in losing his standing; his brother-in-law, the Earl of Rutland, also lost his. Despenser now joined the disgruntled nobles led by Rutland. However, conspirators are often fickle folk, and it was Rutland himself who betrayed the group at Cirencester in January 1400. Despenser managed to evade capture and escape to his castle at Cardiff. He hoped to get away from Wales by ship, but the master of the vessel had other ideas, docked at Bristol and handed him over to the city fathers.

The name Despenser had never been popular in Bristol, and Thomas followed a family tradition which he had probably hoped had been abandoned: he was beheaded. So ended the recorded deeds of a colourful family who carried the baggage of a seemingly irrevocable death wish. Or was it the end?

In 1999 Charles Spencer, the 9th Earl of the name and brother of the late Diana, Princess of Wales, published a family history. In it he recorded the belief that the modern Spencers are descended from the Despensers seven centuries earlier. If so, it is tempting to believe that the sense of family tragedy is undiminished.

NOTES

1 The family is normally called Despenser, although it may be correctly styled le Despenser. The name appears to come from the Norman French and describes a steward, i.e. one who dispenses.

2 The dispute between later sprigs of the Plantagenet line (York and Lancaster) became known long after that event as the Wars of the Roses and ended with the defeat of the last of the Plantagenets, Richard III, in 1485 at the Battle of Bosworth Field.

3 Originally, the marshal was appointed as senior court official overseeing military affairs – a cross between a modern defence secretary and chief of the defence staff. Later, this office became Earl Marshal. From the thirteenth century, the appointment was held hereditarily by the earls – and later the dukes – of Norfolk.

4 Although we speak of the barons being against Henry III, it is clear from the king's gathering of supporters at, for example, Northampton and, disastrously, at Lewes in 1264, that not all were.

5 Mise: from the Norman French, meaning an arrangement.

6 See Chapter 4.

7 Although that earldom became extinct in 1306, the appointment of Earl Marshal of England continued and in 1644 the office became that of the Howard family (now Fitzalan-Howard). Its holder is still titled Earl Marshal and Hereditary Marshal and Chief Butler of England.

8 The second Battle of Dunbar took place over three centuries later, on 3 September 1650, when Cromwell defeated David Leslie's Scots.

9 Wallace was eventually captured and condemned, and was executed in 1305.

10 *Vita Edwardi Regis.*

11 After the defeat of the Despensers and Edward II's murder in 1327, Isabella and Roger Mortimer ruled England. But Edward III (Isabella's son) had him arrested in 1330 and Mortimer was hanged at Tyburn (at the Marble Arch end of the modern Bayswater Road in London).

FURTHER READING

Froissart's *Chronicques*, ed, Kervyn de Lettenhove.
McKISACK, May, *The Fourteenth Century 1307–1399*, OUP, 1959.
POWICKE, Sir Maurice, *The Thirteenth Century 1216–1307*, OUP, 1953.

CHAPTER FOUR

THE MORTIMERS

The Mortimers lurked about the thrones of thirteenth, fourteenth and fifteenth-century England. One ruled England with his mistress, the widow of Edward II whom he had murdered. Another was the heir to Richard II but, instead of becoming king, ended up Lieutenant of Ireland. Another was Marshal of England and the Yorkist claimant by marriage for his wife to the English throne. Another became Edward IV.

Most will remember the Mortimer name through Roger de Mortimer, who, as noted in Chapter 3, was the lover of Edward II's wife Isabella; he helped her to overthrow her husband and for three years to rule England. Inevitably our hero was hanged, drawn and quartered and the heroine became a nun. That is the way of English history in the Middle Ages. But the family's story appears to start much earlier and end much later than the forty or so years in the life of Roger de Mortimer, royal lover and 1st Earl of March.

The name Mortimer probably comes from the name of the place where the tenth- and eleventh-century family lived, Mortemer-en-Brai in Normandy. An earlier Mortimer lost the castle, through bad political judgement, to William the Conqueror. Later, the Mortimers showed up in the Welsh border country of Herefordshire and Shropshire, where William the Conqueror handed them the castle at Wigmore.

Certainly by 1086, the time of the Domesday Book, Mortimers held lands in Herefordshire, Shropshire, Hampshire, Wiltshire, Somerset, Oxfordshire, Leicestershire, Yorkshire and Lincolnshire. In the rising against King Rufus in 1088, Ralph de Mortimer was with the rebels. But the affair was settled the following year and, although he took royal money to build defences against the French, Ralph spent much of his time extending his estates along the Welsh borders. What happened after that is unclear; the best we can do is jump a generation to Ralph's grandson Hugh de Mortimer, who lived in the reign of King Stephen (1135–54).

The saga of Stephen and his cousin, the Empress Matilda,[1] is another of those colourful yet ruthless accounts of rivalries for medieval thrones. When Henry I died in 1135 there were two contestants for the throne: Stephen and the Empress

Matilda. Stephen was the grandson of William the Conqueror, Matilda the daughter of Henry I. In 1127 the Anglo-Norman barons (including Stephen) swore that if their king, Henry I, had no sons, they would recognize Matilda as queen. But when Henry died the barons went back on their collective oath and elected Stephen as king. These were times of constant wars, and the barons believed it would be impossible to have a woman as monarch.

By this time the Empress Matilda was married to Geoffrey of Anjou. She was determined not to give up her claim to the English throne, but she had to bide her time. Her first task was to fight for that throne in France because Stephen was by inheritance also Duke of Normandy. While the Empress was preoccupied in Normandy, Stephen, very much organized by his wife Matilda of Boulogne, contained opposition in England. This caused a delay in the confrontation that had been inevitable since the death of Henry I. In 1139 the Empress Matilda landed in England. Again, thanks to the other Matilda, Stephen's wife, and because the Empress had an arrogant nature, the support she might have expected did not materialize. Even when Stephen was captured at the Battle of Lincoln in 1141, the Empress failed to consolidate her authority and gain the throne for herself. She made her camp in the West Country, as had so many in opposition to the throne before her. There she bided her time and regrouped but, under pressure, retreated in 1148 to Normandy and her son, the future Henry II.

For once, it seems, the Mortimers were not players in the contest for the throne of England. The earliest Mortimer about whom much is known appears to have avoided taking sides. Instead, Hugh de Mortimer decided that he should consolidate his position as one of the senior marcher lords, those guardians of the straggling and rarely peaceful border with Wales. But Hugh de Mortimer's writ ran strongly in Shropshire, so he could not entirely divorce himself from the conflict between the king and his cousin. Miles, Earl of Hereford, for example, did not have full authority of Hugh de Mortimer's lands. This was by special patent of the king. When the Earl of Hereford challenged de Mortimer's authority, he did so as a baron who supported Matilda, not Stephen. So Hugh de Mortimer, like all other lords of the time, had to defend his rights with sword as well as patronage. Mortimer's long dispute with the lord of Ludlow, Joce de Dinant, was an example of uncompromising feuding which could so easily have ended in the death of one or other of them. In the end, de Dinant captured Mortimer and incarcerated him until he came up with a huge ransom. Mortimer's Tower, part of Ludlow Castle, was probably built over the site of his cell.

Other conflicts did not end so bloodlessly. In 1145 Hugh de Mortimer captured the Welsh prince Rhys ap Howel and put his eyes out; a year later, his kinsman Maredudd ap Howel was killed by de Mortimer. The king would not have minded; after all, the marcher lords had a duty to protect the kingdom against marauding Welshmen. By the time the Empress Matilda's son became Henry II in 1154, Hugh de Mortimer was one of the most powerful of the marcher lords and had taken many castles, including the king's at Bridgnorth.

Henry II did not behave as Stephen had, and would not be kept from his own castles. Hugh de Mortimer prepared to hold out against the full might of Henry II's forces and, seeking an ally, made up his differences with the Earl of Hereford – or so he thought. Hereford knew he could not succeed and gave over to the king. Defending one castle against the might of a king, especially one's own king, thus reducing the chances of making any allies, is a venture not without considerable risk. Hugh de Mortimer had three castles, therefore three chances of failing. Henry II sent a division of his army against each stronghold. The castle at Cleobury fell with little real resistance. Bridgnorth (the king's) and Wigmore (de Mortimer's seat) held out for nearly three months. Wigmore had particular importance to the Mortimer family as their spiritual home.

In July 1154, Hugh de Mortimer was forced to bend his knee to Henry; but he kept his head, which suggests that he was a powerful baron. Organizing the defence of three castles, especially since his most important ally had deserted him, must have taken a wide range of skills: there must have been considerable support for Mortimer in the marches. From that point, Hugh de Mortimer is all but forgotten except for one landmark in the border counties, Wigmore Priory. The building had been started in earlier days by a steward to the family and was endowed by Hugh, though it was not until 1174 that the church was consecrated. By 1181, when Hugh de Mortimer lay dying, he was so truly pious that he was made a canon.

The story of the Mortimers now shifts to another Roger, the 6th Baron Wigmore, who was born in about 1231. It is from this point that the family become highly influential in English history rather than just leading marcher lords. So how did this Roger de Mortimer achieve his rise to fame?

In 1247, when his father Ralph had been dead less than a year, Roger de Mortimer inherited the family estates and married a wealthy heiress, Matilda de Braose. She owned a third of the Brecon lordship as well as estates in South Wales and Ireland. With this single act of marriage Roger de Mortimer, still just sixteen years of age, became one of the important landowners in England. Six years later, Henry III dubbed him knight at Winchester.

From our modern perspective, what happened during the next few years is not without irony. Through his mother's Welsh family Mortimer was related to the Prince of Wales, Llywelyn ap Gruffudd. In those days, this did not mean a line into the English royal family – this Prince of Wales was most decidedly not the son of Henry III. Llywelyn was a continuously angry Welshman who raided the marcher lords' estates – many of the holdings held on behalf of the king and his family – and succeeded in capturing land from Roger de Mortimer. So serious was the problem that Henry III gave him money to buy soldiers to defeat Llywelyn, and when a truce was declared Mortimer was appointed one of the king's commissioners charged with working out its terms. It did not last many months – these things rarely did. Once more we are made aware of the significance of distance in medieval England and the importance of the marcher lords to the monarch.

The possessions of the king and his princes were scattered throughout the kingdom. There was never a time when members of the royal family by themselves could hope to protect their estates, manors and castles. The distances were too great, the logistics of defence and maintenance too cumbersome and the opportunities for enemies too easily come by for any king to rule his kingdom without the good will and active support of his barons.

So when, in 1260, Mortimer failed to beat off a Welsh attack on Builth Castle it was the king's son, Edward, who was the immediate loser – it was his castle which Mortimer, as a marcher lord, was expected to defend. Edward was not pleased that Mortimer had not held his castle; whether or not the Welsh had been simply too powerful on the day would not have crossed the prince's mind. Favour and patronage demanded certain returns: hanging on to a royal castle was one of them.

For eight hundred or so years of English, indeed British, history, questions of loyalty must have been recited in the morning catechism of every monarch. This was especially true in the thirteenth century, and perhaps Edward had reason to suspect Mortimer's enthusiasm for defending his estates. When, in 1258, the barons had yet again confronted the monarch, Mortimer had been committed to the baronial cause. He was, for example, one of the twelve lords elected by the barons to reform the way in which the kingdom was managed – a senior commissioner. But he was also the leading marcher lord at the time when the war was taken to the Welsh, so it is difficult to see how he could have done very much other than look after his border interests – and, in doing so, those of the monarch.

Also, by this time, the rebellious baron Simon de Montfort was successfully in league with Llywelyn, Mortimer's main enemy. When de Montfort's inevitable break with Edward came, Mortimer broke away from the baronial opposition. But that did not wipe his slate of constitutional sin; only the monarch could do that, and shortly before Christmas 1261 Mortimer was pardoned. Unlike the case of some of the reprieved barons, his pardon was justified, for he would remain a royalist. A measure of Mortimer's authority is that the other marcher lords followed him and immediately the borders were seen as a royalist stronghold. However, that hardly made for a quiet life with the neighbouring Welsh, who time and again attacked Mortimer's estates and lands and drove him from his four great castles at Bleddva, Cevnllys, Knucklas and Radnor. Mortimer's own tenants were now for the Welsh prince.

Marcher lords had no walls to protect their military and political back, so while Mortimer struggled with Llywelyn his English enemies struck. This was the period of the Barons' War against Henry III and his son, the future Edward I (see p. 40). The confrontation was leading to the infamous Battle of Lewes on 14 May 1264 and, more conclusively, to the Battle of Evesham the following year. Mortimer and the marcher lords who followed him took the king's side and therefore he found himself (really, chose to find himself) in hot pursuit of Simon de Montfort and his brother Henry. When Northampton was taken and Simon de Montfort captured it was Mortimer and his increasingly bloodthirsty band who were to the fore of that assault. They might so easily have suffered an unromantic end if they had not then escaped when the baronial forces defeated the royalists at Lewes and the king and young Edward were captured. Mortimer and his marcher lords got away – or more realistically, were allowed to escape back to the West Country. Yet how could there be any comfort at home?

Mortimer's long-running conflict with Llywelyn had been in part sustained by support from other parts of royalist England. Now de Montfort's baronial party ruled, and Mortimer and his marcher lords understood perfectly that the advantage must now lie with the Welsh. The barons of de Montfort and the Welsh of Llywelyn proved a formidable enemy, ravaging Mortimer's lands and those of his friends. The best the marcher lords could hope for was some sort of truce. It came, but the terms were as harsh as the savagery that had brought them about: Mortimer was to be banished from the kingdom. Time and again during this period apparent victories dissolved into inconclusive truces and a rapid return to the status quo ante. The very disunity that brought about the conflict was usually the element that turned triumph into farce – thus the return of Mortimer before he had departed.

The barons could not hold together. The Earls of Gloucester and Leicester were at each other's throats and, while they grappled, the marcher lords regrouped, with Gloucester more or less forcing Mortimer into an alliance. Here we reach a moment which from today's viewpoint seems bizarre at first glance. De Montfort, no longer sure of his authority, led his forces into the West Country against Gloucester and the recharged marcher lords. To add to his security, de Montfort took with him what he believed would be his stoutest shield – Edward, the future king. The concept was not new: the hostage taken to the battle was a form of insurance, and seven hundred and more years later the procedure is sometimes no more sophisticated.

Mortimer, however, knew what had to be done to swing the advantage away from his enemy. It was he, Roger Mortimer, 6th Baron Wigmore, who devised the ploy that would see the end of Simon de Montfort. Mortimer successfully plotted Edward's escape and returned with the future king to his estate at Wigmore. He did more: it was Mortimer who was largely responsible for bringing the prince together with Gloucester. The alliances were set for the imminent civil war.

When the main battle was fought at Evesham, on 4 August 1265, Mortimer was given command of the royal rearguard. His marcher lords and warriors fought fiercely and without quarter. At the end of the day, de Montfort lay dead. As a final ignominy his head was sliced from his trunk and the bloody object sent as a gift to Mortimer's wife, who was waiting for news of the conflict at Wigmore.

However, these were no times in which to rest on battle laurels. In May the following year Mortimer escaped by the skin of his teeth as his army was slaughtered about him by the Welsh at Brecon. He who fights and runs away lives to fight another day, this time gloriously at the siege of Kenilworth. It was here in Warwickshire that the rump of de Montfort's supporters had held out against

Henry III. Their estates had been taken away by the victorious royalists, and de Montfort's people promised to surrender if their lands might be restored to them. The Dictum of Kenilworth, pronounced in October 1266, agreed the restoration and, although the Dictum had later to be rewritten, the siege was undone.

It was this rewriting that nearly undid Mortimer's further wealth and glory. His holdings increased because the monarch went out of his way to reward his marcher lords, in particular Mortimer. For example, he became sheriff of Herefordshire and the custodian of its castle. Like so many medieval barons Mortimer saw about him land that was weakly held and grabbed at anything he thought he should have or could have. With this sense of greed and power came a harsh sense of justice, again common at a time when any baron needed to be uncompromisingly stern in order to hold on to what was his – including, sometimes, his life. Meanwhile, the Dictum of Kenilworth had been revised and those disinherited supporters of de Montfort were being pardoned and reinstated. Mortimer saw this compromise as a threat to his own wealth and position: it was not unlikely that he would lose the affections of his allies. Pertinently, he fell out with Gilbert of Gloucester – one of the more important barons and hitherto on Mortimer's side – because Gloucester strongly supported the cause of the disinherited. Although there is no direct evidence, there was a great deal of suspicion that Mortimer had gone as far as plotting the assassination of Gloucester.

However, Mortimer's great ally in his unquestionable royalist role was the future king, Edward. He was so trusted that when Edward left the country to go on a crusade in 1270 it was Mortimer whom he asked, together with his brother Richard and the Archbishop of York, to be guardian of the royal children and estates. Henry III died in November 1272, so Mortimer effectively became one of the three regents ruling England in the new king Edward I's absence. This was not a short-term task because the king was away until the late summer of 1274. In the hands of the regents, and in particular those of the leader of the marcher lords, Edward's kingdom seems to have been a safe place in which to live. When some, including the northern barons, thought to take advantage of the king's back being turned, it was Mortimer who speedily put down their rebellion.

When Edward returned, although the country was in good fettle, the constant enemy, Llywelyn of Wales, was once more on the march. The king appointed Mortimer his regent for Herefordshire, Shropshire and Staffordshire and all the marches, so that he could have absolute authority to defend the king's interests. Once more he took the fight to the Welsh, inflicting defeat after defeat on the badly organized and often disunited followers of Llywelyn. He was rewarded, yet again, with more men and the liberates of the territories he had won for the king.[2]

But Mortimer was growing tired. He was now in late middle age and had spent much of his life doing battle with both sword and intrigue. In 1279 he decided to retire from his greater royal duties and gave what we might call a splendid retirement party. It was held at the castle at Kenilworth in Warwickshire, the scene of so many triumphs and not a few failures. Now he created there a latter-day version of Arthur's Camelot, with dozens upon dozens of knights in tournament and ladies in attendance. Three years later he was dead. Mortimer died of an illness, perhaps cancer, rather than on the battlefield – although, ironically, his end came during Edward's last battle against Llywelyn of Wales.

The depth of Edward I's feeling for Mortimer must be measured by the unusual royal decree that virtually discharged Mortimer's debts on his death. Instead of the exchequer having first call on Mortimer's estate, as was the custom, his debts would be collected at some later stage by arrangement with his heirs. In October 1282 Roger de Mortimer, 6th Baron Wigmore, was buried in the family ground at Wigmore Priory.

This was the passing of a great and powerful marcher lord. Yet it was merely the introduction to even more remarkable deeds by that family. By his wife Matilda de Braose, who survived him by nearly twenty years, Mortimer had two 'important' sons. His eldest, Ralph, had been appointed sheriff of Shropshire and Staffordshire during Mortimer's regency but had died seven years before his father. This meant that the second son, Edmund, was Mortimer's heir. Edmund had been intended for the priesthood, but though he may have been a pious man he was no medieval wimp. It was Edmund, who before 1282 was out did what his father had never managed to do – defeat Llywelyn of Wales. He married the daughter of William de Fiennes from Picardy, who was related to Eleanor of Castile through her mother, the Countess of Ponthieu.[3] The importance of this marriage was that Eleanor, of course, was the wife of Edward I. The importance of Edmund was that he was to be the father of Roger Mortimer, the 1st Earl of March.

This Roger Mortimer (the fourth member of the family to be called Roger) was born in 1286 or 1287 – the records are unclear. His father Edmund had died in 1304 and so Roger became the 8th Baron Wigmore whilst still in his teens. He was to be the most famous of them all. Since he was still, in medieval law, a minor, Edward I decided that he should have a guardian. The young Roger Mortimer was put in the charge of Piers Gaveston, the homosexual lover of Edward's son, then Prince of Wales, the future Edward II. Both Piers Gaveston and Edward II, as explained in Chapter 3, were to meet terrible ends.

Roger Mortimer disliked the arrangement with his guardian, and paid 2500 marks to buy himself out. This did not, however, upset his relations with royalty, and at the Great Whit celebrations in 1306 he was dubbed a knight at Westminster. Two years later, when the old king died, the fifteen-year-old Mortimer was bearer of the royal robes at the coronation of Edward II. By then Mortimer had married – one of the rights he had secured by buying himself out from Gaveston's guardianship. His bride was Joan de Genville, whose family included the lord of Ludlow in Shropshire, himself a marcher lord. Moreover, the family had land and estates in County Meath in Ireland. Because Joan de Genville's sisters had become nuns, she brought to Mortimer on their marriage the quarterings of her noble family and considerable lands in the marches. These estates could be added to those that Mortimer had himself inherited along the Welsh borders and his own lordships across Ireland.

On parchment, at least, the teenage Mortimer was both powerful marcher lord and Irish landowner. The lordships had been handed out by successive monarchs in order to preserve those territories from the grievances of marauders who, quite often rightfully, thought the English king an intruder on their traditional lands. Consequently, Roger Mortimer spent much of his time looking to his own estates rather than noticing the development of animosity towards Edward II, particularly as regards his relationship with the increasingly powerful Gaveston.

At first the matter of Ireland appeared simple. In 1308 Roger Mortimer went to Ireland and there met his wife's uncle, the head of the Genville family, who handed over the keys and deeds of the Irish estates to Mortimer, clasped his hand in farewell and took himself off to a Dominican friary. As might be imagined, not all the Irish relations thought this a good arrangement: for example, the Lacys of Trim and Meath saw no good reason to give up what had traditionally been theirs. Roger Mortimer was far from home but not out of his depth. He had the wit and courage to settle with and outmanoeuvre the recalcitrant elements of his wife's family, and in fact it was the Lacys who eventually gave up the struggle and took themselves to Scotland to plot the invasion of Ireland with Edward Bruce, the brother of Robert the Bruce, king of Scotland. This was no idle, rabble-led threat.

In 1316 Bruce indeed invaded Ireland and won a telling victory at Kells over Mortimer, who was forced to escape to England. But ever since 1171, when Henry II had invaded Ireland and had become generally accepted as its overlord, if not king, the island had been an English possession. Edward II was not about to let Bruce usurp the English throne. Once again, a Mortimer was given unusual powers and authority in the king's name. On 23 November 1316 Edward II appointed Roger Mortimer Lieutenant of Ireland, which meant that he was viceroy and that all the English barons with land in Ireland had to send soldiers for his army and, where possible, support him in person. Clearly, many barons could not leave their own estates in England for fear that they too would be overthrown. Many, however, did send troops and captains on a pre-calculated scale in accordance with the size of their landholdings. Mortimer had a single task: to prepare an invasion force and defeat Edward Bruce.

In 1317 the English army under Roger Mortimer's command sailed from Haverfordwest in west Wales and landed at Youghal just before Easter. Edward Bruce could not have been so confident of his authority in Ireland when he heard of the pending invasion. His brother, King Robert, had sailed from Scotland to help him. However, when the two men saw the size of Mortimer's army, perhaps as many as fifteen thousand including cavalry, Robert abandoned his brother and returned to Scotland whilst Edward retreated to his fort at Carrickfergus. Some of their supporters were left behind in Leinster and Connaught, and Mortimer showed them no mercy.

That summer he turned his attention to his very distant relation by marriage, Walter de Lacy. It was the Lacys who had opposed his wife's family in the struggle to secure the lordship of Meath. Walter de Lacy was, as we have seen, the instigator of the Scottish adventure into Ireland. In June 1317 Mortimer defeated him in a couple of minor battles and then declared that the family were felons and enemies of the king. This proclamation by the viceroy effectively made the Lacys outlaws – outside the law's protection as well as breakers of its code.

The Lacys escaped into County Connaught. Mortimer sent his troops in pursuit knowing full well that skirmishes with the clans could so easily escalate into major defeats for his and therefore the king's policy. He was successful – but at an enormous cost. He may have been the viceroy, but he still had to pay for the loyalties of those who had sent troops. His men and their commanders had to be fed and armed. Mortimer could not get at the king's exchequer, and the way in which baronies were maintained often meant that it was up to the lord to raise his expenses, either through his own resources or through those granted him by the monarch. With mounting debts, especially for foodstuffs and supplies, Mortimer found it difficult to maintain his authority.

Nevertheless, in the spring of 1319 Mortimer was sent back to Ireland by the king. As well as his role as viceroy he had assumed the office of Justiciar of All Ireland and the constabulary of the towns and castles of Athlone, Rawdon and Roscommon. He now had absolute power. Shortly before Mortimer's return, Edward Bruce had been killed in battle. Mortimer's task was to seek out, not the foot soldiers, but the influential chiefs who had supported Bruce. He confiscated their lands and gave them to men who had remained faithful to him and his master, Edward II.

If we look at what was going on during this period in England, as already described in Chapter 3, we can see that Edward II was an uncertain ally and about to become an opponent. Gaveston had been executed. The Despensers were in power. The defeat at Bannockburn in 1314 had further weakened Edward's authority. Edward regained his position, but that was because the Earl of Lancaster made a mess of running affairs. In 1321, when Mortimer was recalled, the Despensers were banished. They were back the following year; Lancaster was captured and beheaded. It was against this setting that in 1321 Roger Mortimer lost his authority in Ireland. It was an impossible task for anyone to maintain discipline and accountability there. For Mortimer, the return to English politics was not a disgraceful retreat. Nothing much that happened in Ireland after his departure improved matters.

His experience proved invaluable when he once more gave his full attention to his estates on the Welsh borders and in the Principality itself. With his uncle, Roger of Chirk, he had earlier consolidated the Mortimer family authority in North Wales and the pair of them unofficially ruled it as their private kingdom. He had also strengthened the Mortimer and marcher connections by, for example, the marriage of the Powys marcher lord, John Charlton the Younger with one of the Mortimer daughters, Matilda. On his return Roger Mortimer, like so many in the nation, was now openly opposed to the activities of his sometime patron Edward II and the influence of the Despensers.

While he had been on such good terms with Edward he had, at the most, been in the middle ground of the barons and had certainly not openly supported the demands of the Ordainers (see p. 46). In 1318, when the conflict between the Earl of Lancaster and Edward II was so bitterly public, it was Mortimer who appeared at the king's side as a guarantor of the mediation between the two Houses. He became part of the King's Council, that committee of political nannies whose task it was to keep the king's excesses in check. From this he became a commissioner tasked with the reform of Edward's estates and in particular his household.

Although the documentary evidence is vague, Mortimer's role as commissioner and councillor suggests that he must have been at least moving away from Edward. Certainly, his important position made him one of the more sceptical leaders of his fellow barons. From this period, therefore, Mortimer's open opposition to the king can be observed. It would lead to Mortimer's exile and love affair with the queen, and his eventual execution.

Mortimer's relationship with the king was a very good example of how the politics of England could never be manipulated by a single force. There was – and continued to be – a multiplicity of prejudice in the reasons of those who took one side or the other. Moreover, the internal disputes and worse in political oppositions were not simply a feature of later centuries. Politics is not a product of democracy. Politics expresses the self-interests of the most powerful, and the rest either sign up to those interests or not; hence the evolution of the majority and minority of government, at whatever level. So it was in the fourteenth century, although the state was still feeling its way towards regular forms of parliament which would not appear for several hundred years.

Here too was an example of the disparate nature of opposition. The barons were yet again opposed to the monarch; barons had only self-interest. Mortimer, who was a member of that opposition, was another example of the conflicting interests within his own side. Furthermore, his animosities towards the Despensers went beyond constitutional bounds: Mortimer saw Hugh Despenser the Younger as a personal territorial threat.

At about this time, 1320, the Lord of Gower was desperate for funds and put up his estate for sale. His neighbour, Humphrey de Bohun, Earl of Hereford, said he would buy it in order to link his estates at Brecon. Before an agreement was reached, the Lord of Gower died; however John de Mowbray, who succeeded him, agreed that the contract should go through. But Hugh Despenser the Younger owned the adjacent estate of Glamorgan, and he was both greedy and probably right in thinking that the Earl of Hereford's proposed new acquisition of land could at some time threaten his own position. He used his influence with Edward II to claim that Hereford's contract with Mowbray amounted to nothing more than land-grabbing because (and here he may well have had a good point)

Hereford did not have a royal licence to buy the land. Despenser attacked the earl in what became a notorious dispute, into which Mortimer was drawn on the earl's side. As a result Despenser declared the Mortimer family to be his enemies. The Mortimers were doubly angry because Despenser had already taken by force one of the Mortimer castles in South Wales, a holding given to the family by the king – who now looked the other way.

By the spring of 1321 Mortimer and Despenser were openly at war, with the former showing every sign of overcoming the king's current favourite. By now the feelings among the barons against both the Elder and the Younger Despenser were, as seen in Chapter 3, so great that in the Parliament called that summer the king had no choice but to banish his two most senior and trusted advisers. Mortimer had triumphed, although he still needed a formal royal pardon for his actions despite the fact that the Parliament acknowledged that he had been sinned against and was not the sinner. He returned to the safety of his lands along the Welsh borders and in Wales itself. However, the Despensers would not be long gone and the king knew no let-up in his spite.

It would be wrong to give the impression that the whole country was against the king. As mentioned above, the complex animosities among the barons were no less foolish than those that had rendered impossible any victory by the Welsh and the Irish in the face of successive English assaults and occupations. Sufficient numbers still supported Edward, many for their own reasons which included the dislike of the powerful Mortimers and the other marcher lords. Edward gathered his supporters and decided that, although he needed the marcher lords to protect his kingdom, he would not miss this opportunity of setting himself against them and theoretically gaining control over a part of his kingdom that he had lost to his own people.

The Mortimers were in the vanguard of the military opposition to Edward's progress west. They were not entirely successful, for the king captured Worcester and burned the town of Bridgnorth. Part of the Mortimers' problem was that a considerable amount of support that had been promised them had failed to materialize. They had been let down by the most important people in the king-dom – the great earls, including Lancaster himself, who had promised help if Mortimer would stand against the king. Here is yet another example of the governance and opposition in English history being no different from those in any other crude society concerned with little more than self-interest.

In just a couple of years the Mortimers had slipped from being one of the most important families on the king's side in England to being petitioners for their own pardons before the monarch they now despised. In early 1322 Roger Mortimer and his uncle, Roger of Chirk, were thrown into the Tower of London, where the king left them while he set off north to put down the now fragmented opposi-tion. By March the Earl of Lancaster, he who had failed to come to Mortimer's aid as promised, had been killed by Edward. So too had the Earl of Hereford, alongside whom Mortimer had fought. The Despensers were restored to all their powers and virtually told Edward II how to rule his country.

There was no comfort for the Mortimers among their own people who had come to dislike, perhaps even hate, the Mortimers as much as the Mortimers disliked the Despensers. The Mortimers' subjects and tenants petitioned the king to show neither Roger nor his uncle any leniency. Without hesitation the Despensers supported this petition and made it clear to the king that the charge against the two Mortimers was treason. Lancaster and Hereford had been killed in battle, but the execution of a noble in captivity was an altogether uncertain action. Whatever the feelings of Mortimer's Welsh people and those of the king and his closest court, Roger Mortimer was still a powerful figure in the land and represented an extremely potent caucus. So in July 1322, although the charges of treason stood rock solid, the death penalty which should have followed was commuted to life imprisonment for both uncle and nephew.

The balance between the anger that would surely follow execution and the disadvantages of keeping the Mortimers alive was impossible to assess at the time. A gaoler (especially a royal one) who keeps his prisoner alive creates enormous danger for himself: at the very least that person becomes a martyr in some eyes. But equally dangerous, if the prisoner is that important, is the likelihood of his or her supporters either attempting to remove the gaoler and so set the prisoner free, or hatching a simple escape plan. The Mortimers, although stripped of their authority, remained powerful enough for plotters to plan an escape. The story goes that the mastermind was the Bishop of Hereford, Adam of Orleton, who recruited the deputy commander of the Tower of London. On 1 August 1324, guards from the Tower were attending celebrations for the Feast of St Peter ad Vincula. It is said that their drink was doctored. A hole was cut in the cell of the young Roger Mortimer, who supposedly scampered across the rooftops and then slid down a rope to a small boat. He crossed the Thames to find horses as arranged by the bishop, then galloped to the south coast and a ship waiting to take him to France. His uncle, less fortunate, did not manage to escape. Edward should have executed Mortimer for in exile he did not tarry idly. This is the chapter in Mortimer's life that would bring about Edward's downfall and the grisly execution of both Despensers, father and son.

Charles IV of France thought it a good idea to set up a close friendship with Mortimer who, across the Channel, was seen as a powerful noble. This was no escaping rabble – Charles could see that Mortimer retained an enormous amount of support in England. Those friends were under particular pressures, and even Mortimer's mother Margaret was arrested and put away in a convent.

However, the French king needed no outside encouragement to think the best of Mortimer, for Charles's sister was Isabella, the wife of Edward II. Isabella had been humiliated by her husband's infatuation with the Gascon Piers Gaveston, maltreated by Edward and further humiliated by his arrangement with Hugh Despenser the Younger; Charles IV was not unaware of this situation. As was the custom of the times, the English queen was sent on an embassy, a diplomatic mission, to her brother. This was an unwise act on the part of Edward II, who would have done better to keep his very intelligent and single-minded as well as independently minded wife within rather than without arm's length. Having arrived at the French court in early 1325, she remained there throughout the summer and was joined by her son, the future Edward III, who ostensibly had gone to France in the capacity of Duke of Aquitaine to pay his respects to his mother's brother. Isabella had not been an open supporter of Mortimer, nor could she have been. However, one of her close advisers was Bishop Adam of Hereford who had effected Mortimer's escape. Mortimer was still at the court of Charles IV; he and Isabella became conspirators and lovers, an affair which they hardly bothered to disguise. Edward II, the Despensers and probably the whole of chattering England knew of this affair. But the fact that the king was a cuckold was less significant than the political and military consequences that by then most people of importance understood.

Charles IV, as we saw in Chapter 3, did not approve of Mortimer and Isabella's dangerous liaison: it is said that he was embarrassed, and the morality of the situation was probably questioned. More importantly for Charles, by harbouring the lovers he was implicated in their plotting, which was grounds enough for war between England and France. Mortimer and Isabella left France for the Low Countries. There, in an overtly political act, the queen's fourteen-year-old son Edward was betrothed to Philippa of Hainault. This alliance immediately brought in troops and money from Hainault and the neighbouring German states – always a good source of mercenaries. On 24 September 1326 Mortimer took command of this force and landed in England from the River Orwell. There was no surprise at their return and Adam of Hereford, as well as the Lancastrian lordships, joined forces with them. Edward II had no stomach for this fight. He escaped to the west of England hoping to find safety in the estates of his two advisers, the Despensers.

Here we return to the true strengths of the lordships of medieval England. The king could not point a finger at the invader and summon all the baronies to his side to expel what were, after all, a committed traitor and his mistress. By going to the West Country Edward clearly thought he would be safe in lands controlled by the Despensers. Yet these were the lands of all the marcher lords, of which Mortimer, even in exile, was the most important. On 16 November Edward II was captured. The following day Mortimer encouraged Queen Isabella to order the beheading of the Earl of Arundel, one of the most powerful supporters of the king. Exactly a week later Mortimer sat in judgement and took his bitter revenge on Hugh Despenser the Younger. He too was beheaded. A similar fate was meted out to Hugh the Elder.

Parliament met six weeks later, in January 1327. Edward II, still imprisoned, was formally deposed and his young son became Edward III. One of Mortimer's first tasks was to go to the City of London and promise that it would remain for all time independent of the state. This was a significant declaration, for the independence of the business centre of England was jealously guarded and would remain so, even to the extent of having its own constabulary and official entry point, known as Temple Bar and originally barricaded, right up to the present day.

The king's coronation on 1 February 1327 was for show: Mortimer was the real ruler of England, even more powerfully so than his mistress. So it was easy to give his three sons coronation knighthoods, and to declare formal proclamations of pardon for his escape from the Tower and for any offences that the justices and Parliament may have laid at his door. His old uncle, Roger Mortimer of Chirk, who had not escaped from the Tower with him in 1324, had died there. The nephew, however, included his uncle in the pardons, which meant that all the Mortimer estates and holdings were immediately restored. Even this was not enough for Mortimer, who proved as greedy and as ruthless as the Despensers he had beheaded. He amassed authority, estates and powerful offices by means which included taking lands from young nobles not yet in their majority. There was no question of them buying themselves freedom, as he had done from Gaveston's wardship.

No one doubted Mortimer's power; this was especially so in Wales, where in 1327 he was formally appointed justiciar of Llandaff and then justice of the whole country, which gave him authority over the Welsh marches. He then took the title of chief justice of the peace of Hereford, Stafford and Worcester, as well as the custody of Glamorgan. He had, in modern parlance, tied up the whole of Wales and the border counties, and with his custody of Glamorgan had taken for himself the lands owned by his enemy the late Hugh Despenser the Younger. To consolidate his wealth and possessions, on 29 September 1328 it pleased His Majesty to create Mortimer the 1st Earl of March. And in case there were any who had escaped his baronial and magisterial influence, in November that year he was given the justiceship of Wales for the rest of his life which, although he did not know it, would not be long.

Isabella may have been intelligent, influential and vengeful, but she was clearly under the command of Mortimer. She had to be in full agreement concerning all the powers and wealth that Mortimer was grabbing for himself and, let us not forget, for his long-suffering wife Joan, whose family estates, which she had brought to him when they were married, had been the first extension of his comparatively modest landholdings within the marches. Isabella continued to make sure that his requests were unopposed, even going so far as to give him her castle, Montgomery. She made sure, too, that his bad debts to the exchequer were written off and that he was given renewed authority over land that had been in dispute in Ireland, for example Trim and County Meath.

Mortimer's uncontrollable avarice did not blind him to the need to protect the interests of his powerful supporters. He made sure that those whom he regarded as influential friends found their holdings, their offices and therefore their incomes greatly increased – not through Mortimer's own pocket, of course, but through the public exchequer.

What might be thought curious is that Mortimer had not taken for himself the one office that this trail of land-, office- and wealth-gathering led either to or from. He did not choose to become regent, as had the justiciars in time past when they had acted to defend the rights, interests and future of a monarch still in his minority. In fact Mortimer held no office whatsoever in the ruling of the country. He did, however, make sure that the person he trusted most of all (or, perhaps, at all), Adam, Bishop of Hereford, had the most pertinent appointment of all: the Royal Treasurer. Another ally, Bishop Hotham of Ely, was appointed Chancellor.

Mortimer, therefore, ruled England through Isabella, and took what he wanted from England through her, the Chancellor and the Treasurer. Curiously, for such a resourceful and undoubtedly powerful man, Mortimer was a very bad ruler. He made no attempt to encourage others to believe that England would be a more comfortable place in which to live, nor one in which justice might be admired. By this time he and Isabella had disposed of the one person who might have become a rallying point for the opposition. If Edward II had made the mistake of allowing Mortimer to live once he had him in the Tower, Mortimer made no mistake about Edward II. It is impossible to believe otherwise than that he and Isabella were entirely responsible for the king's ghastly murder in 1327 in Berkeley Castle in Gloucestershire (see Chapter 9).

Mortimer also seems to have been the person who arranged the 1328 treaty of Edinburgh with Robert Bruce, the Scottish king who had retreated from Ireland before Mortimer's invasion several years before. That treaty, described not much later as a shameful agreement, recognized Bruce as king of an independent Scotland. Mortimer's enemies were growing in numbers because of his new powers. They believed that the Scottish treaty was, in fact, a preliminary to Mortimer's long-term ambition to take the crown from his mistress's son, with Robert Bruce's help, for himself.

Moreover, the growing opposition to Mortimer's wealth and position was partly encouraged by the fact that when one man assumed so much power it meant that others lost theirs. This was particularly true of Henry of Lancaster. Lancaster had supported Mortimer and Isabella on their return from Flanders. He had done so partly to bolster their cause, but probably more so as an act of revenge. Thomas, Henry's brother, it must be remembered, had been killed in battle by Edward II. Also, while Lancaster had his powers reduced, Mortimer had loaded much of the responsibility on to Lancaster's public position. In the autumn of 1328, when Mortimer was given his earldom at the Parliament held at Salisbury, Lancaster did not attend. The significance of this was not lost on the young Edward III. This was Lancaster openly defying the king and declaring his total opposition to Mortimer.

After the ceremony at Salisbury, the king returned to London with Mortimer and Isabella in attendance. All seemed well, but the illusion was broken within three months. At the beginning of January 1329, when Edward, Isabella and Mortimer were away from London, Lancaster and his forces marched into the capital. This was more than defiance. Lancaster now publicly called for the removal of Mortimer just as the barons, including Mortimer, had called for the removal of Gaveston and the Despensers from the court of the now murdered king Edward II.

Within days Mortimer had retaliated by taking his Welsh army to plunder Lancaster's estates. Lancaster, full of confidence, ordered his army to march north to meet Mortimer. But their enemy had a fearsome reputation and many of Lancaster's followers, fearing the worst, deserted him. Mortimer, again exhibiting both guile and ruthlessness, pardoned many of Lancaster's supporters but not their leader. Then, with unquenchable confidence, Mortimer arranged a trumped up charge against another of his supposed enemies, Edmund, Earl of Kent, who was tried for treason and executed. The young king was helpless, because although the Earl of Kent was his uncle, Mortimer's court was far more powerful than his own. More than that, Mortimer's Welsh army was a gang of bloodthirsty, plundering looters and marauders who took what they wished in Mortimer's name.

The king needed an ally: someone who could take on Mortimer for him. By the late spring of 1330 Edward III was in the same position his mother had been in five years earlier – totally humiliated. He was also expecting his mother's loyalty to be tested at any time when Mortimer demanded his crown. To Edward's side came the man who would become the 1st Earl of Salisbury, William Montacute. In October 1330 the king summoned Parliament. At some time during that gathering Edward and Montacute planned to overthrow Mortimer and Isabella. Yet this was no splitting of the camps, with one side in one half of the country and the other retreating to their strongholds in the marches. All the parties concerned were in Nottingham Castle.

Mortimer ordered his Welsh swordsmen to stand guard over the king and to let no one through without Mortimer's or Isabella's express permission. Clearly Mortimer knew what was happening, but was so sure of his own power and authority that on 19 October he publicly accused the king of taking part in the conspiracy against him (and therefore the Queen) with Montacute. There was no ambiguity – he was accusing the monarch of treason. What Mortimer probably did not know was that Montacute had allies in the very castle in which he was supposedly prisoner. In fact, Montacute was no longer in the castle. In the great tradition of adventure stories, he had been shown a secret passage and had escaped to gather around him not a Welsh rabble, but a determined and organized force. He returned with them whence he had come – quietly through the secret passage – to where the young king waited in the castle courtyard.

The king led a picked band of knights up to the chambers where Mortimer and Isabella were lodged. Edward himself is said to have led the assault on the room where Mortimer was in conference with his chancellor. It was a quick and bloody confrontation. Isabella, who is said to have cried, 'Fair son, have pity on the gentle Mortimer', was swept aside. On 27 October 1330 Mortimer was returned to the Tower of London, and this time there was no intention of allowing him to escape.

The king announced that there should be no doubting that he, Edward III, had taken charge of his kingdom. Mortimer was accused of treasonably causing dissension at the time of the king's father, Edward II. He was further accused of arranging the murder of Edward II and of misappropriating power, property and position during the regency of the young Edward III. Furthermore, the indictment continued, he had plotted and lied to bring about the execution of the king's uncle, Edmund, Earl of Kent. He had also lied to the king about the intentions of Henry of Lancaster, so much so that Edward had believed Lancaster was an enemy when he was not. He had been guilty of the most terrible acts of taking money for himself and, finally, had been responsible for acts of great cruelty, especially in Ireland. In all, it was decided there was no health in Mortimer.

None would make the mistake of allowing him time. On 29 November 1330 Roger Mortimer, 1st Earl of March, was hanged, drawn and quartered on Tyburn gallows. Why such an execution and not, for a noble, at least the dignity of beheading? This was the final revenge. He was executed in exactly the manner that he had ordered for Hugh Despenser the Younger just four years earlier.

The boy who would one day be the 2nd Earl of March was just three years old when his grandfather, Roger Mortimer, was executed and his father, Edmund, would have succeeded. However, Edmund died almost immediately after Roger. So this infant, the fifth member of the family to be named Roger Mortimer, was now in line to succeed to the title. However, a title could not be assumed without the express approval of the monarch, in whose grace all honours rested. Moreover, because of the possibilities of the sins of the father being visited on the son, the child could so easily have had a miserable time suffering the penalties of the 1st Earl's treason. Certainly there was no question of the estates and everything that went with them being handed over to him and his trustees as if nothing had happened. The 1st Earl's treacherous life would have been seen as far more than the act of an individual: the Mortimers as a family were disgraced and suspected of the most evil intentions.

It was not until the young Roger was about fifteen years of age that he began to come into his inheritance, when the monarch gave him the old castle of Radnor and four other Welsh estates. However, the other castles, including Knucklas (the most important in that region), were given to him in care; in other words, he did not directly inherit them and instead they were held in the name of his stepfather, William de Bohun, the Earl of Northampton.

But in 1343 Roger Mortimer was returned to the family seat, Wigmore, and taken back so firmly into the royal favour that he took part in the king's invasion at St Vaast-de-la-Hogue in 1346, the landing before the Battle of Crécy.[4] Mortimer was dubbed a knight by the new Prince of Wales, Edward, known as the Black Prince. So we find the young Roger Mortimer at the Battle of Crécy, where the Black Prince won his spurs; and in the September of that year Edward III gave Roger all the outstanding Mortimer estates and, perhaps more importantly, dubbed him one of the first knights of the Most Noble Order of the Garter in addition to his first knighthood.

A further sign of favour was that Roger persuaded the king that his notorious grandfather was not the treasonable character suggested by his actions and the sentence on the 1st Earl was reversed – though obviously the consequences stood. It was not, however, until the autumn of 1355, twenty-five years after the death of the 1st Earl, that Roger Mortimer was summoned to Parliament under his title. It had taken that long for the king to recover his confidence sufficiently to allow a Mortimer once more to bear the earldom with him.

There was no doubting the importance of the 2nd Earl, who became Constable of Dover Castle, one of the most important appointments of the crown and certainly not just a piece of symbolism. Strategically sited, Dover Castle was the most important stronghold in the south east of England. He was also made Lord Warden of the Cinque Ports.[5] It was about this time, 1355, that Joan de Genville, his grandfather's widow, died. Her estates, which came to the 2nd Earl, included Ludlow and its castle, to which Mortimer now moved from Wigmore. In 1359 the family estates were extended even further when the earl was made Constable of Corfe Castle and of the infamous Bridgnorth which had been burnt in 1321 by Edward II.

The young 2nd Earl was totally trusted by Edward III and had succeeded in restoring the estates, the name and the loyalties of the Mortimer family. When, in October that year, the king invaded France, Roger Mortimer was one of his principal commanders, leading fifteen hundred men into battle, capturing Saint-Florentin and participating in the invasion of Burgundy. But as the king's army camped near Avalon in February 1360 Mortimer suddenly died; there is no record of battle wounds or illness, only surprise. His remains were returned to the family graveyard at Wigmore Priory and a solemn Mass said at the King's Chapel, Windsor.

The 2nd Earl had married the daughter of the 2nd Earl of Salisbury, William de Montacute, and their son was named after his grandfather, Edmund Mortimer. Young Edmund Mortimer was born in 1351 and so was just nine when his father died. Such was the affection of the king for his late father that the boy became a ward of Edward III, although his practical tutelage was undertaken by William of Wykeham, the Bishop of Winchester, together with Richard Fitzalan, the Earl of Arundel.

Where his father had healed the wounds of animosity towards the Mortimer name, his son strengthened the political base. When he was seventeen he married the thirteen-year-old Philippa, daughter of the second of Edward III's five sons, Lionel, the Duke of Clarence. Within a year of the marriage, in 1368, Philippa's father died and so, even before he had reached his majority, Edmund Mortimer had considerably increased the family and patronage. He now had landholdings in Herefordshire, in Shropshire and throughout Wales, together with the controversially defended Irish estates in County Meath. He was now Lord of Ulster and Connaught, Earl of Ulster and Earl of March.

Historically, the most significant development of the marriage to Philippa was the royal line. The family tree from Edward III now included a Mortimer, who sat on the branch that stretched to the House of York. Richard Plantagenet, who founded the House of York and started the Wars of the Roses with the House of

Lancaster, claimed royal descent through his mother, Anne Mortimer, who, through Edmund and Philipa, was descended from Edward III.

Spectacular through the associated heraldic display might be, we should also remember that, in spite of the favour and affection of royalty, Mortimer still had to wait for all his emblazoned dignity to be official. It was not until the year after the death of the Duke of Clarence that the still very young Mortimer assumed the title of Earl Marshal of All England, one of the highest offices in the land and one which he honoured for the next eight years.

Edmund Mortimer was no weak courtier. He fought against the French and was appointed ambassador of the king to seek their truce, as well as that of the Scots in 1373. It is at this time, however, that we begin to see the old conflicts emerging in new forms. For decades the Mortimers and the House of Lancaster had been too often at loggerheads for any residual trust to survive. So it might not be of any surprise that Mortimer's friendship with the Prince of Wales would set him against the House of Lancaster in the form of John of Gaunt.

John of Gaunt (the name is a corruption of Ghent in Flanders where he was born) was Edward III's fourth son and had acquired the title of Duke of Lancaster through his first wife, who had died in 1362. John had served his father well in the various campaigns of the Hundred Years' War that were fought between 1367 and 1374. Edward, now in late middle age, was showing signs of the stress of his office; moreover, the apparent onset of senility meant that he was increasingly dominated by Alice Perrers, his mistress. John of Gaunt would, in effect, come to run the country. Mortimer believed that the eventual succession, when Edward died, should include his wife and son through the line of the late Duke of Clarence. From his family history he understood only too well that playing constitutional politics was likely to be more effective than out-and-out rebellion.

In 1376, because the war against France was going so badly and taxation to support it was so high, Parliament was summoned. It lasted for four months. Mortimer's influence in that Parliament – known subsequently, although not at the time, as the Good Parliament – was considerable. The parliamentarians successfully tried the king's chamberlain for corruption and fraud, and Alice Perrers was banished – although she was quickly restored to the ageing monarch. During that Parliament news was received of the death of the Black Prince, which presented a constitutional crisis. The Black Prince's son was Richard, who would eventually become Richard II. John of Gaunt wanted Parliament to approve Richard as the successor to his grandfather Edward III on the latter's death. Here, then, was the direct cause of conflict between Lancaster and Mortimer, because the latter's wife, the Countess of March, had a very good case for becoming queen with Mortimer as consort. But in spite of Mortimer's undoubted influence and support in the Commons, there was not sufficient strength in this alliance for him to succeed.

The Good Parliament was distinguished by one particular event, an appointment that was to survive into the twenty-first century. The commoners in that

Parliament (as opposed to the courtiers) appointed as their Speaker of the Commons Sir Peter de la Mare, Mortimer's steward. It was the Speaker who led the constitutional attack on the profligacy of the king's court, but it was not a successful assault. At least the Parliament was able to establish a permanent King's Council, some members of which were always to be with the monarch.

If the parliamentarians and Mortimer had imagined this to be a constitutional triumph, they were soon disappointed. No sooner had Parliament been dismissed than Mortimer's opponent proved conclusively who ruled England. It was not Parliament, it was not the king, it was John of Gaunt. He threw Speaker de la Mare into prison and instructed Mortimer to go to France to inspect the English defences at Calais. Mortimer, probably right in thinking that as soon as he stepped beyond the relative protection of England he would be murdered, resigned his office of Earl Marshal. This was in 1377. In June of that year Edward III died; Richard, the son of the Black Prince, came to the throne as Richard II and the House of Lancaster remained the power in the land. However, Mortimer's own position could not be described as feeble. In fact he carried the regalia at the coronation on 16 July 1377. Richard II was only ten years old and it was not surprising that he was controlled by his uncle, John of Gaunt. Interestingly, if Richard II had died, the heir apparent would have been Mortimer's son.

Mortimer now became something of an elder statesman, even though he was still only in his twenties. He became one of the nine members of the new King's Council and took part in the seemingly continuous trek of truce- and peacemakers to Scotland. The main aim of the House of Lancaster was to keep Mortimer away from the king and the court, in spite of his titles and offices. This was probably why he was appointed Lieutenant of Ireland in the autumn of 1379. It was not an agreeable task, as the Mortimers had always known. Many English efforts, and indeed their practitioners, lay buried in the bogs of the island of Ireland. It was to be so with the 3rd Earl. In December 1381, while crossing the River Shannon, he caught a winter chill; his condition rapidly deteriorated and he passed away at the Dominican friary at Cork. It was said at the time, and much embellished later, that Mortimer, 3rd Earl of March, had done much to quell the terrible habit of wars in Ireland. His passing, therefore, was much mourned, although for different reasons at the English court. Parts of his body were returned and laid to rest near the high altar at Wigmore.

Throughout the years of redeeming the Mortimer name, fighting at the king's side and politicking in the king's court and Parliament, the 3rd Earl had never forgotten the importance of Wigmore Priory. He had started the rebuilding and in his will left money to continue this work. The 4th Earl, his eldest son Roger, was only seven years old at the death of his father and his mother was already dead. He succeeded to his title without the obligatory years of contention that seemed to surround the Mortimers and was also, despite his tender age, made Lord Lieutenant of Ireland. This office allowed him to pocket all the tithes and dues from the estates, which were in practice overseen by his uncle, Sir Thomas

Mortimer. This matter really was a farce, and when the Irish Parliament assembled, his lieutenancy was removed from him – not unceremoniously, but certainly conclusively. Once more, through the family line to royalty, a Mortimer became a royal ward and in 1388, when he was still only thirteen years of age, the 4th Earl was married to the king's niece, Eleanor, the eldest daughter of the Earl of Kent.

In some ways this Roger Mortimer (the sixth) did not take sides in the debate between Lancaster and the royal household, but he certainly became associated with both through marriage and patronage. His controversial and potentially dangerous position was sealed, however, when he was only eleven years old: in 1385 Richard II publicly proclaimed the 4th Earl of March and Ulster his heir presumptive. When he was nineteen, all his estates were formally and heraldically assigned to him. As with so many of the Mortimers (some of them would have thought too many), the earl had to concentrate his resources, if not his personal intentions, on Ireland. Richard II was persuaded to think Ireland so important that he visited it personally in 1394, naturally enough accompanied by Mortimer. As Earl of Ulster, an appointment with no authority, he was beholden to one of the great chieftains, the O'Neill. It was this man who pledged his loyalty to the king during that visit and, perhaps in response, Richard II gave Mortimer further appointments as Lieutenant of Ulster and Connaught and, eventually, the full lieutenancy of the whole of Ireland.

It would have been very easy for the Earl of March and Ulster to have aligned himself with Richard II and accepted the fortune that would have followed. But the king was growing more despotic. Moreover, it is unlikely that their personalities would have survived closer friendship. Mortimer was said to be enormously popular because he was personable, cheerful and not a little loose of living. Equally, this generous noble had a reputation as both a very brave knight and a good and fair administrator. His caution towards Richard II was not without its perils.

His uncle, Sir Thomas Mortimer, was openly against the court. He had been summoned to court, and it was part of the young earl's duty to make sure that his uncle appeared. Richard wondered aloud why he who had received his favour as heir to the throne should now seem reluctant to support him. Mortimer, inevitably in Ireland, was ordered by the king to attend his Parliament at Shrewsbury. The people were not unaware of his potentially dangerous position. When Mortimer returned from Ireland to Shrewsbury the crowds turned out to greet him, thus increasing Richard's paranoia. However, the earl behaved impeccably. He approved those things which the king wished to have approved and disapproved of those things which had angered the monarch. This done, he sensibly returned to Ireland.

He was not to survive there: within the year he was killed fighting at Kells. It is said that the earl was killed not by the enemy, but by his own people. He had, contrary to his own laws, dressed in the Irish kilt and style; in the heat of the skirmish, and unrecognized by some of his own men, he was set upon and hacked to pieces. Those that were found were returned for burial at Wigmore.

Whatever his suspicions, Richard II regarded the death of Mortimer as a national affront. He had, after all, declared him the future king. Richard's campaign of revenge in 1399 proved disastrous, for while he was in Ireland Henry Bolingbroke, son of John of Gaunt, returned from exile and invaded England. Richard hurried back but got no further than Wales before he had to surrender at Conway. He abdicated and was incarcerated at Pontefract, where he died.

Now we come, not to the last Mortimer, but the last who will interest us for the moment. The 4th Earl, who had died in a skirmish in Ireland, may have been suspected of all sorts of disloyalties by even the king, Richard II, but was nevertheless the only person to be proclaimed by Richard as his heir. This, remember, was through the line of the Countess of March to Edward III; so the new Earl of March continued that line. He was Edmund, son of the 4th Earl, who, born in 1391, was therefore only six when his father died. At first the royal court regarded him as his father's heir, who should therefore take his father's place as the eventual successor to Richard II. This gave the young Mortimer enormous position, but only as long as the king still had his. So in 1399, when Richard II was thrown into prison in Pontefract, the Lancastrians took young Edmund Mortimer to Windsor Castle – not in pomp and state, but rather under a form of house arrest. To make sure there were neither mistakes nor rallying points, the Lancastrians also took the earl's young brother, yet another Roger, and confined him under guard at Windsor. The new king was Henry Bolingbroke, who now became Henry IV.

Just as Henry's ascent to the throne had been a violent affair (see Chapter 8), so too was his occupation of that place. This was the time of the Welsh rebellion of Owain Glyndwr. It was also the period of the famous warrior Hotspur, the son of Henry Percy, Earl of Northumberland. Hotspur was famously killed in battle in 1403, but this did not put an end to the rebellions against the king by Northumberland himself, by Mowbray, Duke of Norfolk and by Scrope, Archbishop of York. The very nature of the times, the clear animosities of the baronial and court factions and the way in which Richard II's throne was usurped naturally caused the new monarch to be suspicious of everyone who might have even a distant claim to his title. A child locked in Windsor Castle was seen as no less a threat. That threat receded when the first Parliament of the new king dismissed any claim to the throne by the Mortimer family through the Earl of March, when it proclaimed the young Prince Henry heir to his father's crown. This did not encourage the king to let him go far from Windsor, and in 1402 the then eleven-year-old was sent to Berkhamsted Castle in the care of Sir Hugh Waterton.

The supporters of Richard II had not entirely melted away. Moreover, there was a conspiracy by Owain Glyndwr and some of the English barons who were against Henry to recognize Edmund Mortimer as king and not simply as the heir to the throne. Glyndwr even tried to spring the young earl and his brother from their confinement at Windsor. There is a small irony here in that the person charged with attempting to smuggle the Mortimer boys away from the king's custody was a descendant of one of the Mortimer enemies. She was Lady le

Despenser, mistress of the Earl of Kent who in turn was the boys' uncle. In 1409, by now in his teens, Edmund Mortimer was given over to the custody of Prince Henry and remained under quasi-arrest until the death of Henry IV in 1413.

Here was the great test of the monarch and his opponents, as well as of Mortimer himself. Would Edmund, 5th Earl of March, be championed as king against Henry IV's son? The revolt never came, and Henry V, instead of keeping Mortimer under guard, went in the opposite direction: he gave him back all his lands and his seat in Parliament, and personally made him a Knight of the Bath. The 5th Earl was determined to respect the king's confidence, but his so-called friends and supporters were not so easily defeated. Mortimer's sister Anne was married to the Earl of Cambridge, who tried yet again to whisk him away to Wales where the supporters were gathered to declare him king of England. It is not clear why the Earl of Cambridge believed that Mortimer would go along with this very dangerous scheme. Certainly the plotters would not have attempted the plan on the off-chance that their hero would abandon the monarch who had restored his fortunes and position. The conclusion must be that Mortimer knew about the plot and had decided to go along with it, but changed his mind either when he saw the king's generosity or when he realized his supporters' foolhardiness. Whatever the truth, we do know that Mortimer divulged to the king himself what was going to happen. Cambridge was arrested and the king put Mortimer to the ultimate test by appointing him to the council or commission which condemned Cambridge and ordered his execution.

This was 1415, the year of the Battle of Agincourt. Mortimer rode with Henry V during the preceding siege of Harfleur and was set to ride with his horse-archers and men-at-arms at Agincourt itself. There is some evidence that he was taken ill before the battle and returned to England. Whether or not he was present at that battle, the following spring Mortimer most certainly went as a captain of the king's army to the relief of Harfleur. For the next half-a-dozen years Mortimer more than repaid Henry V's confidence in him, always fighting either at the monarch's side or leading punitive forces in France.

When Henry V died of dysentery in 1422 his one-year-old son became Henry VI, and a regency was established under the joint command of the Duke of Gloucester and the Earl of Lancaster. Henry VI was never to be a warrior king. He suffered long and frequent bouts of insanity that could only encourage the differing factions that sought to control rather than merely administer the kingdom. Mortimer was one of the members of the regency council, which first sat in December 1422. But the troubles of the young king and the nation were as nothing to Mortimer's own. It seems to have been the lot of his family to be lieutenants of Ireland, with all the attendant complications and tragedies. Both his father and grandfather had perished there in sad circumstances. Mortimer had no wish for history to repeat itself in that manner, and so decided to stay in England and to appoint his own regent in Ireland, the bishop of Meath. However, the traditional Mortimer troubles would not recede. His kinsman, Sir John Mortimer, accused as a traitor to the late king, had escaped but in 1424 was recaptured and executed. If that was not enough, the young king's two regents insisted that Mortimer go to Ireland. There, the family curse caught up with him. He had been in Ireland just eleven months when, like his father and grandfather before him, he was struck down not by a sword but by the plague.

The monk at Wigmore who delivered his funeral eulogy described Mortimer thus: 'Severe in his morals, composed in his acts…wise and cautious during the days of his adversity…surnamed The Good by reason of his exceeding kindness…' It is curious then that over so many generations the Mortimer family was so terribly cursed.

NOTES

1   Not to be confused with King Stephen's wife, Matilda of Boulogne. Empress Matilda was so called because her first husband was Henry V, the Holy Roman Emperor.

2   In this case a liberate effectively meant payment of dues for the liberated land.

3   Eleanor of Castile (1245–90) was the daughter of the Comtesse de Ponthieu and Ferdinand III of Spain (1200–52).

4   A moment in the so-called Hundred Years' War (a nineteenth-century term). It began in 1337 over the territorial authority of the English in France, trading differences between the English and the French, French backing for Scottish independence, and English claims to the French throne. The English victories at Crécy and (in the following year) at Calais were followed by a seven year truce.

5   The Cinque Ports (so called because there were originally five: Hastings, Hythe, Dover, Romney and Sandwich) were established in the eleventh century. They supplied the monarch with his (later, her) Channel Fleet. The Warden was first appointed in 1268 and until 1855 was responsible for the region's civilian (but not military) jurisdiction.

FURTHER READING

McKISACK, May, *The Fourteenth Century*, OUP.
STUBBS, William, *Constitutional History of England*, (completed in 1878).

CHAPTER FIVE

THE MacMURROUGHS, FITZGERALDS AND O'NEILLS

Just as the early Anglo-Normans became preoccupied with their conflicts in France and often perished there, so the monarchs and magnates who followed them squelched through the political and military swamp that was Ireland. Here were the families who had few politics that could be developed to give long periods of stability. Like the Scots, the Irish families were better described as clans. For this reason alone there was little prospect of building a long-lasting, political and military unity with others to outwit the English monarchs and their envoys.

Until the fifth century, Ireland was an almost unknown wilderness sanctuary. Even with the coming of Christianity in the middle of that century it assumed little importance to foreigners. The island was, after all, too far away and therefore too dangerous a target for those with ambitions in the later years of the Roman Empire. It did, however, represent a refuge for stormbound invaders of England; and those who came from the north could secure a base here from which to make a landing on the English west coast. In fact Dublin and Limerick were founded not by the Irish, but by the Vikings in the ninth century.

By the 1100s, the island of Ireland was split into mini-kingdoms – Ulster in the north, Munster in the south, Leinster in the south-west, Connaught in the west and Meath in the east. Each monarch spent much of his time defending his kingdom from the other four and, equally, from the other families within his own realm. So although the island in, say, the twelfth century had a single social identity, at the same time it represented a poisonous cauldron of political ambitions and animosities. In Ulster the O'Flynns, the O'Carrolls, the O'Neills and the O'Donnells fought each other. In Connaught the O'Rourkes, the O'Connors, the O'Dowds, the O'Flahertys, the O'Shaughnessys and the O'Kellys did the same. In Munster the O'Briens, the O'Donovans and the O'Sullivans were as wretched to each other as were the O'Tooles, the MacMurroughs, the McGilli-patricks and the O'Dempseys in neighbouring Leinster.

That century also saw the arrival of Norman influence – the Butlers, the Clares, the de Burghs, the Nugents, the Tyrrells and the Fitzgeralds. That connection came about because the king of Leinster, Dermot MacMurrough, had been beaten in battle by Roderic O'Connor, the king of Connaught and deposed. He needed mercenaries to help him reclaim his throne. The best and nearest supply was in Wales, where Norman knights had helped defeat (for the moment anyway) the recalcitrant Welsh princes. In 1169, MacMurrough sought the permission of Henry II of England to buy a mercenary force from the Norman leader in Wales, Richard de Clare. The advance party was successful enough for de Clare himself to think an Irish excursion worthwhile, and in 1170 he landed at Wexford. The arrival of the disciplined Normans proved a great success. They could easily match the bloodthirstiness of the Irish, and they brought with them the ability to plan and execute punitive raids as well as the strategic planning to preserve the advantages they had gained.

The Norman connection was sealed that year when de Clare was given Dermot MacMurrough's daughter in marriage. Father and son-in-law then joined forces to march on Dublin and capture it. O'Connor, MacMurrough's enemy, was the most successful of all the Irish chieftains. Seeing the apparently successful return of MacMurrough he marched to join battle with this force, but was defeated outside Dublin in 1171. He retreated to Connaught to plan his revenge. It was at this stage that the history of Ireland came under the domination of the English, an occupation that would continue for almost eight hundred years. Why should this have been?

The story involves the only English pope, an excommunicated king and a murdered archbishop. For a quarter of a century, the Church in Rome had been angered by the actions and defiance of their priestly flock in Ireland. The Irish Church was not alone in defying the authority of the popes, but with the Irish Rome felt particularly helpless. In 1154 an Englishman, Nicholas Breakspear, became Pope Adrian IV. The following year he published a papal bull, *Laudabiliter*, which gave papal authority to the newly crowned Henry II to rule Ireland in the pope's name. The catch to this apparent *carte blanche* was that Henry would first have to conquer Ireland. This was hardly an enviable task and, with much diplomatic clearing of throats, it was not one to inspire the new king of England.

However, in 1170, the great tragedy in twelfth-century English history occurred. Thomas Becket, Archbishop of Canterbury, who had quarrelled with the King, was murdered in Canterbury Cathedral. Henry II was damned by the current pope, Alexander III. Here, then, was an opportunity for Henry to do penance by launching a crusade against the Irish using the old papal bull as his authority. This tied in nicely with his immediate concern. Having given permission for Dermot MacMurrough to make an alliance with the Norman knights, Henry was now very disturbed by their success. He could easily see a situation arising in which the Normans ruled Ireland and therefore threatened his kingdom.

So, dusting off the papal bull, in 1171 Henry II landed in Ireland and claimed, through that most holy of documents, that he, the English king, was the true lord of Ireland. This was the starting-point for a series of tragedies that would stain English and Irish history right up to the present day.

Dermot MacMurrough, or to give his correct Gaelic spelling, Diarmaid MacMurchadha Ui (the modern version is Murphy), was an unsavoury character who had followed his father as king of Leinster. The reason for the king of Connaught attacking him and driving him out of Leinster was not simply territorial gain. MacMurrough had gone off with the wife of an important follower of the king of Connaught; the code broken, and the excuse offered, invasion took place. As mentioned earlier, Richard de Clare had married Dermot's daughter Aoife – the English equivalent would be Eva. So when Dermot died, de Clare rightly claimed the throne of Leinster through that marriage. The story of the two men became famous in Irish history and literature. When Henry II arrived, de Clare had no option but to submit as one of his nobles – he was the 2nd Earl of Pembroke. Two years later de Clare fought fiercely alongside Henry II in Normandy and, partly as a result of that, was granted the estates of Dublin, Waterford and Wexford. His nickname, Strongbow, suggests that he was a feared warrior; he was certainly an uncompromising foe, and the story goes that he even killed his own son for being a coward.

Henry II's fears that the Norman knights would become too well established in Ireland were not unfounded. Centuries later, it was almost impossible to trace some of those families further back than their Irish histories. Let us take one such family – the Fitzgeralds. When Dermot went to South Wales looking for Norman knights, one of those recruited was Maurice Fitzgerald. He was of noble birth, being the grandson on his mother's side of Rhys, king of Wales; his father came from the eastern side of England, where he had manors. Fitzgerald's credentials as a Norman warrior were impeccable: his wife, Alice, was the granddaughter of Roger Montgomery, who had led the vanguard of William of Normandy's knights at the Battle of Hastings a century earlier.

Maurice Fitzgerald's interest in joining the contingents to go to Ireland was certainly not based on boredom. He and his kinsman, Robert Fitzstephen, had been promised by the deposed king of Leinster that if they came to fight for him – and, presumably, were successful – they would be given Wexford.

Fitzstephen and Fitzgerald were so successful that they had started to restore Dermot to his kingdom before the arrival of Strongbow. So eager was Dermot to cement relationships with his mercenaries that he offered his daughter to either Maurice or Robert. But they were both already married and, in spite of their thirst for enemy blood and estates, honoured that institution. This is why, when Strongbow eventually arrived, he found the young princess without a husband and was able to fill that role himself.

It was Maurice Fitzgerald who was, perhaps, the true hero of the famous lifting of the siege of Dublin, mentioned above. Maurice organized the astonishing counter-attack, when fewer than one hundred Norman knights and followers sprang from the city with such suddenness that about thirty thousand of the Irish were said to have fled in terror. It is said that the reason Maurice was so keen to counter-attack was that his half-brother, Fitzstephen, was trapped with a handful of knights in the very vulnerable fort at Carrick.[1] But Maurice Fitzgerald's daring was too late to save Fitzstephen. Word had reached him at Carrick that Dublin had fallen and he therefore surrendered to the Irish warriors of Wexford.

When Henry II arrived, Robert Fitzstephen was set free by the Wexford army. Whilst both Robert and Maurice welcomed their freedom, the king was in no mood to hand over the territories which he believed Dermot had been wrong in giving to his Norman kinsman by marriage. However, although Henry took Wexford, Waterford and Dublin for himself – as, in theory, he took all of Ireland into his lordship – the king was forced to leave cities and estates in the steward-ship of those loyal supporters he could muster. Maurice Fitzgerald was made a senior commander of Dublin.

Fitzgerald now seems to have made his home in Ireland. Because the English believed that arranged marriages for their daughters and sons were still the best way of creating stability between otherwise warring factions, Maurice married his daughter Nesta (named after her grandmother) to Hervey of Mountmaurice. His son married Alina, Strongbow's daughter.

The intermarriage of the Fitzgeralds and the de Clares improved Maurice's estates, which now included part of north Kildare and, more importantly, Wicklow Castle. The marriage of Nesta to Hervey put the Fitzgeralds firmly in opposition to Hervey 's great enemies, the Geraldines. This hardly bothered Maurice Fitzgerald because it was the Geraldines who had captured his kinsman, Robert FitzStephen, at Carrick. Little more is known about Maurice. He has been variously described as *the* invader of Ireland and the bravest of all the Norman knights. He was said to be very fair and just, but uncompromising with the unjust. He died in 1176, apparently of old age, which suggests that when he sailed for Ireland to help Dermot he had been no young adventurer. The original monu-ment over his grave in the Greyfriars monastery at Wexford survived until the seventeenth century. Clearly Maurice Fitzgerald's memory was honoured long after his death.

The Fitzgeralds continued to prosper, and were given great titles. In *c.*1193 the next Maurice Fitzgerald was born, who would become the Baron of Offaly, which was one of the lands granted to his grandfather by Henry II. He became the justiciar of Ireland when he replaced Richard, the leader of the Burke family, the great rivals of the Fitzgeralds. This Maurice was involved in all sorts of political scandals and plots, for the Irish barons were just as vulnerable and evil minded as those in England during this period.

The interaction of English and Irish should not be ignored. In England, the barons were once more directly opposing the monarch, and in many cases each other, as they took sides and manoeuvred for political status and greater wealth. As we saw in Chapter 3, for example, by the 1230s Henry III had left the restrictions imposed on him because of his youth and assumed full powers to rule. This was the time when Hubert de Burgh was removed from office, and of the so-called Marshal Rebellion. Henry had married Eleanor of Provence, the placing of whose relations in key posts of English government angered the barons. It was the time, too, when Simon de Montfort appeared in English history with his marriage to Henry III's sister, Eleanor. The Irish baronies, including the Fitzgeralds, could not be separated from all this. Maurice Fitzgerald appears to have taken the side of Henry III and was persuaded to raid and plunder the Irish estates of the king's main constitutional enemy, Richard, the Earl Marshal, after whom the Marshal Rebellion was named;. he was the 3rd Earl of Pembroke and therefore a descendant by marriage of Strongbow. When, against the odds, Earl Richard was defeated on the Curragh of Kildare and wounded, he was taken to his castle at Kildare. This, however, was in the hands of Maurice Fitzgerald. In the middle of April 1234 the earl died of his wounds and suspicion fell on Fitzgerald, whose physician had been treating him. All England believed the earl had been murdered. Unsurprisingly, the Fitzgeralds and Pembrokes would never be friends and although Maurice Fitzgerald was supposedly cleared of any part in the Earl Marshal's death few believed his innocence. As a mark of penitence, perhaps, Maurice Fitzgerald endowed a monastery in the earl's name in County Sligo.

Fitzgerald may have been remembered as a poisoner, but his survival depended upon more brutal means. The Fitzgeralds had originally come to Ireland to counter the invasion of Leinster by the king of Connaught, Roderic O'Connor. After he died, in 1198, Connaught was ruled by his brother Cathal for more than a quarter of a century. It was long enough for the many different claims upon his throne to fester. When Cathal died in 1224 it took eight years to find a new ruler, Ædh O'Connor, Roderic's second son. Ædh lasted only twelve months before he was usurped by his cousin, Felim, who proceeded to destroy the castles of Richard de Burgh. De Burgh was very much of the Norman persuasion, and he and Maurice Fitzgerald took their armies into Connaught to seek revenge. For the next two years, with astonishing consistency Felim and Maurice respectively won and lost their battles against each other. Eventually Henry III intervened and in 1240 Maurice Fitzgerald was ordered to treat Felim as an equal under the law. There followed an example of that frequent and not entirely farcical situation in the Middle Ages, as former enemies now joined against common foes.

Much of Fitzgerald's time was spent raising taxes for Henry III, which could never make him popular. He would receive messages from the king telling him that more money was needed and that he should take arms against a particular castle and empty its coffers in the king's name. Eventually he fell out with Henry III, as most barons did at one time or another. When, in 1237, the king decided to look at Fitzgerald's own finances, he was forced to resign. Fitzgerald had taken more than his share of monies which should have gone to Henry. He was fined heavily, although never made to pay off all the money – this was often the case in the thirteenth century. But Henry needed physical as well as financial support, so by the end of the 1240s Maurice was back in favour and once more strapping on his sword in the king's name, not in Ireland but in Gascony. Yet he still found time to invade Connaught once more and oust his erstwhile enemy-cum-ally Felim

O'Connor. It was probably in 1257 that he died. He had taken charge of most of the royal estates in Ireland at one time or another and was constable of their castles. In spite of political and constitutional difficulties, Maurice Fitzgerald had been a loyal servant to Henry III.

The Fitzgerald name continued through the titles gathered in Ireland. For example, the present Duke of Leinster is the 33rd Baron of Offaly and the 28th Earl of Kildare. The Fitzgeralds are also Earls of Offaly, Viscounts of Leinster and Marquesses and Barons of Kildare. And all of this began when a man named Dermot MacMurrough ran off with a vassal's wife.

It is interesting to see how former enemies and vengeful families come together. When the first Fitzgerald had given his daughter to a Hervey, she had married into a family whose sworn enemies were the Irish Geraldines. Yet if we jump to the eighteenth century we see familiar names in the same family tree. For example, James Fitzgerald was the 1st Duke of Leinster, 20th Earl of Kildare – and by now the head of the ancient Waterford family of Geraldines. In 1745 he raised his own regiment to fight against the Young Pretender in his abortive bid for the English throne. Two years later he became Viscount Leinster; this was not an Irish title, but Leinster of Taplow, because he had inherited from his uncle the Taplow estate in Buckinghamshire. The peerage came when he married Emily Lennox, daughter of the 2nd Duke of Richmond.

But this Fitzgerald did not abandon Ireland: he built Leinster House in Dublin and became one of the most powerful politicians in the island. This was a time of political rather than military differences between London and Dublin. There was a continuing movement for Irish political independence.[2] Fitzgerald was extremely influential in supporting the English cause in Ireland. He became Master General of the Ordnance in Ireland and founded the Royal Irish Regiment of Artillery, and it was for his efforts at this time that he became Earl of Offaly and Marquess of Kildare. More was to come. For all the close connections between the English peerage and the monarch and Ireland, there were, surprisingly, no Irish dukedoms. Fitzgerald, although a marquess, could only guarantee his seniority in Ireland by being elevated in the peerage. In March 1766 George III created Fitzgerald Duke of Leinster.

Fitzgerald had seventeen children, for one of whom the king would most certainly never have created a dukedom. It all began rather well for Lord Edward Fitzgerald. Shortly after the old duke died in 1773 the Duke of Richmond lent the family a house in France. Through tutors and the Ogilvy family, into which his widowed mother had married, Edward got a good education. He fancied himself as a soldier and as his uncle, the Duke of Richmond, was colonel of the Sussex militia, Edward joined up and learned the basic skills of an eighteenth-century army officer. He served in Ireland, and in 1781 was to be found with the 19th Foot in America during the War of Independence. At a skirmish in August that year he was wounded and left for dead, but a negro slave called Tony found him, looked after him and from that moment the two were devoted to each other.

Not long after he returned to Ireland he became a member of Parliament, but, though still nominally in the army, was soon back in North America. He went off on his own as a buckskinned frontiersman and trapper, became an honorary member of a tribe of Indians and tracked his way down the then little-explored Mississippi. He got to its mouth, New Orleans, and then made his way home.

Even by eighteenth-century standards of adventure, the young Fitzgerald had an independent spirit. He got caught up in the sense of revolution that was stirring in France and went to Paris, where he became a friend of Tom Paine, probably the most exceptional revolutionary in modern British history. He saw himself as Citizen Fitzgerald and, given the chance, would have dismantled the whole hereditary system of England, Scotland and Ireland. Not surprisingly, he was cashiered from the army and thrown into gaol for describing the Lord Lieutenant of Ireland and his followers as the worst of all the king's subjects.

Until this point Fitzgerald might have been regarded as no more than an eighteenth-century swashbuckler. But now, in 1796, he could no longer be seen in that light. At the age of thirty-three he joined the Society of United Irishmen, a revolutionary secret society founded in 1791 in Belfast by a group of Protestants who held radical views about England. Its leader, Wolfe Tone, found his inspiration in the French Revolution. The mixture of republicanism and uncompromising Protestant zeal led the society's members to the conclusion that Ireland should become an independent state. Tone was deported and found a natural base in Paris, where in 1795 he started to organize an armed invasion. It was launched the following year but, like so many armadas from the eighth to the twentieth century, was swept aside by inclement weather.

Fitzgerald, with his equally revolutionary friend Arthur O'Connor (how often old family rivals turn up as conspirators centuries later), had gone to France to encourage others to finance and join in the movement, and had been instrumental in the planning of this invasion Curiously, at this stage Fitzgerald was held in some suspicion by the would-be backers of the United Irishmen. None doubted his personal commitment; however his wife, Pamela, was a relation of the Duke of Orleans and that family was establishment and royalist. So, much to his annoyance, Fitzgerald was excluded from what we would today call revolutionary fundraising activities.

The crucial year in Irish history at this time was 1798. The United Irishmen had moved on from being a political organization and now had a military wing – rather like Sinn Fein and the Irish Republican Army of the late twentieth century, but on a grander scale and with a more open plan of attack. Fitzgerald was given command of the military committee, and it was estimated that in early 1798 the United Irishmen had more than a quarter of a million men under arms waiting to join up with the French reinforcements for the overthrow of Ireland. Inevitably there were weak links in the command. For example, the apparent plan to assassinate dozens of Irish noblemen was too much for some members, who leaked the scheme to the would-be victims, and in March that year the Provincial

Committee of Leinster was arrested. Fitzgerald thought he had escaped suspicion, but he was wrong; he only got away because of a last-minute warning from the ever-faithful Tony, his servant. From that moment Fitzgerald, often disguised, went into hiding, but continued to be one of the leaders of the rising planned for the third week of May. A price was put on his head and he was betrayed, probably by one of his own bodyguards, for one thousand pieces of silver. During his arrest he was wounded; the wound became infected, and he died as a result. He was buried in St Werburgh's church in Dublin. There were other Fitzgeralds to continue that family name, but compared to Edward they paled into insignificance.

The Fitzgeralds became related to one of the most famous of Irish families, the O'Neills. Back in the late Middle Ages the 8th Earl of Kildare, Gerald Fitzgerald, had a daughter called Alice who married Con O'Neill. They had a son, Con Bacach, known as The Lame. This Con O'Neill was born sometime in the 1480s. He would become the 1st Earl of Tyrone, and in 1519 he became head of the Tyrone family.

The connection with the Fitzgeralds/Leinsters is as important to his story as it is to ours. It shows how arrangement between families can bring former enemies together, how they can cause enormous jealousies that often end in bloodshed, and how they can unite sometimes warring factions of families against a common enemy. This was the case with the O'Neills and the Fitzgeralds – the Tyrones and Leinsters.

During this period Henry VIII was king of England. Henry was determined to tame Ireland and to make it a benign province of his kingdom. For any British monarch and government, this ambition was always unlikely to be fulfilled.

At that stage the English did not pretend that they ruled Ireland in anything other than name. In fact, English law was only recognized over a small area around Dublin known as the Pale. Beyond the Pale there was but unlawful society and savagery – hence the expression. The Pale obviously varied in size depending on the strength of the English monarch and the weakness of the Irish families. As we saw earlier, powerful English families spent considerable time and effort in attempting to subdue Ireland in the king's name. Many, like some of the Mortimers, perished trying to do so. In the 1300s those families were successful – to a point. As many as six counties – Kildare, Kilkenny, Louth, Meath, Trim, and of course Dublin – were safe places to exercise the king's authority. But by the sixteenth century, Henry VIII found it necessary to attempt to reassert his writ.

And so, when the Earl of Surrey arrived as viceroy in the king's name, Con O'Neill regarded it as his first duty as the new Lord of the Tyrones to invade the Pale. It was not a successful adventure, for not all the powerful Irish actively opposed the English – hence Henry's belief that he could indeed anglicize the island. The Earl of Ormonde, for instance, uncompromisingly supported the king's viceroy, while the O'Donnells instinctively opposed O'Neill.

O'Neill was beaten but not vanquished. Henry VIII understood what a power-ful enemy the Lord of Tyrone might be; later monarchs, including Elizabeth I, would find this to be true. The king sent his good wishes to O'Neill and accepted his submission. He created him a knight and gave him a collar of gold in the king's livery. This was indeed a royal honour, but it was not enough to buy an O'Neill. Having paid homage to the Earl of Surrey, O'Neill was reasonably expected to provide troops for any excursions made in the king's name. However, the O'Neills were as ever preoccupied with either defending themselves against or attacking the O'Donnells. Hugh 'The Black' O'Donnell was a continuing enemy: immediately O'Neill had promised his forces for an expedition by the viceroy, O'Donnell attacked him and in 1522 decimated O'Neill's troops at the memorable Battle of Knockavoe by Strabane.

Two years later O'Neill's kinsman, the Earl of Kildare, succeeded the Earl of Surrey as viceroy. But this was the time of the terrible politics that moved favour and power by political rumour, insecurity and plotting. Kildare was replaced in Dublin by the Earl of Ormonde. This was a temporary arrangement, but Kildare could see the damage Ormonde would cause by disregarding the political balance in Dublin and O'Neill, on Kildare's behalf, openly attempted – often with considerable success – to disrupt Ormonde's rule. In 1532 Kildare was restored to Dublin Castle; O'Neill was restored to what he did best, plundering. There followed five years of O'Neill either supporting or instigating rebellion and causing havoc throughout the English Pale. He also attempted to regain some of the fortunes and position that his relatives, the Kildares, had now lost. In 1539 he even made a pact with Manus O'Donnell of all people, in order to get back for the youthful Gerald Fitzgerald the earldom of Kildare.

The next envoy was Lord Leonard Grey who was quite against the Fitzgeralds. Grey invaded O'Neill country, Tyrone. This was open warfare. In turn, O'Neill and O'Donnell together led a huge army and once again invaded the Pale to avenge the ravaging of Tyrone by Grey. Too successful for their own good, they plundered and looted at will and thought themselves invincible. Grey thought them very vulnerable indeed and scattered them at the Battle of Ballahoe.

O'Neill and O'Donnell retreated, and there followed a year of double-talking in an attempt to resolve all differences. It was doomed to failure. The Lord Justice, Sir William Brereton, was plotting to split O'Donnell from O'Neill, and O'Neill was trying to get mercenaries from Scotland. Brereton invaded Tyrone. O'Neill invaded the Pale. Back to Tyrone went Brereton, and O'Neill was humbled as no O'Neill had ever been before. Henry VIII saw the simple solution as beating O'Neill into submission and then giving all Tyrone to English settlers, a concept fraught with difficulties wherever it has been tried out at any time in history, from Scotland to Palestine.

O'Neill made promises that were totally alien to a lord of Tyrone. He promised to be an unquestionable subject of the king, to rebuild all the churches he had destroyed and, at the time most significantly, to renounce the pope. The inevitability of this should not be underestimated. This was 1542. Henry VIII had made his break with Rome and been excommunicated four years earlier; the last of the

1 Decorated initial depicting King Cnut from *Liber Legum Antiquorum Regum, c.*1321.

2

AROLDO:
REGIS

HIC RE
REX:AN

SIDET:HAROLD
GLORVM:

STIGANT
ARCHIEPS

3

2 The Coronation of Harold from the Bayeux tapestry. Archbishop Stigand can be seen to the right of the king. PHOTOGRAPH: MICHAEL MOLFORD

3 Twelfth-century fresco in the Chapelle de Sainte Radegonde, Chinon, France showing Eleanor of Aquitaine and her daughter-in-law Isabella of Angoulême followed by two knights. THE ART ARCHIVE/DAGLI ORTI

4 A late fifteenth-century depiction of the execution of Hugh Despenser the Younger, from *Froissart's Chronicle*. THE BRIDGEMAN ART LIBRARY/BIBLIOTHÈQUE NATIONALE, PARIS

5

6

Dolose agunt fily iniquitatis

FH

Tyrone defired a parley with the Lord Lieutenant.

8

5 Fourteenth-century illuminated manuscript showing Isabella of Angoulême and her troops at Hereford.
BRIDGEMAN ART LIBRARY/BRITISH LIBRARY

6 Engraving showing the Earl of Tyrone ('The Great O'Neill'), meeting the Earl of Essex at a crossing in the River Lagan at Kinsale.
BRIDGEMAN ART LIBRARY/PRIVATE COLLECTION

7 Sixteenth-century portrait of William Cecil, Lord Burghley (detail).
BRIDGEMAN ART LIBRARY/BURGHLEY HOUSE, LINCOLNSHIRE

8 Photograph of the Marquess of Salisbury taken for the cover of the *Illustrated London News* in 1893.
BRIDGEMAN ART LIBRARY/ILLUSTRATED LONDON NEWS PICTURE LIBRARY, LONDON

9 Portrait of John Churchill, 1st Duke of Marlborough, *c*.1690 (detail), attributed to Robert Byng.

10 Portrait of Lord Randolph Churchill at his writing desk, by Edwin Ward.

10

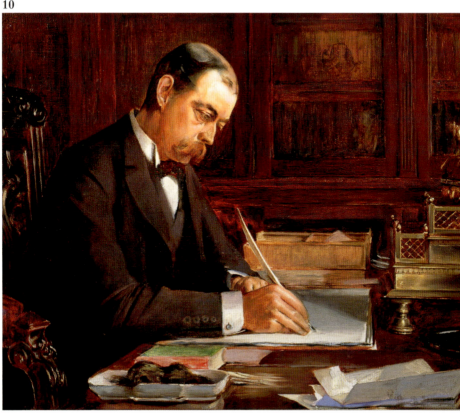

11 Henry Percy (kneeling) from 'The Earl of Northumberland's Oath', *Histoire du Roy d'Angleterre, Richard II*, 1399.
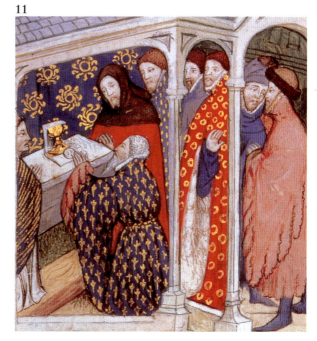

12 Georgiana, Countess Spencer with her daughter Lady Georgiana Spencer (detail), by Sir Joshua Reynolds.

13 Sir Robert Walpole, Earl of Orford, first Lord of the Treasury and Chancellor of the Exchequer, in a portrait by Michael Dahl.

monasteries had been suppressed. In 1540 Henry had pronounced himself head of the Church in Ireland and, to show he had no fears to overcome, had that very year, 1542, chopped off Catherine Howard's head.

O'Neill was now the king's man, and in the autumn of 1542 he became the 1st Earl of Tyrone. The following year he achieved what he could not have done with his sword: he was given grand estates in Dublin. This was no ordinary thrashing of a rebel. The O'Neills of Tyrone carried great authority and embodied the spirit of an Irish sense of independence. When O'Neill was made Earl of Tyrone, and submitted to Henry VIII at his palace at Greenwich on the banks of the Thames, many in Ireland saw in this auspicious moment the hope for some form of stability in their island. Everyone knew the character of the O'Neills. It was as if Ireland would have to hold its breath for a decade or more to see if this would be a proper reconciliation between two seemingly opposing forces, or a mere blip in the nature of the O'Neills to be rectified by a later generation. In the year of Con O'Neill's return to Ireland, 1543, all seemed well. Yet beneath the celebrations there was a feeling that the acceptance of an English title was a degradation of the names of O'Neill and Tyrone; O'Neill began to lose his authority over the family. The leader of the unrest was Shane O'Neill,[3] who saw the importance of the independence of the family and was as ruthless as any of its members. Shane usurped the earl and, following peace attempts, failed reconciliations, plots, counter-plots and assassinations, Con O'Neill, 1st Earl of Tyrone, took refuge in the place he had first attacked as the symbol of all he hated: the English Pale. He never returned to Tyrone, and died in the Pale in 1559.

Perhaps the most influential O'Neill was Hugh, the 2nd Earl, born in or around 1540. His father was Lord Dungannon, who may or may not have been a son of the 1st Earl of Tyrone. Whatever the legitimacy of the succession, Hugh O'Neill became the 2nd Earl after his older brother was murdered by another O'Neill, Turlough Luimeach. Clearly, even at the age of twenty-two or so when he inherited, Hugh O'Neill was vulnerable to plots against his life. Shane O'Neill, the warlike leader who had usurped the 1st Earl's authority, died in 1567 and was succeeded as leader of the O'Neill clan by the murderous Turlough.

In 1568, at the age of twenty-eight, Hugh O'Neill was thought by the government to be the best chance it had of re-establishing its authority in Tyrone. With considerable protection Hugh returned from the relative safety around Dublin to Tyrone, or at least part of it, with his mentor and royal bodyguard, Sir Henry Sidney, and the more military-minded Sir Nicholas Bagenal. Here was a classic case of internecine warfare – O'Neill against O'Neill. At this stage, Hugh O'Neill had inherited the barony of Dungannon but had not yet been advanced to his grandfather's title of Earl of Tyrone. First the title was still in the king's gift and, second, the 1st Earl had had tenure of the title but was not free to pass it automatically to his next of kin.

O'Neill had a close ally in Walter Devereux, the 1st Earl of Essex, whose eldest son had such a famous understanding, albeit a fatal one, with Elizabeth I.

The previous year, 1573, Essex had been commanded to conquer Ulster, and Hugh O'Neill had helped him in the battles against Brian MacPhelim O'Neill. Essex's campaign was not successful. Even so, he tried to persuade Elizabeth I's court to raise O'Neill to the earldom of Tyrone. If Essex had been successful in Ulster, his recommendation might have been acted on; in the circumstances, it was not. Moreover, there was always the suspicion that an O'Neill was an O'Neill whatever his present manifestation.

At that stage, Hugh O'Neill appears to have been abandoned by those who would have supported him. He was now hunted by Turlough O'Neill and clearly was in some danger of being overwhelmed. The government of Ireland was in a tricky situation. Its best chance of restraining the O'Neill family was to keep them divided, and Hugh O'Neill was its safest pawn in this often played game. If he were to become subjected to Turlough, or to an equally villainous relative, Henry MacShane O'Neill, this would not suit the elaborate plan of those who attempted to rule from the Pale. So Hugh was rescued by the government, given a small contingent of his own cavalry and proceeded to fight on the government's behalf. Some indication that the government was correct in its suspicions of his nature was given when, having heard that Turlough had been murdered, Hugh was said to have tried to get himself elected leader of the O'Neills. The fact that it was a false alarm or a false hope, depending on which cause was followed, did not deflect the government's view that he was by now sufficiently trustworthy to be given command of large enough forces to defend the borders of the English Pale. This view does seem to have been short-sighted, for it is not unlikely that the original sceptical assessment was sound. Hugh was no different from the other O'Neills, and prized above all things the lordship of the clan.

Perhaps what reined in Hugh O'Neill's immediate ambition was his joining the war against the Ulster Scots under the command of the English general Sir John Perrot. His credentials, then, were sound and in 1585 he became the 2nd Earl of Tyrone. With his earldom came an arrangement that he should be given part of Tyrone for himself. It was not a satisfactory arrangement: he was a bad, unjust and sometimes cruel landlord. He still agitated for the return of the lands that had been given to his grandfather, Con O'Neill, by Henry VIII, and even went to London for a royal petition to be heard. But he was neither important enough nor sufficiently trusted to get any more than Perrot had made possible for him in Tyrone.

His grumblings against the decision were very audible and even Perrot began to doubt Tyrone's loyalty. He could not be content, probably rightly so, with his lot. After raising a force he tried to unseat Turlough (who clearly had not been murdered, as some thought) and yet another O'Donnell, Nial Gary. But they were far too good for him and he was lucky to get away. He found no sympathy in Dublin, where Perrot thought it was the best news he had heard since arriving in the wretched island. The 2nd Earl tried again and again, and was so unsuccessful that Turlough was bold enough to demand a small amount of land in Tyrone that the earl had left. The earl replied that he would defend every last sod of turf to the death. At first the government in Dublin was inclined to support Turlough, but then reasoned that another branch of the family, the Shane O'Neills, would think that if Turlough could get away with making such claims they too could demand more or less any land to which they thought they had some title.

The obvious result was that the O'Neills continued to fight each other. It was an uncompromising affair, and on one occasion the earl was accused of personally hanging one of his enemies from a thorn tree. Called to Dublin to explain himself, the earl arrogantly pointed out that, considering the nature of the executed fellow, he had got nothing more than he deserved.

It is a curious story, that of the O'Neills. Hugh O'Neill, though disgraced, distrusted and unreservedly ambitious for greater lands and authority over all the O'Neills, was still trusted by the government in Dublin. The confusion of enemies and families had something to do with this. For example, O'Neill had married into the O'Donnell family on the death of his first wife, another O'Neill. This almost Saxon habit of reconciling two warring families would continue for many years; there was little evidence that Hugh O'Neill had married for affection. But although this may just have been true of his third marriage (he married four times in all) it was still hardly an agreeable affair. Mabel Bagenal was the daughter of his one-time mentor Sir Nicholas; her guardian was now her brother, Sir Henry Bagenal. He refused Tyrone permission to marry Mabel, but this veteran of wars with the most fearsome men in Ireland was not about to let a mere brother stand in his way. He eloped with Mabel and persuaded the Bishop of Meath to marry them. Bagenal showed his displeasure by refusing to let the earl have his sister's dowry. The social, never mind the financial, implications of Bagenal's decision were totally unacceptable even in sixteenth-century Irish society, and the earl never forgave him.

Henry Bagenal was probably right in his decision, since the marriage was an unhappy one. The earl had a couple of mistresses, and Mabel Bagenal took him to the Administrative Council. Much good it did her, for she was dead in a couple of years. Perhaps that was just as well, because not much later the earl killed her brother.

There is not much in the 2nd Earl of Tyrone's character to endear his memory to modern readers. For example, although his enduring ambition was to defeat his great enemy, Turlough O'Neill, there were many who believed that he had a more sinister agenda: to separate Ireland from England. Queen Elizabeth had enormous doubts about the earl and at one point ordered him to be apprehended and charged with treason. He did appear to be examined, but in Dundalk – he was too clever to go into Dublin, where he would have few, if any, friends and little chance of escape. The examination was inconclusive, because there was insufficient evidence of any conspiracy to overturn Elizabeth's authority in Ireland. The earl fought on the government side wherever there were skirmishes against recalcitrant chieftains, but he never did wholly commit himself; nor did he do enough in the other direction to land himself in gaol – until, that is, 1595.

There were signs that the 2nd Earl and others were plotting to take over Ireland with the help of the Scots and, worse still, Spanish soldiers sent by King Philip. This was seven years after the Armada, but that had been a somewhat inconclusive event and fear of a Spanish invasion had not left the English court. It was decided that the earl was to be apprehended and defeated: a sound judgement, but made too late to do anything about it. By May 1595 the O'Neill Revolt, led by the Earl of Tyrone and Hugh Roe O'Donnell, the lord of Tyrconnell, was under way.[4] Tyrone was declared a traitor, but the declaration had little military consequence.

Moreover, Tyrone's bitter enemy, Turlough, died and the earl at last became head of the O'Neills. There was no way in which he was going to surrender other than on his own terms. Philip II of Spain entered into correspondence with the Irish rebel. Rebellion by local chieftains is one thing; quite a different and more dangerous situation arises when a foreign power – particularly one which has already attempted an invasion – joins the rebels. In April 1596, Elizabeth agreed to some sort of truce. It was a tenuous truce: Tyrone saw it as a breathing space until the Spaniards agreed to join the rebellion openly .

At the same time he was telling the queen's representatives that, even if all the ships of Spain came to his assistance, he would turn his back on them; he was, he asserted, a devoted and loyal servant of the monarch. You can flatter some of the people some of the time, but…they did not believe him. The earl was attacked and only just managed to escape into the bog land – minus his hat and his horse, so close was it.

Yet a series of misfortunes for the queen's men, including the sudden but natural death of their commander, Lord Burough, gave the earl such an advantage that he could probably have taken Dublin itself. He did not. Instead, shortly before Christmas 1597, from a position of considerable strength, Tyrone submitted to the queen's mercy. He was pardoned and another truce proclaimed. He promptly broke it, and once more he defeated the queen's army. Defeat is perhaps an understatement – few government soldiers left the field except to be buried. The rest of Ireland took great heart from the Earl of Tyrone's victory and the English settlers abandoned their estates. However, O'Neill was not a clever man; he was no more than a voracious killer with an erratic soul who appears to have been incapable of pressing home his advantage.

In 1599 Robert Devereux, the 2nd Earl of Essex, was sent to Ireland to put down the O'Neill Revolt. Essex's story is well known (see Chapter 6). He was the 1st Earl's son and the stepson of the Earl of Leicester, Robert Dudley. Was there ever such a pedigree of disaster? He became Elizabeth's favourite courtier even though she was angered by his marriage to her secretary Sir Francis Walsingham's daughter Frances, the widow of Sir Philip Sidney. Essex was arrogant, presumed too much at court and was successfully conspired against by the devious past-master of English sixteenth- and seventeenth-century court politics, Robert Cecil (see Chapter 6). In April 1599 the much disgruntled Essex landed in Ireland, that graveyard of English aristocratic and political ambition.

Essex had the right idea, but the wrong method. He wanted to take the key territories – Connaught, Leinster and Munster. He failed, and retreated to Dublin. Although certainly safe there from the Earl of Tyrone, he was not safe from Elizabeth's instructions: he was to stop lolling in the Pale and go on the attack. Famously, the two men met in the middle of a crossing in the River Lagan. The nature of that discussion is unrecorded. What we do know is that there was to be yet another truce. It meant little, as both Tyrone – or the O'Neill, as he now called himself, reviving an ancient Irish royal title – and Essex would find out.

In January 1600 the O'Neill started southwards, savaging and pillaging all those and their estates who would not join him, saluting with promises all those who did. He appeared to be progressing well when he was brought short, not by an enemy in front of him, but with the death in a small battle of his most valued ally, Hugh Maguire. The O'Neill retreated to Ulster. By now, his rebellion had not only the active support of Philip of Spain – who was so impressed with the O'Neill victory that he started a blockade of all ships that were not sailing to Tyrone's advantage – but the blessing of the pope, Clement VIII, who told the world that the O'Neill was fighting for the Church. The O'Neill had led a revolt; now he led a blessed crusade. The hand of the pope rested on the O'Neill. The hand of some sound military tactician rested on the queen's forces, especially those commanded by the Earl of Devonshire, Charles Mountjoy.[5] Mountjoy was with Essex, but had not been tainted with the other's impetuous attempt to usurp Elizabeth's throne.

The O'Neill and the Spanish planned to attack the English troops on Christmas morning 1600. But Mountjoy heard, probably from men whom he had bribed, that they had formed against his positions, and the would-be attackers never completed a manoeuvre more complicated than ragged withdrawal to Inishannon.

The end was in sight in the few weeks left to Elizabeth on this earth. In February 1603, the queen gave Mountjoy orders that if the O'Neill would give up many of his rights he should be pardoned. When the O'Neill surrendered to Mountjoy, he probably had no idea that the queen had died in March, some weeks before. When he signed his submission in Dublin it was not to Elizabeth I but to James VI of Scotland in his capacity as the new James I of England.

There now followed a scene not unfamiliar in modern times. The O'Neill, perceived as a murderous rebel and enemy of the crown and the English people, was now received in London with most of his demands met. There was great animosity towards this man, and not a little anger that the government had treated what in later centuries would be called a republican terrorist so graciously. The sceptics in London believed that Irish leopards rarely changed their republican spots, and indeed within a few years, the O'Neill was discovered trying to raise a new revolt in Ireland. He escaped by ship with some followers and his very reluctant wife. They had hoped to get to Spain, but the wind set them on to the northern coast of France and from there they reached the Spanish Netherlands.

He recorded his complaints against the English crown – complaints that to anyone who was unaware of the man's history would seem reasonable. By 1608, the O'Neill had become an exile and headed for Rome, where he was well received, socially and financially, by the pope. He appealed to be allowed to return home, but the English had no reason to have him back. The 2nd Earl of Tyrone died in Rome in 1616.

In Ireland, the order had much changed. The O'Neill estates he longed for were now part of the infamous plantation. After the O'Neill and O'Donnell left Ireland in 1607 – the Flight of the Earls, as it became known – there was no longer any substantial opposition to the implementation of English plans to hand over Irish land to new settlers. This, known as the plantation of Ireland, was intended to 'anglicize' the island once and for all by settling there as many Presbyterian English and Scots as possible. The businessmen of the City of London took part in this plan by sending people to colonize the place that came to be known as Londonderry.

The O'Neill dynasty has continued down to the present day with considerable distinction and colourful doings that suggest the O'Neill instincts did not waste away in 1616. Yet the when the saga of the Great O'Neill, as he became known, ended, so closed the most famous period in the history of the last of the mighty Irish rebel peers. With a few brains to guide his sword the O'Neill might indeed have changed the course of his nation's relationship with England, and thus its history.

NOTES

1 Care should be taken with terminology when talking about Irish houses, castles and forts. These were not like the great stone structures of the Normans in England and France. In Ireland a fort was often akin to the stockades of the American frontiersmen and was usually made of turf.

2 Henry Gratton succeeded as leader of the patriots' party to gain parliamentary independence from England although he failed to prevent the Act of Union.

3 At the time of writing (2001) the present Lord O'Neill (a barony created in 1868) lives at Shane's Castle, County Antrim and his heir is Shane O'Neill.

4 O'Donnell had been captured by the English, but escaped in 1591 and three years later joined up with Tyrone. He was poisoned by an English spy in Spain in 1602.

5 The Dublin prison is named after this Mountjoy.

FURTHER READING

DALRYMPLE, James, *Memoirs of Great Britain and Ireland*, 1771.
O'CLEARY, Michael, *The Annals of the Four Masters* (1630), ed. John O'Donovan, 1857.
O'CLEARY, Michael, *Life of O'Donnell*, 1640.
State Papers, Henry VIII, Public Record Office.
TEMPLE, Sir John, *History of the Rebellion*, 1646.

CHAPTER SIX

THE CECILS

The Cecils came to power among the Tudors of the sixteenth century and continued to influence English public life right into the twenty-first. Their numbers include statesmen, politicians, soldiers, academics, advocates, a Nobel Laureate and even an Olympic gold medallist.

William Cecil, who would become confidant of Elizabeth I and draughtsman of Elizabethan political and diplomatic policy, was born in 1520, the year in which Henry VIII and Francis I of France gathered in such opulent but false friendship at the Field of the Cloth of Gold,[1] and the year after Ferdinand Magellan set out on his circumnavigation of the world. Henry VIII would live until 1547, and would be followed by Edward VI and Mary I before Elizabeth I was crowned in 1558. It was during the difficult 'interregnum' between the death of Henry and the accession of Elizabeth that Cecil learned his craft as courtier, adviser and consummate politician.

As Elizabeth's foreign minister this 'first' Cecil persuaded her to exhibit perhaps more sympathy than she might otherwise have done towards the Huguenots, as the French Protestants were called.[2] The Huguenot immigration that followed in 1567, and that of the Calvinists two decades later, was not as great as would follow the great migration of 1685, when protection of Protestants under French law as a minority sect was removed. However, it was a considerable piece of diplomatic persuasion by Cecil. He became the 1st Baron Burghley in 1571 and then Elizabeth's Lord Treasurer.[3] If he failed in anything, it was that he never convinced Elizabeth to marry. Nor did his son, Robert.

When his father died in 1598 the 'second' Cecil followed him as the then sixty-five-year-old Elizabeth's chief minister. Robert was at her side for the remaining five years of her life. When James VI of Scotland became James I of England[4] on Elizabeth's death, it was the 'second' Cecil's role to ease this very different monarch into the ways of the court and vice versa. Two years after his accession James created Robert Cecil Earl of Salisbury, though he eventually fell from favour because James preferred another courtier, Robert Carr.

Here, then, is the beginning of the story of the Cecil dynasty. Their original home, and certainly the one from which William took his title, was Burleigh in

Northamptonshire although the spelling was changed to Burghley. Little is known about the Cecils before William's grandfather, David, who seems to have been a favourite of Henry VII and, under Henry VIII, was appointed High Sheriff of Northamptonshire. When he died in 1541 his estate included all sorts of rents and benefactions which could only have come with the consent of the king himself. That he had all the wisdom and prudence that was so to distinguish his grandson and great-grandson suggests the mind of a country banker as well as that of an occasional courtier. His son, William's father, Richard, was introduced to the exotic life of the English court at a very early age and appears to have been a page to Henry VIII on the occasion of the Field of the Cloth of Gold, the year in which his only son was born. Richard made good provision for him. He became the Constable of Warwick Castle and High Sheriff of Rutland, gathered estates in both Rutland and Northamptonshire and probably did rather well in storing treasures that before Henry VIII's break with Rome had sat quietly in the monasteries. Richard died in the spring of 1552 when William was thirty-two.

William, although he had a pre-ordained career as a courtier, also possessed a strong intellect and the academic background to capitalize on this opportunity. When he was not yet fifteen he went to study at St John's College, Cambridge – perhaps the highest seat of academic learning in England in the sixteenth century – and became a Greek scholar, something quite unusual in those times. William acquired more than a knowledge of Greek from his then famous tutor, John Cheke; he fell in love with Cheke's sister, Mary. Since she was not a particularly acceptable marital prospect for the High Sheriff of Rutland, William was removed from St John's and deposited at Gray's Inn in London to train as a lawyer. But he did not find the journey between the two places insurmountable. He and Mary Cheke married in secret in 1541 and within a year produced a son, Thomas. Richard of Rutland, his grandfather, may have considered the whole affair rather low, but Thomas would one day be the Earl of Exeter. Sadly, Mary died in February 1544. Although William remarried, there was always a view within the family that his first romance was his only one. Moreover, he never lost his affection for Mary's mother and family and was always a firm friend of his brother-in-law John Cheke, who by 1544 had become the tutor of Edward VI.

Cecil's second wife was Mildred, the eldest daughter of Sir Anthony Cooke, who had a reputation as one of the most intellectual women of her day; her sister was the mother of Sir Francis Bacon. So Cecil truly was at home in creative, intellectual and grand circles. Those circles widened when he became Secretary to the Duke of Somerset, then one of the regents to the young King Edward VI. This was a prestigious position, but also a precarious one.

Edward Seymour, Duke of Somerset, was the virtual ruler of England at this time. Edward VI, born in 1537, was the son of Henry VIII and his third wife, Jane Seymour; Somerset was Jane Seymour's brother and therefore the king's uncle. In the king's name he had sacked Edinburgh in 1545 and two years later, at the Battle of Pinkie, had slaughtered many Scots. Cecil, by now in Somerset's pay, narrowly escaped with his life at Pinkie.

A court faction dominated by the Earl of Warwick (who later became Duke of Northumberland) started to express dissatisfaction with Somerset. Somerset kept Warwick at bay for a considerable time, but when in 1549 the former enforced the use of the first Book of Common Prayer, which replaced the Latin liturgy with English, there was rebellion. Somerset further angered the Warwick set by being sympathetic to yet another rebellion, this time led by a man named Robert Ket in Norfolk. Some sixteen thousand of Ket's followers were protesting against the landowners, who had fenced off common pasture and so prevented the ordinary people from grazing their own sheep as they had done for centuries. Ket demanded the abolition of common land enclosures. The rebellion began to attract widespread support and, as we have seen, some sympathy from the Duke of Somerset. There was a certain element of politicking in Somerset's position. He would, for example, have chosen to see the failure of his rival, the Earl of Warwick. The matter came to a head when the Earl of Warwick led a force against Robert Ket and the rebel leader was executed. Somerset, whatever his motives, was never going to find much support among the magnates of England, all of whom were landowners. Inevitably, Somerset was deposed and imprisoned. Although released in 1550, he was re-arrested and executed on 22 January 1552. Clearly, the Duke of Somerset was not much of a patron to have. William Cecil, too, was arrested in 1549 and sent to the Tower, but within two months was freed on bail. First, it was understood that he might have been Secretary to Somerset, but was not a fellow conspirator. Second, it must have been recognized that he was no ordinary courtier.

By the autumn of that year, 1550, William Cecil, at the age of thirty, had become a Privy Councillor and Secretary of State. A year later he was knighted; so too was his celebrated brother-in-law, John Cheke. Six months later Cecil was elevated to the influential appointment of Chancellor of the Order of the Garter. Soon he added wealth to his position, when in May 1552 his father, Richard Cecil, died and William inherited the vast family estates. He now lived as well as mixed in the highest and most powerful circles. His experience with the Duke of Somerset had taught him the most important lesson of his career: he had intellect, wealth, position and ambition, but none of this would count for anything if he discarded loyalty. William Cecil, and most of the dynasty that followed, had an unambiguous sense of duty, the first ribbon of which was loyalty to the monarch.

Thus, when an attempt was made by the Duke of Northumberland to rewrite the rules of accession to the throne, Cecil refused to support it. Lady Jane Grey's claim to the throne was via a dotted line, as the granddaughter of Henry VIII's youngest sister, Mary. She was married – although the idea had appalled her – to the son of the Duke of Northumberland, Lord Dudley. The marriage was part of an ambitious plan to stop the Catholic Mary, daughter of Henry VIII and his first wife, Catherine of Aragon, becoming queen. Cecil, asked to sign a document apparently endorsing Northumberland's scheme, refused and added his signature only as a witness. This was something of a wise move as well as an honourable one. In July 1553 Jane Grey was declared queen. However, Mary Tudor had far more resourceful followers than Northumberland and 'Queen' Jane lasted but nine days before she and Dudley were executed.

Then Mary Tudor, Edward VI's half-sister, became queen. It was a time for Cecil to remain very much on the fringe of court life, for the perils were obvious. What brought him back was probably the queen's marriage. When Mary I, known as Bloody Mary for her persecution of Protestants, married her cousin Philip of Spain she set in motion two events, both of which were deeply concerning for the stability of England. England became embroiled in Spain's war with France and, as a result, Mary was blamed for the loss of the last English foothold in France, Calais. More immediate was the apparent desire to undo what she saw as the heresy of her father, Henry VIII: she sought reconciliation with Rome. In the autumn of 1554, Cecil re-emerged into public life from his private pastime of enlarging aggrandizing his family seat at Burleigh and his country house to the south-west of London at Wimbledon.

In November 1554, Cecil, Sir Edward Hastings and Lord Paget were sent as royal commissioners and envoys to Rome to discuss that reconciliation. Before the month was out they returned with a papal nuncio, Cardinal Pole. Cecil's sense of diplomacy and loyalty was well tuned enough for him to become a Roman Catholic convert. Three months after the return of Cecil with the cardinal, the bonfires were lit in Smithfield. At least three hundred Protestants perished in the flames while Mary reigned. The torches were carried from London throughout England. No one was safe who professed the Protestant persuasion: the high-ranking churchmen Cranmer, Hooper, Latimer and Ridley were perhaps the most prominent of what were known as the Marian Martyrs.

There is no evidence that Cecil – a Roman Catholic convert, remember – approved this persecution of Protestants in England. That it was religious intolerance is not doubted. Equally, given the events of Henry VIII's reign – during which Cecil's own family had benefited from the persecution of the monks and the destruction of their monasteries – the passions of those who led Bloody Mary's crusade have to be seen in a sixteenth-century and not a twenty-first century light.

The monarch was still an enormously powerful influence on the ways in which people lived. Dissent at even a minor level could be, and often was, seen as raising a voice or committing an action against the throne itself. The Roman Catholic revival had far more behind it, and much greater consequences for England, than the capriciousness of one woman. Mary I could not have carried out her scheme without the endorsement and encouragement of very powerful people in England. It is therefore a measure of Cecil's political skill that he appears to have kept a distance between himself and what was going on in Queen Mary's name.

Moreover, before Mary's death in November 1558, Cecil had made sure that he was well in with Elizabeth, the future queen. He seems to have approved of her enormously and imagined what might be possible in an Elizabethan age. In 1837 Viscount Melbourne became the indispensable adviser to the eighteen-year-old Queen Victoria on her accession. Elizabeth was twenty-five when she came to the throne and, although older than Victoria and certainly far more mature, as any sixteenth-century princess might have been, Elizabeth needed her Melbourne. Into that role stepped Cecil. Whereas Victoria was naïve and demanded advice, Elizabeth, who had lived under the threat of death for so long, needed someone she could trust.[5] There was an indication that Cecil had already been appointed Elizabeth's Secretary of State even before Mary's death: on the day Mary died, it was Cecil who wrote a proclamation of the new monarchy. Three days later, on 20 November 1558, it was Cecil who received the oaths of loyalty of courtiers and barony.

We saw earlier how Cecil would not be distracted by promises of high office and reward. Even as Secretary to Somerset and when he was so close to the Earl of Warwick, he had never lost sight of his first duty – to serve the crown. Elizabeth understood this. Her judgement was not based simply on instinct. Cecil's reputation was the highest and surest in her kingdom. 'This judgement I have of you, that you will not be corrupted with any manner of gifts and that you will be faithful to the state...' These words of Elizabeth about Cecil were to be tacitly repeated about that family for the next four hundred years and more. For William Cecil, the way was now open for him to become the best-remembered monarch's Secretary of all time. It meant also that he would be the subject of innuendo, attempted bribery and malicious plotting. Elizabeth's judgement held fast.

England may have been a green and pleasant land, but it was struck with discontent from within and without. There was great pressure for Elizabeth to marry, and it was even possible that she would have to take seriously the proposal from Philip of Spain. Elizabeth, unlike her half-sister Mary, was a Protestant. Cecil's first task was to get rid of much of the anti-Protestant legislation which Mary had enacted; he did so between 1559 and 1563, by which time the Church of England had become established. He also encouraged the queen to recognize the movement for the reformation in Scotland, where John Knox's Calvinists were bent on reform. It prompted the abdication of the Catholic Mary, Queen of Scots, already damned by a series of scandals, who in 1568 fled to England and became the symbol of those who opposed Elizabeth's Protestantism. Mary was forced by radical lords to abdicate in favour of her son, who became James VI. She was imprisoned, escaped, led a 6000-strong army to regain her crown and failed. Mary then escaped to England where she was arrested and moved from 'prison' to 'prison'. After being held in nine places, she was kept in Fotheringhay and so became a focus for would-be Catholic revolutionaries and the insecurities of her Protestant sister, Elizabeth I. The Protestantism versus Catholicism that would exist in greater and lesser forms into the twentieth century would not go away, in spite of Cecil's best efforts. In 1570 the pope issued a bull entitled *Regnans in Excelsis*, which declared that Catholics in England did not have to pay any allegiance to Elizabeth – she was excommunicated. Although there was not by any means the same level of persecution as there had been under her half-sister Mary, Elizabeth, with Cecil at her side, now introduced orders that most certainly repressed the English Catholics.

Cecil's part in the repression of the Catholics; his unswerving advice that Mary, Queen of Scots should remain imprisoned (it was he who convinced the queen to sign Mary's death warrant); and his increasing dominance, as well as that of other members of his family, at Elizabeth's court could not be accepted by some of the most powerful men in the land. It is inevitable that, just as the barons had plotted against, for example, the Godwines, the Despensers and the Mortimers, so they would against the Cecils – even though that family's expressions of morality and duty were not entirely motivated by personal gain.

The first major expression of this opposition to the Cecils and of anti-Catholicism began in 1569. The leading Roman Catholic among the peers, Thomas Howard, Duke of Norfolk, began something that would be known later as the northern rebellion. It had two aims: to remove the Cecils – or at least reduce their influence on the queen – and to gain the release of Mary, Queen of Scots. He tried to get the Spanish to join their cause, but. initially it all came to nothing and Howard gave in to Cecil and the queen.

However, the rebellion would not so easily be put down. In times past the monarch had always relied on the northern barons to maintain the kingdom. The position of those peers was so important that, for example, there was never a king of all England until they agreed to pay homage to Aethelstan in the tenth century; they then went on to protect the monarch from the Scots and Norse invaders. The monarch, therefore, frequently had to express gratitude to them and was usually not a little in fear of them. So it was now. Having overturned the 4th Duke of Norfolk's somewhat sloppy attempt at an uprising, Elizabeth was now faced by the two most powerful of the northern families: the Percys of Northumberland and the Nevilles of Westmorland. They demanded, then in 1570 tried to effect, the release of Mary, Queen of Scots. Cecil's advice was plain: they must be crushed. Elizabeth's soldiers cantered northwards to a devastating victory and eight hundred of the rebels were executed. But if the northern rebellion was done with, the sense of revolt was not.

Cecil's view was that the sword would not resolve the cause. He saw recent events not as a civil war but as a religious uprising. He had, much earlier, written what centuries later would be called a policy document, or even in parliamentary terms a Green Paper, on the state of English politics at home and abroad. Thus what had happened in 1569 and 1570 could not have caused much surprise. Pius V's bull had been published in February 1570. Many in the queen's council were nervous of Cecil's influence, yet took heed of his warning that the schism amounted to an act of war. This was not hyperbole in the sixteenth century, when the power of the Church remained considerable. It was, too, the centre of much European ambition. The popes still sent their divisions against non-believers.

The year after Elizabeth's excommunication, for example, Pius V, who was often remembered as a quiet Dominican friar, masterminded a Spanish offensive against the Turks. At the time, this was seen as a mighty expression of papal power. Hence Cecil's instinct that an uprising focused on Mary, Queen of Scots was far more dangerous to the crown and the well-being of its kingdom. Few were convinced of his wisdom; more were convinced of his evil. Attempts were made to assassinate him. The life of the queen, too, was continuously threatened. But it was Cecil's life, or rather his death, that was seen as the great prize.

He set up his own counter-intelligence service, which has often been seen, along with Sir Francis Walsingham's network of spies, as the beginnings of the British intelligence service. Walsingham, who in 1573 would come to power as Elizabeth's Secretary of State, was a master intriguer and spy. It was he who discovered the Ridolfi and Babington plots against the queen (see below) and was probably of even greater influence than Cecil in the matter of the execution of Mary, Queen of Scots. Yet the spy networks that both men established were hardly sophisticated – those characters recruited by Cecil might even be described as mercenary thugs. Stories abounded, with some justification, of Cecil's intelligence groups torturing and murdering: they hardly match Cecil's image as a man of honour. His defenders repeatedly point out that the alternative was probably regicide. Is this just a case of the end justifying the means? Certainly it reminds us that this man, whom we first saw as a romantic and academic (he became chancellor of Cambridge University), church reformer and legal and political draughtsman, was also a ruthless politician. His success and character were mirrored in many generations down the centuries.

There were probably just two significant occasions in Cecil's life and in his relationship with the queen that jarred with his image of wise eminence. First, she steadfastly refused to accept his advice that she should marry. But the most difficult time, perhaps predictably, was when the news came that Mary, Queen of Scots had been executed.

One of the attempts to assassinate Cecil, and more importantly Elizabeth, occurred in 1586. As Cecil had predicted, the suppression of the northern rebellion did not put an end to the Catholic revolt. A man called Anthony Babington hatched a plot to assassinate Elizabeth, to free Mary, Queen of Scots, and thus bring the English Catholics and their Spanish sympathizers to arms. Babington wrote secretly, so he thought, to Mary with the details of the conspiracy; but Walsingham's spies got hold of the letter, and Babington and his handful of fellow conspirators were executed. It was Walsingham who showed that Mary was still so powerful that she too had to die. Elizabeth was not convinced. Cecil convinced her. When news came that day in 1587 that the execution had been carried out, Elizabeth turned on Cecil.

It is said that she simply wished people to believe that Cecil had misinterpreted her wishes; those familiar with the story of Henry II and Thomas Becket may find this a familiar emotion. Cecil was banished from court, but not for long; the queen needed him. Her reputation darkened, for the moment. The following year, 1588, was the year of the Armada, and this man in a woman's body rose to the height of her popularity. Protestant England understood all too well her vision, shared with Cecil, of the Catholic threat which successive monarchs would recognize and use to raise funds and troops.

Cecil continued to be Elizabeth's chief minister until his death in 1598 at the grand age of seventy-eight. He had outlived and outlasted most of his friends and his children, except his eldest son Thomas and his second son Robert.

At the age of thirty-five, Robert Cecil then succeeded his father as chief minister to the queen. Not physically strong, he had spent much of his young life at home with tutors. Later, like his father, he went up to St John's College Cambridge, although without any distinction. It is not surprising that he rose to some sort of power through his father – it could not be otherwise. In addition, he became a friend of the queen's favourite, Essex, who was younger than he was. However, he exhibited none of the characteristics of that ill-fated earl and instead quietly worked away in the more courtly style that was to become a hallmark of the Cecil family. Although he took his late father's office, Robert had no political base to sustain his position. Also, he was perhaps sensitive to the thought that Elizabeth was in the autumn of her reign. Moreover, there was no great Cecil family in support, only his brother Thomas, who had become a distinguished soldier and who would lead the successful assault on Essex's rebellion in 1601. As for his cousins, particularly Francis Bacon, they were politically opposed to him and on the side of the Earl of Essex, whose money and élan – something to which Cecils never pretended – attracted friends and admirers Here, then, is an image of a supposedly powerful, but surely lonely, chief minister to the ageing queen.

Curiously, his stock among some who had previously disregarded him rose in 1600 when Essex, against the queen's express command, returned from Ireland where he had been dealing unsuccessfully with the O'Neill Revolt (see Chapter 4). Cecil was undoubtedly influential in rescuing Essex from this moment of stupidity. His advice to Elizabeth was to banish the earl from court, but to allow him liberty. The advice proved over-generous and the opportunity fatal for the Earl of Essex, who staged an abortive coup.

Essex, of course, was hardly a character to acknowledge a debt of gratitude – particularly when his life was on the line. In February 1601 he was put on trial for treason. During the trial he thought to thoroughly discredit Robert Cecil and make him complicit in the offence. The earl claimed that Cecil had given his opinion to the Comptroller of the queen's household, Sir William Knollys, that on the queen's death the Infanta of Spain should become monarch of England.

When we consider what was going on at the time, this was a terrible accusation. The queen was old, she was suspicious of almost everyone, the threat from Spain had never really gone away, the Catholics were always seen as threatening, there had been a very public attempt to overthrow her, and plot and accusation were coming from every credible lip. Even the incredible, in Essex's case, had to be taken seriously when the objects of the attacks were Cecil, the queen's closest adviser, and, by implication, Knollys, her own Comptroller.

Of course the accusation was baseless; yet the damage had been done. Some stain was left on Cecil's credibility, particularly with the natural successor to the queen, James VI of Scotland, and his followers. This was not a time of instant broadcasting and a widely available free press, enabling explanations to be quickly heard and absorbed. The story of Essex's accusation would sound much stronger by the time it had travelled north of the border than would the truth of it which lamely followed.

Nevertheless, the time had come for Robert Cecil to take his father's example and quietly make communications with James VI, in order that the momentous transition from the House of Tudor to the House of Stuart would be as uneventful as was possible. In the early hours of the morning of 24 March 1603 Elizabeth I turned her face to the wall and died. She was seventy years old. Nine hours later Robert Cecil, completely in control of the affairs of state, read to the assembled nobles the proclamation he had written declaring James VI of Scotland to be James I of England. It was Cecil more than anyone else who made sure that matters proceeded smoothly. It might so easily have been otherwise and James, a king of eccentric habits and of sometimes distasteful homosexual yearnings, was indeed grateful for the way that Cecil had masterminded his accession. Roberts's father, William, had had great position and wealth, but Elizabeth never gave him great titles, nor did he seek them. The same was true of his son; nevertheless a grateful James I created him Viscount Cranborne in 1604 and the following year 1st Earl of Salisbury. Although James was much in Cecil's debt, these honours were bestowed for his services to Elizabeth. In 1605 he became a Knight of the Garter, an honour that was only in the king's gift.

Cecil, or more accurately Salisbury, as he was known by 1605, had enormous personal wealth through his father's estates, his grandmother's Lincolnshire estates and his father's second marriage. He collected tithes and funds from various offices of state including the bland-sounding but lucrative mastership of the court of wards. He was also lord steward to Anne of Denmark, James's queen. But his fellow peers and courtiers did not always bow to his wishes, even though he was the most powerful man in the whole country. This was partly because he represented the views of the king and often determined how the king's interests should be heard in Parliament. Many of the nobles did not approve of James I, who, in the early days of his monarchy, was seen as greedy and uncouth – and his Scottish retinue doubly so. A greedy king expected Parliament to give him the revenues he demanded. This early opposition to James meant that Cecil had to stretch his powers of negotiation and political skills to the limit, and he was not particularly successful.

In the Parliament of 1604, king and commons confronted each other on the matter of what revenues and benefits the monarch should have. Some years later, in 1610, Salisbury drew up a scheme called the Great Contract. Until that point –

and certainly all the arguments in 1604 had revolved about it – the revenues due to the monarch had come from feudal dues. Salisbury attempted to reform the way in which the monarch was paid, to produce what many years later became known as the civil list: he proposed an annual allowance determined by Parliament.But James refused to allow Parliament to tamper with the royal prerogative.

The prerogative is a constitutional issue, the instrument by which Parliament recognizes the powers of the sovereign. Even at the beginning of the seventeenth century, there was no question but that the prerogative of the monarch reflected the feudal position of the throne as being above all others and all institutions. It was something akin to kingship in its purest form, where the monarch promises to protect the people from all their enemies, including invaders and government, in return for absolute allegiance. So by preserving that feudal prerogative James I would have absolute power, including the total authority to dispense justice.

Elizabeth, with the help of Salisbury's father, William Cecil, had taken even more powers by insisting that Parliament could not even debate questions about her personal life – for example, whether or not she should marry and who should succeed her to the throne. Here was the fundamental argument that Salisbury had to win: Parliament should be able to set aside money as the income of the monarch instead of the monarch being automatically entitled to feudal dues of wardship, but Parliament could not overturn the prerogative of the crown. Parliament opposed that prerogative and James I refused to budge. Salisbury's hope of constitutional reform failed in that 1610 Parliament. The Great Contract was never signed, and the feudal dues system remained in the monarch's power until 1643.

By now, 1610, the era of the two Cecils was coming to an end. Salisbury's failure to implement the Great Contract had not done a great deal for him in James's eyes – and anyway, the king was already taking more note of his courtier Robert Carr. James was to create Carr Earl of Somerset, but he too would fall from royal favour and be lucky to escape with his life, having been implicated in the murder of Sir Thomas Overbury in 1613. Overbury had tried to stop Carr marrying Frances Howard, the divorced Countess of Essex; Carr and Howard had him poisoned. This was not a happy period, involving as it did opposition to the king; the king's extraordinary behaviour, coupled with that of his Scottish camp followers; more plotting; more poisonings; and constitutional resettlement. These goings on have rarely been political adventure playgrounds for Cecils, but Salisbury survived them to die of natural causes in 1612.

The other two Cecils of this period should be noted, albeit briefly. Thomas, eldest son of William, inherited his father's barony of Burghley and gave the Cecil family another branch in its genealogical tree by becoming 1st Earl of Exeter. His third son was Viscount Wimbledon, otherwise known as Sir Edward Cecil. Both were military men.

Thomas Cecil was not the serious student that his father had been. He was born in 1542 and at the age of nineteen was dispatched on a grand tour of the continent. His father should have known better: the young Thomas cared little for Doric arches but greatly for wine and women. William Cecil, appalled, felt his son could never make his mark in a sensible and respectable profession and might even degenerate to the status of a tennis court attendant. In the spring of 1563, having drunk, gambled and whored his way through Paris, Heidelberg, Frankfurt and Antwerp, Thomas Cecil was brought home and made MP for Stamford.

He also managed to have himself admitted to Cambridge University. The fact that his father was chancellor of that institution was perhaps of some help when the Senate was asked to make him a special case. Thomas Cecil had, however, started to put some of his physical energies to good use. In 1569 he helped put down the rebellion of the northern earls – Northumberland and Neville. He seems to have had an instinct for rough and tumble, and when the Scottish wars began he left Westminster to take part and was later knighted by Queen Elizabeth. He got a command during the wars in the Low Countries and in 1588 is mentioned in the records as going to sea against the Armada. When his father died ten years later the queen commanded that Thomas Cecil should mourn as a great earl – in other words have considerable precedence. The following year, 1599, he was instructed by Elizabeth to hunt out the papists in the north of England. He thoroughly enjoyed the task and filled his coffers not with Catholic gold, but with Roman missals.

He was installed at Windsor in May 1601 as a Knight of the Garter, partly for his services among the queen's enemies in the north, but more notably for his prominent part in putting down the attempted coup by the Earl of Essex. When Elizabeth died, just as his brother Robert continued in office under James so too did Thomas Cecil, and in 1605 he became Earl of Exeter. Five years later he was widowed and subsequently married the daughter of the 4th Lord Chandos, thus bringing together two great families.

Edward, born in 1572, was Thomas Cecil's third son. He did not reconnoitre the inns and bedrooms of Paris with the same determination as had his father, although he did become a soldier and go with his father to the war in the Low Countries. He appears to have been a better soldier than Thomas, and in 1601 led one thousand infantry and cavalry to the relief of Ostend. Queen Elizabeth thought much of him and gave him his knighthood. Very soon he was a colonel of a cavalry regiment himself and in 1610, while his uncle Robert was battling with Parliament for the Great Contract, Edward was leading four thousand English troops at the siege of Juliers. James I, impressed with Edward's reputation as a brave and honourable soldier, used him as an envoy and ambassador. In 1625, under the nominal command of his mentor, the Duke of Buckingham, Edward became lord marshal and general of the sea and land forces. This was in the campaign against the Spanish, which was not enormously distinguished. There were no smart ranks to inspect nor Bristol-fashion fleet to command. Cecil's soldiers were a mixed bag of incompetents and his ships more like Tyneside colliers than those of a lord high admiral. Nevertheless it was after this adventure that the king raised him to the peerage as Viscount Wimbledon.

The raid on Cadiz which he conducted was a fiasco. Cecil had no idea how to use a naval flotilla; nor, apparently, would he accept the advice of his senior commanders who included the Earl of Essex and Lord Cromwell; so he failed to take the fort from the sea. However, it surrendered readily when Sir John Burgh led some of his soldiers ashore and they assaulted the citadel from behind.

The next morning, emboldened by the news from the fort, Cecil landed the rest of his troops not in a proper military manner but more as though they were going on a picnic – except that they had no provisions. The English soldiers were then expected to confront the Spaniards after a day's march, but were tired and hungry. When this was pointed out to Cecil, he observed that with the enemy at his tent flap this was hardly the time for the English soldier to be thinking about his stomach.

That evening his forces discovered a huge store of wine in a cave and the men got drunk. Cecil managed to get them back on board and sailed away, but fiasco now turned into tragedy as disease struck on the ships and hundreds of corpses were buried at sea. Most of the blame was heaped on Buckingham, as he was the nominal commander. Moreover, although the other commanders, particularly Essex, laid formal charges of incompetence against Cecil, the king paid little attention.

Cecil took part in a few other near disasters, and yet when he was made governor of Portsmouth he was considered to be the nation's foremost military authority. At the beginning of the seventeenth century, Edward Cecil had assumed a mystique that later generations reserved for Marlborough and Wellington. On one occasion he was compared with King Arthur's great knights at Camelot. Thus the Cecil dynasty marched on, not even tarnished by the stains on Edward Cecil's military passbook.

Cecils continued to distinguish themselves in each century. For much of the nineteenth century the name Cecil was associated with Robert, the 3rd Marquess of Salisbury. He was born in 1830, went from Eton to Christ Church College, Oxford and in 1853 was elected a Fellow of All Souls'. In the same year he became the Tory member of Parliament for Stamford, a seat occupied by Cecils at one time or another since the sixteenth century. Robert Cecil was an opponent of parliamentary reform, and not simply to safeguard the family seat. He was born just two years before the first Reform Act of 1832; thirty-three years later he was fighting Gladstone's Reform Bill and seen as a coming parliamentary tactician as well as orator. As Viscount Cranborne, in 1866 Cecil joined the Tory government of Lord Derby (though since Derby sat in the Lords the real power lay with Benjamin Disraeli in the Commons). Cecil was given the office of India Secretary, but it was not a colonial matter that caused his resignation. Once more, parliamentary reform was, ostensibly, the problem. Cecil did not like the Reform Bill drafted by Disraeli, for he believed it lowered the franchise too much. At the same time, Disraeli was probably correct in his belief that Cecil disliked him sufficiently to use his opposition to the Bill to embarrass him. Equally, Cecil was not alone in leaving the administration. Jonathan Peel (the former Prime Minister's brother) and the Earl of Caernarfon also resigned.

Cecil, who in 1868 succeeded his father as the 3rd Marquess of Salisbury (his elder brother having died), found enormous difficulties when asked to support what he saw as the too rapid flow of ill-thought-through legislation on such important issues as parliamentary reform, the disestablishment of the Irish church, the Irish Land Act and the Public Worship Regulation Act. When Disraeli died in 1881, it was Salisbury who now led the Conservative Party and from June 1885 to January 1886 became Prime Minister for the first time. Later in 1886, supported by the Liberal Unionists, he became Prime Minister again and would remain so for four years. It was during this time that the Conservatives pushed through the ideas that gave the British greater dominion over Africa. On more domestic matters, it was Salisbury's government which, in 1888, set up county councils. The Conservatives lost office in 1892, but Salisbury came back in 1895 and remained as Prime Minister until 1902 – although very clearly he would like to have gone earlier.

This Cecil was almost a caricature of a late nineteenth-century Tory. He most certainly had deep suspicions about getting too involved in the realignment that was going on in continental Europe. Towards the close of the nineteenth century there had been strenuous efforts to bring about some Anglo-German alliance. Given that the British monarchy had been German since 1714, that on the death of Victoria in 1901 the king's family name was Saxe-Coburg and that the German Kaiser was Edward VII's nephew, the discussions about the proposed alliance went far beyond the normal diplomatic channels. In the mid-1890s Joseph Chamberlain had encouraged his Cabinet colleagues to reach some agreement with Germany. Chamberlain was mindful of German arms going to Britain's enemies in the Boer War. Also, with political adjustment in Europe, Germany had new colonial ambitions in Africa. It is not surprising, therefore, that Chamberlain believed that an alliance with Germany could prevent some future confrontation. In addition, there was concern in some quarters that the emphasis on Empire would produce a sense of isolationism in British policy. But Salisbury would not support Chamberlain's proposed treaty.

The Kaiser was in a quandary. His naval lobbyists could always point to the lack of a formal treaty between Germany and Britain, plus the increasing building programme in the Royal Navy as a very good reason to fulfil the Kaiser's ambitions to build a huge high seas fleet; yet he also wanted a treaty. The Kaiser, not always the most careful of thinkers, simply believed that a High Seas Fleet would give Germany authority and encourage others to sign treaties. He was, after all, supporting one of the oldest principles of naval warfare doctrine: that a powerful navy will keep enemies in port and their ministers willing to sign peace treaties. There was a further complication which Salisbury recognized. In 1899 the Russians held a world peace conference in The Hague. One of its themes was an arms limitation agreement, and neither the Germans nor the British were going along with that. Salisbury's view was that the important question in Europe was the possibility of a Franco-Russian axis. He was certainly not going to line up with the Germans to oppose that or anything else for the moment. Salisbury also suspected all German motives. After all, the Boer War was being fought in Southern Africa at this time and the British believed that the Germans were supplying the Boers.

Equally complicated was the sometimes erratic diplomacy practised by Kaiser Wilhelm. For example, he lobbied his uncle, Edward VII, to impress upon Chamberlain and the apparently dull Foreign Secretary, the Marquess of Lansdowne, the need for an Anglo-German pact. The Kaiser's view was that an agreement was an obvious piece of diplomacy and that the people who were getting in its way, that is, Salisbury and Lansdowne, were nothing more than 'noodles'. Salisbury held firm. Furthermore, Salisbury did not accept that such an alliance would act as a guarantor for European peace. He also accepted the argument that more effort should be made to stop the Russians getting a stranglehold on the lucrative commercial region of the Far East, as well as establishing some strategic domination. The Japanese, not unnaturally, were equally nervous of Russian ambitions. The Germans quite liked this idea, probably because it would worry the Russians. When, in 1901, Salisbury agreed a draft for an Anglo-Japanese treaty, Edward VII told the Kaiser about it. The Kaiser told the Tsar – why not? They were all cousins and uncles. What the Kaiser failed to understand was that as a result the Russians would intensify their interests in Europe and the Middle East, thus threatening Germany's security and trading interests.

Here was an example of how increasingly difficult international diplomacy was at this time, especially among leaders who imagined that those difficulties were best resolved by their personal ideas. Towards the end of 1901, an outline treaty between Germany and Britain was prepared. Salisbury, in a manner after William Cecil himself, added a cryptic note to the draft – more of a veto than a cautionary sentence. The timing was perfect, because this was the moment when the German press were running articles about British concentration camps in the Boer War, and Chamberlain was guilty of an injudicious retaliation. The treaty was never signed; the Germans began building their ships; and Salisbury seemed to know that the late W. E. Gladstone's observation that German naval power was an indication of inevitable war was coming true.

Salisbury was tired and unwell and for some time had wished to move into retirement. There were two reasons why he could not leave office when he wanted to. First he had to see through the coronation of Edward VII. Victoria had died in January 1901, and after a year of official mourning the coronation was fixed for June 1902. Unfortunately Edward VII then had appendicitis, so the ceremony was postponed until August. The other reason Salisbury could not leave office was the Boer War. In 1900, after good news from that conflict, Salisbury, probably against his better judgement, was persuaded to call a general election. This was known as the khaki election, after the new colour of the British Army's uniform. Salisbury won with a majority of 134, and so there was no great reason for him to cut and run. It was not until the peace treaty was signed at Vereeniging in May 1902 that Salisbury, now in his seventies, who had been born when the Duke of Wellington was Prime Minister and who had been in government and opposition since 1866, could at last leave the political arena. It was not a long retirement. Robert Cecil, 3rd Marquess of Salisbury, died the following year, 1903. He was the last Prime Minister to lead his government from the House of Lords.

To the general reader Lord Salisbury is not famous for very much except for being powerful – this is quite often the lot of the truly powerful. Yet there is one Salisbury legacy that is commonplace. Towards the end of the nineteenth century an expression was coined that lasts until this day: 'Bob's your uncle.' It is said to have come from the fact that Lord Salisbury, Robert Cecil, gave the job of Minister for Ireland to his rather dull nephew Arthur Balfour – a piece of nepotism. Balfour followed Salisbury as Prime Minister until the general election of 1906, and was perhaps best known for the Balfour Declaration of 1917 which promised a homeland for Zionists in Palestine.

When Salisbury died, so too did the era of grand Victorian power politics. Certainly, the world that he had influenced had been the subject of enormous change. There are those who say that Britain declined as a world power from this point. The balance of power in world politics was indeed beginning to shift. The USA was, for the first time, appearing as an international force and as an industrial nation. Germany, too, was moving into manufacturing and industrial markets hitherto dominated by the industrial revolution in Britain during the previous hundred years.

However, the Britain Salisbury left behind in 1903 remained the most powerful industrial nation, and the most politically influential, on earth. The vast majority of cargoes were carried in British ships and they were insured in London. The commercial and financial exchanges were dominated by London contracts and rates. Except for 'the sixth continent', South America, there was not a region in the world that did not recognize British influence in terms of commercial, economic and political leadership. Within a decade or so that authority would be weakened. After all, with the political emergence of America, Germany and soon Japan, change was inevitable. Somewhere, over the next hundred years, Cecils would be part of the emerging new Britain.

Not all the Cecils were movers and shakers in the palaces and ministries of London. In the year of Salisbury's death, 1902, David Cecil was born. He became famous as an Oxford literary don and the biographer of William Cowper, Max Beerbohm and Lord Melbourne, the mentor of the young Queen Victoria. He was in many ways the most famous of all the twentieth-century Cecils because his apolitical career and scholarship made him more nationally known through broadcasting and journalism, almost until his death in 1986. His contemporary in the other branch of the Cecil family was the 6th Marquess of Exeter, who was known by the oldest of the Cecil titles, Lord Burghley. It was this Cecil who was the great athlete and who in 1928 won for Britain an Olympic hurdles gold medal. His name became synonymous with the Amateur Athletic Association – the three As – and it was Burghley who organized the 1948 Olympic Games in London.

Perhaps the most powerful, politically, of the twentieth-century Cecils was the 5th Marquess of Salisbury, Robert Gascoyne-Cecil, known in the House of Lords as Bobbity Salisbury. Born in the 1890s, he went into politics as the MP for Dorset South in 1929, became a junior foreign office minister in 1935 and three years later resigned, along with his boss, Anthony Eden, because he disagreed with the government's so-called appeasement of Mussolini. Then Viscount Cranborne, he succeeded his father, the 4th Marquess, after the war. Most importantly, he led the Tory opposition in the Lords after the general election of 1945 until the return of the Conservatives to power in 1951. He was seen by his contemporaries as one of the wisest members of the Lords, and became teacher and example to that intake of sometimes disillusioned young peers following the Conservative defeat in 1945.

Most of all, it was this Cecil who introduced something which became known as the Salisbury Convention. Naturally, during this period of socialist reform, approximately 1945–50, many Tories could not accept the changes proposed by the Labour government of Clement Attlee. Even though Labour had been elected on a programme of nationalization, the Tory instinct in the Lords, based on their centuries-old baronial power and prejudice, was to block that legislation in the hope of preventing it getting on to the statute book. Salisbury said this was wrong. He saw the Lords as a place for tidying up badly drafted legislation and revising it when it made sense to do so, and did not believe that the Lords in the second half of the twentieth century had the right to block government legislation on ideological grounds. Salisbury's view was that, if a government had been elected to do certain things clearly defined in the election manifesto, then that government had a perfect right for its legislation to become law.

Salisbury was wise enough also to understand that if the Lords, with its in-built Tory majority, attempted to destroy the socialist legislative programme when the mood of the country clearly expected it to be implemented, then the Labour government would be well justified and have unquestionable public support if it decided on a radical reform of the Upper House. It was the Salisbury rules of how an opposition should behave in the Lords that saved the House and the country from the sort of constitutional crisis that could not be afforded in such austere times. Although there were blips along the way, Salisbury's wisdom prevailed to the end of the twentieth century.

It should not be thought, however, that this Robert Cecil was a dyed-in-the-wool reactionary. He was a champion of House of Lords reform, but he wanted it done quietly and thoughtfully. It was his example that was followed by other peers, notably Lord Carrington. Yet the reforms when they did come, did so not from that place, but from a government seemingly beset with spite rather than possessing a clear idea of what, constitutionally and democratically, should replace the chamber whose greatest value was to be a check against the excesses of government majorities in the House of Commons.

So it is not surprising to find that by the end of the century it was once again a Cecil who was right in the thick of the negotiations to reform the Lords. Here was another Robert Cecil, bearing a barony created in 1603, the year in which Elizabeth I died. He was born in 1946 and was the son of the 6th Marquess of Salisbury. He too became the Conservative MP for Dorset South – in the year that Margaret Thatcher became Prime Minister, 1979. He then went to the House of Lords and in 1992, sitting with the family's courtesy title of Viscount Cranborne that dates from 1604, became a junior defence minister. Two years later he became leader of the House of Lords and would remain so until the Conservative defeat in 1997; he then became leader of the opposition in the Lords. It was in this role that all the backstairs and wardrobe diplomacy of the Cecils reappeared. It was Robert Cranborne who negotiated the reform of the Lords so desired by the new government of Tony Blair. He agreed that the majority of hereditary peers would go, but the then new leader of the Conservative Party, William Hague, did not like the idea of his leader in the House of Lords reaching agreement with government, and sacked him. Nevertheless Cranborne's formula was more or less implemented.

For four hundred years the Cecils have been accustomed to power and to the idea that they might be discarded by those in higher office. Interestingly, not a single holder of higher office from Elizabeth I to Elizabeth II has inaugurated a dynasty that could ever imagine having the Cecils' influence over British political and constitutional life.

NOTES

1 In June 1520 the two kings met at Calais and set out a banquet of such extravagance, with fountains of wine under bejewelled silken canopies, that it became known as the Field of the Cloth of Gold. Within a year, England and France were declared enemies.

2 The origin of the term Huguenot is uncertain. It may have came from a Swiss German word, *Eidgenoss*, meaning 'confederate'.

3 The title Lord Burghley survives. William Cecil, the 1st Baron, had two sons, Thomas and Robert. Through their lines, the earldoms of Salisbury (Robert) and Exeter (Thomas) appeared. The title Burghley survives through the Exeter title, and Cranborne through Salisbury.

4 His mother was Mary, Queen of Scots, but he became king of England by way of being great-grandson of Margaret Tudor, the eldest daughter of Henry VII.

5 Since the execution of her mother, Anne Boleyn, in 1536 and Parliament's declaration that she was illegitimate, Elizabeth had lived a very insecure life. The accession of her sister, Mary I, brought dangers because of her religion and Elizabeth was certainly vulnerable to the accusation that she was involved in the Wyatt rebellion, which was why she was locked in the Tower in 1554.

FURTHER READING

AIKIN, Lucy, *Memoirs of the Court and Times of Queen Elizabeth*, 1818.

BLACK, J. B., *The Reign of Elizabeth*, OUP, 1936.

Calendars of State Papers, Public Record Office.

FROUDE, J. A., *History of England from the Fall of Wolsey to the Defeat of the Spanish Armada*, 1862–70.

READ, Conyers, *Mr Secretary Cecil and Queen Elizabeth*, Jonathan Cape, 1956.

WEIR, Alison, *Elizabeth the Queen*, Pimlico, 1998.

WILSON, John Dover, *Life in Shakespeare's England*, CUP, 1911.

CHAPTER SEVEN

THE CHURCHILLS

To most contemporary readers, any title that contains the name 'Churchill' inevitably draws attention to Sir Winston, the World War II British leader and, later, Conservative Prime Minister. Other people would make the connection with the 1st Duke of Marlborough and, others perhaps, Lord Randolph. The Churchill line is longer than three names and justifiably so. Furthermore, the Churchills are often associated with Chartwell in Kent and Blenheim Palace. Their origins are further west – Somerset and Dorset.

The first Churchill of any fame was one of the great seventeenth-century lawyers, Sir John Churchill. The family had come from Bradford-on-Avon in Somerset and certainly the lawyer's father and grandfather (both named Jasper) had been squires of some distinction. The young John Churchill, according to the lists of Lincoln's Inn, became a law student in March 1639 and eight years later was called to the bar. In the seventeenth century, lawyers became rich when they practised in chancery; John Churchill became very rich in his capacity as a successful businessman as well as that of lawyer. In 1661 he became an MP in Dorset. By 1670 he was knighted, and four years later he had become a king's counsel and attorney general to the royal Duke of York. But the following year we find Churchill heading for the Tower. It all began when he was appointed as one of the lawyers to act for a man named Sir Nicholas Crispe in an appeal case. The difficulty was that the defendant, Thomas Dalmahoy, was an MP. The Commons were very jealous of their privileges and wary of losing any form of independence, which could only be taken away by the Lords. The House of Commons, rightly, regarded anyone who appeared at the bar of the House to prosecute a Member of Parliament as having usurped that member's privileges. In June 1675, therefore, the serjeant-at-arms was instructed to arrest Churchill by MPs, who then voted to send the lawyer to the Tower since he was in contempt of the authority of the House of Commons. The response was simple but drastic: the king prorogued Parliament and Churchill was freed. This did nothing to damage his career. In 1682 he became Recorder of Bristol, and in 1685 Churchill succeeded Harbottle Grimston as Master of the Rolls and became member of Parliament (in the Lords, of course) for Bristol. He took up both offices in 1685. Much good it did him, for he died that October. He may have been a fine lawyer and a good businessman, but the manor house in Somerset in which the family lived had to be sold to pay off his debts.[1]

John Churchill and his wife Susan had no son, but four daughters. The connection with the modern Churchills is that through a different branch of the family he was an ancestor of another John Churchill the 1st Duke of Marlborough. The father of the 1st Duke was a seventeenth-century Sir Winston, who was born in comfortable circumstances in Dorset, in a hamlet called Glanvilles Wootton, a few miles south of Sherborne in or around 1620.[2] His wife, Elizabeth, was the daughter of Sir John and Eleanor Drake from Ashe in East Devon, close to the Dorset border. Eleanor, Churchill's mother-in-law, was the daughter of George Villiers, the Duke of Buckingham.

Winston, even in the seventeenth century satisfying the twentieth-century view of that family, was a royalist during the Civil War. Given the outcome of that struggle it is hardly surprising that he and his family fell upon hard times and retreated to Ashe during Cromwell's rule. Yet once the monarchy was restored so were the Churchill fortunes, and Winston was allowed to return to his estates and his life as a politician and a historian of some note. In 1664 he was knighted and became a Fellow of the Royal Society. The Society, then in its very early years, had begun as a series of meetings among scientists and philosophers in the 1640s and received its royal charter in 1662. Churchill was in good company: Sir Christopher Wren and Sir Isaac Newton were also Fellows, as was Churchill's friend and the diarist of the restored Charles II's London, Samuel Pepys.

Churchill became a friend of that monarch and was also a trusted courtier of his brother and successor James II. He is probably best remembered, apart from his influence on two kings, for something he wrote and for two children he sired. One connection between this seventeenth-century Churchill and his better-known namesake, the twentieth-century wartime leader, is their leaning to be loyalist historians. The earlier Sir Winston was the author of *A Divi Britannici*, sub-titled '...A Remark upon the Lives of all the kings of this isle, from the year of World 2855 until the year of grace 1660...'. His greater mark on British history was the fact that he was the father of Arabella and of John, the famous 1st Duke of Marlborough.

Arabella was born in 1648, a terrible time in English history. The previous year, Charles I had been imprisoned at Carisbrooke Castle. The year after her birth, the king was executed, the House of Lords and the monarchy abolished, the Commonwealth declared and Cromwell ordered the massacres of Drogheda and Wexford. In 1649 the Scots had proclaimed Charles II king and in 1651 he was crowned at Scone and invaded England, only to be defeated at the Battle of Worcester. It was not until 1660, when Arabella was twelve years old, that General Monck instigated the return of the monarchy and what was to become the twenty-five-year reign of Charles II. For the Churchill family, as for the whole nation, those first twelve years of Arabella's life were difficult; a time when powerful dynasties were forced into taking sides. The civil war pitted family against family, father against son and none escaped its ruthlessness. It was a true test – sometimes willingly taken, sometimes enforced – of loyalties either to a distressed monarchy or to a traumatic adventure into republican thinking.

By the time the monarchy was restored the Churchills had made their mark as loyalists to the Stuart House, and so their futures were assured – even though they would later fall from grace. Just as Sir Winston Churchill was brought by his father into the court of Charles II, his own children were similarly favoured. His daughter Arabella was appointed a lady-in-waiting to the new Duchess of York, Anne Hyde. Her husband the Duke was the second surviving son of Charles I and Henrietta Maria; during the Civil War he had taken refuge at first in the Low Countries and then in France. His importance, of course, was that he was Charles II's brother and, in the absence of any legitimate sons of Charles's, would one day be James II, king of England. The two daughters of James and Anne would also become monarchs, Mary II and Queen Anne. Thus the Churchills were very close to the monarchy – Arabella closer than her brother, for, whilst still in her teens, she became the future James II's mistress. When she was nineteen they had a bastard daughter, Henrietta, followed by two sons, James Fitzjames and Henry Fitzjames, and a daughter, also called Arabella, who went into a convent. Henrietta married a Waldegrave, a member of the famous Somerset family which had in 1381 provided one of the earliest Speakers of the House of Commons, Sir Richard Waldegrave. The marriage of the illegitimate Henrietta (legitimacy was a fact rather than a stigma in the seventeenth century) thus produced a dotted line between the Churchills, James II and the present earls at Chewton, the latest of whom is the brother of the twentieth-century Conservative Cabinet minister, William Waldegrave.

The two illegitimate sons also went on to some fame. The second, Henry Fitzjames, was created Duke of Albemarle when his father was king. His older brother, James Fitzjames, became the celebrated 1st Duke of Berwick, and is remembered in British history as fighting to defend his father's right to remain king and for taking part in the Battle of the Boyne in 1690. In continental Europe, Berwick was at least as famous as his uncle John Churchill, later Duke of Marlborough, and in later life he was created a Marshal of France. It is a curiosity of seventeenth- and eighteenth-century warfare that two commanders from the same family might easily be found on opposing sides. Thus there came a point, when the French king Louis XIV was offering peace terms to the Dutch, that Berwick was negotiating a truce with his uncle, the Duke of Marlborough. He never much enjoyed anything but soldiering and, perhaps appropriately, was killed in battle – he was downed by a cannon ball at the siege of Phillippsburg during the War of the Polish Succession.

Arabella's time with Anne Hyde, apart from her affair with the king, was inevitably governed by politics and the rise and fall of her brother. John was born at Ashe during the time of his mother's retreat to her parental family home because of the excesses of the Civil War. Unlike his father, John was no scholar. But he did well enough at St Paul's School and then left to become, through his father's influence and the court's gratitude, a page to the Duke of York, the future James II. At about the time his sister Arabella was giving birth to James's daughter Henrietta, John Churchill enlisted as an ensign in the Foot Guards. Here lay his career and his future. Almost immediately he was called a hero: in 1672 his gallantry at the siege of Nijmegen was the talk of the court. A year later at another siege, this time at Maastricht, he volunteered with a handful of others to go with the Duke of Monmouth on a remarkably successful attack. On his safe return Monmouth is said to have told his father: 'I owe my life to his bravery.' The importance of this early friendship between Churchill and Monmouth should not be overlooked, for James Duke of Monmouth[3] was the bastard son of Charles II; hence the king's gratitude to Churchill. Everything about him was remarkable, including his love life. He fell in love with Sarah Jennings, a lady-in-waiting to one of the Duke of York's daughters, Princess Anne. They married in secret, much to the annoyance of his parents who felt he should have married into more money.

He had little time to relax in this new arrangement. Both Charles II and Churchill's current mentor, the Duke of York, used him as an emissary in their negotiations in the Netherlands with the Prince of Orange. Charles II was convinced that he should make some continental pact against France: known as the Triple Alliance, it would unite the English, the Dutch and the Swedes against the common enemy, the French.[4]

Churchill was committed to the Duke of York and when the Duke went into self-imposed exile in 1679 following anti-Catholic legislation and so-called popish plots against the crown, Churchill and his wife Sarah went too. In the autumn they were allowed to return, but only to Scotland; Churchill, following his master, went to Edinburgh. He was used as a go-between. In 1681 it was Churchill who tried to bring Charles II to James's way of thinking that he should be allowed to return to England and that Charles II should abandon Parliament – that is, rule without it. For the moment this could not be, but in 1682 the negotiations and the atmosphere in London at least allowed the Duke of York to come back to England. But the future James II's return nearly resulted in disaster when the ship carrying him, Churchill and their retinue foundered. It is said that it was the future king's efforts which saved his loyal subject, the future Duke of Marlborough. Neither then had any notion that within six years Churchill would be changing sides and giving his allegiance to William of Orange, with whom he had discussed the future of Europe the previous year.

The whole matter of Roman Catholicism and Protestantism would dog British constitutional history for the next three hundred years. It was because James II was a Catholic that he was eventually so hated and feared. His supporters were, naturally, Catholics too. That support came also from overseas, and therefore Catholicism was seen as not just a religious persuasion; it was identified far more as a physical and military threat to the nation and therefore to the monarchy.

Churchill was not a Catholic: he was devoted to the Church of England, as was his wife Sarah. In fact when Sarah's mistress, Princess Anne, married the Protestant Prince George of Denmark she asked Sarah to become her closest lady-in-waiting. Princess Anne and Sarah Churchill (by now Lady Churchill, after her husband had been created Baron Churchill of Aymouth at Christmas 1682) became the firmest of friends. Here too was a conflict of religious and therefore political interests. Much effort was made to convert the Churchills to Roman Catholicism, but in spite of his then allegiance to the future James II, Churchill, and therefore Sarah, resisted.

In an age in which principles were easily redrafted on account of politics, John Churchill's feelings towards the Church of England were, if not exceptional, certainly important. They tell us something about his character. In those days the Church of England represented more than a religious viewpoint. Churchill was by instinct what was then relatively new: a properly defined Tory.

The Tory Party (the term 'Party' was quite common and had been for centuries) was a political grouping that emerged in the 1680s. The name 'Tory' was a pejorative term derived from the Irish Gaelic *toraidhe*, meaning 'outlaw'. The 'outlaws' were those who were against the attempt to stop the Catholic Duke of York becoming king. Instead of being particularly angered by the term, the 'outlaws' liked it enough to adopt it and were known as Tories until the nineteenth century. The people who opposed them were the Protestant Whigs, members of the country party which had done the opposite of the Tories and tried to stop the Duke of York becoming king. The term 'Whig', also originally pejorative, has obscure origins but may derive from a casual Scottish expression, 'Whiggamore'. This was applied to rebels, and probably came from a Scottish term for a horse thief.

Here was the basis for nineteenth-century British politics. The Whigs, often aristocratic but nevertheless usually liberal-minded in their politics, naturally became the basis for the Liberals. The Tories, equally aristocratic, were, however, more usually reactionary and emerged in the 1830s as the Conservatives.

Churchill could not be anything but a Tory – in the late seventeenth-century sense. This contradiction (he was a Protestant) is perhaps explained by two factors: his utter dislike for extremism and, perhaps in the way that William Cecil had in Tudor times, an inner understanding that, whatever one's private dealings, the ultimate loyalty should be towards the crown – or at least until such time as that crown could no longer be trusted in the interests of the people. John Churchill had – and continues to have – many critics. Sometimes this simple factor in his personality is overlooked.

When James II was crowned on 23 April 1685 Churchill was raised further in the peerage, to the barony of Sandridge, and became one of the king's most intimate courtiers – a gentleman of the bedchamber. By this time the affair between Churchill's sister Arabella and the king had run its course. Moreover, King James was far from secure on his throne.

When Charles II died, his bastard son the Duke of Monmouth was in the Netherlands, where he had been exiled after intrigues to have himself declared heir. As an exile Monmouth had lived very much on the indulgence of his father, King Charles. He had lived rather too well, mostly in the arms of his mistress, Lady Wentworth. His position in Holland depended very much on his circle of fellow exiles, most of whom longed for the 'good old days' in Charles's Merrie England. More importantly, Monmouth stayed on sufferance of William, Prince of Orange.

William, grandson of Charles I through his mother, and whose wife Mary was James II's daughter, had every reason to remain above suspicion but had his own secret agenda for the future of the English throne. Equally, he did not wish to be seen to be harbouring a pretender, as Monmouth clearly was. Once James was king William therefore immediately told Monmouth to leave the Netherlands. He went so far as to suggest that he try his hand at soldiering in Asia Minor. Monmouth's friends in the Netherlands were keener that he should try his hand at soldiering in England and claim his throne. He truly believed that all England would come to his clarion call. The issue was very simple: he, the Duke of Monmouth, was a legitimate heir to the throne of his father Charles II, and he was a Protestant. In theory, the country might well have been unwilling for a Roman Catholic to rule England. However, at this stage the significance of the impact of James II's religion was not felt by the general public, only by a typically anxious and suspicious clergy.

So Monmouth sailed for England and on 11 June 1685 arrived in Lyme Bay off the Dorset coast. His reception was encouraging. Having issued a decree stating that he was, through his mother, the true heir and should therefore be declared as the true James II, Monmouth found a steady line waiting to take his shilling and enlist in his cause. But the king was not dreadfully put out by the landing. The powerful men at Westminster pledged their loyalty and, although he had no large standing army, he did have regular infantry and the dragoons of John Churchill; furthermore, the part-time militia were called up. The Earl of Feversham was given command of the army.

Monmouth, who seemed to have no great tactical command of the situation, now began a great circuit with his six thousand or so supporters – most of whom were enthusiastic rather than militarily efficient. They marched from the south coast up to Taunton, then to Bridgwater and from there to the great prize, Bristol. Bristol turned him back. He then marched on a few miles to Bath. There was no point in being there, so he marched south into the steep valley that leads to Frome and then, wearily, back to Bridgwater. Churchill's assessment was that Monmouth had no support other than the rough-and-ready force that marched behind him. His supporters who had landed in Scotland – hardly a strategic pincer movement – had been captured. He knew also that Monmouth had no brilliant military mind to get him out of a tight spot. Feversham had camped at Sedgemoor on the Somerset levels, where Monmouth attacked him; although it was an inconclusive engagement, the king's forces were certainly not getting the best of it. At this point

Churchill led his dragoons and cavalry against the West Countrymen. He gave no quarter. When Monmouth's supporters were not killed in battle they were hunted down and, without hesitation, executed. Monmouth, apparently not one to stand and fight, escaped, only to be captured at Ringwood, taken to the Tower of London and then, without ado, to his execution. His last words, 'I die a Protestant of the Church of England', gave him, his supporters and the clergy little comfort.

It was at this moment that King James sent one of the most infamous lawyers in English history to clean up the remnants of the Monmouth rebellion. After Chief Justice Jeffreys had ordered the execution of more than two hundred and deported four times that number to Barbados James felt supremely confident. He appointed Catholics to senior posts in the army and civil administration. Some men, like the Earl of Sunderland, Robert Spencer, were happy to live with their eye on the main chance, so they converted from Protestantism to Catholicism. James then assaulted the two treasures of England: its part-time army, the militia, and the established Church of England. The Church was a comfortable place in which to worship without the uncompromising dogma of Rome. The militia, a descendant of the Saxon *fyrd*, provided a community-led military fire service. More importantly, the militia made unnecessary a large standing army; such an institution was feared by the ruling classes, who saw it not as an instrument of foreign policy but as a threat to English civil liberties as it had been under Cromwell. The army, while professing loyalty to the monarch, did not like the monarchy, and therefore, whatever James II's motives, his ambitions were seen as foolhardy as well as dangerous.

James got his way, and did so by the simplest of means: he prorogued Parliament and it never again met during his reign. When, for example, the courts questioned his plans to revoke the Test laws – legislation passed in Charles II's time which was intended to prevent Catholics from holding political office and military rank – he merely appointed new judges. When the Church asserted its rights he ordered the dismissal of offending clergy including Henry Compton, the Bishop of London (see Chapter 11).

King James was also concerned about his succession; he was determined that the future monarch should be a Roman Catholic. The obvious scheme was to make his daughter Princess Anne, married to Prince George of Denmark, convert to Catholicism. But Anne was a devout Protestant and she had at her side three people to protect her and help her resist all pressure; her chaplain, Henry Compton, the deposed bishop; her closest friend, her lady-in-waiting, Sarah Churchill; and Sarah's husband John. With their encouragement Princess Anne stood firm. By now, the end of 1687, the confrontation between James and so many in high as well as low places who hitherto had supported him was reaching its zenith.

Moreover, William of Orange was watching from the Netherlands. The Dutchman had played a clever diplomatic game. On the death of Charles he had ordered out James's rival, Monmouth, and had offered James assistance when the rebellion took place. It was now clear that the time was fast approaching when he could make his move and would be encouraged to do so. James understood that there was no chance that Princess Anne would convert; but his wife, Mary of Modena, was pregnant, and on 10 June 1688 gave birth to a son. Or did she? Certainly there was a newborn male child in her bed, but so fearful of the consequences were the Protestants that a rumour gained credence that the baby was not the queen's and had been smuggled into St James's Palace in a warming pan.

Now, those who were determined that James II had to go and be replaced by William of Orange (ostensibly by his wife, Mary, to continue the Stuart line) wrote to William in the Netherlands. The letter, smuggled by a disguised admiral to the king, was perfectly clear in its meaning, if not in its wording:

> ...the people are so generally dissatisfied with the present conduct of the government in relation to their religion, liberties and properties and they are in such expectation of their prospects being daily worse, that your Highness may be assured there are nineteen parts of twenty of the people throughout the kingdom who are desirous of change, and who, we believe, would willingly contribute to it if they had such a protection to countenance their rising as would secure them from being destroyed before they could get to be in a posture able to defend themselves...

The letter was careful not to offer the crown, but no one had any difficulty reading between its urgent lines. In the third week of October, William of Orange put to sea for England. This was yet another armada blown off course by the wind and currents. William had planned to bring his mixture of Scots, English, Dutch, Swedes and not a few Huguenots to a landfall in the north of England, where he had been promised reinforcements. Instead, he ended up in Torbay where he landed on 5 November – unintentionally, but ironically, on the anniversary of an infamous plot.

James, realizing there was no diplomatic means of stopping his son-in-law, must have been proud of his foresight in raising a standing army. Yet just as Parliament had been sceptical about trusting a mythically loyal British army, so James II now suffered. Many of the commanders, either because they saw which way the political wind was blowing or because they sincerely wanted a Protestant monarch, began to melt away from their sovereign. James's final attempts at reconciliation had been to reverse many of the anti-Protestant decrees and proclamations – everything from getting rid of lord lieutenants, magistrates, even Protestant academics at Magdalen College, Oxford. It was too late.

When James II arrived on 19 November with the bulk of his army in Salisbury, he appeared to have a sound defence against the invader. Although the commanders, including some of his best men, were deserting, he still had most of the soldiery; yet this did not amount to a fig leaf of resistance. John Churchill had personally promised James that he would die rather than leave his king. At the same time, Churchill was writing to William of Orange via his intermediary, the Whig, Henry Sidney, one of those who had put their names to the original letter to James's son-in-law.[5] There can be no doubting Churchill's double-dealing.

…Mr Sidney will let you know how I intend to behave myself; I think it is what I owe to God and my country. My honour [William] I take leave to put into your Royal Highness's hands, in which I think it safe. If you think there is anything else that I ought to do, you have but to command me, and I shall pay an entire obedience to it, being resolved to die in that religion that it has pleased God to give you both the will and the power to protect…

On 24 November, Churchill, along with the Duke of Grafton, left James to join William of Orange. Sarah Churchill now hurried Princess Anne northwards to protect her from the very real possibility that James II would try to have her kidnapped.

Churchill and his fellow army officers were not alone in their disloyalty to the monarch. The original plotters had scattered throughout the country and were taking on the king's men; resistance was low. Rebellion in the cities was unanimous and the navy reported to William that they were with him and that the fleet and the great base of Portsmouth were his to command. One of those who immediately went over from the navy was John Churchill's younger brother George, at the time one of James's fleet captains.

By December 1688 King James II was done for. London panicked with news of massacres, but somehow the council, which had so recently been the king's to persuade, restored some form of command. James escaped, was caught and allowed to escape again, and never returned. Although something close to being a zealot, he had remained true to his beliefs and for that was, outside of England, always respected and honoured.

Churchill had abandoned his patron and monarch. He had done so because of his religion, but it is difficult to believe that his religious beliefs were not somehow bound to a greater ambition. He went on to become one of the greatest generals Europe has ever seen. He was created Duke of Marlborough and a grateful nation paid for him to build Blenheim Palace, with Capability Brown laying out its gardens to represent the forces at his famous victory of the same name in 1704 during the War of the Spanish Succession. Later, perhaps at the height of his popularity amongst the British people, he was accused of greed and misappropriation of funds; such matters are often raised as a result of jealousy. John Churchill's unquestionable thirst for prosperity and fame was not unique. His equally famous descendant exhibited similar moments of inspiration from his time as a soldier-cum-correspondent at the end of the nineteenth century and then through more than fifty years of not always successful but ever spectacular political life. The main difference between the two men is important: Winston Spencer Churchill, unlike his hero John Churchill, could never be accused of disloyalty.

John Churchill's younger brother, George, was not a credit to the family line. Although he eventually became an admiral and, indeed, a very important one, he was generally thought arrogant and inefficient and owed much of his career to his brother. When George Churchill joined other captains and went over to William of Orange, his career suggests that he had been at sea since 1666, which would have made him a volunteer midshipman at the age of twelve – a common enough age to join up. He was already, by the time of William's landing, a senior captain and was in command of a ship called the *Newcastle*. Whether or not his commands were sea-going was not always certain: in the seventeenth century some commands of regiments and ships were similar to livings in the Church in that the incumbent was not always required to be physically present. George Churchill probably suffered from the king's annoyance. William III, as William of Orange became, grew to dislike the Churchills, although all this was to change. Much later, in 1699, the Churchills made an uneasy truce with William, after which George was promoted to admiral and, when Queen Anne came to the throne, rose even further in flag rank. There is no evidence that he was particularly good at managing the navy and in fact was often accused of mismanagement, to the nation's detriment. He did, however, manage to inspire unrelenting dislike among most of those who met him, and to amass a considerable fortune. Having few friends and fewer gifts other than to antagonize, George Churchill eventually retired to a house at Windsor where he reared exotic birds until his death in 1710.

The nineteenth century produced another John Churchill and, more famously, Lord Randolph Churchill. This John Churchill was born in 1822 and on the death of his father became the 6th Duke of Marlborough. He was born not at Blenheim but in Norfolk, and then followed the familiar path of Eton, Oxford, the army and the Commons. After joining the Oxfordshire yeomanry, he became in 1844, as the Marquess of Blandford, Tory MP for Woodstock. Unfortunately for him, John Churchill voted for free trade, certainly against his father's wishes, and was in no uncertain terms told to give up his seat at Woodstock, which was more or less in his father's gift. He eventually got it back and held on to it until 1857 when he succeeded as Duke of Marlborough.

John Churchill became a courtier, a Knight of the Garter and Lord President of the Council. Disraeli thought him a wise and fair man and, after one refusal, persuaded him to become Lord Lieutenant of Ireland. Yet this was a Churchill who did not look for spectacular appointments, and when he died in July 1883 he was probably remembered as a quiet duke who did good works, supporting charities for shipwrecked fishermen and poor agricultural workers. Most particularly, he and his wife, the eldest daughter of the Marquess of Londonderry, demonstrated their beliefs during their time in Ireland. After the terrible potato famine of 1845–50 the Churchills set up a special relief fund. Uncomplicated and apolitical, its purpose was to help people other than the Churchills – not always a family trait.

Another George Churchill became the 7th Duke of Marlborough; it was this man who was the father of Randolph Churchill and therefore the grandfather of Winston. Randolph, his parents' third son, was born in 1849 and had a conventional upbringing for his class – Eton and Oxford. At the age of twenty-five he became MP for Woodstock and married a New York heiress, Jennie Jerome. In 1877 the 7th Duke became viceroy of Ireland and his son, Lord Randolph, went with him as his private secretary. When his father died, Randolph appears to have been so deeply upset that he wanted to get away from England. He and his family travelled, not always happily, on the continent for more than a year. It was a typical journey at a typical time for a typically rich and aristocratic family.

But Randolph Churchill was not a comfortable Tory. In 1884 he decided that he would stand for Parliament again, but for a seat in Birmingham. Woodstock, with its electorate of about a thousand people, was about to disappear as the last of the pocket and rotten boroughs,[6] which officially had gone about half a century before, but Randolph's decision to go to a non-Tory area such as the midlands had far more to do with his political principles. He believed that the Conservative Party should be reformed and develop into an organization that looked after the interests of the entire people – the concept of one-nation politics. In 1880 Churchill and three like-minded political souls, Salisbury's nephew Arthur Balfour (an interesting political philosopher rather than an exciting politician), John Eldon Gorst and Drummond Wolff, formed what became known as the Fourth Party.

Gorst was a Lancastrian who had made a name for himself as an administrator among the native Maori population of New Zealand. Although he entered Parliament as a Tory he was one of many who were rethinking their politics. His time as a member of Churchill's Fourth Party did him no harm; in 1885 he was appointed Solicitor General by Salisbury and received a knighthood.

The Fourth Party is not much remembered, though its ambitions were not idle. In 1883 Churchill and other members of the Fourth Party founded another society, the Primrose League, which did last because it represented a much more identifiable ideal. Gorst was typical of its membership, who were devoted to the form of Conservatism promoted by their hero, Disraeli, and the League was so named because the primrose was supposed to have been his favourite flower.[7] The Fourth Party wanted what Churchill called Tory Democracy, but this was no wishy-washy theoretical thinking. He was very much a radical, and he wanted the Conservative Party to stand up to Gladstone rather than wait for him to trip up.[8] Churchill believed that radical Tories had a duty to exercise radical politics and to launch parliamentary and oratorical ambushes on their opponents. In some ways, they were learning the lessons offered by the Irish radicals at Westminster.

Lord Randolph may not have been a reactionary – but then nor was he a man-of-the-people-style barnstormer. He failed to win the seat at Birmingham. Considering that his opponent was John Bright, that was hardly surprising, for Bright was one of the great British radical orators and son of a Rochdale cotton spinner. With Richard Cobden he had founded the Anti-Corn Law League, which had campaigned for free trade in the late 1830s and 1840s – something which had affected a previous Churchill. Bright was a great campaigner for parliamentary reform and in 1885 was above suspicion among the voters of Birmingham. Lord Randolph was not. However, he did find a seat closer to home – South Paddington. This was the time of the first government of Lord Salisbury (see Chapter 6). Lord Randolph had spent the previous few months in India, and when Salisbury formed his administration he was made Secretary for India.

Salisbury quickly lost the confidence of the House and in 1886 went to the country again. The circumstances of that election meant that there was much greater Irish influence, and the man at the centre of it was not Salisbury but Joseph Chamberlain. Gladstone's change of mind about Ireland had led him to promise that if his Liberals were elected the government would introduce a Home Rule Bill. Lord Randolph threw himself into attacking the whole idea of Home Rule. He believed that, should the Liberals get in and push their Bill through, then 'Ulster will fight'. This became the theme of Unionist Ireland during the campaigning. The Conservatives now needed the support of the Chamberlainites – Joseph Chamberlain and seventy or so of his friends in the Liberal Party who opposed Home Rule for Ireland and had broken away to become the Liberal-Unionists. Churchill did much to persuade them to go in with Salisbury, and there were easily enough of them to represent the balance of power. With this coalition, Salisbury was able to form a government: it marked the beginning of the Conservative and Unionist Party, the full title of the Tories, which survives into the present day and which Randolph's son, Winston, would lead.

Salisbury now made Randolph Chancellor of the Exchequer. Churchill was deeply concerned at the state of government finances, and in 1886 made a very bold speech at Dartford in Kent. His premise was basic economics: it was his task, he said, to cut government spending, and to do so he had to take on the increasingly powerful military and armaments lobbies. Churchill had deeper concerns than monetary policy: he was truly alarmed at what he believed to be the growing dangers of militarism, especially in Europe. He certainly would not have supported the twentieth-century concept that diplomacy is best enforced with a gun barrel. Moreover, his one-nation politics could not tolerate the idea of the increasing tax burden coming from government expenditure. Churchill insisted that the army and navy should reduce their demands for at least the coming year. The two services refused, knowing that they had the backing of Lord Salisbury who was no great supporter of Churchill's philosophy. In December 1886, having been Chancellor of the Exchequer for but a few months, Churchill contemplated resigning. Those particularly close to him, including the editor of the *Times* newspaper, suggested that his value would be diminished if he left government.

Churchill, however, could not simply accept that the Admiralty and the War Office should have such power that they made a direct contribution to the large tax burden on the country. He felt that if he did not resign he should at least formally warn Salisbury that he was deeply unhappy and that, unless something was done about the situation, he would probably have to go. He wrote to the Prime Minister that he did not 'want to be wrangling and quarrelling in the Cabinet and therefore must request to be allowed to give up my office and retire from the government…'. But the Cecils had three hundred years' experience of political intrigue. Moreover, Churchill's rise to power had made him enemies, most of whom despised his primrose politics. Most of all, Salisbury was not interested in whether or not Churchill really intended to resign. No one threatened a Cecil. The Prime Minister immediately accepted Churchill's 'resignation' as the real thing. Churchill was out of government by the Christmas of 1886 and never returned.

In 1892 the Conservatives lost power. This was considered something of a political disaster for Salisbury's government, although there were plenty who believed that, once the Conservatives were out of government, Churchill might regain his place on the party's front bench in opposition. As his son, Winston, observed much later, 'one could not grow up in my father's house…without understanding that there had been a great political disaster…'.

Randolph Churchill was not to be taken back into the party's bosom. If he had been, it is doubtful that he would have done much good. By now, 1894, he was suffering increasing mental and physical problems. In the summer, he decided that he and his wife, with a doctor accompanying them, would embark on a world tour. The Churchills were seen off by the new Prime Minister, Lord Rosebery. It was more than a formality: bearded and increasingly drawn as he was, no one expected to see Randolph again. In Japan his illness began to overtake him. By the time they reached Hong Kong his doctor, George Keith, was reporting that his speech patterns were so disrupted that he was hardly coherent. From India, at the end of November, Keith reported again to London that Randolph had little time to live. Jennie Churchill now had to decide what was best for her husband; he could make no decisions himself. At first, she thought they had best go to the South of France. However, Lord Randolph was ranting so loudly and suffering so greatly from delusions that he had to be strapped into a straitjacket, and on Christmas Eve the couple arrived back in London. The Prince of Wales, a close friend of the Churchills, consulted his own doctor as to the seriousness of Lord Randolph's illness. The polite description was that he was suffering from 'general paralysis'. What it concealed was that he was exhibiting symptoms of syphilis and that, from the advanced nature of his condition, he had probably contracted the infection anything up to twenty years earlier. On 24 January 1895, at the age of forty-five, the sad, tortured image of Randolph Churchill faded and he died. He was buried in Bladon churchyard outside the grounds of Blenheim Palace where he had been born.

Sometimes, Randolph Churchill is seen as a sad and misunderstood fellow. The truth is he was a poor father to Winston and an equally poor politician. As one of his biographers, Roy Jenkins, wrote, 'He had the gift of insolence…nearly all his political attitudes were dictated by opportunism and not by any coherent corpus of belief...'[9]

Randolph's son Winston was still a cadet at Sandhurst when his father died. It is unlikely that he knew that his father had died from syphilis, and even less likely that he would have known how he had come by the infection. Winston imagined that his father had simply followed a pattern amongst the Churchills. They were not a healthy family. Lord Randolph's eldest brother, the 8th Duke of Marlborough, had died in his forties, and the other three brothers had died when they were children. Winston himself was a sickly child and did not anticipate a long life. Apart from his natural enthusiasms, this might have contributed to his youthful quest for adventure and glory. In fact he need not have worried. Winston Leonard Spencer Churchill was the longest-lived of them all: he was ninety-one when he died in 1965.

This is not the place to go into an account of Churchill's life. There is hardly a library shelf without its comprehensive Churchill section. There are Churchill societies throughout the world. The Churchill Centre in Washington has a continuing debate on his life and career. There are monuments and memorials throughout the world. He has time and again been described as the greatest British leader of the twentieth century. There is hardly a revisionist historian who has not felt it his or her duty to debunk the Churchill reputation – a reasonable sign of its strength. His books are still read and some, like *A History of the English-speaking Peoples*, are still in print nearly half a century after first being published. Churchill came to signify the wartime spirit of some imaginary bulldog breed. His voice and speeches became the most mimicked of all politicians of the twentieth century.

However, if it had not been for World War II would Churchill have been much more remembered than his father? The answer is probably yes, but only by political historians. He was a successful politician in so much that, come World War II, he was able to replace Chamberlain as leader of the coalition. He was, in short, an image long before the spinning fantasies that brought Tony Blair to power in 1997. Cynics might say the big difference was that, while Churchill's policies were sometimes misconceived or for that moment irrational, at least he believed in them.

Two years after his father's death, young Churchill became a subaltern in the 4th Hussars. In those days a young officer still had the freedom to make his own career pattern and to mix it with other affairs; this was particularly so if that young man had reasonable means, good family and therefore good connections. In 1897 in India Churchill joined a punitive force of the north-west frontier troops at Malakand. Both he and his mother were enormously ambitious for him, but it was not their intention that he should make a splendid career in the army. Winston's future had to be in public and therefore in politics. Jennie Churchill used her charm and influence to persuade the *Daily Telegraph* to carry, as 'Letters from the Frontier', her son's reports. Winston was not much pleased when they appeared as by 'A Young Officer'; he would much have preferred to see his full name as this, he felt, was the quickest way for the public and therefore the electorate to get to know him. He was never one to shirk publicity.

It should not be imagined, as sometimes it has been portrayed, that Churchill's excursion in India was superficial. In one action, against the Afridi, two of his colleagues were hit by gunfire and one of them hacked to death; Churchill shot the attacking Afridi. He then helped rescue one of his wounded Sikh soldiers and for an hour had to defend a very dangerous position with his revolver and an abandoned rifle. He was decorated, and the general view of his commander, Bindon Blood, was that Churchill was a truly gallant officer and would win either a VC or a DSO, even though that might be posthumously. Throughout his life, Churchill was all for medals and the opportunities to win them. After India, thanks to his mother, he again went off in search of excitement, medals and head-lines: he took part in the famous Battle of Omdurman in the Sudan, where he was engaged in the charge and hand-to-hand fighting against the Dervishes. Equally famously, he was captured while acting as a correspondent during the Boer War and escaped – which made an even better story.

In 1900, Churchill was elected MP for Oldham during the khaki election. Like his father, he had ill-concealed differences with the Conservative Party. He became friends with the young and equally ambitious Lloyd George. In 1906, and with considerable theatrical timing – a talent both men possessed – Churchill deserted the Conservative Party to cross the floor of the House and sit as a Liberal. Some never forgave him. Two years later, in 1908, he became President of the Board of Trade and introduced the concept of labour exchanges. In 1910, still only thirty-six, Churchill was made Home Secretary and, somewhat sensationally, became personally involved in what was called the siege of Sidney Street; a Russian anarchist known as Peter the Painter had holed himself up in a house in London's East End. Churchill then became First Lord of the Admiralty and imme-diately designed for himself a sailor suit complete with peaked cap to be worn on as many official occasions as possible. It was a uniform that continued to be worn by many of his successors, including Lord Carrington, who, while not feeling uncomfortable in it, always found it odd since he had once been a Grenadier Guards officer. Churchill's task was to organize the navy for the war which almost everyone at his level knew to be inevitable. When it came, so too did disasters and tragedies. In 1915 he was forced to resign over the Dardanelles fiasco.

In 1915, the war in France was at a stalemate. Churchill, badly advised as it turned out, pushed through an idea that British forces could attack, not in France but through the narrow strait of the Dardanelles in an attempt to kick Turkey out of the war. In March, Churchill's navy failed miserably. Instead of recognizing the futility of the operation, Churchill believed it important to press on. Between April and August 1915 ten divisions of British and Australian troops were landed in an indefensible position on the Gallipoli peninsula: the casualties were horrendous. The campaign was abandoned shortly before Christmas 1915 and

Churchill had to go. Instead of skulking on the back benches, he arranged to join his regiment in France; he was, almost naturally, promoted. He was still an MP, of course, and regularly returned to London to keep up with news and appearances. In 1916, Lloyd George usurped the authority of Asquith and became Prime Minister. The following year, Winston Churchill was in his friend's Cabinet as Munitions Minister.

After World War I, British politics underwent radical reform. The Labour Party had become a proper and influential power. The Liberals had had their time – although they would continue, as a mostly ineffectual political group, into the twenty-first century. If Churchill were to stay in politics and reach high office once more, there was only one place he could do that – the Conservative benches. In 1924 he became MP for Epping, choosing to describe himself as a constitutional supporter of the Conservatives. This mockery served him well until 1929. He became Chancellor of the Exchequer, arguably as incapable of managing the economy as he had his schoolboy finances.

The national government of the 1930s did not do Churchill much good. He felt ineffectual and by and large was exactly that. However, in the middle of that decade the Prime Minister, Stanley Baldwin, believed that Churchill should not be given any strenuous office now but should be saved to exert all his energies as a national leader during the war with Germany that both he, Baldwin, and Churchill believed would come.

So it was in May 1940 that Baldwin's successor Neville Chamberlain, an increasingly sad figure who had advocated appeasement and been proved so wrong, and Lord Halifax, a prime ministerial contender but with no political support, made way for Churchill to lead the wartime coalition. The memory of many who lived through that conflict suggests that Churchill's reputation as a leader and source of inspiration throughout the Allied world is easily justified; revisionists have rightly pointed to his mistakes and fallibilities. Yet the image remains sound and the criticisms are often too clever and unimportant. As the war came to an end, Churchill found he could not hold on to power. In fact it was Clement Attlee who saw out the final stages of the war as Prime Minister. Churchill went to disagreeable extremes to cling to power, even making unstatesmanlike assertions that a Labour government would need a Gestapo-like fist to implement its reforms. But Lord Carrington, in 1945 a decorated Guards officer, remembers that people, although determined to continue with the social revolution that had started in the 1930s by voting Labour, still sometimes believed that Churchill would continue to be Prime Minister.

Churchill may have been out of power, but no pronouncement other than his Fulton, Missouri 'Iron Curtain' speech of 1946 is remembered from that period. Even among those who had never read it, it took on the same aura as his wartime 'fight them on the beaches' speech. Moreover, it is probably true that no other British politician uttered such memorable words until Harold Macmillan's 'wind of change' speech in 1960. Britain, after World War II, had the biggest political figure that it would ever possess during the whole of the twentieth century. By 1952 the nation also had a new queen.

Just as the earliest Churchills had been confidants of princes, princesses and monarchs, so Winston Churchill became the closest adviser of the young Elizabeth. There were moments when his advice was enormously firm. For example, when George VI died, Lord Mountbatten attempted to have the royal House change its name to the House of Mountbatten. Dickie Mountbatten had unrelenting ambitions for himself, his wider family and the Mountbatten name – an anglicization forced upon his father in 1915 when Battenberg was seen as too Germanic for the British to stomach. Mountbatten's ambitions for the young Greek prince, his nephew Philip Mountbatten, had become clear while Philip was still at Dartmouth naval college and the princess in her early teens. He regarded their eventual marriage as a triumph – hence his determination that the family name would become that of royalty. It was Churchill who immediately informed the wavering royal household and the new queen herself that this was not to be. Hers was the House of Windsor.

Winston Churchill, like John Churchill, could have become a duke. The queen thought that was the least that might be done. Churchill said no. He clung to power for as long as he could; the sad figure of Anthony Eden almost pleaded for Churchill to go so that he could be Prime Minister in his place. There is no evidence to suggest that Churchill greatly admired Eden. More importantly, Churchill wanted to stay Prime Minister to fulfil his great post-war ambition: a great peacetime conference between Stalin, President Eisenhower and himself, an echo of the wartime one at Yalta. Eisenhower fended off the idea; Stalin died in 1953. Churchill still believed that the three-power summit was the way to peace in a still unsettled world. It was almost an obsession. He even sent his wife, Clementine, to collect his Nobel peace prize because he was due to attend a meeting with the American President.

In 1955, he left politics – he really was too ill to hang on much longer. Ten years later he was dead. His funeral was an international occasion. At one poignant moment the gaunt Thames dockside cranes dipped in salute as his coffin was borne past on a naval barge. It was an unexpected and memorable moment, which rather summed up the last of the celebrated Churchills.

NOTES

1 Not far from Bristol, it was called Churchill Manor. The village of Churchill, which has survived, is on the A38 trunk road heading south from the city.
2 The manorial home of the thirteenth-century Glanvilles (earlier spelt, Glaunuill).
3 1649–85.
4 There were two other alliances of this name in history. In 1717 Britain, France and the Netherlands joined against Spain, and in 1788 Britain, the Netherlands and Prussia agreed a pact in an attempt to maintain continental security and stability.

5 The signatories were the four Whigs, Henry Sidney, Edward Russell, the 4th Earl of Devonshire and the 12th Earl of Shrewsbury, together with the three Tories, Bishop Henry Compton, Lord Lumley and the Earl of Danby.

6 Pitt the Elder coined the term 'rotten borough' – he thought the idea of a constituency (often in name only) was a rotten element of the constitution. A rotten borough was one in which the voters were openly and often bribed. A pocket borough was one 'owned' by a patron; he had the votes in his pocket.

7 It is often believed that, on Disraeli's death, Queen Victoria sent a posy of primroses to be placed in his coffin as a mark of her deepest mourning for a man whom she had first detested, then loved as her closest political friend.

8 Disraeli believed that England could be brought together, fairly, by balancing the traditional and natural talent of the aristocracy to lead the caring and radical programmes championed by the politically romantic Young England movement.

9 Roy Jenkins, *Churchill*, Macmillan, 2001.

FURTHER READING

CHURCHILL, Winston S., *Marlborough: His Life and Times*, Scribner's, 1933–8.
GILBERT, Martin, *Churchill, A Life*, William Heinemann, 1991.
JENKINS, Roy, *Churchill*, Macmillan, 2001.
MACLOUD, John, *Dynasty, The Stuarts*, Hodder & Stoughton, 1999.

CHAPTER EIGHT

THE PERCYS

There is surely a case for claiming that, for close on a thousand years, the most powerful family in England has been the Percys. In the early Middle Ages, the Mortimers and Despensers proved exciting copy for the historic doodlers. Later the Berkeleys were, perhaps like the Norfolks, always somewhere in the make-up of British constitutional life. From the sixteenth century the Cecils were constantly in the corridors of power and at the elbows of the strongest lawmakers and monarchs. In the nineteenth century it was perhaps the Russells, and in the twentieth the newspaper barons, who overtly exercised power. Yet from the very day of the Conquest the Percys, through one branch or another of the dynasty, have always been in the lists of English pageantry and power.

The dynasty begins with the birth in 1030, in Normandy, of William de Percy, who sailed with Duke William in 1066 and took part in the great Conquest. Part of his task was to secure for William the lands beyond the southeast that still resisted him, and in this he was successful. He became part of the Norman elite that at first imposed its will on Saxon England and then became very much part of what was to be a new nation, the Anglo-Normans. In payment for his loyalty to Duke William, by now William I of England, de Percy was granted great estates, at first in the south – Essex and Hampshire – and then in Lincolnshire and Yorkshire. Eventually the Percys, along with the Nevilles, would be the great northern earls. To have those great estates did not mean that a baron could be a backwoodsman – there was rarely such a being during the early Middle Ages. This was feudal England, where power was exercised, even at local level, as an absolute autocracy. Nor was there unquestionable respect for the monarch.

These were the very early days of making laws work without putting total power in the hands of the lawmakers. The late Saxon kings had united the country until it was a single state under one royal banner. The Saxon monarch could offer kingship; the right of the monarch to expect the obedience of all his people, including the barons, in return for protecting them against their enemies. These enemies might be invaders. They might also be the early form of government, which was often oppressive.

The picture book vision, therefore, of the powerful king leading his country is an illusion. True, the king was usually immensely strong politically and from very early times was considered to rule by some divine right. His (only much later 'her') most powerful enemies were not necessarily foreign usurpers or even a disgruntled peasantry. Consistently, the threat to a monarch came from the noble dynasties of England. It was not until the early 1700s, with the last of the Stuarts and the constitutionally contrived accession of the Protestant Hanoverians, that an English monarch could rest easy from the notion that the great battle might well be against the barons rather than any other threat. Thus it was in the twelfth and thirteenth centuries when, for example, the peers began to understand that they should take control of the monarchy. The Percys would always play an active part in the cabal to challenge the power of the king. So we find Richard de Percy as one of the barons who forced King John to accept Magna Carta at Runnymede in 1215, the year before the king died.

The strength of the Percys clearly came from the great lands they controlled in the north of England, but it was not derived simply from their membership of the band of baronial brothers. Their great estates and holdings enabled the barons to raise their own armies to defend the king's realm. The Percys ruled Northumberland. Imagine the consequences of this task in, say, the days of Norman and Plantagenet rule.

Distance was measured not so much in miles, but in the time that it took to travel those miles. The king, with all his major interests tucked away in the south-east of England or across the broader belt of Wessex, would always be vulnerable because of his inability to move great forces over long distances in time to defend against invaders. This, as we have seen, was the origin of the marcher lords on the border between Wales and England. But the greater threat had always come from the north. The Romans had understood this, which is why Hadrian's and the Antonine Wall were built. It was no different for the Saxons, the Normans or the Angevins.[1] The Norsemen had landed in Scotland and on the North Sea coast. Moreover, a persistent threat to English monarchs had come from the Scots, whom the Romans had not been able to keep out other than by stationing enormously superior forces in their garrisons along the walls. Now, in the Middle Ages, the monarchs in London needed their own legions in the north, which is why the Percys became so powerful. The king relied on them, and so when Edward I marched north against the Scots in the late thirteenth century, it was Henry de Percy who gathered his forces to help put down the rebellions. Edward needed the support of this family and its warriors at Dunbar in 1296 and at Falkirk two years after that. But when Robert the Bruce rallied the Scots a few years later, the Percys had to retreat; Edward II stripped Bruce of his earldom of Carrick and gave it to the Percys.

The connection with the modern Percys began in 1309 when Henry de Percy bought a barony – a perfectly reasonable fourteenth-century agreement – from the Church. This was Alnwick, which has survived as the Percy family seat to the present day. It was Henry de Percy, now Lord Alnwick, who sired some of the fierce fighters of the family. His son, also Lord Alnwick, led the charge in the Battle of Neville's Cross on 17 October 1346. This was the time of the Hundred Years' War – England's meandering conflict with the French. The Scots, under King David II, had once more penetrated south of the border; the Scots had long been the allies of the French, so this was more than a punitive raid on their part. But when King David's forces arrived just outside Durham, Percy defeated him and captured him. The significance of this battle was that the Scots were now spent and the French could not rely on them to establish a second 'front' in their war with England. In the August of that year another Percy, Henry's grandson, had been fighting in France with Edward III and the young Black Prince at the Battle of Crécy.

Yet another Henry, the 4th Lord of Alnwick and great-grandson of the 1st, became the king's most important courtier and political magnate. In 1377, Henry Percy became Marshal of England and was created Earl of Northumberland. Here is another illustration of how barons who might in one generation be very close to a monarch could rapidly become perceived as traitors.

Henry Percy, the 1st Earl of Northumberland, was as famous a warrior as he was a political figure. Described as the warden of the Scottish marchers (just as the Mortimers controlled the Welsh marchers), he led the force which captured Berwick in 1378. It was also his army which, in his home territory of Northumberland, defeated the Scots at the Battle of Homildon Hill. However, it was also this Percy who led the rebellion of the barons against Henry IV in 1403, and two years later he joined forces with the rebels Edmund de Mortimer and the Welsh prince Owen Glyndwr (see Chapter 4) against Henry. As with so many rebellions, support fell away and it failed. Ironically, considering the role of the Percys since the Conquest, the 1st Earl took refuge in Scotland and then became a raider himself. For the family it was a disaster. In February 1408 the Percys brought their force south, still intent on overthrowing Henry IV. In the battle which took place at Bramham Moor, not far from Tadcaster in Yorkshire, the Percys were defeated and Henry, their first earl, killed.

This is the time of perhaps the most famous of all the Percys. The 1st Earl's son, also named Henry, was made famous by Shakespeare in *Henry IV Part I*. Nicknamed Hotspur, he was by all accounts a fearless knight who had made his reputation in France. Although he had, in 1399, been one of those who had supported Henry Bolingbroke in his challenge to the authority of Richard II, he later joined his father against Bolingbroke, subsequently Henry IV. He met his end in 1403 at the Battle of Shrewsbury. In the third week of July that year Hotspur led the army of rebellious barons, which included the Duke of Norfolk, against Henry IV's army at Hateley Field just north of Shrewsbury. It was not even a close-run thing: the rebels were defeated and Hotspur killed. He was not the only member of the family not to survive that day: the Earl of Worcester, his uncle, was captured and executed.

But no monarch could do without the Percys for long. Moreover, although grudges might have been held for a considerable time, as happened after many insurrections they were soon healed by pragmatism. So it was when Henry V came to the throne in 1413. The war with France was resting in an uneasy truce and, in spite of a tenuous alliance with Burgundy, everyone understood that hostilities would resume. Two years later Henry V beat the French first at Harfleur and then, more famously, at Agincourt; he also, in 1418, captured Falaise, birthplace of the mother of William of Normandy. By 1420 Henry had negotiated through the Treaty of Troyes a suitable peace and a promise that he would be heir to the throne of France itself. That never came about, although successive kings and queens of England referred to themselves as monarch of France. In 1422, just nine years after he came to the throne, Henry V died and the infant Henry VI was created monarch.

So in 1413 the Percys were forgiven for their rebellions, including the part they had played in the uprising organized by the Archbishop of York, Scrope. By then, Hotspur and his father were long dead and old Henry's grandson was the head of the family. It was he who found favour with Henry V, and he to whom the title was restored in 1414. As a further mark of the esteem in which he was held, as well as of the need for the Percys, it was this earl who became High Constable of England. When he died at the first Battle of St Albans, in 1455, his son took the title, but he too was killed in battle. For this was the start of what were later called the Wars of the Roses, the thirty-year struggle between the Lancastrians and the Yorkists for the throne of England.

The house of Lancaster descended from Henry III's second son, the Earl of Lancaster, whose earldom dated from 1267. In 1351 the current Earl became Duke of Lancaster, and when he died, the title and all the holdings passed to John of Gaunt, one of the sons of Edward III. It was Gaunt's son who was Henry Bolingbroke, later Henry IV. He was exiled by Richard II, but successfully challenged him for the throne with the help of his powerful supporters, including the Percys.

The House of York was descended from the 1st Duke of York, who was another son of Edward III; there lay the origin of a claim to the throne. When the 2nd Duke was killed at Agincourt in 1415 it was his nephew, Richard, who became the 3rd Duke of York. Richard claimed the throne additionally through a line to his great-grandfather on his mother's side, the 3rd Earl of March, Edmund Mortimer (see Chapter 4). In 1460 Richard, Duke of York was recognized as the rightful heir to Henry VI. But war does not always take notice of constitutional niceties: Richard was killed at the Battle of Wakefield in the same year that he had had his claim to the throne accepted, 1460. It was his son Edward, Earl of March, who was now crowned Edward IV. In 1483 he was succeeded, briefly, by his son, Edward V, and then controversially by his brother, Richard III.

There is the background to the two Houses. The succession to the English throne was complicated by the fact that Henry VI was just a baby when he became king in 1422. Two regents were appointed – his uncles Lancaster and Gloucester. The conflicts within the regency council and the length of Henry VI's minority meant that the barons had plenty of time and reason to plot the downfall of factions against them. Moreover, the war with France had gone badly, the peace arrangements were supposedly contrived to England's disadvantage and the people themselves were becoming a factor in the power struggle to control the throne. Local government was collapsing and there were mini-civil wars throughout the shires.

Edward IV reigned from 1461 until his death in 1483 when he was succeeded by Edward V, who was immediately imprisoned with his brother in the Tower by Richard of Gloucester. Although the evidence is inconclusive, it is often assumed that Richard of Gloucester had the two princes murdered there. He was proclaimed king, but two years later Richard III, the last of the Plantagenets, was killed at the Battle of Bosworth Field. Of course, a Percy was there in 1485 at the end of the Wars of the Roses, though his part was not a success. This was the 4th Earl of Northumberland, who since 1482 had been Great Chamberlain. Far from being loyal to the end, it was this 4th Earl who betrayed Richard III on the battlefield; he gained little from his treachery, for he was later murdered by a crowd of ruffians. After Bosworth Field Henry VII was crowned king, initiating the Tudor dynasty.

In the early sixteenth century the Percys were once more separated from their estates. The 6th Earl, who in the 1520s had been one of Anne Boleyn's lovers (before Henry VIII was, and so quite safe), died in 1537 without producing an heir. The title might have gone to his brother, Sir Thomas Percy; but, unfortunately for the family line, this Percy had just been executed. Sir Thomas, not a fan of Henry VIII, became a ringleader in what was probably the sharpest rebellion against the way in which the kingdom was ruled during the sixteenth century. This uprising, known as the Pilgrimage of Grace, took place during a short period over the end of 1536 and the first few weeks of 1537. It had an odd name for such widespread unrest in the country. A short explanation of the different elements of the uprising will reveal its historical significance and show why families such as the Percys found themselves involved.

Henry VIII came to the throne in 1509, and, for nearly two decades afterwards all was reasonably well in the kingdom. True, there was the ever-present threat and then reality of war with France (in 1512 it became compulsory to practise archery), yet by and large there was a sense of culture abroad in England. In 1515 Henry's powerful Chancellor Cardinal Wolsey had started to build his magnificent palace on the Thames at Hampton Court. Thomas More had published *Utopia* in 1516, Thomas Linacre had established the Royal College of Physicians in 1518 and in 1526 the painter Holbein was in London. Then it all began to change. In 1527, Henry tried (and failed) to divorce Catherine of Aragon, to whom he had been married for eighteen years but who had failed to provide him with a male heir. In 1529, Wolsey's grip slipped and for the next seven years the so-called

Reformation Parliament would sit.[2] In 1532 the clergy submitted to Henry VIII and in 1534 he was declared, by the Act of Supremacy, the temporal head of the Church in England. In 1535 the Bishop of Rochester, John Fisher, who had fought against Protestantism and, worse for him, against Henry's determination to divorce Catherine of Aragon, was executed. So too was Thomas More who, like Fisher, refused to acknowledge the Act of Succession. In 1536 Catherine of Aragon died, as did her successor Anne Boleyn (but by harsher hand); the Act of Succession was passed; and the ten articles laying down the theology of the new Church along with the reform law, were published. This was also the year in which the suppression of the lesser monasteries started, although, considering how much personal wealth the monks and friars had amassed, few tears were shed – it was the principle behind Henry's reform which caused concern rather than the acts which characterized it.

Against this background came the Pilgrimage of Grace. It started with a moderate dispute in Lincolnshire: those who opposed the suppression of the monasteries, the traditionalists, rose in groups for their protests to be heard. The movement swelled to become a general protest and was joined by the peasants, who were threatened by land enclosures, and then by the barons who decided they would no longer tolerate the controls Henry had imposed on the north of England, always regarded by its earls as an unofficial principality. The rebels called themselves Pilgrims, hence the title eventually given to the uprising. The northern leader of the Pilgrims, Robert Aske, was joined by the traditionally rebellious Percy family in the guise of Sir Thomas. By February 1536 the rebellion was all but over, largely because it was badly organized. The ringleaders, including Aske and Percy, were for the moment spared, but when the rebellion looked to be reviving they were executed. With this, life was snuffed from the Pilgrimage of Grace too.

The title of Northumberland now took leave of the Percy family. As the 6th earl had no children and Sir Thomas Percy, his brother, had no head, Edward VI gave the title to the infamous John Dudley, Earl of Warwick. This was the figure who for a time became the most powerful man in England. It was Dudley who got rid of the Duke of Somerset, uncle of the young Edward VI and thus his protector, and brother of Henry VIII's third wife, Jane Seymour. Somerset was a distinguished soldier and for nearly three years from 1547 had ruled England as Edward VI's regent. It was Somerset who guided through the legislation that forced people to use the first Book of Common Prayer, the cause of Catholic uprisings. He had no sympathies with the Catholics, but did with some of the peasants who were rebelling against land enclosures (see Chapter 6).[3] The uprising was put down by Dudley. Somerset was arrested and, although he was later released, Dudley (now Duke of Northumberland) usurped his position and Somerset was hanged.

Northumberland now pushed for even more use of the revised version of the Book of Common Prayer. More immediately, he persuaded Edward VI to make his (Northumberland's) daughter-in-law heir to the throne. The sad figure of Lady Jane Grey was proclaimed queen, but her reign lasted only nine days before Henry VIII and Catherine of Aragon's daughter Mary rightfully became queen instead. John Dudley, Duke of Northumberland was executed in 1553.

Four years after John Dudley's death, Queen Mary I gave the earldom of Northumberland to another Percy – Thomas, the son of the Sir Thomas Percy executed for his part in the Pilgrimage of Grace. This Percy, and a few who followed him, did not enjoy the honour for very long. These were terrible times for nobles who decided to stand up for their own rights, for the rights of others or simply for schemes from which they thought they would do exceptionally well. Many did not. Many lost more than their titles.

Thomas Percy, the new 7th Earl of Northumberland, took a leading part in the Northern Earls' Rising of 1569–70. The principal protagonist of that rebellion was the Duke of Norfolk. He and his northern supporters, including the Percys, were against the Cecils, who they believed exerted too powerful an influence in Elizabeth I's court. Norfolk – then leader of a family which would be seen for centuries afterwards as the guardian of British Roman Catholicism – quickly gave in to Elizabeth. But the Percys and the Nevilles refused to acquiesce and demanded that the Church of Rome should be restored to what they saw as its rightful place in English religious life. They also wanted Mary, Queen of Scots, imprisoned in England, to be returned to Scotland. The rebellion was intense, but foolish in its belief that it might succeed. Thomas Percy was executed at York in 1572.

The next Earl of Northumberland, the 8th, was Thomas's brother Henry. He too was far from being a backwoodsman. In 1583 he took part in yet another piece of skulduggery, the Throckmorton Plot. The plan, led by Francis Throckmorton, a young Roman Catholic, was to get rid of Elizabeth I and replace her with Mary, Queen of Scots. This ambition was supported by the Spanish and by English exiles in France, who hoped to mount an invasion under the Duc de Guise, kinsman of Mary Queen of Scots' mother, Mary de Guise. The conspiracy was blown when one of the plotters was interrogated. Throckmorton was executed and Henry Percy was sent to the Tower where, before he too could be publicly executed, he was murdered, or so the Catholics claimed.

His son, the 9th Earl, also had little chance of a quiet life. In 1605 he found himself wrongly accused of complicity in the Gunpowder Plot. Most certainly the earl was an ardent and uncompromising Catholic; he may even have sympathized with the plotters; but there is no strong evidence that he was a member of the cabal. Nevertheless he was fined £30,000 (a huge sum then) and was sent to the Tower for fifteen years.

Algernon Percy, the 9th Earl's son, was born just six months before the death of Elizabeth in 1603, and succeeded as 10th Earl at the age of thirty. Here was another example of the importance of the old and powerful families. Algernon Percy was the most important northern peer. The uprisings by the northern earls that had disrupted the reign of Elizabeth I in the previous century were likely to be repeated, and they were not all based on the conflict between Catholics and Protestants. There was a new sense of unrest, more and more to do with the way in which the country was governed and therefore against the authority not of the monarchy, but of the king.

English history is scattered with examples of the vulnerability of the individual, especially when the nation needs a strong monarchy. So it was with Charles I. This king needed Northumberland's support and, three years after his succession as 10th Earl, Charles made him a member of the Order of the Garter. The following year, 1636, Percy became Admiral of the Fleet. It was a grand title which achieved, perhaps because of the ineffectualness of the king, almost nothing. That could certainly not be attributed to Percy's lack of enthusiasm, for he produced one of the most comprehensive assessments of the navy ever seen and whose like would not be seen again for another hundred years. Percy produced lists of examples of maladministration and blatant corruption among the commissioners, but the king took no notice. The corruption and mismanagement continued and Percy became despondent. Even Thomas Wentworth, who, along with William Laud, Archbishop of Canterbury, was the king's most efficient administrator, supported Percy. Nothing came of it. Percy was created Lord High Admiral of England, but could only keep the post until the Duke of York – the future James II – was ready for it. He had no power.

Historically, when they weren't harrying the monarch, the Percys were best suited to defending the state's interests on land. When so minded, they were the king's friends in the north. So it was that in 1638 Algernon Percy, the 10th Earl of Northumberland, became one of the privy councillors charged with resolving the differences in Scotland. That too was a hopeless task.

Here was the beginning of the Bishops' Wars – the events which would eventually lead to the execution of Charles I. Through Archbishop Laud, Charles insisted that the Anglican Communion be imposed on Scotland: the Scots were told to use the English Book of Common Prayer. The national assembly in Scotland retaliated and abolished the episcopacy. The first so-called Bishops' War did not develop into physical conflict. The truce negotiated at Berwick was supposed to become a peace.

When it did not, Charles summoned Parliament. He wanted money to carry on the war against the Scots; Parliament refused. At the instigation of Wentworth, Charles turned to the Irish Parliament; it promised help but no strength. The Scots invaded England in 1640 and defeated Charles's army; the treaty of Ripon, signed in October that year, ended the war. This again was a truce, not a conclusion, for the Scots held Northumberland, the land of the Percys, plus a considerable subsistence – that is, financial deposits – until the matter could be finally settled. The king called the Long Parliament (so named because it sat from 1640 to 1660) to settle the arrangements with the Scots, and then his whole campaign fell apart. Wentworth, recently ennobled as the Earl of Strafford, and Laud were impeached.

In December 1641 Parliament presented the king with the Grand Remonstrance – a manifesto demanding redress for grievances, the dismissal of Charles's advisers and a curbing of the power of the bishops. And in August 1642, the English Civil War began.

Percy, the 10th Earl of Northumberland, had been given command of the army against Scotland during the first Bishops' War, but he had had enormous doubts. He did not want an invasion of Scotland; logically, he could not see how any military operation against the Scots could succeed if there was no money to pay and supply the army; moreover, he had begun to doubt the wisdom of those who had encouraged the king. In spite of all this, he had felt it his duty – for the moment at least – to lead the army and had drawn on his own money to help fund it. His command had not lasted long, however, because he was ill, and Strafford took over. Percy had found it impossible to continue to support the king and his men. In the Long Parliament he had started to side with those who had drawn up the Remonstrance. His was a difficult situation in that he did not believe the extreme accusations levelled at Strafford; that he planned a Catholic dictatorship, had subverted many laws and was plotting to import the army from Ireland to enforce his authority. But at the same time Percy accepted that Strafford was guilty of some of the charges, including subversion of the law. Yet he would not accept the extremist view that, in going to the Irish Parliament for help, Strafford's real plan had been to use the Irish army against the English opposition. Charles I attempted to get Percy to commit perjury on behalf of Strafford; Percy refused. By the beginning of 1642 the Earl of Northumberland was seen as a defector from Charles I's camp. He was nominated by Parliament for the lord lieutenancies of Anglesey, Northumberland, Pembroke and Sussex and kept his appointment as Lord High Admiral. This meant that the parliamentarians, through the earl, had control of large numbers of supporters in those four counties and, for what it was worth, command of the navy. In June 1642, Charles, determined to exercise his constitutional might over Parliament, sacked Northumberland from his senior posts. It was too late.

It is easy to understand that this Percy saw the way Parliament was leaning and felt his interests would be best served by tilting his loyalties. It is equally understandable that Charles felt bitter and disappointed. The king had made Percy a Knight of the Garter, the most honourable and personal order of the king. He had given him high office. He had treated him with great kindness, as a friend and as a trusted confidant.

Percy may have crossed the floor, but he persistently claimed that his ambition above all else was to obtain an agreement between the king and the people. In November 1642 he was entrusted by Parliament to present a peace proposal to the king, but it proved abortive. In March 1643 he led the parliamentary commissioners in an attempt to negotiate with Charles at Oxford, to where he had moved his court and capital from London. That too was a failure. Curiously, Percy's image as a peacemaker made him suspect in the eyes of many of the rebellious parliamentarians whom he represented. Consequently, he was spied upon and even accused of plotting against Parliament. At one stage he left Parliament altogether, totally disillusioned and probably very wary of the consequences of such accusations, no matter how unfounded. Executed men do not hear posthumous apologies. But he did not stay away for long; he was back by 1644 (the year of the parliamentarians' decisive victory over the royalists at Marston Moor) and the following year he became the guardian of three of the king's children including the Duke of York, the future James II. The mood of Parliament during that war was one of continued suspicion. Percy, the 10th Earl of Northumberland, found it impossible to avoid accusations that he was really for the king and not simply for the peace. At another point, he was accused of financing Charles I. At the same time, the committee that met to draw up plans to support the army against more radical elements who would have withdrawn from Parliament did so in his house, Syon Park at Brentford in Middlesex.

Northumberland's relationship with Charles could not have been openly bitter. After all, Percy was the guardian of some of the king's children. Indeed at one stage Charles, believing hope should never be abandoned, went so far as to propose that the Duke of York marry one of Percy's daughters. But Northumberland was not willing to go over to the king. It is certainly true that at this time he found it more and more difficult to act as guardian to the children and when in April 1648 the young Duke of York escaped his guardianship and managed to get to the Low Countries, Northumberland, who could so easily have found himself in the Tower for apparently helping the king, was absolved from all responsibility. He was able to persuade Parliament to relieve him of the duty of looking after the remaining children, Princess Elizabeth and Prince Henry. However, the guardianship did not stray far from the Percys. His sister, by now married to the Earl of Leicester, became their official governess.

Percy now made his biggest attempt to distance himself from all that was going on in politics. He refused to sit in Parliament. The House of Lords of course would be abandoned, as would the monarchy. Northumberland made it very clear that he thought that the Lords should be restored as part of any settlement. After Charles was beheaded on 30 January 1649 in Whitehall, Northumberland always maintained that he had had no part in bringing about this most infamous act of regicide. Northumberland avoided taking sides in the Parliament which followed the death of Charles I. He spoke against an unconditional restoration of the House of Lords. When the time came to restore the monachy, Percy supported the idea of an indemnity for those who had brought about the late king's execution. He believed that the very seriousness of that act would be enough to deter such a future event. In other words, a witch-hunt would be fruitless.

It is difficult to see how the 10th Earl of Northumberland could have been perceived as a particularly agreeable character by Charles II. Yet in May 1660 when the monarchy was restored he was sworn in as a privy councillor, and in 1661, at the coronation, it was Northumberland who performed the role of Lord High

Constable. But that was his final great public act: Northumberland was finished, although not disgraced, and died in 1668.

Sixteenth- and seventeenth-century courtiership threw up some unexpected relationships, such as Northumberland's first marriage to the eldest daughter of the 2nd Earl of Salisbury, William Cecil. Percy's father, who had gone through enormous difficulties himself, never approved the match. How could he? The two families had been on opposing political and religious sides. It was said that the blood of a Percy and the blood of a Cecil, if poured into a dish, would not mix. His second wife was Lady Elizabeth Howard, a daughter of the Earl of Suffolk. It was through this marriage that the mansion that had been the London home of the Howards came into the Percys' possession. It was now renamed Northumberland House and remained so until 1874, when it was pulled down to make way for a great thoroughfare leading off Trafalgar Square, to be known as Northumberland Avenue.

The 11th Earl, dead by 1670, was perhaps the most important because he was the last of the male line of that part of the family. But of course the Percys and the dukes of Northumberland were not finished. After the late 11th Earl's daughter, Baroness Percy, married Charles Seymour, 6th Duke of Somerset, they had a son. In 1749 he was created Lord Warkworth and Earl of Northumberland. It was his son-in-law, Hugh Smithson, who restored the old name of Percy. In 1766 he became the Duke of Northumberland, and the full power of the Percys was up and running again.

When a dukedom is moved from one family to another, or is revived after having become extinct because a family line has ended, it is said to be a new creation. So when Smithson became Duke of Northumberland, this was the third creation of that dukedom. Born in 1715 in Newby Wiske in Yorkshire, he inherited his baronetcy from his grandfather (an earlier Sir Hugh). While still Sir Hugh Smithson (before changing his name to Percy), he became the High Sheriff of Yorkshire. When he married in 1740, it was to Elizabeth Seymour whose grandfather was the 6th Duke of Somerset, the one related by marriage to Joseline Percy, the 11th Earl of Northumberland, who had died without a son. When the Duchess of Somerset died in 1722, she was the 11th Earl's heiress and therefore had in her will the Percy family estates, which would have gone to Sir Hugh Smithson's brother-in-law; but he died. Through this complex detective work we discover how a relatively obscure Yorkshireman came by one of the great estates and most powerful names in English history – because Sir Hugh's wife, Lady Elizabeth, now inherited the Percy estates. The Duke of Somerset, her grandfather, was furious and tried to block the will. The plot then becomes even more complicated because, by way of this erratic dotted line of inheritance, Lady Elizabeth's father was created Earl of Northumberland in 1749. Through Lady Elizabeth, the title would now go to the Smithsons – which it did the following year, when her father died. So in 1750, Hugh Smithson got the title of Northumberland, changed the family name and assumed the coat of arms of the

Percys. It was not the first restyling of a family name, nor would it be the last (see Chapter 16).

The new Hugh Percy soared in the social and political firmament. He became Lord Lieutenant of Northumberland, a Knight of the Garter and Lord Chamberlain to Queen Charlotte. True to the caste, and instinctively following the Percy model of political controversy at the highest level, Hugh Percy became a close friend of the Earl of Bute, the most controversial political figure of his day, and became related when Bute's daughter married Percy's son. Bute had been the friend and tutor of George III, and urged him to be more than a symbolic monarch. Bute told him he should get into politics and, more importantly, get among the politicians. When George III became king he could not do without Bute and for a year between 1762 and 1763 he replaced Newcastle as Prime Minister. Hugh Percy was Bute's closest ally; together they ran an inner Cabinet for George III.

This northern and Scottish cabal was so politically controversial and widely unpopular that the infamous newspaper called the *North Briton* was set up to challenge their influence. The 'North Briton' was, of course, Bute. The paper's editor, John Wilkes, was unrelenting in his determination to rid George III of his *eminence grise*. In April 1763, in the forty-fifth edition of the paper, Wilkes accused the king of having been forced to lie in his proclamation proroguing Parliament. In the most sensational court case of its day the Prime Minister, George Grenville, started proceedings that led to Wilkes's prosecution for seditious libel. Wilkes was acquitted. The Bute junta – for indeed that is what it was – was discredited, and Bute himself was forced to go. Hugh Percy felt the sting of that political and legal rebuke, for he was equally implicated. He was, nevertheless, a powerful man and, although Grenville had no liking for him, he could not get rid of him. He did the next best thing.

Hugh Percy was now appointed Lord Lieutenant of Ireland – but he would not disappear among the pomp and style he affected in Dublin. The king still relied heavily on Northumberland's political skills and – without much effort – he persuaded Northumberland to plot Grenville's downfall. In fact, George III suggested to Grenville's fellow Whig William Pitt (the Elder) that a new government should come into being and that Percy should be First Lord of the Treasury – effectively Prime Minister. Pitt was not entirely against this proposal although he did not want Percy to have the Treasury; in other words, he would agree but only if Percy were a token first minister. Pitt saw himself returning and Percy becoming a member of the Cabinet.

There was one very sound objection to the idea of Percy having any political advancement. It came from Richard Temple, Grenville's brother and Pitt's brother-in-law. He had been a prime supporter of Wilkes during his defence and against the Earl of Bute. Furthermore, he still regarded Hugh Percy as Bute's right-hand political man. In 1766, Temple fell out with Pitt who formed the new government, although it was the Duke of Grafton who was supposedly Prime

Minister. Percy wanted some high and courtier-like office, and the king wanted him to become the Lord Chamberlain.

Then came an example of how the great and powerful families all seem related, however distantly. Instead of Percy becoming Lord Chamberlain, the appointment went to the Marquess of Hertford, who was a Seymour. Percy was very put out. Pitt suggested that, as he was so favoured by the king, he could easily ask George III for an important peerage. The king thought he would make Percy, like Hertford who had taken his job, a marquess. Percy was quite fed up with the whole business by now and said that he felt he should have a dukedom. Pitt (by now himself the Earl of Chatham) said he thought that was a good idea. George III, for all his liking of Percy, felt it was going too far. However, against his better instincts, on 3 October 1766 Hugh Percy was created Duke of Northumberland, Earl Percy and Viscount Louvaine of Alnwick – the Percy seat. Northumberland was reasonably satisfied, although in his original demand – respectful suggestion – to the king he had in fact mentioned two dukedoms.

The new duke hardly distinguished himself. At one time shortly after his creation, there was talk that Northumberland might become Prime Minister and form some administration with the king's supporters. It came to nothing. He generally supported Pitt and spent much of his time trying to do down John Wilkes, which did not do him much good because Wilkes remained a popular figure. He went through the indignities of being forced, apparently by a mob, on one occasion to drink Wilkes's health in public. There was talk of him being prosecuted for murder when a man was killed during an election. He was ridiculed as Master of the Horse because he was enormously overweight and stricken with gout, and during the Gordon Riots of 1780 he was pulled from his carriage and robbed because his travel companion was thought to be a Jesuit priest. The riots occurred after Lord Gordon offered a parliamentary petition against the recently introduced Roman Catholic Relief Act, and the anti-Catholic rioters brought London into chaos. Northumberland was probably lucky to escape with the loss of his watch, because between 2 and 9 June that year some three hundred people were killed . By now Northumberland had retired from public life; and on 6 June 1786 he died, and was subsequently buried in the family vault at Westminster Abbey.

As a footnote to Hugh Percy, the 1st Duke of Northumberland, it is rarely remembered that he had an illegitimate son. His name was James Smithson and he became more famous than his father, because it was he who founded the Smithsonian Institution in Washington DC.

NOTES

1 Henry II was the first Angevin king of England when he came to the throne in 1154 after the death of King Stephen. He was the son of Geoffrey Plantagenet, Count of Anjou, and Matilda, the daughter of Henry I. Henry II's sons, Richard I and King John, are called

Angevins. After John, although the dynasty descended from the counts of Anjou, the ruling English kings were known as Plantagenets – Henry III, Edward I, Edward II, Edward III, Richard II. Then the dynasty split to produce the House of Lancaster: Henry IV, Henry V, Henry VI, followed by the return of the Yorkists with Edward IV and, lastly, the final Plantagenet king, Richard III.

2   In 1529, Henry as king (for no one else could) summoned Parliament. Thomas Cromwell drafted a series of laws which destroyed the authority of the Church of Rome in England. In 1534, by the Act of Supremacy, Henry (and successive monarchs) became the supreme head of the Church of England.

3   Ket's Rebellion of 1549, led by Robert Ket.

FURTHER READING

AYLMER, G. E., *The Struggle for the Constitution*, Blandford Press, 1963.
McKISACK, May, *The Fourteenth Century 1307–1399*, OUP, 1959.

CHAPTER NINE

THE BERKELEYS

Any family which can give its name to one of the most fashionable squares of London must be of more than passing interest. So it is with the Berkeleys dynasty. It is said that at one time they could hunt from Bristol to London without leaving their own land. Somewhere behind that bold statement lies the story of yet another remarkable dynasty in British history.

For most people, with a passing and perhaps gory interest in history, the name 'Berkeley' is associated with the castle in which Edward II was murdered in 1327. It is not surprising that the name rests on such detail; it was, after all, a terrible affair. Regicide is usually so. More significant is the thought that to have been entrusted with Edward II's death meant that the keeper of the family castle was no Johnny-come-lately.

As with so many of the stout and long-lived English lines, the Berkeleys appeared with the Conqueror. We know from *Domesday* that a Roger Berkeley had estates in Gloucestershire and Wiltshire.[1] Given that the basis for *Domesday* was written before the Conquest, the Berkeley seat has its origins earlier than the mid-eleventh century and the manor (that is the land) was held by the Godwine family.

On Roger Berkeley's death the estates were inherited by William Berkeley. The holdings included Berkeley Castle, which was built by William Fitzosbern and was already established as one of the great houses of the West Country. For example, in 1120 the Berkeleys entertained Henry I during the most important date in the Christian calendar: 'the king spent Easter at Berkeley, and thereafter on the Whit Sunday he held a great court at Westminster...'.[2] It is very likely that, although the castle was in the Berkeleys' hands, like many fortresses it was really owned by the king, who gave barons rights to build for their own use but in his defence.

William Berkeley's son, another Roger, was the master of this powerful seat, and the family demanded allegiance across a wide part of Gloucestershire. Like high ground, Berkeley was harder to hold than to take. The Berkeleys had enemies enough, including some fellow marcher lords. The Herefords captured Roger Berkeley and, according to the *Gesta Stephani* – the chronicle of the life of King Stephen who followed Henry I – cruelly tortured him until he was forced to give up the castle.

Roger Berkeley still held many of his estates, but he lost other holdings including perhaps the most important of them to the other powerful family of the region, the Fitzhardings. Here was an example not simply of changes in fortune due to local feuding, but also of the judgement of the monarch as to who would best protect his interests. Some of the old Berkeley lands had been handed by the monarch to the Fitzhardings. And, as ever in these times, reconciliation was agreeable: although grievances might last in the minds for decades, most of the barons were pragmatists. The less charitable view was that they would change sides and agreements to protect themselves, which, considering the violence of the age, was a realistic enough position. The usual way to resolve differences, albeit temporarily, was a marriage between the two families. This was the case with the Berkeleys and the Fitzhardings. Roger married off his daughter Alicia to the eldest Fitzharding son, Robert, and she took with her as her dowry Slimbridge.

The Berkeleys of Roger's branch of the family existed mainly in the Durseleys, who became extinct in 1382, and in the Cubberleys, who disappeared with the last of the line twenty-two years later. So the Berkeley line would descend from the Fitzhardings. The original Fitzhardings were Saxons who were courtiers to Edward the Confessor and Harold Godwineson (see Chapter 2). Certainly from *Domesday* we know that they had Gloucestershire estates and had held them from Edward the Confessor's time. In 1421 the 1st Baron Berkeley was created, and the line has remained unbroken to the present day.

The twelfth-century Robert Fitzharding consolidated the family's interests in Bristol, a place which truly became a Berkeley city; it was he who established the priory of St Augustine in the city. But his religious foresight, rarely coupled with political ambivalence, did not protect him or his family from the hectic events of the next four centuries. For example, when Robert's grandson, also called Robert, became one of the barons who set themselves against King John, the king confiscated Berkeley Castle. This Fitzharding was, despite whatever prayers were said for him in St Augustine's, excommunicated. Young Robert's brother, Thomas, got the castle and the estates back in 1220 because he was in favour with the new king since 1216, Henry III. The monarch needed the Berkeleys, politically and strategically. With his lands in the West Country, Thomas Fitzharding defended the king's interests against the Welsh, later riding with his troops to the northern marches against the Scots and then south again to cross the Channel to fight the French during the Hundred Years' War.

He had become a great supporter of Edward I and when in 1295 Edward summoned Parliament Thomas Fitzharding was one of those called to attend. The Model Parliament (as so often a nineteenth-century label) was called because Edward needed money —the only reason in those days that a king ever allowed Parliament to sit. In these and relatively later times it was effectively a grand committee of England, in this instance consisting of the seven earls, about forty of Edward's barons, the most important clergy including the abbots and priors of the monasteries, two knights from each of the shires and two burghers from each of the major towns and cities. Edward wanted funds to fight on various fronts. That year the Welsh were in rebellion. The following year Edward was leading his army in Scotland at the famous Battle of Dunbar which dislodged John Balliol from his throne. In 1297 the Scots retaliated, pillaged northern England and massacred the English troops at Stirling Bridge. In 1298 came the Battle of Falkirk: William Wallace was defeated by Edward but managed to elude the English until 1305 when he was captured and executed.

Here, then, was the atmosphere of the final decade of the thirteenth century. The writ that called Thomas Fitzharding to that 1295 Parliament gave him a special standing in the nobility and as a result he was perhaps the first of the Berkeleys to be given a hereditary peerage. Again, this was no protection from the violently expressed politics of fourteenth-century England. By then the Berkeleys had large estates in and around Bristol including the areas of Bedminster and Redcliff. The city fathers saw the Berkeley holdings as a direct threat to their authority, so the Berkeleys went to war with the burghers of Bristol. For the moment, the Berkeleys won.

Bristol was then one of a handful of important cities in England. It had become a township in the tenth century and had received its city charter in 1155. In 1353 it was to become a staple town, one of the most important labels to be given any city. Because of restrictions on trade (largely the wool industry) and the need to control duties and prices, the political masterminds of the fourteenth century made a price-fixing arrangement with certain parties in continental Europe. This act, predating the politics of the twentieth-century Treaty of Rome, established a series of towns that held a monopoly for the sale of goods to foreigners. In 1326 there were fourteen so-called staples, including Bristol, and the Statute of Staples in 1354 named fifteen towns in England and Ireland in which such trade could be conducted.[3]

The Berkeleys were always expanding their interests and their riches. Thomas, Lord Berkeley, for example, had great agricultural estates, but was shrewd enough to see little sense in farming for himself. He took his money from the land in rents, which were collected far and wide. By now the Berkeley holdings stretched from the Welsh marches to eastern England. We know, for example, that when this Thomas Berkeley was in London he had bread sent up to him from his manor of Wenden in Essex.

However, it was not trade which kept the interests of the Berkeleys in the West Country. The profits were great, but the family were also involved in warfare and politics and we come to yet another example of one family linking with another to make a strong political and historical alliance. Thomas died in 1321, seventy-six years old. The new baron was his second son, Maurice, who married the daughter of the Earl of March, Roger de Mortimer. This demonstrates how he had tied himself in with the highly political and ambitious Mortimer family (see Chapter 4), and Maurice Fitzharding now joined his father-in-law in the war against the Despensers (see Chapter 3).

The Despensers, father and son, were the favourites of the king, Edward II. So they should have been: they were keeping him in power. The Berkeleys and the Mortimers prepared to take their fight from the West Country across all the Welsh holdings of the Despensers, and in 1321 forced Edward II to banish the detested family. As we saw earlier, the Despensers were not long away from England. The following year, Edward II had regained his power and the marcher lords had to bend to his authority. The Berkeleys were thrown into prison at Wallingford and there Maurice Fitzharding and his son, Thomas, stayed until 1326. Maurice died before he could be released, but Thomas was pardoned because that was the year in which Mortimer, who had escaped to France, returned with his mistress, Edward II's queen, Isabella, and an army, took much of the country and, without a second thought, executed the Despensers.

It was at this point that the Berkeleys were involved in the single act for which at least the castle of that name is remembered. Roger de Mortimer had no sense of forgiveness, Queen Isabella even less. She had been humiliated by her husband's infatuation with first Piers Gaveston and then the young Hugh Despenser. She and Mortimer decided to incarcerate Edward II and place her young son Edward on the throne as Edward III. In this they were successful, because no one would defend Edward II's position.

The northern nobles had always felt threatened by Edward II and the Despensers on account of the way in which they had mismanaged the war with Scotland. The Welsh marcher lords were, by and large, with Mortimer. Probably only Edward's Chancellor, Robert Baldock, and Robert Holden, his Controller of the Wardrobe, were loyal to him.[4] Yet despite the lack of support for Edward II Isabella and Mortimer could never feel safe, even though Mortimer's arrogance suggested otherwise. He was, however, no fool.

In April 1327 the king, whom they had locked up in Kenilworth, was taken to Berkeley Castle and put in the charge of Lord Thomas Berkeley and his fellow conspirator Sir John Maltravers. The Mortimers and the Berkeleys were not alone in their dislike of the king and, more particularly, of the way in which the Despensers had seized so much power and wealth. However, the marcher lords had many enemies of their own. There were at least two plans to rescue Edward and restore him to his throne – though those who were prepared to plot for him did so only because they disliked Mortimer. Shortly after Edward was taken to Berkeley Castle, he was sprung from prison and spirited away to Corfe Castle in Dorset. The trouble was that the rescuers did not know what to do with the king – there was no popular rising for his return. Edward was recaptured and sent back to Berkeley Castle, and his rescuers were dispensed with. But the matter had not rested there.

By that summer of 1327, Isabella and Mortimer were rightly concerned that another attempt would be made to get the king out. The obvious direction from which it would come would be the west. The Mortimers, indeed most of the marcher lords including the Berkeleys, were disliked by the Welsh and seen as no better than the Despensers.

In September 1327 the decision seems to have been made that Edward had to be killed. Exactly what part Berkeley played in the king's death is not known. It is assumed that the deed was organized by Berkeley's friend Sir John Maltravers and another knight from Somerset, Sir Thomas Gurney. Edward II was, it has been said, ghoulishly executed with red-hot pokers that left not a mark on his body. There is no certain documentary evidence for this; yet, whatever the circumstances of the king's death, he was certainly murdered in Berkeley Castle.

It was in the 1400s that the Berkeleys and their estates expanded. Apart from Gloucester, they now had manors across the West Country at Portbury, Beveston, and Stoke Gifford in Gloucestershire; at Bruton and Pyle, close by each other in Somerset; and even more lands in Middlesex, Kent and Essex. A new Thomas Berkeley, the grandson of the Thomas Fitzharding who had survived imprisonment under Edward II, was one of the most powerful barons in England. In 1399 he appeared as one of the commissioners who felt forced to present Richard II with the abdication documents which led to Henry IV becoming king.

Bolingbroke, the future Henry IV, had returned from exile and landed in England at Pevensey, and his triumphant march against Richard II's supporters led at one point to Gloucestershire and the Berkeleys. The King's Council, whose members included Berkeley, had tried to persuade Richard to return from his refuge in Ireland, and had headed for the West Country in the expectation of meeting up with the king on his return. This strategy was foiled by Bolingbroke, who sent his troops to intercept them. Most of the council, led by the Duke of York, took refuge with Berkeley in his castle, but when Bolingbroke set about the fortress they quickly surrendered. Berkeley seems to have decided very quickly where better interests lay and that the king too should submit. Bolingbroke swept Richard aside, imprisoned him, and was then crowned Henry IV. The following year, Richard II was murdered.

When he died in 1417, this Thomas Fitzharding was to have been succeeded by his nephew, James Fitzharding. However, Berkeley Castle was taken over by his daughter, Elizabeth, Countess of Warwick. The dispute arose because, as his daughter, she reasonably claimed that she was more a Berkeley than a nephew could be. The matter was not settled – legally, that is – for four years, when Parliament decided that James was the rightful heir through his uncle. James Fitzharding was then summoned to the Parliament as the Baron Berkeley, and it is this establishment of the barony which has existed in an unbroken line to the present day, through a family easily traceable and always influential.

Lord James Berkeley was not allowed a quiet tenure of his title nor of Berkeley Castle. He may have won the legal argument in his case to inherit Berkeley, but his cousin, Elizabeth, did not give up. Her son, Lord de L'Isle, was constantly warring, and not simply through the courts. The Earl of Shrewsbury took sides through his relationship with de L'Isle, kidnapped Lord James Berkeley's wife, Isabel, and never returned her. She died in his hands at Gloucester.

Lord James and the Berkeleys held their own. William, his eldest son, was created a viscount by Edward IV in 1481, raised as Earl of Nottingham by Richard III in 1483 and finally, five years later, as Marquess of Berkeley by Henry VII who had come to the throne on the defeat of Richard at Bosworth Field.

But the fine honours bestowed on William did little for his succession. He had no son and so the titles, apart from his barony, disappeared and the castle itself was again out of the hands of the Berkeleys until the death of Edward VI. Only in Elizabethan times were the Berkeleys and Berkeley Castle re-established on a firm footing. Elizabeth so liked the castle that she tried to appropriate it for the Earl of Leicester, her favourite; she failed.

The later Berkeleys never hunted with the political pack to the extent that their ancestors had in the twelfth and thirteenth centuries. Perhaps there was no need. The family contented themselves with being enormously wealthy, mostly long-lived and always quietly influential. None was boring.

For example, the 8th Baron, George Berkeley, who was born in 1601, just two years before the death of Elizabeth I, did nothing remarkable, yet his interesting and charmed life was typical of the Berkeleys. He was created a Knight of the Bath for no great reason other than the family's standing as courtiers, spent most of his time travelling, was considered something of a linguist and was one of the early landowners in America. His youngest son, George, became the 9th Baron and quietly sat for a few years as a canon commoner at Christ Church, Oxford, but was no scholar. Although he had no need to do so he married well, to Elizabeth, one of the daughters of the treasurer of the East India Company, John Massingberd – another name which would survive well into the twentieth century. This George established the family's holdings far from Gloucester in what was then, in 1663, the unexplored tip of southern Africa. A particularly lucrative and far-seeing negotiation resulted in his Royal African Company picking up shares in the territory for a thousand years. By the 1680s he had further expanded the overseas interests of the family. This time the venture was in the eastern Mediterranean and for good measure he expanded the family interests by joining the board of the East India Company. Although the family gave every indication of being rich and nothing more (Pepys, in 1666, notes one of the daughters being well decked in jewels), George had not abandoned the Berkeley tradition of political power, and he was one of those sent to the Netherlands to invite Charles II to return as king. Having welcomed Charles in 1660, in 1688 George Berkeley encouraged the departure of James II. He was a member of the council which governed the country during the short interregnum until the arrival of William of Orange and Queen Mary.

The seafaring tradition of the Berkeleys was certainly maintained by James Berkeley, the 3rd Earl, and he remained true to the family habit of being present at great historical moments. He became Lord Berkeley early in 1704 and joined a ship called the *Boyne* under the command of Admiral Sir George Rooke. Berkeley found himself in the Mediterranean and did rather well with Rooke at the Battle of Malaga. Most importantly, it was in this campaign that they captured Gibraltar from the Spanish. The Berkeleys continued to have an interest in the colony, never believing that it should be given back to Spain. One of the other commanders serving under Rooke was Sir Cloudesley Shovel.[5] In 1707, Berkeley was back in the Mediterranean in command of his own ship in the squadron of Sir Cloudesley, recently promoted to admiral. Berkeley found himself in August that year taking part in an attack on Toulon, which failed. The squadron was ordered back to England, with the admiral flying his flag in the *Association* and Berkeley commanding *St George*. In thick fog off the Scilly Isles on the night of 22 October the two ships were in close company, feeling their way for the English Channel, but hit the rocks. A strong swell swept the *St George* off and, although badly damaged, she survived. The *Association* was wrecked and went to the bottom, Admiral Sir Cloudesley Shovel with it. His body was washed ashore and later buried in Westminster Abbey.

Berkeley, now promoted to vice-admiral, found himself serving with yet another famous commander – and one whose son would become more famous still, but for tragic reasons. Berkeley was given command of HMS *Berwick* as deputy to the flag officer, Sir George Byng. This was in 1708 and the two were in the Scottish flotilla, which protected the North Sea ports; it was an uneventful time. In May 1710 Berkeley went ashore and later that year, following the death of his father, he became the 3rd Earl and went about the business of looking after his estates in Gloucestershire. This was very much the time of land battles. In 1704, while Berkeley was involved in the taking of Gibraltar, Marlborough (see Chapter 7) was defeating the French at Blenheim. In 1706 the famous general was victorious at Ramillies and in 1708 at Oudenarde. In 1709 he won the Battle of Malplaquet. Yet in 1711 Marlborough was dismissed, his enemies in the queen's council momentarily successful and his foes on the battlefield astonished. Berkeley, an admirer of Marlborough, was also removed from his one high office, that of Lord Lieutenant of Gloucestershire.

When George I became king on the death of Queen Anne in 1714, Berkeley's fortunes returned and he became the first lord commissioner of the admiralty. In 1718 he was the commander-in-chief of the Channel fleet during the war with Spain. Byng, his old commander, was back in the Mediterranean having a good war. He had four sons. One of them, John, would be a very popular and successful admiral. Sadly, when he sailed for the Mediterranean in 1756 to relieve the garrison in Minorca he was accused of refusing to engage the enemy more closely, as the naval instruction would have it. Byng the younger was executed to, as Voltaire observed, encourage the others.

As for Berkeley, he had gone into retirement except for the portfolio of courtly honours and duties expected of the aristocracy in the eighteenth century. He did, however, add to the diagram of the Berkeley family tree when he married Louisa Lennox, daughter of the 1st Duke of Richmond. Thus the Berkeleys became related to the families of the Dukes of Richmond and Gordon. There was an interesting footnote to this, yet another example of aristocratic intermarriage and resultant relationships between the great dynasties. In earlier times the Berkeleys had been trusted marcher lords; they had married into the Mortimer family who had first held the title Earl of March. The connection in the eighteenth century between the Berkeleys and the Richmonds was that the latter family now included the earldom of March in its list of noble honours. As an indication of how some of the titles appear in different forms, the Duke of Richmond's title was created in 1675. In the same year the Scottish dukedom of Lennox was created. In 1876 the Duke of Richmond and Lennox became the Duke of Richmond, Lennox and Gordon. The earldom of March was given to Richmond in the same year as the dukedom was created, 1675. Also that year, the earldom of Darnley was created, and so the Duke of Richmond, Lennox and Gordon is also the Earl of Darnley. He is, too, the Duc d'Aubigny, a French personal title granted in 1684. On 17 August 1736 James Berkeley, the admiral, died at Richmond's chateau at Aubigny in France.

A far more exciting character was another George Berkeley. Born in 1753 he was one of the 4th Earl's sons. When he was thirteen he joined the navy, perhaps because his cousin was the very famous junior admiral Augustus Keppel. Thirteen years before George was born, Keppel had circumnavigated the globe with George Anson. That famous four-year voyage gained Anson his flag rank and Keppel his reputation as a rising star. This was not the time to be a social naval officer. Berkeley sailed with James Cook in the *Resolution* and took part in the survey of Newfoundland. He then joined a frigate called the *Alarm*, whose captain was John Jervis. Jervis was as distinguished as Keppel and Cook, having been in Wolfe's expedition to North America at the time of the Seven Years' War.[6] Later he would become equally famous when he defeated the Spanish off Cape St Vincent and was created an earl for his trouble.

Berkeley then combined his naval career with politics – or tried to. He spent tens of thousands of pounds trying to become MP for Gloucester but failed, and again it was his cousin, Keppel, who got him back into the navy. He became a lieutenant in HMS *Victory*. For the next decade, Berkeley commanded smaller ships and spent most of his time looking for smaller skirmishes. In 1793, during the Revolutionary Wars with France, he got more than that. He was in command of the 74-gun *Marlborough* which was severely damaged and took more than a hundred casualties, including Berkeley, who was so badly wounded that he could no longer command. It would seem that George Berkeley was something of a hero, although there were those who accused him of cowardice.[7] He was cleared of being a 'shy cock' as the terminology had it, but the stain was never bleached from his reputation.

Undoubtedly not all the Berkeleys were 'gallant gentlemen'. One, Gilbert Berkeley, was Bishop of Bath and Wells in the sixteenth-century. Another, the 1st Baron Berkeley of Stratton, was a seventeenth century soldier and what is generally described as a courtier. This man, John Berkeley, came from Bruton in

Somerset; the 'Stratton' of his title refers to a place not far from Bruton, and the home of the abbey that became Downside School.

This Berkeley appears to have been a cheerful soul, full of self-confidence, and one who in modern jargon would be considered something of an aristocratic net-worker. Charles I appointed him ambassador to Queen Christina of Sweden. He must have been reasonably successful at his embassy, because the king knighted him for his efforts. He was very much a loyalist and at one time, in 1641, was locked up in the Tower because Parliament accused him of being involved in a conspiracy to swing the army over to the king. Parliament was probably right: this was the eve of the Civil War.

Berkeley was bailed from the Tower and joined the Marquess of Hertford at his headquarters at Sherborne in Dorset. He was promoted, as so many were. John Berkeley was on home territory and in May 1643 led his forces with élan in the battles and skirmishes around Stratton and Wells. The royalists, in need of good leaders, accepted him as the commander of all their forces in Devon and that autumn forced the Earl of Stamford to surrender his parliamentary forces at Exeter.

He continued to do rather well from Cornwall to Somerset until, in 1646, the parliamentarians led by Fairfax got down to some proper soldiering and in April Berkeley had to surrender at Exeter. He was lucky to escape with his life. He decamped to Paris and became a courtier to the king's wife, Queen Henrietta Maria. She, apparently, rather liked him. It would not have been proper to stay too long and because he believed his role to be that of intriguer and go-between the queen recommended him to her husband. Certainly in the summer of 1647 Berkeley had secured some form of proposal from Cromwell that might well have brought about an agreement between Charles I and the parliamentarians. At least that was Berkeley's view. It was one the king did not share, and in November that year Berkeley found himself running from Oxford with the king down to Lymington in Hampshire. Here was the crossing point to Carisbrooke Castle. The governor was Colonel Robert Hammond who Berkeley believed would give the king a sympathetic hearing. Instead, Charles was imprisoned at the castle. Berkeley was allowed to leave for London to negotiate with the army the king's future. The following year, the Civil War resumed and Parliament proposed a treaty in the wake of its decision in January to break off any negotiations, including Berkeley's somewhat futile attempts at rapprochement. The Newport Treaty, named after the main town on the Isle of Wight, was supposedly the nearest Charles would get to some safe agreement. It would, in theory, give him the army, though this was hardly likely as the army now controlled the country. In truth it controlled even Cromwell – which was perhaps why, much later, when Cromwell was offered the throne, after much deep thought (or was it indecision?) he turned down the opportunity because he knew that the army would kick him out. Contrary to popular belief, soldiers, perhaps the military in general, have never been 100 per cent devoted to the monarch except on ceremonial occasions. The military has always regarded its duty as being to the state.

Charles I was executed the following year, 1649. Berkeley, seen as a royalist and something of an opportunist, was not trusted by the army. He took the hint and left England, once more for Paris, where he lived by a courtier's wits. He tried to marry the Countess Morton, the governess of Henrietta, the daughter of the now widowed queen. She turned him down, not necessarily because he was not much of a catch but because of court intrigue. Edward Hyde, the future Earl of Clarendon, thought about as much of Berkeley as had the army; Hyde had considerable influence with the countess, and persuaded her to keep her suitor at a distance. Berkeley took this rather poorly and went off with the Duke of York (the future James II) for more soldiering against the Spaniards. The duke thought a great deal of Berkeley, especially on account of his loyalty as a soldier through three years' hard campaigning. In 1658 – in exile, of course – Berkeley became Baron Berkeley of Stratton. Once the monarchy was restored in 1660, Berkeley too was restored to his titles and became a commissioner of the navy and Lord President of Connaught. The diarist Samuel Pepys noted a dull formal fellow offering prayers for 'The Right Honourable John Lord Berkeley, President of Connaught'.

By this time, whatever Pepys may have thought of him, Berkeley was doing exceedingly well for the family name and had a palace built in London just off Piccadilly.[8] In 1670 he was appointed the king's Viceroy in Ireland for two years during which time he showed every sign of converting to Roman Catholicism. He even told the Archbishop of Dublin that he hoped to have High Mass at Christ Church in Dublin. He fell into poor health, including fits, and in August 1678 died at the age of seventy-two. He was buried in the churchyard at Twickenham in Middlesex, probably because he had added to the Berkeley land bank by buying the splendid estate of Twickenham Park – although it did not survive in the family for long beyond his death. Pepys tells us that most people thought Berkeley's extraordinarily influential career, his ability to find himself in high-placed positions, mostly lucrative, together with a sense of courtly survival beyond his wit, was largely due to family influence. His kinsman was the Earl of St Albans – one of the influential men at court – and the Duke of York was his patron.

This Berkeley was yet another character in British family history rarely brought to anyone's attention, but never during his lifetime without considerable influence, simply because he was part of that self-perpetuating nomenklatura which has truly ruled England for a thousand years. For example, John Berkeley's son might simply have been an obscure naval officer. But, as described above, he survived the Revolution of 1688 and became an admiral. He served with other famous names such as Dartmouth and Herbert and Sir Cloudesley Shovel; even with old Admiral Benbow and the revered Sir George Rooke. Berkeley became a commander-in-chief without ever carrying out a distinguished action.

There was a similar career for a later Berkeley, Maurice, who in the nineteenth century became an admiral too. His uncle, who was commander-in-chief, made sure that the young man was appointed his flag lieutenant and nine months later made further sure of Maurice's career by giving him his first command. Most of his time was spent ashore on the admiralty board, or as MP for the city of Gloucester. For his loyal pains in 1861 he became Baron Fitzhardinge, thus perpetuating the twelfth-century family name of the Berkeleys. Maurice also married rather well. He was another to ally himself with the Duke of Richmond's family when, in 1823, he married Charlotte Lennox. After Charlotte's death, Berkeley married another Charlotte, Lady Charlotte Moreton, the daughter of the first Earl of Ducie.

The Berkeley name has not always passed down the male line. In modern times, for example, the family standard might have been seen flying over Pickade Cottage in Great Kimble in Buckinghamshire. That was the home of the 17th Baroness, whose title was created in 1421. The eighteenth holder of the barony is Anthony Fitzhardinge Gueterbock, a civil engineer and sometime public affairs manager on the Eurotunnel project – no Berkeley since the time of the Conqueror ever ignored the quickest route between France and England and vice versa.

NOTES
1 *Domesday*, Volume 1 and *Monasticon*, Volume 1.
2 *Anglo-Saxon Chronicle*, Laud Chronicle, 1121.
3 Under the Statute of Staples of 1354, the staple towns were Bristol, Canterbury, Carmarthen, Chichester, Cork, Drogheda, Dublin, Exeter, Lincoln, London, Newcastle, Norwich, Waterford, Winchester and York.
4 May McKisack, *The Fourteenth Century 1307–1399*, OUP, 1959.
5 Later, the Royal Navy base at Gibraltar was named HMS *Rooke*. Apart from the matter of seniority, it is doubtful whether HMS *Shovel* would have had quite the right ring.
6 1756–63.
7 In a battle in June 1794, the *Marlborough* came under heavy fire and some 120 of Berkeley's ship's company were killed or wounded. Berkeley himself received a head wound. Later, rumour had it that he hid in his cabin during the engagement.
8 It was burned down in 1733.

FURTHER READING
JACOB, E. F., *The Fifteenth Century*, OUP, 1961.
POOLE, A. L., *Domesday Book to Magna Carta*, OUP, 1951.

CHAPTER TEN

THE CAVENDISHES

The name 'Devonshire' is one which sits comfortably on English streets, squares and houses. In towns along the south coast of England there always seems to be a Devonshire something-or-other. In London W1, Devonshire Street and Devonshire House are but a short walk from Cavendish Square. So do famous families slip easily into the public consciousness, though few people usually understand why. So it is with Devonshire and Cavendish – the latter the family name of the former.

The popular image of the Cavendishes must be the family seat of Chatsworth in Derbyshire, brought into the family by the marriage of Elizabeth of Hardwick to Sir William Cavendish in the sixteenth century. But the name comes from Cavendish in Suffolk and the first Cavendish noted in history was the fourteenth-century Sir John, the chief justice who in 1381 had his head cut off by rebels during the Peasants' Revolt.

There have been eleven dukes of Devonshire since the first one was created in 1694; he, of course, was a Cavendish. The first Baron Cavendish was created in 1605, in the third year of the reign of James I. By 1618 the barons had become earls. The 'modern' Cavendishes include a famous Civil War general, an art-collecting early-nineteenth-century duchess and a scattering of field marshals and generals. There was the colourful Georgiana, the duchess who was the daughter of the 1st Earl Spencer. There was Lord Frederick who was in Gladstone's Cabinet; Lord John, a Chancellor of the Exchequer; the 4th Duke, William, who was Prime Minister; and Henry Cavendish, one of the most celebrated scientists of his day. He is commemorated, of course, in the Cavendish Laboratory at Cambridge. There is even a Cavendish island near Bermuda named after perhaps the least remembered of the family – William Cavendish, the 1st Earl of Devonshire, who was born some time in the late sixteenth century and died in 1626. In all, this is certainly not a boring family.

The Cavendishes were very well connected and moneyed in the fifteenth and sixteenth centuries. When the William Cavendish who was to become the 1st Earl was born, the family were very close friends of the Shrewsburys, so much so that when old William Cavendish died, young William's mother married George

Talbot, who was the 6th Earl of Shrewsbury. The family estates of the Cavendishes were, as they are today, in Derbyshire, and in 1595 he became High Sheriff of the county. Ten years later he was created a peer and took the title of Baron Cavendish of Hardwicke. Most of his money came from his mother and because, although his older brother, Henry, had inherited their father's fortune, he had died young. Already established in Elizabeth I's court, Lord Cavendish, as he now was, became a courtier to James I, and it was this king who created him Earl of Devonshire. Sometimes peerages were happily and openly bought: there is every likelihood that Cavendish would have paid, at seventeenth-century prices, about £10,000 for his earldom. He left no remarkable stamp on the family history apart from his interests in what was then still very much the New World, and was instrumental in the colonization of Bermuda. The place was named after Juan Bermudez who discovered it and its neighbouring islands in 1503, after which they remained uninhabited for a hundred years. In 1609 Sir George Somers, who was a founder of the South Virginia Company, was shipwrecked there with some of his friends. Somers claimed the islands for Britain and a whole group was renamed after him; one of the individual islands was called after one of Somers' colleagues, William Cavendish.

The 1st Earl died in 1626 and was succeeded by his second son, also William. The family already lived at Chatsworth and it was there that this Cavendish was educated by one of the most formidable philosophers of his day, Thomas Hobbes. Hobbes was born in the year of the Armada, 1588, and became a political philosopher at Oxford; his most famous work was the *Leviathan*. His reputation would not have been so easily made had it not been for the patronage of the Cavendishes: Hobbes went to live at Chatsworth, travelled with the family as tutor and thus found himself debating his hypotheses with intellectuals such as Ben Jonson, Descartes, Gassendi and even Galileo. When he was forty Hobbes studied the geometry of Euclid; this uncomplicated setting of order that had amused philosophers from classical times, and was to continue to do so down to fictional figures of twentieth-century popular literature such as Agatha Christie's Hercule Poirot, formed a template for his developing political theory. Institutions such as the banking system, the insurance markets and the fledgling political parties, and their effects on order and disorder, were re-emerging in the early seventeenth century, and Hobbes was at the forefront of this debate. His first major work was not his own, but a translation of Thucydides' *History*, which he dedicated to William Cavendish, the 2nd Earl's son.

That the 2nd Earl survived his father by only two years was probably due to what politely might be called his love of life – he lived extremely well and his excesses probably killed him. They certainly put a strain on even the Cavendish finances, and he went so far as to obtain an Act of Parliament to allow him to sell off some of his tied estates so that he could pay his creditors. Having done so, he dropped dead in his London house, which was big enough for it later to be redeveloped as a whole square of houses, appropriately called Devonshire Square.

His eldest son, another William, the 3rd Earl, was also tutored by Hobbes and the pair of them, philosopher and pupil, travelled across Europe between 1634 and 1637. The family were great royalists and in 1625 Cavendish had become, at the tender age of eight, a Knight of the Bath in honour of Charles I's crowning. The connection with other great families was further made when Cavendish married Elizabeth, one of the daughters of William Cecil, the 2nd Earl of Salisbury (see Chapter 6).

Their loyalty to Charles I was for some time to cost the family dearly. At the beginning of the Civil War in 1642, the Cavendishes went to Charles I's colours. As a result, the 3rd Earl became one of the peers who were impeached by an angry Parliament for high crimes, almost amounting to treasonable conduct, against the House of government. If he had been captured, Cavendish would have been dispatched at least to the Tower, probably to a higher place. So he wisely left England, and all the Cavendish estates were taken over by the parliamentarians. He stayed away for three years until in 1646 Parliament pardoned him, but only returned a small portion of the Cavendish landholdings. However, when the monarchy was restored in 1660 so too were all the estates.

We should not ignore Christiana, the 3rd Earl's mother, who strongly influenced her son. It was she who encouraged his education and the attentions of Hobbes. Furthermore, as was only right in the daughter of a good Scottish gentleman, Bruce of Kinloss, she took charge of the Cavendish estates when her husband died in 1628, increasing what was left of the family fortune. Nor was she strictly a businesswoman. Distraught at the actions of the parliamentarians, in 1642 she was already one of Charles I's staunchest supporters. Her second son was named after the king, who was the boy's godfather.

A year after the war began, in 1643, this son was killed trying to break the siege of Gainsborough. This only increased Christiana's determination and support for the king. The execution of Charles I in 1649 made her doubly certain that the royalists had to have their revenge and right to rule. She became a focal point of the surviving loyalists at home and in continental Europe, and it was she who took charge of Charles II's effects after the Battle of Worcester in 1651 when he was so decisively trounced by Cromwell's forces; the royalists never really mounted another attempt for a decade. She survived the interregnum well enough, and when it was time for the Commonwealth to end General Monck made sure that the Religious Lady, as she was often called, knew that Charles would be returning. When he had done so in 1660, Christiana Cavendish frequently acted as the king's hostess at her house in Roehampton and became perhaps his most intimate friend outside the royal family. She died in January 1675, the year work started on Wren's new cathedral of St Paul to replace the one destroyed in the Great Fire of 1666.

The 4th Earl became the 1st Duke, by which time the family was clearly well integrated with the rest of the aristocracy. For example, the 1st Duke's mother was the daughter of William Cecil, the 2nd Earl of Salisbury, after whom he was named. This William Cavendish was born in 1640 during the Civil War; although that conflict severely damaged the fabric of English life, in some ways young William benefited from the social and constitutional disruption. He was sent to the continent for his education, and by the time of the restoration of the monarchy, was very suited to take his place at the court of Charles II. At the king's coronation in 1661, Cavendish was one of Charles's train bearers. He then went to Ireland and it was there that he married Mary, a daughter of the Duke of Ormonde. Young Cavendish, as was the style, became an MP, having been given a seat at Derby. He was a great Protestant believer and was one of those who spoke, if not actively campaigned, for the suppression of Roman Catholics.

He must also have been something of a strong willed character. There is a story of how, while in Paris, he managed to get into a fight with three Frenchmen on the stage of a theatre. Swords were drawn and he looked done for, but fortunately he was rescued by an obliging friend who threw him down into the orchestra pit. He bore the scars of this encounter for the rest of his life. Not long after that, back in England, he found himself in the Tower. He had got into an argument in the House of Commons over an apparent breach of privilege and insult. Challenged to a duel, he was subsequently accused of ducking it. Cavendish then denounced his accuser as a poltroon – the ultimate form of cowardice. Both the supposed coward, a man called Howard, and Cavendish were dumped in the Tower until the Commons could deal with them, but they were soon released and apparently reconciled. As a result of Cavendish's action, the House of Commons tried to bring in an Act of Parliament that would have banned duelling; it failed, but only narrowly.

Cavendish did not feel at all upset by his brush with Parliament and in fact saw it as a way of influencing not simply the laws of the nation, but the very constitution. In this part of the seventeenth century the parliamentary system was split broadly into two parties, the Whigs and the Tories (see Chapter 7). Cavendish saw himself as not against royalty or the monarchy, but as against its domination and undue influence. It was a philosophy that would have been recognized, although for quite different reasons, four hundred and fifty years earlier at Runnymede. For example, Cavendish wanted to enforce an Act which dated from the fourteenth century and the time of Edward III, which would require annual Parliaments to be held. In the 1670s Parliament could simply be prorogued, and if a session were ended for more than a year it was dissolved. Cavendish failed in his aim, but it was not a futile gesture. In 1677, English soldiers were fighting for the king of France. Cavendish thought this wrong and was also being done without the authority of Parliament. This was revolutionary politics in the seventeenth century. So he introduced a bill to bring the troops back to England, and when it looked as if it was going to become law the king ordered that Parliament should be adjourned. When Cavendish got to his feet to ask, on a point of order, by what right the adjournment was to be made, the Speaker, Sir Edward Seymour, is said to have run from the building. The House came back two months later and Cavendish was immediately on his feet again questioning the legality of the adjournment. So the

House was adjourned again. This nonsense carried on until January 1678, when the matter was finally dropped. Yet Cavendish had succeeded, in that he had gathered support for constitutional reform, thereby warning the monarch that on major issues Parliament would challenge him. This, by seventeenth-century standards, was a modest, but real success for Cavendish.[1]

After this, Cavendish continued to be deeply involved against the Catholics and what he saw as a sinister side to the creeping influence of the pope. This, 1678, was the year of the so-called Popish Plot. Very briefly, the plot did not exist – only the rumour of it. It was said that the Jesuits were planning to assassinate the Protestant Charles II, put his brother James (the Catholic Duke of York) on the throne in his place and, for good measure, massacre non-Catholics. The credibility of the plot was not helped when genuine correspondence between a secretary in the York household and the French court was discovered. The whole thing came to nothing except for the apparent conspirators, who were executed.

Cavendish was also the man sent to the king with the news of Parliament's intention to impeach Thomas Danby. Danby, created an earl just four years earlier, was Charles II's chief minister, a position that later would have been called Prime Minister. He was one of the seventeenth-century political manipulators and exploited the custom of bribery and patronage in order to build up a political loyalty in Parliament for the king – generally called the court party. He was commendably (for those times) anti-French. It was Danby who was instrumental in bringing about the marriage of the king's niece, Mary (the daughter of the future James II), and William of Orange – who was a Protestant and against the French.

However, Danby's darker dealings got the better of him, though not of Parliament. It was he who had arranged, in absolute secrecy or so he thought, for large sums to be paid by Louis XIV of France to Charles II in return for keeping the English out of the French war with the Spanish Netherlands. When Cavendish delivered the news to King Charles that Parliament had taken the decision to impeach Danby, the monarch knew what was the simplest way to protect his chief minister: he dissolved Parliament. He also gave Danby a royal pardon. But Parliament was no longer so easily fobbed off. With Cavendish in the van of the opposition to the court party and therefore to the monarch, Danby was impeached and sent to the Tower in 1679; there he stayed there for five years.[2]

Little wonder that Cavendish and his fellow peers were able to tell the king eagerly that the laws against the Roman Catholics should be tightened. So, in April 1679, Cavendish was one of the main draughtsmen of a bill against popery. His anti-Catholic speeches were so popular that they caused diplomatic hysteria abroad when published in a newsletter, *A Speech of Lord Cavendish*. The pamphlet was sent to the House of Commons for examination of its apparent seditious nature. Nothing came of the exercise and Cavendish continued with his caustic style of oratory.

With Danby gone, so was the influence of the court party. The best way to balance the enthusiasms of the sometimes headstrong House of Commons was to establish a powerful privy council in the Lords. This was to be led by Lord Shaftesbury, who was to have the foremost of the powerful peers at his table. Cavendish was one; the others were Lords Essex, Halifax and Russell (see Chapter 12). Parliament was still an unreliable instrument, and the king spent much time calling it and then sending it quickly home once his cherished political ambitions had been settled: for example, putting Protestantism above all other religious denominations. The concept of a coalition of interests between the country party and the court party might have succeeded if there had not had been a constitutional crisis. In January 1680, Cavendish left the council. The complete split in Parliament, with Cavendish to the fore, was caused by the fact that the Duke of York, shortly to become James II, was hardly a model of Protestant monarchy.

It is at this point that Cavendish, for all his reputation as a constitutional revolutionary, is seen as a calming and judicious influence on the English political system during the period of Charles II's unconscionable time in dying and James II's turbulent reign. It is easy to get some idea of the disruption in political life if we look at three or four events between, say, 1678 and the death of Charles II. In 1678 there was the Popish Plot and all the paranoia that it produced, even though it was found to be a fiction. In 1679 Parliament met only for five months, there was a confrontation with the king and Danby fell. The country party tried to stop the Duke of York from becoming king because of his Catholicism. Also in the same year, one of England's most important pieces of judicial legislation was enacted: the Act of Habeas Corpus, of which Cavendish was a leading supporter, thus making him a confidant of Anthony Ashley Cooper, the 1st Earl of Shaftesbury, who drove it through. This Act established the procedures to be used for the issue of criminal writs and provided for officials to be prosecuted if they chose to ignore those procedures – as they commonly did. Moreover, the political battles were actually taken to the streets and countryside where, among the extremists, for example the Covenanters, there was considerable violence.[3] In 1681 King Charles, so out of sorts with the likes of Cavendish, dissolved Parliament and ruled without it until his death. It was also the year when the fallout from the Popish Plot was still obvious, with the execution on trumped up charges of the Roman Catholic Archbishop of Armagh, Oliver Plunket.[4] In 1682 Shaftesbury, whom Cavendish had supported in his anti-Catholic campaigns and with whom he had stood shoulder to shoulder on the most controversial antipopery issues, tried to stage a revolution. It failed, and he fled to that haven of all Protestant anarchists, the Netherlands, where William of Orange watched and waited. There was more to come.

The next year, 1683, there was an apparent plan to assassinate Charles II. The Rye House Plot, seen as an attempt by the Whigs to seize power, was so called because the assassination was supposed to have taken place as Charles II and his brother James travelled to Newmarket races via Hertfordshire, where they would have met their ends as they passed Rye House. They never went to the races and the plot came to nothing, but it did add to the political sensitivities of the hour.

Cavendish did his best to distance himself from the would-be plotters or, perhaps more accurately, from the plots. For all his constitutional politics, he appeared to be reluctant to stand as firmly as did Shaftesbury and Russell, with their talk of removing so many of the monarch's powers. Lord William Russell, a son of the 1st Duke of Bedford, was one of the Rye House plotters. The evidence presented against him for his part in the Rye House Plot was nonsense, but that hardly mattered in the political and religious fever of the time. Russell was sentenced to be beheaded in the Tower. According to the historian Gilbert Burnet's account,[5] Cavendish offered to take Russell's place in the Tower but this was refused.

Although Cavendish had tried to keep his distance from those who campaigned for James's exclusion from the right to the throne, it was hardly surprising that in some quarters he was always suspect. His friendship with Russell could not have helped. It was this schism among the courtiers that led to a lasting difficulty for Cavendish.

When the Duke of York became James II he appointed Cavendish to his court. Although Cavendish again professed his innocence, he was forced to leave the court, albeit briefly when James, Duke of Monmouth, Charles II's bastard son by Lucy Walter,[6] landed in England to claim the throne (see Chapter 7). This departure of Cavendish was a brief affair. When Cavendish returned he met up with an old adversary, a Colonel Thomas Colepeper. The colonel's regard for Cavendish was particularly low, and he publicly informed him that as he was an Excluder he should not be at court. The diarist John Evelyn[7] noted that Colepeper then boxed Cavendish's ear and that the injured man struck back and felled the colonel. The business was viewed with some alarm by the Court of the King's Bench: Cavendish was fined £30,000 and sent to prison until such time as he should pay this not inconsiderable sum.

The prisoner escaped and took refuge at the family seat, Chatsworth. When the sheriff of Derby was sent to arrest him he promptly overpowered the sheriff and his men and held them until he had arranged a bond to pay the fine. The matter seems an insignificant incident; it is not. It tells us something about the way in which power was and still is exercised at the highest levels. How many times, right from the start of this book with the Godwines, have we seen people apparently banished from powerful positions, perhaps even from the kingdom, only to turn up within months in equally powerful positions? Although some fell violently – or at least their heads did – the pattern hardly changed through the centuries. Even at the beginning of the twenty-first century we could all name people who seemingly fell from grace, only to return. So it was with Cavendish.

Cavendish's mother had promissory notes left over from the Civil War, for the family had helped finance Charles I – two monarchs and one Cromwell ago. These notes were, in theory, worth twice as much as the fine imposed by the king's bench. James II would have none of it. Parliament was no less eager to have a go at the Earl of Cavendish, but here was a curiously bigger issue. Was the king's bench correct, because surely a breach of the privilege of Parliament was involved here? The judges, summoned to the bar of the House, decided that the imprisonment was illegal and thus the Cavendish case constituted a valuable precedent. However, the earl was wise enough to understand how close to the wind he had sailed. The act that had brought about his committal to prison remained a breach of the peace. He may have been free of the gaoler's grip; he was not free of the obligation to pay his fine.

Cavendish returned to Chatsworth and it was he, the 4th Earl, and the architect William Talman who started on the rebuilding of the great house. They began in the spring of 1687 and pressed on for nine years until shortly before Cavendish's death in 1707. This building coincided with the so-called Glorious Revolution of 1688 and the usurping of James II by his son-in-law, William of Orange, who became William III. It rapidly became fashionable to impose Dutch styles on to English houses, but Cavendish stuck clearly to his sense of classical Italian design. In terms of architectural taste this was not particularly surprising, for the Cavendishes of this period were classically minded. It was a taste that would continue within the family. For example, in 1811 Elizabeth Cavendish (1758–1824), later Duchess of Devonshire, went to live in Rome, following the death of her husband, the 5th Duke, after just two years of marriage. She kept one of the most fashionable of Rome's salons and financed excavations in the Forum. She built a collection of sculpture, paintings and engravings by the likes of Marchetti, Canova and Cavaccioli. Joshua Reynolds painted her and she was a friend of the historian Edward Gibbon for the last seven years of his life.[8]

Cavendish may have retired to Derbyshire to work on Chatsworth, but he was by no means at a distance from one of the most crucial developments in British constitutional history. James II, sceptical of Cavendish's loyalty, ordered him to come to London and attend on the throne. His cousin, the Duke of Newcastle, was sent by James to persuade him, but failed. Cavendish was keeping his distance. He was actively plotting with, among others, Berkeley, Russell and Shrewsbury – of the so-called 'Immortal Seven'[9] – to get William of Orange and his wife, James II's daughter Mary, to come and take the throne.

Once it was announced that James II had an heir in 1688, it was clear that the plotters would either have to give up or accelerate their efforts. As we know well (see Chapter 7), they did the latter. Cavendish's signature is to be found on the secret letter sent to William on 30 June that year. The letters and intelligence sent to William through Russell and Henry Sidney left the Dutchman in no doubt that support among senior figures of the British aristocracy was sufficiently encouraging for him to fulfil his ambition.

Cavendish joined with others including his one-time foe, the Earl of Danby, to plot the uprising against James II. Danby, a considerable figure in this event, had in a short space of time established himself in key government positions including that of Treasurer of the Navy and eventually Lord High Treasurer. It was Danby who had figured so largely in the enforcement of laws against Roman Catholics. He also had been influential in persuading William of Orange to marry the young

Princess Mary. Having recovered from his temporary downfall in 1678 as a result of his impeachment for intriguing with Louis IV of France, Danby was now very much on the same side as Cavendish. The uprising would involve Danby taking the city of York, and Cavendish Nottingham. However, when Cavendish heard that, instead of landing in the north of England as planned, William had been blown south to Torbay, he took his forces to Derby, his home territory. It was here that he read to the local populace his Declaration in Defence of the Protestant Religion. They were enthusiastic to start with, but grew less so when rumours spread that William was not doing so well in his advance on London (quite untrue) and that James and his supporters thought they had a chance of over-turning the rebellion.

In the November of the uprising Cavendish was instrumental in abducting Princess Anne, James's daughter and the future queen, who was travelling north from London to escape the dangers of the uprising. He intercepted her party and harboured the princess until it was time for him to take her to join her husband, Prince George,[10] at Oxford.

Cavendish was in the forefront of the Lords who met at Westminster on Christmas Day 1688, urging and effectively authorizing William of Orange to govern until such time as a convention could be brought together to discuss the future of James II, as well as what had effectively become the regency of Prince William. The conundrum for the peers was not whether King James II should be deposed – that was agreed – but whether William should then be appointed as monarch or rule as regent. The argument was not so easily solved as might be imagined. Eventually of course, James fought against his usurpation and failed. Cavendish was a key figure in the debate and in the administration that was formed to rule for the Dutch monarch. On 11 April 1689, at the coronation, it was Cavendish who carried the king's crown; his daughter held Queen Mary's train. Together they perfectly symbolized the powerful position of the Cavendishes – at the head and hem of one of the most significant monarchs of the past three hundred years.

In May 1694, Cavendish was created 1st Duke of Devonshire and Marquess of Hartington. That was the year that Queen Mary died. William III had never been popular; with the death of Mary he became even less so. He had done reasonably well in moving the government of England towards some form of stability after such turbulent years. The government now controlled a better economy, having established a National Debt, and it was in 1694 that the Bank of England was set up.[11] The king's preoccupation had always been warring with France. Although these adventures were expensive and politically debilitating, William had the guile and the military intelligence to establish an army and something of a navy that would form a basis for the forces that would, in the next century, be so skilfully commanded by John Churchill, later Duke of Marlborough.

However, with the death of Mary, William started to spend more time away from affairs of the English state. Here, then, appeared another example of the power of the Cavendish family. With the Archbishop of Canterbury, Tennison, the 1st Duke effectively ruled England between 1694 and the death of William III in 1702. This was no housekeeping role. Devonshire, as he was now more correctly called, was deeply involved with the controversial Irish legislation that would have disrupted the grants of valuable estates in Ireland. William III granted estates to friends and supporters – often his Dutch followers. This largesse pleased those who believed they had a right to expect such grants and angered those – especially the Anglo-Irish – who resented royal 'hand-outs' of Irish land. Considering the numbers of great families who profited from those grants (some of which were in land, others financial, to maintain granted estates), this was politically sensitive: there was a great risk of William's popularity and support sinking even further. If it had done, the result would have been wide-reaching. After all, since 1688 this had been the great experiment and the stern path that would guarantee that England, Scotland, Wales and some of Ireland would be forever, or so they thought, ruled by a Protestant. On the death of William and the accession of Anne, James II's daughter, it was Devonshire who successfully held the ring against those Tories who would have had Parliament believe rumours that Anne was not fit to be queen because she had, supposedly, Jacobite sympathies.

His last contribution to British constitutional history related to the manoeu-vrings that brought about the Union of England and Scotland. As one of the commissioners (that is, one of those 'commissioned' by Parliament to explore ways of uniting Scotland and England) he had tried, but failed, to negotiate the Union as early as 1703. In 1706 an acceptable way was found for the two states to form a union, and the Act became law in 1707. At nine o'clock in the morning on 18 August that year William Cavendish, the 1st Duke of Devonshire, died at Devonshire House in Piccadilly.

He may have appeared caught up in the solemn and sometimes scary moments of what in later times might be called 'power politics'. Yet the 1st Duke was a man of considerable learning. He may in early life have been influ-enced by Hobbes, but when he had had so much experience of the realities unrealized by the political philosophers he tended to dismiss Hobbes's hypotheses as damnable. He was something of a poet, as might be expected of one who was more than familiar with Homer, Horace and Plutarch, and John Dryden thought his verse on the death of Queen Mary at the very least commendable. His contemporary, Robert Walpole, who became the first Prime Minister, thought Devonshire a patriot among the men, a corydon among the ladies. He managed to find time in between insults, lawsuits, politics, revolutions and mat-ters of state to father a good many illegitimate children, including a daughter who was married off to one of the sons of the Earl of Dysart. In his later years he was taken by the charms of at least one actress, not an unfashionable pastime. By the start of the eighteenth century, the Cavendishes had long been one of the most fashionable families in Britain. The Devonshires and Chatsworth had become one of a handful of grand dynasties and houses that would survive, even thrive in, the complex changes in British politics, society and economic life that were fast approaching.

The 4th Duke, another William, reached the highest political office, albeit briefly. This Cavendish became Prime Minister without having any particular political acumen and at an entirely impossible time for one of his abilities. He went off to Ireland as Lord Lieutenant in 1754. He was not particularly clever, but was a very personable fellow and by all accounts a popular figure. He succeeded his father as 4th Duke shortly before Christmas 1755. The following year, the Seven Years' War broke out. Britain was allied with Prussia and the Electorate of Hanover (whence came George I *et al.*) against a coalition of Austria, France, Russia, Saxony, Spain and Sweden.

The conflict began because Britain opposed French ambitions in India and North America. The French attacked the Mediterranean island of Minorca, which was British. The Prussians invaded Saxony. This was the time of Clive of India and General Wolfe of Quebec, of vigorous diplomacy and often spectacular and historically memorable battles. Into this arena stepped the rather ill-distinguished 4th Duke of Devonshire – though perhaps that is a cruel characterization, in the context of the strange nature of English politics at this moment.

It was believed that the Prime Minister should be an amiable diplomatic soul content to be a figurehead, with Pitt the Elder in charge of running Britain's part in the war. Pitt was enormously popular throughout the country and there was a great movement to bring him back into government. When the Prime Minister, Henry Pelham, died in 1754, his brother, the Duke of Newcastle, succeeded him. The obvious thing to do was to make Pitt Prime Minister, but Newcastle soldiered on until 1756. Once more we see how dynasties, especially political families, influence and often control great affairs of state. The majority of Whigs would not let the king appoint Pitt as Prime Minister and Pitt refused to serve under Newcastle.[12] In fact, he criticized Newcastle's handling of the war.

There had to be a compromise. Devonshire, a genial figure and rising light among the Whigs, was asked by the king (who had previously consulted Pitt) if he would become Prime Minister, with Pitt running the war. On 16 November 1756 he became First Lord of the Treasury – the official title of the Prime Minister. Devonshire was not a success. His instincts for the pleasant diplomacy of Ireland, as then it was, and his reputation as a very clubbable Whig were not at all suited for high political office. Moreover, the mucky battle of political point-scoring at the beginning of the Seven Years' War took place in the Commons. Pitt had to confess that, if he were to make a dramatic effect on the management of the war, as it was a coalition of muddles, he would have to shake hands with the Duke of Newcastle. In the spring of 1757, Devonshire handed back the keys to the Duke of Newcastle and assumed the far more agreeable appointment of lord chamberlain of the king's household. In October 1764 he dropped down dead, a nice man of forty-four.

Lord John Cavendish was the fourth son of the 3rd Duke of Devonshire. He too became a senior albeit unmemorable politician, even if he did become Chancellor of the Exchequer. In the Rockingham administration of 1765 Cavendish was one of the Treasury lords but, as Rockingham could not hold on to office, Cavendish could not hold on to the Treasury. When Pitt offered him a Cabinet job he refused, because he would not desert Rockingham. When Rockingham became Prime Minister again in 1782, Cavendish became Chancellor of the Exchequer. Once more, he had hardly opened the nation's accounts before he was out of office. Rockingham, who had returned to power in March 1782, died on 1 July; Cavendish resigned. In 1783 he was back at the Treasury: Pitt had been forced to resign and the Duke of Portland had become Prime Minister. Here again, we see the intermarriage of political aristocracies. Portland was married to Cavendish's niece. Cavendish was appointed by Portland as Chancellor of the Exchequer. He is not remembered for very much except that, since the country was broke, he was the first Chancellor to propose the idea of a national lottery. Nor can this Cavendish be remembered as a speaker in the House, although notably he did speak against the expulsion of John Wilkes (see p. 140) and was all for religious freedom (not always a popular idea among Cavendishes). Altogether, Lord John was probably too upright a fellow for the continuingly grubby ways of eighteenth-century politics.

More interesting among the Cavendish dynasty of this period is Henry, born in 1731, who was neither statesman nor courtier; when he died in 1810, he was well known as a scientist and philosopher. The grandson of the 2nd Duke, he was a very private person. Not much is known about his time up at Cambridge other than that he did not take a degree, which was not unusual in those days. He was principally a mathematician during his early adulthood, but his first published experiments to fire debate inquired into the results of combining hydrogen and oxygen: he deduced that the single product of the combustion of these two elements was water. He was also the first person to identify nitric acid. Cavendish appears to have been a placid soul, yet his conclusions and discoveries caused enormous controversy. It was a time when experimental chemists were making startling claims. In 1774 both Joseph Priestley and Karl Scheele announced, separately, that they had isolated oxygen. By 1766 Cavendish had established the precise composition of the atmosphere, of which one-fifth was oxygen.

Much more of Cavendish's work was original and successful than many imagined. His remarkable reluctance to get into a debate with other scientists, indeed even to find out what they were doing, led to all sorts of accusations that he was not important and that he had not made the discoveries he so clearly had; but no one should doubt his original research. For example, his discoveries about the composition of water were made at the same time as similar claims by James Watt. Only after his death was it admitted that Cavendish had anticipated most of the great discoveries of electricity. He also produced a system for estimating the density of the earth, known as the Cavendish Experiment.

That little is known of his private life is partly due to the fact that he rarely spoke to anyone and most certainly did not have a social life. He apparently ate alone at his house at Clapham and even left notes for the servants to tell them what food he wanted rather than speaking to them. With few friends and almost no conversation, Cavendish would have made a good companion in a closed order of friars. His lasting visible monument is the building named after him at Cambridge, the Cavendish Physical Laboratory.

If the eighteenth-century Cavendishes were a curious mix of brilliance and mediocrity, the nineteenth-century family was equally comfortable in those echelons of society that were on the fringes of power and even at its epicentre. At the start of the 1800s William, the 5th Duke, was best remembered – perhaps only remembered – for having been the husband of the spectacular Georgiana Spencer. Daughter of the 1st Earl Spencer, she married in 1774 at seventeen and immediately became the most talked about hostess in London. She was beautiful, graceful and very intelligent. Horace Walpole called her a phenomenon; Boswell wrote of Johnson visiting the Devonshires at Chatsworth, and the writer Nathaniel Wraxall [13] remembers her hanging on to the learned doctor's every word. She followed, too, every political utterance of the celebrated Charles James Fox and worked hard and sometimes flauntingly for his election in 1784. Fox was an inspiring liberal figure in late eighteenth-century politics. He had uncompromising views on the American colonies, the reform of the East India Company and the slave trade, and, somewhat controversially, was an admirer of the French Revolution. Georgiana saw Fox as a great hope for the political system, particularly in his opposition to Pitt the Younger. Fox and Georgiana died in the same year, 1806. He was buried in Westminster Abbey, she in the family vault at Derby.

The 6th Duke was Georgiana's son William. In a family expected to produce exceptional personalities, William George Spencer Cavendish left only one landmark. It was certainly not political, although he naturally took his seat in the House of Lords on the Whig benches – if he had any political influence, it was exercised in quiet drawing rooms. He carried out his duties as Lord Lieutenant of Derbyshire and High Steward of Derby with great care, but he was never a public figure and, considering the political revolutions of the first two or three decades of the nineteenth century, was almost totally mute in the Lords: there is no record of the 6th Duke ever having made an intervention in any of the great debates.

His main interest was far from the politics of Westminster – the gardens of Chatsworth. At some time he was president of the Horticultural Society and had the good judgement to make Joseph Paxton his estate manager. It was Paxton who built the Chatsworth conservatory, an enormous glass building 60 feet high, 300 feet long and 145 feet wide. This very special gardener-cum-architect used his experience of Devonshire's glasshouse when he designed the Crystal Palace for Prince Albert's Great Exhibition of 1851. Paxton is probably better remembered than his master at Chatsworth, who died a bachelor and thus sent the dukedom to his cousin, another William Cavendish, who was then the Earl of Burlington.

Perhaps the most famous of the Victorian Cavendishes is remembered for the most tragic circumstance. Lord Frederick Cavendish was Gladstone's brother-in-law and became Irish Chief Secretary. On 6 May 1882 Cavendish and his under-secretary, T. H. Burke, were walking in Phoenix Park in Dublin when they were set upon by members of the so-called Irish Nationalists and stabbed to death. Five of the terrorists were captured and hanged. The British government responded to its own considered instincts, and to the publicly expressed feelings of outrage in England. The result was a system of tribunals, each with three judges but without juries. A similar system was introduced in Northern Ireland a hundred years later. These tribunals came from the Prevention of Crimes Act 1882, a direct response to the murders of Cavendish and Burke. Ireland had once more inflicted misery upon a famous family.[14]

NOTES

1 Speaker Seymour was not re-appointed when the new Parliament met in March 1678.

2 Danby was eventually released, abandoned the by then restructured court party (James II was now on the throne), and was one of the people who put his signature to the request to William of Orange to invade England. He became William III's chief minister, but was once again impeached for corruption. The charge did not come to anything, but Danby's career was over even though he had been created the 1st Duke of Leeds.

3 Covenanters were supporters of the National Covenant, a manifesto with its origins in 1638 and written to oppose the religious policies of Charles I. By Charles II's time, Covenanters were oppressed for fighting against episcopacy. The minor rebellion in 1679 was put down by the Duke of Monmouth, the king's son.

4 He was canonized in 1976 as St Oliver.

5 Burnet (1643–1715) was a clergyman and noted historian, a friend of Russell's who was with him as chaplain on the scaffold. Burnet fell from Charles's favour and it was under William of Orange, whose chaplain he became in 1688, that he became Bishop of Salisbury. His pastoral letter on William's right of accession was thought so contentious that Parliament – which was not happy that William should be king, only consort to Mary – ordered it to be burned by the public hangman.

6 Lucy Walter (1630–58) was sometimes called Mrs Barlow. She and Prince Charles (later Charles II) had an affair after they met in the Channel Islands.

7 1620–1706.

8 1737–94.

9 The Immortal Seven were the seven signatories to the invitation to William of Orange to 'invade' England in 1688. The seven were Cavendish (above), Edward Sidney, the Earl of Shrewsbury, Lord Lumley, Edward Russell, Bishop Henry Compton and the Earl of Danby (Thomas Osborne).

10 Second son of Frederick III of Denmark.

11 The Bank of Scotland was founded in 1695.

12 Pitt the Elder, known as The Great Commander, had never been as popular with the Whig establishment as he was with the people. As a young MP he was a friend of Frederick, Prince of Wales, who was at odds with his father, George II, and was heavily critical of the Prime Minister, Robert Walpole. His strong views on policies and people made him more political enemies than friends.

13 In 1815 Nathaniel Wraxall (1751–1831) published his famous *Historical Memoirs of My Own Time*, usually called *Wraxall's Memoirs*.

14 Gladstone's record on Ireland begins during his first administration (1868). He disestablished the Irish Church and brought in a Bill of Compensation for Irish tenants. He had always felt Home Rule for Ireland to be wrong, until, that is, 1886, when he believed Home Rule to be the wish of the Irish people. His U-turn split his party. In 1893 he eventually got his Home Rule Bill through the Commons, but it was thrown out by the Lords. The following year he resigned.

FURTHER READING
LEES-MILNE, James, *The Bachelor Duke*, John Murray, 1991.

CHAPTER ELEVEN

THE COMPTONS

Kings and queens are crowned by the Archbishops of Canterbury. With the exception of Harold (who was crowned by the Archbishop of York in 1066), that is the rule. Only once has it been broken. In 1689 the Bishop of London crowned William of Orange King William III of England; and his wife, Mary Stuart, Mary II. The story of this break with holy tradition tells us a great deal about the traumatic events that settled once and for all the British political and constitutional paranoia over Roman Catholicism. It tells too of a seemingly unremarkable aristocratic family, and yet one which at times has been influential in the governing of England. That family is the Comptons.

The senior member of the Compton family is the Marquess of Northampton who is also the Earl of Compton; the Northampton titles date from the early seventeenth century. The 1st Earl, created in 1618, was William Compton. It is his son Spencer Compton, the 2nd Earl, who first attracts attention. Like his father, he was a royalist; but his loyalty to the monarch mattered more than his father's because he would find himself one of Charles I's strongest supporters in the Civil War.

Earlier, at the age of twenty-one in 1622, Spencer Compton had set out for Spain with the young Prince Charles and the extraordinary George Villiers, the newly created Duke of Buckingham. This was no ideal vacation: the trip to Madrid was the cause of enormous anxieties in the Spanish capital as well as London. Villiers was powerful in the political corridors of the king, James I, who loved him. He was also very rich, having married three years earlier Katherine Manners, the heiress to the Earl of Rutland's fortune. And finally he was insatiably ambitious. Villiers, unsurprisingly, had great powers of persuasion at court – hence the journey to Madrid. It was he who convinced James that he should marry his heir to a Spanish princess. Given the national fear of Catholics, the plan was more than bold – it was political dynamite.

This was to be an arranged marriage of the highest order. It would bring together Spain and England in some sort of alliance although, given previous examples, it was no guarantee of peace between the two countries. Quiet negotiations had been opened with the Spanish court for the betrothal of Charles and the Infanta Maria. No one was surprised, because the possibility of the marriage was by then six or seven years old.

The impetuous Villiers, with Compton in tow, talked the future Charles I into a wild scheme. They would travel to Spain in disguise and tell no one of their real mission, which was to have the young prince personally convince the Infanta of his charm and the suitability of their marriage. Compton was caught up in these youthful but dangerous enthusiasms, but could not have been unaware of the political sensitivities because Prince Charles would have had to convert to Catholicism if the match were to be agreed.

As it turned out, the visit to the Spanish court was a fiasco and the prince returned empty-handed. Young Compton, in the thick of the plot, was fortunate to have been taken ill shortly before this bizarre mission actually reached Madrid. If it had come to a marriage there could well have been an uprising against the monarch, with even more serious consequences than the one that was later to confront Charles I.

But as it happened Spencer Compton did himself no harm and stayed in favour with both James and, more importantly, Charles. Compton also remained a friend of George Villiers, who very quickly had made himself the most power-ful man in all England. It was he who arranged the marriage of Charles with Henrietta Maria of France in 1625 – a religious and political coupling that caused as much alarm as a marriage with Spain would have done. Compton became Master of the Robes and quietly established his own political base within the court, especially after the curious assassination of Villiers in 1628 by a mal-content, John Felton.

When the impasse between king and Parliament became obvious, Compton, by now the 2nd Earl of Northampton, followed Charles to York, where his sup-porters would, he supposed, protect him from the wrath of Parliament. This enraged Parliament and Compton was impeached. With notable exceptions, impeachment and threats of impeachment would be frequent ploys in the civil confrontation that was about to take place. Compton turned out to be a very competent commander of Charles's troops. He fought successfully in Warwickshire and, although he did not take Warwick Castle, managed to cut off the parliamentary re-supplies before attacking Banbury and stealing the guns from under the parliamentary noses.

Compton raised his own dragoons, consisting of a hundred minor aristocrats and gentlemen. Fleet and brave, they joined Prince Rupert, himself famous as a cavalryman in the successful skirmish at Worcester in September 1642.[1] The following month, Compton led his hundred dragoons alongside Charles I and Prince Rupert at Edgehill, the first big battle of the Civil War. It was, as most battles tended to be at that stage, indecisive. However, it was also the point at which Charles, with the advice of Prince Rupert and Compton and his other commanders, felt confident enough to reject any suggestions from the parliamen-tarians that enough was enough and that there should be peace.

The Compton family were irrevocably involved in the war. After Spencer Compton had taken Banbury, the king gave him the whole area about Banbury to defend, with instructions to expand his gentlemen of the horse into a full regiment. The command of the enlarged force was given to Compton's eldest son, Lord James, while his second son, Sir Charles, became the regiment's lieutenant colonel. The third son, William Compton, was given command of the castle at Banbury, which was immediately attacked by the parliamentarians; it was only the timely arrival of Prince Rupert's cavalry that saved the castle and the whole Compton family. For the moment the family was safe, with Spencer Compton, perhaps too proudly, at their head. King Charles had told him that it was an impossible task to hold on to Banbury and that he should burn it to the ground if he felt he could no longer defend it.

Spencer Compton was a brave man and extraordinarily proud. In March 1643 he set out for Stafford where the royalists were under siege. The parliamentarians sent extra forces under their famous commander Sir William Brereton, and Compton met them at Hopton Heath. If he had not been so bold, even arrogant, he might have survived. At the beginning of the battle he led the charge against the parliamentary cavalry, which he scattered. He then captured their artillery. But there were still the foot guards to contend with; they did not, perhaps could not, scatter too easily, and stood firm. Compton found himself outnumbered. He could probably have surrendered and later even have been let go. But to him, those who opposed the monarch were nothing but baseless rogues. He refused to give in, and so they killed him. There is a footnote which encapsulates the bitterness of this confrontation. When his eldest son, formerly Lord James Compton and now, sadly, the 3rd Earl of Northampton, asked for his father's body, the parliamentarians would only hand it over if their eight artillery pieces were returned.

The third son of the late earl, Sir William, was at the time of his father's death just eighteen. Perhaps by modern standards he possessed a bravery beyond his years, but then who did not in that terrible civil war? For example, at the taking of Banbury this teenager led his often frightened men from the front in such vicious skirmishes that he had two of his horses shot from under him. It was after the successful third attack that he had been given the command of Banbury Castle, and the king knighted him at Oxford shortly before Christmas 1643.

He now returned to Banbury, mindful of the king's instructions to his late father that if all seemed lost he should scorch the place to the very reed tops. In the summer of 1644 the parliamentary forces fell upon the town, ordering him to surrender or they would kill all the inhabitants. It is said that young William Compton's response was that, as long as anyone was left inside the castle, that person would defend to his own death the king's majesty. The parliamentarians set up a siege that was to last more than three months. Not once did William go to bed. At all hours of day and night he was to be seen patrolling Banbury, urging his troops to keep at least one eye open for the enemy. William Compton became an almost mystical figure, inspiring his men to resist the darkest doubts that must have assaulted them during the thirteen weeks of the siege.

On 26 October 1644 it was all over: his elder brother, the new 3rd Earl of Northampton, arrived and drove off the parliamentarians. It must seem a wonder that, with stories like that of the Comptons, the Civil War went the way it did. The Comptons were a perfect example of inspired and loyal commanders of men.

In that same year were fought the three important battles of Marston Moor, Lostwithiel and Newbury. The second Battle of Newbury, in October 1644, was probably a turning point for the parliamentarians. They should have been able to capture Charles and his inferior-sized force, but failed. The result was the establishment in February 1645 of a force of more than twenty thousand men, known as the New Model Army and commanded by Sir Thomas Fairfax. This new fighting machine was capable of the kind of co-ordination that had been obviously lacking in the early parliamentary forces. For example, at that second Battle of Newbury there were three separate armies that should have been brought together to capture Charles, but were not and so did not. The creation of the New Model Army was largely the doing of Oliver Cromwell, until then a minor figure. After Newbury, he forced through Parliament a bill called the Self-Denying Ordinance. The old generals were sent packing, Fairfax was given command and Cromwell became his deputy and Lieutenant-General of Horse – in command of the cavalry. This new military set-up was the prime factor in the royalist defeat in 1645 at Naseby, a battle sometimes seen as the beginning of democracy in England.

This was also the year of the execution of William Laud, Charles I's Archbishop of Canterbury. He had been impeached five years earlier by the Long Parliament, tried in 1644 under an atrocious form of justice and after the Bill of Attainder was, much to the disgrace of Charles, executed.[2]

The following year, 1646, Charles had surrendered to the Scots. What he did not realize was that the Scots would eventually hand him over to the English. For the Comptons, Charles's surrender meant that the armies had to surrender to the parliamentarians. But they avoided imprisonment; and in fact, in May 1646 the terms of surrender were not unreasonable: they would be able to keep their weapons and horses and be given safe conduct to wherever they wanted to go. This was the period when the royalists and the parliamentarians were trying to bargain their way out of the confrontation that Parliament still appeared keen to avoid.

Two months after the Comptons had surrendered Parliament offered Charles I peace proposals, known as the Propositions of Newcastle because at that point he was still a prisoner of the Scots in that city. There were nineteen major points to be agreed, including Parliament's control of the army and the prosecution of Charles's leading supporters, including the Comptons. The king rather hoped that he could make good allies of the Scots, who were less than enamoured of the parliamentarians. He failed, as did the Propositions.

It was at this point, 1647, that the Scots, fed up with the whole matter and playing their own double game, handed over Charles to the parliamentarians. In the same year the king was imprisoned in Carisbrooke Castle on the Isle of Wight, although he subsequently escaped. In 1648, the Civil War started again, this time with Charles having made some agreement to set up a Presbyterian Church in England in return for Scottish help in getting him back to power. The whole thing was a nonsense, as was made clear in August 1648 at the Battle of Preston. It was here that Cromwell proved for the first time his right to lead the parliamentarians, when his brilliant tactics and command of the New Model Army destroyed the Scottish attempt to restore Charles to his throne.

Young Sir William Compton, still only twenty-three, was now a royalist general and present at the seige of Colchester. This was no Banbury. Fairfax was now well organized and well drilled, and even Compton found little to inspire the resistance. The siege was so severe that Compton's men, knowing that they could never expect to escape alive, first killed off their horses for their meat, then ate the dogs of the town and finally the very grasses about the grain stores. They were forced to surrender. Cromwell rather admired Compton: he called him a 'godly' cavalier.

He did not suffer, as did Charles I outside the Banqueting House in Whitehall.[3] In fact, Compton escaped and survived the Commonwealth and Cromwell. He became a member of a small and dangerous group of ardent royalists known as the Sealed Knot (a title readopted in the twentieth century by enthusiasts whose hobby it is to re-enact the battles of the Civil War). Compton, Lord Bellasis, Sir John Grenville, Sir John Russell, the Earl of Oxford and Sir Richard Willis were the main movers in attempting, on eight occasions between 1652 and 1659, to bring Charles II to the throne. Time and again they found themselves in prison for their pains.

When Charles did return in 1660, Sir William Compton became a member of Parliament for Cambridge and, for good measure, Charles made him Master General of the Ordnance. Three years later, at the age of just thirty-eight, he collapsed and died in London's Drury Lane.

William was Spencer Compton's third son. The sixth son, Henry, was probably the most interesting and influential of all the Northampton family. Henry was not born until 1632 and yet, even though not much more than a child, he had been involved in the Civil War and once claimed that he had actually fought in it. He was sent off to Oxford at the age of seventeen in 1649, the year in which Charles I was beheaded. For three years he studied divinity before being sent to Italy, where he was schooled in state and ecclesiastical law.

Henry Compton kept away from England until Charles II was restored to the throne in 1660. Although inclined to the Church, he now got a commission with the Royal Horse Guards in a similar manner to his late father – but in different circumstances, of course. By most accounts he was a good soldier, but he really did not like the profession and in 1662 took holy orders. Four years later he was rector of the village of Cottenham in Cambridgeshire. Not long after that, he was a canon of Christ Church, Oxford and appeared at the celebrations to honour benefactors of what was then the new theatre in Oxford, the Sheldonian. From this point Henry Compton was recognized as a serious churchman, although, according to the diarist John Evelyn, 'not much of a preacher'. There were many who, for reasons of personality and sometimes politics, were indeed indifferent pulpit performers. That did not stop Henry Compton, at the age of forty-one, becoming Bishop of Oxford in 1674 and, shortly afterwards, Dean of the Chapel Royal and Bishop of London.

How was it that Compton could win such advancement in the Church, particularly as he does not appear to have been either a strong personality or an academic theologian? There are probably three reasons, each of which tells us more about the ways in which a few families influenced so much in British history.

First and foremost was the fact that he was a Compton, that his father had been such a celebrated royalist and that the family had continued along such loyal lines. Second, he was a very close friend of Thomas Danby, the Earl of Danby and the man who would be the 1st Duke of Leeds. As we have seen, it was Danby who had negotiated the marriage of Mary, daughter of the Duke of York (later James II), with Prince William of Orange and was thus close to the throne. Third, Compton's anti-Catholic views were so strong and so publicly expressed that, whether he liked it or not, his persuasion resulted in much political credit – not something he openly sought. There was a drawback to his open hostility towards Catholics. The Duke of York had recently become a convert and, like many converts, was so adamant in the expression of his beliefs that in 1673 he refused to swear the constitutional oath against Catholicism, resigned all his offices, including that of Lord High Admiral, and married a prominent Catholic, Mary of Modena.[4]

Moreover, the Duke of York was never entirely happy with the influence of Compton in Charles II's court and the way in which the bishop became responsible for the education of the Duke's daughters, Anne and Mary – both of whom would become queens. It is curious that the Duke of York did not or could not dismiss his children's tutor. There could be no doubt that Henry Compton was making sure that the princesses were being brought up good Protestants. Such was his influence that Compton got rid of Mary of Modena's personal courtier because he was a Catholic influence. In 1676 it was Compton who officiated at the confirmation ceremony of Anne and Mary. It was he too, who married first Princess Mary and Prince William of Orange in 1677 and then, in 1683, Princess Anne to her Danish prince, George.

By this time, Compton's authority was clear and he appears to have had his own way – with one important exception. When the Archbishop of Canterbury, Gilbert Sheldon,[5] died in 1677, Compton believed that he should succeed him. So too did his influential friend the Earl of Danby. In terms of Church dignity there was every reason for him to do so, for Sheldon had been Bishop of London himself before his own translation to Canterbury. It was probable that the Duke of

York blocked Compton's preferment. Moreover, might there still have been a feeling that, in spite of the Protestant nature of the Church, Compton was not suitable because he was married?

The appointment to Canterbury was almost entirely political, as confirmed by the fact that Compton failed to get the job when it came up again. It was one thing being anti-Catholic; it was quite another balancing his strong Protestant views with those of the dissenters in his own Church. Thus he was now upbraided, sometimes wickedly so, by members of his own Church because of his moderate attitude towards the Nonconformists.

The importance of the schisms within the Church of England should not be underestimated. Nonconformists, sometimes called Dissenters, were so called because they refused to conform to the ideals and liturgy of the established Church of England. So disruptive was their influence that from the time of Elizabeth I they had been on occasions prosecuted. After the Civil War started in 1642 the Nonconformists, particularly the Baptists and Congregationalists, became increasingly influential.[6] The Nonconformists were protected during Cromwell's Commonwealth, but under the 1662 Act of Uniformity, which became law two years after Charles II came to the throne, they were not allowed to worship. The later Act of Toleration of 1689, the year after the Glorious Revolution, restored their rights.

Thus we can see that Compton was treading on controversial, if not always hallowed, ground in his belief that the Church of England should moderate its position towards Nonconformists. In 1683, pamphleteers demanded that Compton should be removed from office because of his views. That he survived all this showed that he must have been well supported among other courtiers and that the anti-Catholic feeling had not lessened. None of this much impressed Charles II or the future James II. It is said that, when Charles was dying, he acknowledged no comfort from the words of his Bishop of London. Here were two men of quite opposite personalities: one, warm and frivolous; the other, apparently cold and uncompromising.

Once James II was on the throne, he exercised his hostility towards Compton. Since James had refused to swear a constitutional oath against the Catholics there was now a confrontation between Church and monarch and a test of Compton's position on Nonconformism. In 1685, the year James came to the throne, the king wanted to abolish the Test Act, a means of preventing Nonconformists holding high office. Such people had, for example, to be Anglicans, worship in Anglican churches, swear the monarch's supremacy as head of the Church and, particularly, reject the Catholic doctrine of transubstantiation – the Roman Catholic belief in the actual conversion of bread and wine into the body and blood of Jesus Christ. In Parliament, Compton spoke against James, insisting that the very constitution of the realm would suffer. Little wonder, then, that James relieved him of his post as Dean of the Chapel Royal and took away his membership of the privy council.

In 1686 Compton was further outraged when James prohibited what he thought were anti-Catholic sermons. John Sharp, the Dean of Norwich Cathedral, ignored the king and produced a tirade against Roman Catholicism; the king ordered Compton to suspend Sharp. Compton's skill as a diplomat and politician was now tested to the full. He told the king that Sharp had not actually broken any law and made it known that he had asked the dean to be, for the moment, a little more circumspect. James would have none of it; he called on his Lord Chancellor to commit Compton before a tribunal for refusing to obey the monarch. It happened that the Lord Chancellor of the day was the most notorious judge in English history, George Jeffreys, who was unlikely to listen sympathetically to Compton. Nor did he, refusing to let Compton see any of the written evidence against him. Compton declared that, as Bishop of London, he had certain rights and should be tried by his peers, not by Lord Chancellor Jeffreys. Compton was suspended from his bishopric.

Perhaps what the king had not anticipated was the level of public feeling in favour of Compton. The diarist John Evelyn observed that the proceedings had been universally resented. Moreover, William of Orange made it clear that he disagreed with the action against Compton and thought his father-in-law, James II, was wrong. William's wife, Mary, wrote to her father asking him to relax what she privately saw as a persecution of Compton, her old tutor and dear chaplain. James told his daughter to mind her own business. This was just two years before the invasion of William and Mary to usurp James's throne. The king was not unaware of what would be in the mind of his son-in-law; nor was he blind to the fact that the events of the tribunal and the protests of Compton and his lawyers had been circulated in Dutch for a wider and more dangerous audience.

For the moment there was nothing Compton could do other than literally to retire to his garden and tend his plants. He was a keen botanist, an interest shared by many Comptons through the centuries. Henry Compton was more than a casual gardener, for he built Fulham Palace and laid out its great gardens. He also became the official collector of plants sent from the colonies; it was he who introduced to England the tulip tree and the honey locust. Another, more modern connection with splendid gardens was initiated at this time, though in the most roundabout manner. One of the bishop's employees at Fulham Palace went off to design the gardens at Newbury Hall in Yorkshire, then owned by the Blacket family. Almost three centuries later the Comptons bought Newbury Hall, and their aristocratic green fingers continued work started in the seventeenth century by their famous clerical ancestor's man.

It was inevitable that, when emissaries sped between Holland and England in 1687, Compton would be involved in the plans to overthrow the Catholic James II and replace him with his Protestant daughter, Mary. (It should be remembered that it was, constitutionally, Mary who was coming to the throne, even though the means of doing so would be her husband, Prince William of Orange, and that it would be tacitly understood that William would be king with her.) Compton's personal warmth towards Mary and his regard for her husband were clearly important at this stage. Equally, Compton was important to the plans of William of Orange. The prince believed that the bishop would be able to square many of the dissenting clergy who might otherwise have been nervous of the consequences of this elaborate palace coup.

Compton, again through his close friend the Earl of Danby, became one of the secret inner circle of revolutionaries who met at the Earl of Shrewsbury's house. On 30 June 1688 Compton put his name alongside that of the six other conspirators to the letter to be sent to William of Orange entreating him to invade England.

Word got out that Compton was part of the plot against King James, and he was twice brought before the king to explain what was going on. Twice he denied any knowledge. Princess Anne, Mary's sister, was thought to be in great danger. Compton smuggled her out of London and was by her side all the way to Nottingham. It was at this point that Cavendish, the Earl of Devonshire, met up with the vulnerable group of Princess Anne, Bishop Compton and just forty horsemen to protect them (see Chapter 10) and foiled their plans. Once more a Compton buckled on a sword to protect a monarch, but not the existing one. James fled. On 30 December 1688, Bishop Compton gave William of Orange communion in London.

Compton had not quite pulled the rest of the clergy together, but such was his political strength that his and that of Bishop Trelawny of Bristol were considered the important votes in the House of Lords when they agreed with the majority that a king should occupy the vacant throne. In other words, there was still nervousness that what was happening had been inspired by a small group and amounted to a constitutional outrage in offering the throne elsewhere, whatever the lineage of Prince William and Princess Mary.

It is often thought that the whole country was against James II and was only too eager to line the streets to welcome William and Mary. Moreover, because of the strong anti-Catholic feeling, some of it based as much on political and military fear as on religious grounds, it is thought that the whole Church would be for a Protestant monarch. This is not so. For example, the Archbishop of Canterbury, William Sancroft, refused to acknowledge the new monarchs. He was the leader of the so-called nonjurors – clergymen, as well as senior laymen, who could not bring themselves to swear an oath of allegiance to William and Mary because they believed it to be morally wrong. They had after all sworn an oath of allegiance to James II: what value was that oath if it could be so easily discarded?

It should not be forgotten that the Church had believed for centuries, and would continue to believe, in the importance of the consecration of the monarch. Every English monarch up to and including Elizabeth II has been anointed with consecrated oils to signify God's blessing and the divine right to be monarch. Sancroft, eight of his fellow bishops and perhaps as many as four hundred priests could not so easily lay aside their oath relating to the divine right of kings.

This was the reason that 11 April 1689 was the only occasion on which an archbishop failed to crown an English monarch. Henry Compton, Bishop of London and once more Dean of the Chapel Royal, crowned William and Mary joint king and queen at Westminster Abbey. Sancroft was sacked – though it was not Compton who became archbishop in his place. John Tillotson, the Dean of Canterbury, described by Gilbert Burnet as the best preacher of his age, was preferred (a small irony was that Tillotson was married to a niece of Oliver Cromwell). Compton never quite recovered from what he regarded as a snub and out-and-out politicking by the Whigs.

He continued as Bishop of London, and when William III died and James II's daughter became queen in 1702 he received even greater favour. Queen Anne cared very much for Compton. She had never forgotten his kindnesses and loyalties through some of the most difficult years in her life. And so he ended his days as a continuing influence on the monarchy and, by now a Tory, on the political goings and comings at Westminster.

He died in July 1713, at the age of eighty-one at his house at Fulham. Gilbert Burnet believed that Compton was too easily influenced by other people and was therefore essentially a weak man. This suggests why he never made the final stretch to Canterbury. Yet it is difficult to reconcile this view with the influence that he exerted on such strong-minded individuals who were so prominent at this stage of English history. Perhaps Danby and Prince William thought Compton malleable enough to do their bidding and bring the Church with him when their revolutionary time came; yet they must also have thought Compton strong enough to do so. On balance, it seems that the 2nd Earl of Northampton's sixth son was probably not a leader, yet he was one of those intriguing figures upon whom leaders rely to remain in power.

Another Spencer Compton was the third son of the 3rd Earl of Northampton. He was born in 1673 and so grew up in the atmosphere of the new English political and constitutional court. The Protestant monarchy was established and the country was moving towards a form of government which would be recognizable today. It included the moment in 1721 when Robert Walpole became the first Prime Minister of Britain.[7]

Compton, member for the rotten borough of Eye in Suffolk, had swapped political sides at an early stage of his parliamentary career. The political ideologies in the late seventeenth and early eighteenth centuries were not so easily separated as they would be in, say, the mid-nineteenth and twentieth centuries. Modern readers who grew up with easily distinguishable Labour and Conservative viewpoints became, after the 1997 election, hard pushed to see much difference between the two main political parties. It was really more a question of which party could convince the country that it was best able to implement very similar policies; thus it would be not too difficult for, say, a Tory supporter to switch to New Labour. Later it might even be possible for that process to be reversed. So it was in the seventeenth and, to some extent, the early eighteenth century. To describe someone as a Whig or a Tory did not mean that they were set in that mould for the rest of their political lives. Issues that might have easily divided the aristocracy – the effective ruling class in the seventeenth century – would include, for example, attitudes towards Catholicism and the authority of the monarchy, including his or her divine right – in the true sense of the term – to rule. The Comptons had been Whigs, then had become Tories. Now, Spencer Compton abandoned the Tory ideas of his dynasty and returned to the Whigs. In 1705 he became chairman of the parliamentary committee of privileges and elections. Two years later he was appointed treasurer to Prince George of Denmark, the husband of Queen Anne who had come to power on the death of William III in 1702.

This was the period of the Duke of Marlborough's great victories at Blenheim, Ramillies, Oudenarde and Malplaquet. It was the time when the monarchy made its last stab at absolute authority: in 1708 Queen Anne vetoed a bill to restructure the Scottish militia, but no monarch was ever allowed such power again. It was the time, also in 1713, when Minorca became British, the period when the *Tatler*, *Spectator* and *John Bull* were first published; and George Frederick Handel came to live in England.

Queen Anne died in 1714 and so the British throne (following the Act of Union with Scotland in 1707 it was no longer simply the throne of England and Ireland) passed to a German, George I. The Hanoverian age had begun.[8]

In 1715 Parliament met for the first time under the reign of George I. Spencer Compton, by now MP for Sussex, was elected Speaker of the House. As was the custom for a new Speaker, he expressed his preferment in modest manner – the Speaker is traditionally dragged to the chair. Compton showed further reluctance in his acceptance speech, protesting that he had neither 'memory to retain judgement to collect, nor skill to guide their debates'. The king, who could not speak English and therefore was unlikely to listen to those parliamentary deliberations even if Compton had had such skills, confirmed him in the appointment. In fact Compton was not being unduly modest – he was being quite honest. So for twelve years – the entire reign of George I – Compton remained Speaker and, supposedly, influential backstairs man at Westminster. But he left no great mark. It may simply have been that he was not an exceptional parliamentarian. He certainly had intellectual limitations, although politically he became very close to actually running the country.

When George II became king in 1727 (incidentally, the year Isaac Newton died) it was Compton's job to produce the first declaration for the king. In spite of the fact that he had been Speaker for twelve years, he did not know the form of words to be used. It was Robert Walpole who had to write the declaration for him; Compton thanked him very much, but not sheepishly, and happily took the document along to the king for him to read in public.

George I and George II were completely taken with Compton. The latter thought him such a fine chap and such a good friend that he wanted him to replace Walpole as Prime Minister. The king may have liked the idea; his queen,

Caroline of Ansbach, most certainly did not. Walpole, who was friendly with Caroline, used her to get at the king. The king still pushed Compton to form an administration; but Queen Caroline and her friends won the day – helped, ironically, by Compton himself. Just as he had confessed that he really was not up to being Speaker of the House, he now confided in George II that he felt he was not best suited to what he saw as a somewhat arduous task. The king was disappointed, Caroline triumphant, Walpole not a little relieved. They all agreed that Compton was a nice man and he was created Baron Wilmington in 1728.

Walpole did not abandon Compton who, after all, did have influence at the highest levels – particularly with the king, who was not always Walpole's greatest fan – and with other peers. In 1730 Walpole asked Compton if he would like to be Lord Privy Seal; when he accepted, he was further raised in the peerage as the Earl of Wilmington and Viscount Pevensey. He then became Lord President of the Council. The king showed his further appreciation by creating Compton a Knight of the Garter at the first opportunity when one of the existing holders died.[9]

Queen Caroline had never much admired Compton's political skills and had kept him out of office. She was, too, a great champion of Walpole, so had some influence in keeping him in office. In 1737 she died, an event which Compton saw – as did his supporters – as an opportunity for him to think more positively about becoming Prime Minister. He was a member of the Cabinet and very much represented the views of George II, a warlike monarch. George would shortly become the last British monarch to lead his troops into battle, at Dettingen in 1743. This king, as had George I, saw great advantage in being monarch of Britain – as opposed to mere Elector of Hanover – because he could use British forces in his battles in continental Europe. This situation seemed to contravene the 1701 Act of Settlement, which forbade the monarch to send armies in defence of foreign parts not owned by the crown unless Parliament had sanctioned it first; but by then the general view was that, if the political decision to go to war was taken in Parliament, no serious legal argument could be put by the constitutional lawyers.

In 1739 this whole matter was put to the test in Cabinet. The king wanted to go to war with Spain. Moreover, looming was the eight-year War of the Austrian Succession, to which Britain seemed inevitably drawn. The war with Spain in 1739 involved one of the more bizarre moments in eighteenth-century British history. To understand it we have to go back eight years to 1731. This was the time when the British were harrying the Spanish in an attempt to break into what was then Spain's monopoly over trade with Latin America. Apparently the Spanish had captured a British sailor called Captain Jenkins and during the fracas his ear was cut off. A bottle containing this purported extremity of skin and gristle was shown to the House of Commons, which, as might be imagined, expressed proper indignation. The real story of the War of Jenkins' Ear was trade, and what happened was that the Anglo-Spanish grudge merged into the bigger picture, the War of the Austrian Succession. This conflict grumbled away from the Atlantic through Europe and even to India.

Behind it was the question of who had the right to rule the Hapsburg Austrian Empire, which was not an insignificant debate. In 1713 the Emperor Charles VI announced to his ministers that on his death all the Hapsburg lands would go to a daughter, should he fail to have a surviving male heir. His son, then a sickly child, died the following year, 1714. Three years later, Charles's daughter, Maria Theresa, was born. Most of the European powers had to agree to his edict because they each had economic interests in the efficiency of the Empire, as well as territorial ambitions (or concerns that others did), and thus were effectively being asked to declare their support. It also meant that the Emperor would probably have to make certain political, territorial and economic agreements and concessions with those countries in order for him to get his wishes accepted. It took a long time, but by the early 1730s most of the states had gone along with Charles VI's pronouncement. However, when he died in 1740 Frederick II of Prussia saw his opportunity to grab the Empire and backed out of the agreement. Thus started the War of the Austrian Succession. The Prussians began the war by taking Silesia, which was an Austrian province. George II came in on the side of Maria Theresa. The French, who inevitably were not on England's side, were opponents along with Spain. England was not only fighting the French over the rights of Maria Theresa, but was also taking the opportunity to battle with them in North America and in India where they had similar interests.

Back in London, in 1739 the Cabinet was split over going to war with Spain and had not yet come to the point of taking on the world. The king wanted to fight Spain; Walpole did not; Compton thought whatever the king thought.

The move to get rid of Walpole was unstoppable. Once again Compton was reluctant to get into the more messy areas of palace revolution. The prime mover was John Carteret, who for more than a decade had been battling against Walpole's authority. To get him out of the way, he had been sent to Ireland as Lord Lieutenant – as we have seen throughout this book, a common enough practice. Now it was he, Carteret, who was urging Britain to take Maria Theresa's side in the War of the Austrian Succession. One of the accusations against him – for he was not a universally popular man – was that he was no longer English, nor British, but Hanoverian. Compton too was seen as very much in George II's pocket. Carteret had ambitions to be Prime Minister (and nearly did so in 1746), but had to settle for an earldom. He was created Earl Granville and more or less disappeared from British politics. The hapless Compton did not disappear.

In 1741, Carteret had laid down a motion of no confidence in Walpole. Compton, who was a Cabinet minister, should have voted against the motion; he did not. The following year Walpole was defeated in the House of Commons and so his administration fell. Here at last was Compton's second chance of becoming Prime Minister. Imagine the consternation in British politics: Walpole was deeply unpopular; there was war with Spain; the king was fighting on the continent. There was a great need for a calming influence, and Compton's friends told him that his hour had come: he should not make the mistake of being too cautious, as he had fourteen years earlier.

Compton did indeed become Prime Minister. It was hardly more than a charade, yet it was to last from January 1742 until July 1743. In truth the main characters were Carteret, the Duke of Newcastle and Lord Pulteney. William Pulteney, now Earl of Bath, had long been Walpole's enemy. It was he who managed to bring the different groups together to form the administration supposedly run by Compton. Everyone knew that poor Compton was neither a leader nor a political intellectual; he was not the first who needed to be reminded to catch up with the political parade as he was supposed to be its master. Consequently he became an object of fun, particularly as he uttered very few words upon which ordinary men could hang.

Yet he was only disliked by his political opponents. Many people had a simple regard for this man of unremarkable habits and less memorable achievement. Even in his personal life, Compton left no mark. He never took a wife, and when he died at the age of seventy, in 1743, his only distinction was that he was one of the few prime ministers to die in office. As he had no children, his titles became extinct.

However, his death did provide a link with an earlier part of our story. Compton's estates had to go somewhere: they therefore passed to his brother George, the 4th Earl of Northampton. This earl had a great-granddaughter called Elizabeth who married the Earl of Burlington. He, as we have seen, was Lord George Cavendish. And that is how the Wilmington estates came into the Cavendish dynasty. Although only connected through the family name, there is a link between Spencer Compton and a later member of the family, Charles Compton, the 9th Earl of Northampton. In 1812 Spencer Percival became the only British Prime Minister to have been assassinated. The 9th Earl's second son, Spencer, was given Percival's vacant seat, Northampton. The link of course, was the unfortunate deaths of two premiers in office – a rare event.

The member for Northampton was by all accounts a short-tempered character who often saw the practice of politics in a simplified manner. His views on taxation, for example, might be summed up as taking a straight percentage from a person's income and nothing more, whereas the practice developed in the eighteenth and early nineteenth centuries was what today would be called indirect taxation. He was a lawyer who was probably ahead of his time, especially on the vexed question of what were and were not seditious meetings and who were and were not classified as aliens. Compton was also one of the group of men who rallied about William Wilberforce in his long-term battle to change Britain's policies on Africa and slavery.

Once more, here is an example of a member of a distinguished and influential family who remains unremarkable, partly because other members of the family were so memorable. To follow the examples of one ancestor who was influential in appointing a foreign prince as king of England and then crowning him, another

14 A cartoon of Lord John Russell, from *Vanity Fair*, 1869.
BRIDGEMAN ART LIBRARY / VICTORIA & ALBERT MUSEUM, LONDON

15 Bertrand Russell (3rd Earl) and his wife (Patricia Helen Spencer) with their baby son in the garden of their home at Hartling, Hampshire, May 1937.
THE HULTON ARCHIVE

16 Portrait thought to be of Catherine Howard, fifth wife of Henry VIII, by Hans Holbein the Younger.

17 Henry Howard, the Earl of Surrey, son of the 3rd Duke of Norfolk by Guillim Stretes, 1546.

ANNO·1546
ÆTATIS·SVÆ·29

SAT
SVPER
EST

HENRY HOWARD EARL OF SVRREY

18 John Graham, 1st Viscount Dundee by David Paton.
19 John Dalrymple, 2nd Earl of Stair by an unknown artist.
20 John Stuart, 3rd Earl of Bute by Sir Joshua Reynolds, 1773.

18

19

21 Portrait of William Pitt the Younger by John Hoppner.
BRIDGEMAN ART LIBRARY/RAFAEL VALLS GALLERY, LONDON
22 Lord Carrington, then Foreign Secretary, with Prime Minister Margaret Thatcher during the European Summit in Luxembourg, April 1980.
THE HULTON ARCHIVE/KEYSTONE COLLECTION

Overleaf
23 Lord Rothermere with former Prime Minister, David Lloyd George in 1927.
THE HULTON ARCHIVE
24 Lord Beaverbrook celebrating his 83rd birthday with Sir Winston Churchill in 1961.
THE HULTON ARCHIVE

23

24

who was a gallant soldier and yet another who, even by default, was Prime Minister is something of a tall order. There was no indication that the 10th Earl was heading for a particularly celebrated career.

And yet if we look at Compton's life outside Westminster, indeed outside England, we see another aspect of influence. In 1820, having lost his seat in the general election of that year, Compton went to live in Italy, a country still fragmented into a number of small, often repressive, states. Italy was not yet a single State. That didn't come about until 1861. The land of the Italians was very much that of broken States which would take another forty years to be in some ways united. For ten years Compton's estate became a focal point for revolutionaries and others who had been persecuted in that land, and Compton himself achieved fame as someone who understood the problems of those who suffered at the hands of cruel regimes. He might have stayed longer if his wife, Margaret, had not died in Rome.

In the spring of 1830 he returned to England and Parliament, and yet again made no particular mark. His name appears on few boards of recognition, except that he was once president of the Royal Society and one of the first presidents of the Geological Society; and in the family he is still remembered as a poet.

But a sense of political life was never very far from the Comptons and some of their relations. For example, through marriage the Earls of Ripon are related to them. It was the 1st Earl (created in 1833) who was Prime Minister in the nineteenth century. Before he was ennobled he was known as F. J. Robinson and became President of the Board of Trade and then Chancellor of the Exchequer, all between 1818 and 1828. He was very influential in getting rid of the old and prohibitive Navigation Acts, which had first appeared in 1382 and were designed to protect English shipping from commercial rather than military marauders. In the mid-seventeenth century the Acts declared it unlawful for foreign ships to carry cargoes from English colonies and, in order to stop people circumventing this legislation, at least three-quarters of merchant crews had to be English. Moreover, because the Dutch were clever and persistent traders and able to breach this legislation (it was very difficult to enforce), an amendment to the Navigation Act of 1660 stated that some colonial cargoes could be shipped only to England.

If this attempt at restrictive practice appears today as less than bright, it has to be remembered that by the early seventeenth century the whole concept of the country's economy was based on trade. This economic philosophy, known as mercantilism, meant that customs and excise duties, direct taxes and restrictions on transport provided the most swingeing means to control economies since the introduction of the staples at the time of Edward I (see Chapter 9). Robinson (he was not created viscount until 1827) worked hard to repeal the Navigation Acts, which now ran counter to the growing philosophy of free trade, a phrase that was to keep emerging in British political debate for two centuries.

In 1827, Robinson was created Viscount Goderich and briefly became Prime Minister. It is doubtful whether anyone could have held the Tory Party together, and in January 1828 he resigned. He is probably better remembered at the Board of Trade and the Treasury. His time at the latter prompted the political and social commentator William Cobbett to call him Goody Goderich. In 1833 he was ennobled as the Earl of Ripon.

His son, George Ripon, was not a Tory. He became a Liberal MP and then had successful junior ministries right up until 1905 when he was made Lord Privy Seal. He was also the second Viceroy of India, between 1880 and 1884 (until 1876 the post was that of Governor General). The Comptons today may not have political bishops, royalist commanders and modest political figures among their numbers, yet the present marquess and earl (the 7th Marquess and 15th Earl), Spencer Compton, is known for his wise counsel in the quieter corridors of power. The botanical interests have continued. Perhaps the instincts of Henry Compton, the warring seventeenth-century Bishop of London and sometime botanist, stir in the earl's younger brother. Jamie Compton is a botanist of considerable standing at Reading University and his wife, Tania, the gardening editor of *House and Garden* magazine. But there is no bishop lurking in the family to make ecclesiastical or constitutional history.

NOTES

1 Prince Rupert of the Rhine (1619–82). His mother was Elizabeth of Bohemia, Charles I's sister. He lived in exile and was effectively a royal mercenary, which is why he joined his uncle, Charles I, in the Civil War. When he was not in the saddle swinging his sabre, or trying his hand at piracy against Cromwell's merchant ships, Prince Rupert was something of an amateur scientist and artistic figure who introduced the craft of mezzotint into English printing.

2 'Attainder' is derived from the Norman French *attaindre*, meaning 'to convict'. A Bill of Attainder was also known as a Bill of Pains and Penalties, and the first one was put before Parliament in the mid-fifteenth century. Monarchs tended to use them to get rid of political opponents, because these Bills removed the rights of anyone sentenced to death or to be outlawed (to be put beyond the protection of the law). This is what happened to Laud, thus there was no final appeal.

3 Charles I was beheaded on 30 January 1649. The execution was witnessed by a crowd which included the diarist Samuel Pepys, who could clearly see it. The irony was that the Banqueting Hall had been built by Inigo Jones for James I, Charles's father.

4 Their son, James Francis Edward Stuart, became known as the Old Pretender after Mary had fled abroad with him following the Glorious Revolution of 1688. The Old Pretender's youngest son, Henry, was the last Stuart claimant to the throne and died childless in 1807.

5 After whom the Sheldonian Theatre in Oxford is named.

6 The first Baptist church was established in Amsterdam in 1609 by an Englishman, John Smyth, who believed that Born Again Christians would come together through adult baptism. In 1580, Robert Browne opened the first Congregational church in Norwich. The Congregationalists were Calvinists and, in their early days, suffered terrible persecution. Two leaders, Henry Barrow and John Penry, were executed for their Nonconformist beliefs.

7 Sir Robert Walpole (1676–1745), later Earl of Orford. He was the Whig leader of the Commons, imprisoned in 1712 by the Tories for allegedly being involved in corruption.

8 Sophia, Electress of Hanover, also died in 1714. If she had not, she would have been the first Hanoverian monarch of England. Under the Act of Settlement, if both William III and Queen Anne died without leaving an heir, the throne of England and Ireland would go to Sophia or her descendants as long as they were Protestant.

9 The Most Noble Order of the Garter, the senior Order of Chivalry, founded by Edward III in 1348. The first members were Edward III and the Prince of Wales, the Black Prince. Edward declared that there should be twenty-four Companion Knights, all of whom were military men. Their patron saint would be St George, and today the banners of the Knights rest in St George's Chapel at Windsor Castle. In the fourteenth century George was seen less as patron saint of England and more as patron saint of soldiers – a decision made by Richard I, Coeur de Lion, at the end of the twelfth century. The Order is limited to the original number, and therefore a new knight may not be installed until an existing one has died.

FURTHER READING

COWARD, Barry, *The Stuart Age*, Longman, 1994.

HARRIS, Tim, *Politics under the Later Stuarts*, Longman, 1993.

JONES, J. R., *The Revolution of 1688 in England*, Weidenfeld and Nicolson, 1972.

KENYON, J. P., *The Nobility in the Revolution of 1688*, Hull Press, 1963.

CHAPTER TWELVE

THE RUSSELLS

When we read about the Godwines, the Cecils and the Churchills, we almost expect them to be examples of great and powerful families. Even if we do not know their exact contributions to English history, we have a sense that they are sometimes sinister, sometimes glorious characters in Britain's historical tapestry. And then there are others who at first glance appear to be standing in the shadows, their contributions often hidden by the personalities and historical images of others. So it is with the Russells.

For the general reader the only famous Russell was Bertrand, the twentieth-century philosopher. Yet he was a member of one of the most important Whig families. They were descended from a wine merchant who traded with the French in the early 1400s; he was Henry Russell, who, in between importing tuns, became member of Parliament for Weymouth. After him came politicians, naval commanders, generals, writers, philosophers, earls, marquesses and, most famously, the Dukes of Bedford, who in the seventeenth century built the well-known family seat, Woburn Abbey in Bedfordshire.

Like many aristocratic families with land in London they gave their names to famous thoroughfares. As the eighteenth century turned into the nineteenth, Francis Russell built Tavistock Square and neighbouring Russell Square. Another Francis was responsible for the development of Covent Garden. Later, the family was linked with the very twentieth-century Sackville-Wests, the family name of the Earls De La Warr. It should not be thought that the Russell family, during its five hundred years of almost continuous involvement with monarchy, political thought and moral leadership, was ever boring.

For example, the 1st Earl of Bedford, born in *c*.1486, was John Russell, a courtier of Henry VIII and one of his most trusted envoys, whose name is found time and again in the archives of discreet negotiations abroad. He carried out the king's wishes well, and in 1554 was entrusted with one of the most delicate journeys of the time. Mary Tudor, 'Bloody Mary', was by now on the throne and had decided that she would marry Philip II of Spain. This decision, coupled with her fervent belief that she could restore Catholicism to its former authority in her kingdom, was greeted with widespread anger.

One consequence was Wyatt's rebellion, when in January 1554 Sir Thomas Wyatt led three thousand Kentish men to London in revolt against the idea. He was determined that the young Princess Elizabeth should replace Mary on the throne. But the queen was made of sterner stuff than Wyatt had imagined, and his rebels were beaten by Mary's loyal forces. Wyatt and dozens of his immediate followers were executed. So too were another Protestant claimant, Lady Jane Grey, and her husband. Princess Elizabeth was sent to the Tower. Both spiritually and militarily, Mary Tudor was not inclined to take prisoners. It was she who in 1555 had the bishops Latimer and Ridley burned at the stake, followed by Cranmer the following spring. Of course, much that happened in these times and circumstances did so in the name of the monarch rather than by his or her direct command; so Mary should perhaps not be too readily blamed for all the cruelties committed in her name. It meant also that surrounding her in positions of great power were those who relied on absolutism and intrigue to maintain their authority.

So it is clear that the position of John Russell in 1554 must have been enormously important, when he was commanded by the queen to go to Spain and return with Philip II for her marriage. Little wonder that we find him as Comptroller of the Royal Household and Lord Privy Seal. Equally, the way in which he gathered wealth as well as influence for the Russell family should not be surprising. This Russell accumulated Covent Garden and Long Acre in London, Woburn Abbey in Bedfordshire and Tavistock in Devon during a triumphant as well as a trying time for a family which would be celebrated for its Protestant values and Whiggish politics.

His son, Francis Russell, later the 2nd Earl of Bedford, was very much involved in the Lady Jane Grey affair. She was married in 1553, much to her anger, to Lord Guildford Dudley, the Duke of Northumberland's son (see Chapter 6). Northumberland had persuaded the then king, Edward VI, that she should be queen on his death, and on 9 July that year she was so proclaimed. Northumberland gathered supporters to enforce his daughter-in-law's claim to the throne against that of Mary Tudor. Francis Russell was a participant in Northumberland's plans. When they failed, he escaped from England and remained abroad until Elizabeth became queen, when he came back and received a series of minor offices. The interest in this Russell was the family's continuing involvement in schemes to preserve the Protestant character of England and particularly to keep Catholics off the throne.

The 2nd Earl's youngest son, William, was born in the year that Elizabeth I became queen, 1558, and was given a typical upbringing for an Elizabethan young gentleman. At Magdalen College, Oxford he was tutored by the celebrated cleric Laurence Humphrey, although there is no particular evidence that William was much of a scholar. Then he went travelling throughout continental Europe until, in about 1579, he seems to have been commissioned by the Church to command a company of soldiers in the wars against the Irish. His enemy, Fiagh Mac Hugh

O'Byrne, was never captured in the subsequent bloody fighting although his band of followers were.

Five years later William, now Sir William (knighted for his successful blood-letting in Ireland) was off to the Low Countries with the Earl of Leicester's expeditionary force to fight the Spanish. From a mere company commander against the Irish rabble, Russell was now a lieutenant general of cavalry. He was considered so bloodthirsty that at the skirmish, perhaps minor battle, at Warnsfeld he led a charge so terrible that the enemy 'reputed him a devil and no man'.[1] Shortly afterwards Russell became the governor of Flushing, wearing a magnificent suit of gilt armour left to him in his will by his dear friend, the much better-remembered Sir Philip Sidney, the previous governor, who died of a wound sustained when he and Russell were engaged in an attack on a Spanish arms shipment destined for Zutphen.

As governor Russell planned forays against the Spanish and the forces of their ally the Duke of Parma.[2] But although he was a hero of the military conflict, he fell foul of its politics. He was inclined to promote the idea of parts of the Netherlands becoming an English protectorate, but what exactly lay behind this rather rash plan is not easy to understand. It might have had something to do with the carving up of the various regiments and Russell losing his authority. It could easily have been an example of the ill-disguised animosity between Russell and the Prince of Orange. Fortunately, Elizabeth saw the danger and said that she did not want the breakaway communities anyway.

Russell's life could have taken a completely new and vigorous twist at this point. He wanted to be appointed governor of the entire Netherlands, and again it was the Earl of Leicester who supported him. But the court's favour and ear were better tuned to one of the petitioners against Russell, a harsh soldier from Munster by the name of Sir John Norris. Norris was not a fan of Leicester, nor did he have much regard for Russell and he tried, but failed, to block that appointment. A further problem for Russell was that Leicester had been replaced by Peregrine Bertie, Lord Willoughby de Eresby. (A much later generation of Willoughbys became related in the nineteenth century to the Carringtons, thus sharing the royal appointment of Lord High Chamberlain; see Chapter 16). Russell could not really stay much longer as governor of Flushing and in May 1594 he made that well-rehearsed aristocratic trek to Dublin where he was appointed Lord Deputy of Ireland.

His immediate task was to decide what he should be doing about the one man who continuously threatened the peace of the island, Hugh O'Neill, the Earl of Tyrone (see Chapter 5). The crown would have been rather pleased if this troublesome Irishman had been captured. Russell had the opportunity to take O'Neill, but stupidly let him go. Elizabeth was not amused. Almost immediately he was on horseback heading north through the dangerous country of Athlone, Roscommon and Boyle to relieve the siege at Enniskillen. He was successful and in some short measure redeemed himself; but he still had not got O'Neill in his grasp. What he needed, and requested, was a very smart general with a good following of troops to help him. Elizabeth thought that a fine idea. Russell was quite pleased also, until he found that the new general was none other than Sir John Norris. Russell was not happy. He set about trying to lay hands on his old adversary Fiagh Mac Hugh, who was now officially cited for treason. As with O'Neill, Fiagh's men were killed but he himself escaped.

Russell had to leave his northern army in Norris's command. It is reasonable to suggest that Russell was determined to play the diplomat, but Norris was not content with simple relations of command because he remained officially junior. Norris did not care for Russell and by suggesting the latter's inefficiency, tried to discredit him. (Earlier, remember, Norris had tried to stop Russell's appointment to the Netherlands.)

As almost every envoy and viceroy has discovered, attempting to control opposition in Ireland is a thankless and terrible task. So politically and physically dangerous is the role of authority, and so sinister and uncompromising is the nature of the enemy, that few emerge unscathed from the Irish experience. Russell found himself caught in a crossfire of warfare and personal and political animosities, but eventually he succeeded where others had failed and in the late spring of 1597 captured Fiagh Mac Hugh in the badlands of Wicklow. Russell's achievement was received with great acclaim, yet he knew full well that the greater prize would be to rid himself of that place.

Russell now went into some semi-retirement. He had been, in as much as anyone could be, successful in Dublin; thus he was an authority to be quizzed on the vexed matter of how to govern the people of Ireland. Now he looked for a quieter life, although hopeful yet of some relatively unstressful position of authority. He had hoped to become governor of Jersey, with its clement climate and less than arduous duties – although one eye had to be kept open for the French and another for the possibility of a new Armada. He had but one competitor for the appointment and, sadly for Russell, lost out to Sir Walter Raleigh.

There is a tailpiece to William Russell's life. While he was governor of Flushing he had become much impressed with the way in which the lowlands were drained and dyked. It was this Russell who started the scheme to apply the same engineering to the fens of Cambridgeshire.

His son Francis became the 4th Earl of Bedford on the death of his cousin Edward, who shortly before Christmas 1594 had married Lucy Harington. Reference to the new 3rd Countess of Bedford is made not so much in court listings and political goings-on as in the world of literature. She appears to have been the darling of poets and playwrights, including John Donne, George Chapman and Ben Jonson. Chapman, in his partial translation of the *Iliad* in 1598, scripted a sonnet as a dedication 'To the right noble patroness and grace of virtue, the Countess of Bedford'. Donne dedicated five of his poems to her. Such was her popularity, undoubted beauty and wit, that she aroused jealousies among writers and poets who did not benefit from her patronage. For example Michael Drayton, author of such works as the 'Ballad of Agincourt' ('Fair stood the wind for France') and 'Polyolbion', made similar dedications until either he fell out of favour or she transferred her patronage. When his 'Mortimeriados' was published in 1596, there were the familiar references and dedications to Lucy Russell. When it was reprinted in 1603, Drayton had erased his dedication and every reference to the literary countess. She and her husband lived at Moor Park in Hertfordshire, where they died, childless, within days of each other in 1627.

It was because Edward and Lucy Bedford had no issue that Edward's cousin Francis became the 4th Earl. Not a great patron of the arts, it was he who returned the Russells to the way of English politics. He was something of an agitator; for example, in 1621 this Russell is recorded as petitioning James I against the king's creation of Scottish and Irish peerages to the detriment of the English nobility. Again, like most Russells, this earl did not much care for Catholics, especially if they chanced to be on the throne of England. In 1629 he found himself running close to the constitutional and political wind when he was accused, wrongly as it turned out, of questioning the monarch's authority.

Wisely, he turned his energies to his landholdings. In the 1630s, with his friend the architect Inigo Jones, he started to build houses in Covent Garden, former convent land which his family had acquired at the time of Henry VIII and where they had subsequently built the grand Bedford House, and started work on the church of St Paul's there. But even here Russell could hardly escape the attention of the authorities, for seventeenth-century planners were just as hawklike as those of today. Russell was summoned to the Star Chamber to explain what was going on.

It was now that Russell became the leader of a consortium to finish the draining of the fens. This was not a benign ambition of seventeenth-century conservationists but a purely commercial venture. If Russell and his friends were able to drain the fens, they would get almost a hundred thousand acres of it for themselves. The whole project was, in a manner familiar to modern ears, hyped by the private investors, who failed to deliver what they had promised. Most of them, including Russell, lost hundreds of thousands of pounds. The king's government took the project on, paid out subsidies and compensation claims and finished the task. Russell never saw the end of it. By the time the fens were finally drained in 1653 he had died of the smallpox twelve years earlier. He was struck down at the time of the controversy which would lead to the execution of Strafford in 1641 for high treason against Charles. Archbishop Laud, who believed that Russell had plotted against Strafford (there is no evidence that he had), thought the pox was God's judgement on him.

William, 1st Duke of Bedford (the 5th Earl, elevated to a dukedom in 1694) continued the famous Russell drainage system. He was by all accounts a taciturn fellow who seemed to be something of a political chameleon. Having fought on the parliamentary side at Edgehill, the first of the great battles of the Civil War, in the following year, 1643, he decided he was a royalist after all and so swapped allegiances. However, when the royalist campaign collapsed at the first Battle of Newbury, when King Charles was heavily defeated and forced to withdraw to Oxford, Russell decided that his political bread would once more be better buttered on the parliamentary side. He lived to the ripe old age of eighty-seven, dying in 1700. He is perhaps best remembered for refining the drainage designs of Bedfordshire and completing the famous Bedford Level.

His son restored the family interest in intrigue and near disaster. Again, it was the family obsession with keeping down the Catholics that charted the rise and bloody fall of Lord William Russell, who had his head cut off for plotting against the monarch. His mother Anne was the daughter of another controversial figure, Robert Carr who had been a great favourite of James I but fell from grace and was imprisoned in 1616 for the murder of Sir Thomas Overbury (see Chapter 6).

William Russell was born in 1639, when religious tolerance was not widespread. It appears that he and his elder brother Francis were brought up by the family chaplain, John Thornton, as nonconformists and were encouraged in their Protestant faith by a French priest named De la Faisse.

For the first twenty or so years of his life William was not a particularly remarkable figure. He had, or tried to have, many affairs of the heart, including one with Queen Christina of Sweden. He appears to have been in debt for much of this time and close to death, either through illness or, on more than one occasion, as a result of a duel. At the age of thirty he married a widow, Rachel Wriothesley, who was a daughter of the Earl of Southampton. The joining of the Russells to the Wriothesleys was a union of temperament: politically and religiously they had similar ambitions.

Russell reflected his upbringing as a Nonconformist when, as a member of the so-called country party, he started to speak out against Catholicism and therefore the perceived threat from France, and against those with influence at court, who were generally mistrusted. The way in which the country was governed at the time by the Cabal of Clifford, Arlington, Buckingham, Ashley Cooper and Lauderdale was coming to a close. First, Ashley Cooper (who would become the 1st Earl of Shaftesbury) lost his job as Charles II's Chancellor.

In 1674 Russell began to emerge as a vociferous opponent of the remaining members of the Cabal. In the Parliament of January of that year it was he who demanded the break-up of the Cabal and particularly the removal of Lauderdale and Buckingham. Russell was full of confidence that his cause was right and his support firm. It was not surprising, then, that the following year he stood up in Parliament and demanded the removal of Danby, who had just been created an earl and who was a well-known user of bribes – both financial and political – to strengthen the court party. But it was the idea that Danby might have secured money from France for Charles II in return for English neutrality in the European wars that spurred Russell on to demand that Danby should be impeached (see Chapter 10). Danby was no fool, however, and Russell's eloquence could not muster as many votes as Danby could manipulate.

Danby went on to arrange the marriage of Charles II's niece, Mary, with William of Orange. This pleased many people, as William of Orange was clearly no friend of France. The great debate was whether or not England should go to war against the French. Danby's idea was that it was all very simple: the French could give the king considerable sums of money and there would be no question of war. In 1678 the French sent the Marquis de Ruvigny to negotiate with the English; the connection with the Russells was that de Ruvigny was the uncle of William's wife, Rachel.

Complicated backstairs bargaining followed. Russell's main concern was that Charles II should not return to a form of absolute rule. Absolutism, the great fear of the time, meant that the king had supreme power in all matters. Russell was not alone in seeing immense danger in something which had been supposedly abandoned after Charles I. The French had the ability to influence both the English Parliament and most certainly the king. Here was Russell trying to satisfy himself that the king of France could actually help the ambitions he held against the court party. The great danger for Russell and the rest of the country party was that they were having secret discussions with the French king, which was very curious because Russell and his friends were always saying that the French were a threat to peace. Furthermore, the French were hardly likely to support his Nonconformist views. Yet here was Russell involving himself in what would be seen as a popish plot. If anything, their crime was to be fooled.

In 1678, a rumour spread that there was a Jesuit plot to kill Charles II and put James, Duke of York, a Roman Catholic convert, in his place. When Parliament met in October 1678, William Russell proposed the Duke of York's banishment from court; his party also wanted Danby impeached. Charles simply dissolved Parliament.

When Parliament eventually returned, Russell and his party found themselves in the majority. Immediately, he began agitating once more against the idea of a Catholic successor to Charles II. With his closest friend, Lord Cavendish (see Chapter 10), Russell resigned from the privy council and supported the bill of indictment against the Duke of York as a Catholic recusant. And when the House reassembled in the autumn of 1680, it was Russell who moved the motion to stop a Catholic successor – in other words, to exclude the Duke of York from the crown of England. Through his influence, Russell saw the Exclusion Bill reach its third reading in the Commons and it was he who took it personally to the Lords. The Lords threw it out.

The Russell family were obsessed with what they thought was a sinister threat that would put Catholics on the throne and in control of the whole kingdom. When Viscount Stafford was involved in the so-called Popish Plot, Russell promised that he would support him if he revealed everything he knew about the Catholic plans to overthrow the monarchy. The plot was nonsense, the whole thing invented by a man called Titus Oates. Although a Protestant, he had entered a Jesuit college in an attempt to uncover information that would lead to persecution of the

Catholics. Oates had implicated Stafford with his lies, and the Catholic peer was condemned to death. This was the point at which Russell offered to help Stafford, in particular if he could find enough evidence to accuse the Duke of York of being involved. Russell's efforts came to nothing and Stafford was beheaded in 1680, although by that time Russell was demanding that, instead of such a quick execution, Stafford should be hanged, drawn and quartered.

Meanwhile, Russell was in almost constant contact with William of Orange and his house was one of those used as a meeting-place for the plotters against the present monarchy. Whilst there are no firm grounds for believing that Russell was willing to go as far as Shaftesbury and start an insurrection, this was ignored when evidence was gathered against those who in 1683 were implicated in the Rye House Plot, a plan to kill Charles II and his brother, the Duke of York (see Chapter 10). When news of the plot was leaked spies were lodged among the conspirators, and it was claimed that Russell not only knew about it but was actively involved. In June Russell was sent to the Tower, and the following month he was taken to the Old Bailey where he was put on trial for high treason. One of the counsel for the prosecution was a young lawyer with a growing reputation: George Jeffreys. Russell pleaded not guilty. He also argued that to be against the way the king's court was run and the Catholic leanings of the Duke of York did not necessarily amount to plotting against their lives and therefore he could not be guilty of treason.[3] Russell also claimed that he did not even know about the plot. This was very hard to prove in spite of the boldness of the two friends who spoke up for him – Lord William Cavendish and the Duke of Somerset.

It is difficult to believe that Russell could ever have been found innocent – the family's reputation against popery was too well established. Moreover, here was the man who had championed the Exclusion Bill to stop the Duke of York becoming James II, simply on the grounds that he was a Catholic. These were particularly tense times in England, and Russell could not be allowed to escape punishment. He was beheaded. His fellow conspirator – if indeed there ever was a conspiracy – was the Earl of Essex who, on the morning that Russell's trial began, was found dead in the Tower.

Not all the Russells were involved in such Machiavellian political manoeuvrings. Francis Russell, 5th Duke of Bedford, was the son of yet another Francis Russell, the then Marquess of Tavistock (one of the family titles dating back to the sixteenth century) who was thrown by his horse in March 1767 and died. His son was just two years old. By the time he was six he had succeeded his grandfather, John Russell, to the dukedom. On paper he looked an erudite lad. He was sent to Westminster School and then, in 1780, up to Trinity College, Cambridge. Sadly, there is no record of him ever having opened a book other than the one used by those who suspected they knew which horse was running well at Newmarket. Although he had inherited the Bedford responsibilities, Francis Russell was not allowed to sit in the Lords until he was twenty-one. Even there he was very reluctant to get to his feet because he could scarcely string a couple of sentences together without displaying an unfortunate mismanagement of English grammar. He adhered to the family line in politics and so was a Whig, and at the time, in the early 1790s, followed the leadership of Charles James Fox.

It was probably his friendship with the Earl of Lauderdale that brought him out of the social and political shell in which he had felt safe. Lauderdale encouraged him to read and to think through rather than follow unimaginatively the politics of the day. This Russell never did become a great orator, yet he appeared to be one of those characters in British parliamentary life who, being aware of their limitations, see rather complex matters in their simplest forms and so, when they do speak, talk a certain common sense.

This was a likeable duke who was good at his loyalties. The Prince of Wales seized upon him as a friend, so much so that Russell was one of the future George IV's supporters – one of the two best men – at his disastrous marriage to Caroline of Brunswick in 1795. Russell had the utmost difficulty in preventing the very drunk Prince George from falling flat on his face during the ceremony. The fact that the prince collapsed into the grate on his wedding night and hardly stirred until the morning was not Russell's fault. But his closeness to royalty could hardly protect him from the enormous criticism of the vitriolic Burke[4] and the spiteful Gillray.[5]

Russell's crime was that his family was enormously wealthy, was apparently influential with the crown and was still, as far as Burke and Gillray were concerned, by the 1790s doing the bidding of Fox. A little confusingly, perhaps, in the caption to one of his caricatures Gillray referred to 'the Republican Rattlesnake Fox fascinating the Bedford Squirrel'. Yet this Russell should not be remembered for disappearing into the hideous mouth of the Whig rattlesnake. The 5th Duke of Bedford was really happy developing the estate at Woburn. He built what was thought to be the most modern farm of its day, devoted to experimental husbandry, particularly cattle breeding. A more everyday monument (though few of the original houses remain) can be seen in central London, where, at the turn of the eighteenth and nineteenth centuries, the 5th Duke built two of the biggest squares in the capital, Russell Square and Tavistock Square, on the enormous gardens of the family property, the adjacent Tavistock House. It was in Russell Square that his statue was put up in 1809, seven years after his death. Quite properly, the statue was not of the 5th Duke of Bedford holding forth in Parliament; it was of Francis Russell gripping a plough, the only instrument of change which he ever really understood.

A slightly later Russell was most assuredly the instigator of political change. Known for much of his life as Lord John Russell, he became one of the more memorable politicians of the nineteenth century, a period renowned for its gallery of great characters of English political history. Lord John's father was the 6th Duke of Bedford, who, before he inherited the dukedom, tried his hand as a soldier in the foot guards and then, like most of the family, went into politics. He too saw himself as a parliamentary reformer and aligned himself with radicals who had become members of the Society of the Friends of the People; this group, which included Charles James Fox and Charles Grey, a future Whig Prime Minister, campaigned for parliamentary reform. He became 6th Duke in 1802 and, although he stayed in politics for the next five years and indeed became a member of the so-called 'Ministry of all the Talents' in the 1806 Parliament,[6] he was soon to return to Woburn to look after the estate.

It was in the role of estate builder and agriculturalist that the 6th Duke of Bedford should be remembered. He renovated both Woburn and the estate at Tavistock, but most prominently it was he who, in the 1830s, rebuilt Covent Garden market much as it still is today. His heart lay more in the land than in political reform. He spent considerable time experimenting with grasses and with new systems of drainage; the publications that he either produced or edited, including a description of some six thousand plants and shrubs at Woburn, remain well known. Even so, he is probably more famous for having been Lord John Russell's father.

Remarkably, for someone who lived until he was eighty and spent much of his time in the difficult world of nineteenth-century politics, Lord John Russell was hardly ever well. His delicate state had something to do with his mother, Georgiana Elizabeth, who was often thought of as frail. Genetically, she should have been as tough as anyone: she was a Byng, from that famous naval family which included John Byng, the admiral executed in 1757 after the abortive attempt to recapture Minorca.

John Russell could not help but be involved in politics at a very early age. His was a family of politicians, with a wide collection of political friends and acquaintances. When the celebrated Charles James Fox came to the house shortly before his death in 1806, young John noted in his diary that, whilst it was possible for someone to be hanged for stealing a loaf, a politician could get away with stealing thousands in public money. His political education continued at Dublin Castle while his father was Lord Lieutenant of Ireland. The duke seems to have taken him along as a travelling companion on many occasions. They went among other places to Spain and Portugal – places that made a deep impression on Russell who had perhaps inherited a combination of his father's feeling for injustice as well as creativity and an understanding of logic. Unlike many of the famous leaders in English history, Lord John Russell was not sent off to Oxbridge. Instead, in 1809 his father sent him to Edinburgh where for three years he had an intellectual apprenticeship under John Playfair. Playfair had been professor of mathematics there as well as professor of natural philosophy. Later, Russell was to remember his time with Playfair as one of extraordinary stimulation – a natural training ground for a politician.

He continued to travel in continental Europe, where he met Wellington and Bonaparte. However, his ambition was not to while away his time being introduced to the great men of Europe, but to enter Parliament. He could not legally do so until he was twenty-one; nevertheless he managed somehow to beat the age barrier, albeit by just one month, and took up the family seat at Tavistock in 1813.

It was not until 1817 that something of his strength of character in political debate emerged. As a very young member of the House he made two speeches of some distinction. The first was in 1817, when he spoke against the movement to suspend the Habeas Corpus Act. Here was a fundamental right in English law. Whatever the circumstances of the day and the difficulties of the civil administration, Russell believed there could be no corruption of such a basic ordinance.

As with his father, his instincts were that the Houses of Commons and Lords needed to be reformed. More importantly to him, the voting system had to be changed. There should be, he believed, wider political voting. Russell believed that more people should be allowed to vote, especially if they were people of some standing – property holders, for example (though not necessarily property owners). He also became something of a writer, and because his stories about the Russell family attracted such attention, so did his personality and therefore his political opinion and his speeches. By the 1820s he was an erudite, perceptive and well-travelled young MP (by now the member for Huntingdonshire) who was seen as one of the new men. He also had depth of character and intellect, not just a family borough in his pocket.

The second speech which brought him to the members' notice was made in 1822. It was Lord John Russell's presentation of argument, supported by statistical ammunition, that impressed the Commons when he moved his motion that 'the present state of representation of the people in parliament requires the most serious consideration of the House'. He lost the motion, but not the argument. He also proposed a bill that would have outlawed bribery and corruption at elections. Much to his disappointment, although not much to his surprise, the bill did not get anywhere because the government of the day would not support it.

The irony of Lord John Russell's campaigning instincts was that some of the very dubious processes that he wanted to reform were really to his advantage. For example, when he was defeated in Huntingdonshire in 1826 he managed to get into Parliament later that year through an Irish borough owned by a family friend, the Duke of Devonshire. In 1830 he again failed to get back into Parliament, though his opponent received the narrowest possible majority. Wellington resigned and Earl Grey, his father's friend, became Prime Minister. Lord John Russell was appointed paymaster general of the army and navy, even though he was no longer an MP. Once again that situation did not last long and another of the family's boroughs, Tavistock, was manipulated in order that he should have a seat.

It was now that Lord John Russell was to become one of the most famous politicians in England. His father had campaigned with Grey for parliamentary reform of some sort. Lord John had made a name for himself inside Parliament with his cogent argument for reform and now, along with a small group of parliamentary colleagues, he was given his head. The group would draw up the plan that would eventually become one of the most important pieces of legislation ever to go through the House of Commons, the 1832 Reform Bill. Grey may not have had Russell in his Cabinet, but he knew there was no one else who could present the government's Reform Bill so well to the House of Commons. On 1 March 1831, Lord John Russell got to his feet and delivered what many political historians believe to have been one of the most important speeches of his career and in the history of parliamentary reform.

Russell's speech was not born of fiery passion. He was not a radical; he did not seek to overturn the whole system; he was against what he called extensive change, because the other institutions upon which government and society strongly relied might well be damaged in the enthusiasm for reform. Moreover, there was no evidence that, although what he was supporting was considered radical politics, he supported radical leaders. Russell's view was that the balance between reform and extremism should not be overlooked. Moreover, the country was hardly indifferent to what was going on. For example, ever since the French Revolution there had been a fear among politicians that this social and political virus could easily spread across the Channel. The fall of Charles X of France with the 'second French revolution' in 1830 had stirred the English sense of revolt.[7] If authority could be deposed in France, why not in England?

The London Radical Reform Association and the Birmingham Political Union, for example, were quite opposed to the present system and managed to agitate the debate after the general election that followed the fall of Wellington's government. Wellington had not gone because he was tired, but because of popular feeling that the government could not do anything about controlling unrest. Politicians of both parties, Tories and Whigs, knew that the demand for parliamentary reform was so great that it could not be put off indefinitely.

In such an atmosphere it was easy to see why Russell, a reforming Whig, thought it important that, while reform was essential, other institutions should not be damaged. Although he was not a Cabinet Minister, Russell became one of the four draughtsmen of the Reform Bill in 1831.[8] The Bill sought to abolish rotten and pocket boroughs and reduce the number of MPs who could stand for small constituencies (those with fewer than 4000 constituents, not necessarily voters). This would mean a redistribution of seats, an increase in the number of voters and increased political importance for some towns – for example, Leeds, Birmingham and Manchester. Altogether, then, a radical piece of legislation. Grey himself was hardly a radical; his Cabinet contained more aristocrats than would any other in the whole of the nineteenth century. Even then, the four members of the Cabinet who were not in the House of Lords included Althorp, who would become an earl, Palmerston, a baronet and another who would get a peerage. And, as has been noted elsewhere, the government included a son, a son-in-law, a brother-in-law and a cousin of the Prime Minister.[9] This was hardly a ministry whose instincts were to change – little wonder that Grey needed Russell's skills as well as his credibility in the Commons. The first Reform Bill brought about change, but did not bring about the redistribution of seats that many had wanted. The reason, as Russell had to reassure the House, was the need to keep a hold on parliamentary power. What Russell was saying was that the system was corrupt and should be reformed. At the same time, he was not promising some panacea for the redistribution of available seats. The skill of the committee that drafted the bill was that the document, whilst not radical, went further than most had expected.

Russell's more intriguing hypothesis was that the Tories would denigrate the bill and therefore the general public would imagine it to be even more radical than it was. Otherwise why would the Tories be against it? But this idea of playing the Tories off for publicity reasons would not get the bill through Parliament. It did get its second reading, but only by one vote and that was thanks to Irish members of Parliament. The Tories had the government on the run, and in April defeated them in committee. The king, reluctantly, had no choice but to dissolve Parliament.

The general election that followed produced a big majority for the reformers; the voters had little time for the Tory objections. So in the summer of 1831 another bill was brought before the House – more or less the same as the previous one, but with a concession which allowed landowners and freeholders to control votes on their estates. In September the Reform Bill got through the House of Commons. It then went to the Lords, where the bishops, of all people, brought about its downfall: twenty-one of them voted against the bill. It was enough for the government to lose the vote.

This was the moment for more rioting. Newspapers were printed with black borders, in mourning for the bill. There was increased agitation in Birmingham, the focus outside London for the reform campaign. People took to the streets in Nottingham, Derby and Bristol; in Bristol a crowd attacked the Mansion House where Sir Charles Wetherell, the recorder of that city, was lodging – he had opposed the bills in the Commons. As the demonstrators became noisier, the militia became uncertain of its authority. The crowd, by now a mob, ended by burning the Mansion House and the bishop's palace. The significance of the Bristol riot was that other cities looked nervously at every street gathering.

In December, a third Reform Bill was introduced in Parliament. There were a few concessions. The king was called to persuade the bishops to vote for the bill or to abstain; and it was now that William IV was asked to create new peers, or to be ready to do so, in order to load the government benches in the Lords to push through the legislation. The threat to change the balance of power in the Lords was enough to persuade many of the peers to vote for the government, and the third bill got its second reading. Yet some members of the Cabinet were still not satisfied that the bill would get through, and Grey pressed the king to create fifty new peers. William wanted no more than twenty, and even then believed that they should be men who would inherit a title anyway. On 9 May the government was forced to resign – though everyone knew it would only be for a few days, because the Tories could not form an administration. Wellington might have been able to, but Peel would not join him. Wellington and Peel had never trusted each other's political leanings: Wellington was to the right, while Peel inclined to the liberal wing. Wellington had refused to join the liberal Tory administration of Canning and only reluctantly became Prime Minister (1828–9) with Robert Peel as his reforming Home Secretary. Wellington and his conservative Tories never really stomached Peel's legislation that allowed Roman Catholics to become MPs. Moreover, it is unlikely that the country would have quietly tolerated a new Tory government because they believed that only the Whigs would put through the parliamentary reform.

It is perhaps difficult to understand nowadays the depth of feeling among the population. This was a defining moment in British parliamentary democracy and Russell increasingly found himself acting as persuader, fixer, go-between, sage and, surprisingly most of all, the symbol that the people appeared to want as the upholder of their right to vote. Not even Russell believed in universal franchise with no restrictions other than age. That would take more than a century to put into place. However, the bill eventually went through and the first Reform Act of 1832 passed into British constitutional history. It was not until 1928 that women could vote at the same age as men, twenty-one. Moreover, it was not until 1948 that plural voting (the ability to vote twice, at home and at university) was abolished.

Russell was an unlikely character. He had none of the enormous presence of, say, Wellington – indeed, he was a small, slight and nervous figure, a great fidget with his tiny hands and feet. He was no booming orator but had a thin, small voice. Yet when he rose to his feet, in the often rumbustious House of Commons, the crammed benches would still and wait on his every word. Like most of the Russells, perhaps even since the fifteenth-century founder of the family line, Lord John Russell was at ease with himself and self-possessed. It was Sydney Smith, the great nineteenth-century clerical essayist, who observed of him: 'Lord John Russell would perform the operation of a stone, build St Peter's, or assume – with or without ten minutes' notice – the command of the Channel fleet; and no one would discover by his manner that the patient had died, the church tumbled down, and the Channel fleet been knocked to atoms.' [10]

What Smith was describing was the impossible task of getting behind the Russell façade. In public, and in particular in politics, Lord John does not seem to have had an ounce of humour or warmth. Yet his reputation as a host was that of a generous figure.

Most certainly Russell, like many of his ancestors and descendants, was a man who questioned the system and, like much of the Whig family he represented, believed in freedom whether it was in religion or political choice. While the Reform Bill was being discussed and prepared, for instance, it was Russell who questioned the idea of secret ballots because they would be vulnerable to corrupt practices. Consequently he found it difficult to trust anyone who did not share his views, and was always bringing in other members of the Russell family to perform important jobs. Yet this should not be seen as patronage or nepotism: it was his way of achieving what he thought was best for the country and its people.

Nor was he remembered only as a politician. It was Russell who brought about Alfred, Lord Tennyson's appointment as poet laureate. In 1846 Russell was asked to be rector of Glasgow University. The largely ceremonial role appealed to him, yet once he heard that William Wordsworth might be a candidate Russell stepped aside to usher in the poet.

After the 1832 Reform Act Lord John Russell's popularity, in spite of his reserved personality, was enormously high. Even Tories who did not like Whigs liked him, for he was seen as someone who was determined that reasonable views should triumph. He said that it was unreasonable that a whispering faction should triumph over the voice of the nation; the sincerity of this belief caught more than the political imagination, and a form of the quote was repeated time and again.

After the Reform Bill, Lord John Russell found himself concentrating on what was going on in Ireland; he had, after all, spent time as a child in Dublin Castle when his father was Lord Lieutenant. In 1833 Russell went to Ireland to see for himself the sources of the unrest in that country. The government wanted to introduce so-called coercive measures to subdue the Irish; Russell opposed them. Moreover, he then attacked the Irish Church, claiming that its clergy and administrators were getting rich beyond the needs of its parishioners. This was more than giving a slight opinion or expressing some personal remarks to the House of Commons. The political sensitivities of the Ireland debate were as great then as they are now: his stand against coercive measures and his attack on the wealth-gathering of the Irish Church not only caught public attention, but upset the political equilibrium that might have been achieved in a sensitive Cabinet. Russell declared that reform of the Irish Church was a first principle of government – or should be. Members of the Cabinet could not live with this vigorous attack and yet had no credible counter to it; they were forced to resign. Grey, the Prime Minister, was among their number and this was the reason that the reluctant Lord Melbourne took the post.[11]

That same year, 1834, the leadership of the House of Commons became vacant. Althorp had succeeded his father as the new Earl Spencer and Lord John Russell was asked if he would like to lead the government in the Commons. The monarch still had considerable influence and in November of that year dismissed the government. Peel now became Prime Minister because the Tories won the ensuing election. Even so, Russell did well by the upheaval and became leader of the Whigs in the Commons. It was not a comfortable period in waiting for the opportunity to return to government. We can already see the embryo of what would become the Liberal party: here were the Whigs, the radicals and not a few of the Irish members; all that was missing was a group of disillusioned Tories.

It may have been a hard task for Russell to hold the Whigs in the Commons together, but he and his family were becoming more influential. Russell blossomed. He took on Peel, no mean performer, and regularly defeated him in debate. Again, on the issue of the Irish Church and its revenues Russell succeeded in splitting the government. In 1835 Peel was forced to resign and Melbourne was once more back in Downing Street with Russell now Leader of the House and Home Secretary.

William IV could not stand Lord John Russell. He did not like the way in which Lord John (a Whig) had brought about Peel's defeat (the king was a great admirer of the Tories and of Peel), nor did he care for the Russell family. The king could count on the Tory-filled House of Lords; Russell could not. Yet he could, and would, overcome the seemingly natural hostilities of the Upper House.

For example, Russell produced such logical argument for something which sounds boring, but in practice most certainly is not – the Municipal Corporations Bill – that he overcame those who would have voted against him simply because they disliked him. In 1835 his Bill got through, which meant that municipal government was now established everywhere, with the exception of London itself. This legislation would reform municipal government so that rate payers could elect councillors for the first time. Urban political corruption would not disappear, but never before had the electorate had such influence – should they choose to use it. Russell went on to draft legislation that would live on into modern times. For example, it was Russell who was responsible for the Act of Parliament that set up registration of births, marriages and deaths. He also managed to force through a reduction in the number of offences for which a felon could be hanged. He reformed the poor laws, and might have achieved so much more but for the death of William IV in 1837. When the monarch died, Parliament was dissolved.

Melbourne was staying in office. In 1839 Peel should have formed a government; but the twenty-year-old Queen Victoria could not bear the thought of him and his Tories, even complaining that her ladies-in-waiting were being removed in some Tory plot against her. Melbourne spent the next three years holding the queen's hand through the difficult transition from young princess to vulnerable monarch. With all the uncertainties and consequent obstinacy brought about through her upbringing by a strict German governess and an enormously ambitious mother, Victoria needed Melbourne perhaps more than the country did.

Lord John Russell was very much part of this transition period. For example, he wanted Melbourne to bring into his Cabinet more people with radical opinions, especially those who held a stronger belief in parliamentary reform than did some of the existing Cabinet members. Melbourne would have nothing of it. Russell for the moment went along with this and consequently had to admit to Parliament that electoral reform was not on his immediate list of priorities. The radicals, most of whom had supported him and vice versa, now mocked him with the nickname 'Finality Jack'.

When in 1839, the queen asked Melbourne to stay on as Prime Minister, Russell became Colonial Secretary and it was he who tried to sort out, moderately successfully, many of the difficulties that beset Jamaica after the abolition of slavery. But his time as Colonial Secretary was probably best remembered for the fact that he pushed through the setting up of New Zealand as a British colony and settled a formal claim for the whole of Australia.

There came a time when Russell was the one person who could form a new Whig administration – or so it seemed. In 1845, Peel had resigned because he was unable to carry his Cabinet with him for the repeal of the Corn Laws.[12] Russell was asked to form a government, but could not do so because some of the other ministers refused to serve in a Cabinet which contained the unpredictable Palmerston as Foreign Secretary. Peel got back into Downing Street and, with a lot of help from Russell, repealed the Corn Laws. It was to be a short stay in power for Peel, and once again the question of a Cabinet for Ireland was to bring about an administration's defeat in the House of Commons. As the Corn Law Bill was being passed in the Lords (26 June 1846), Peel's Ireland Coercion Bill (to give powers to put down by any means the unrest in Ireland) failed in the Commons. Peel's government fell and in July 1846, a year after he had tried to form his first government, Russell succeeded in becoming Prime Minister. Palmerston duly set up his camp in the Foreign Office.

This was not a happy time to be Prime Minister. Ireland, the place for which Russell had such affection, was in the midst of the Potato Famine. The debate on how that disaster was handled by the British government continues to this day: too little, too late has often been the charge. And yet in the twentieth and the twenty-first centuries, with all the advantages of science and communications, there are still many occasions when governments have similar accusations thrust on them for seemingly very public and obvious crises. It is no excuse to point out that in the first half of the nineteenth century the skill of crisis management was barely known. The assessment of a situation in order to analyze its consequences was a slow matter, usually based on personal judgement and prejudice rather than on accurate scientific and social data. That the matter of the Potato Famine was complicated by the politics and eventually the religious arguments of Anglo-Irish relationships meant that, whatever decisions might have been taken, none would have been perfect.

The £10 million given by the government to resolve the consequences of the famine may now appear ludicrously inadequate and, even worse, paid on a basis of indifference to the suffering. That is poor judgement, considering the times. Russell's government was not indifferent; it simply could not find a way out of the fix which would get through Parliament and would be effectual. Recently, Britain has witnessed agricultural diseases which it has found impossible to control fully, in spite of modern science. How much more difficult it was in the 1840s to control a blight that had travelled across the Atlantic from America and then pestered so much of Europe. The Remedial Measures Bill for Ireland was published in 1847. Russell introduced in that Bill an amendment to the Poor Law allowing more money to alleviate hardship. He created a Secretary of State for Ireland. None of this contained the misery or the anger of the Irish people. The unrest in Ireland crippled Lord John Russell's previously expressed moral indignation at the measures necessary to contain it. He now had to introduce the very measures that he had so often opposed. The Cabinet was not of his liking, but necessarily of his doing.

Russell should be praised for the way in which he attempted to make the poor laws easier for the Irish people and for appointing another minister to help the problems of that island. But nothing came of these efforts. He attempted to return to the whole idea of electoral and parliamentary reform, but was defeated by his own Cabinet before he had a chance of putting it to Parliament. He did manage make the Port Phillip district of Australia a separate colony to be named Victoris after the queen, but any warm glow that this may have brought about was not much felt in Ireland.

Russell's difficulty with his Cabinet was hardly new for any prime minister; but his annoyance with, and largely ineffectual control over, his Foreign Secretary, Palmerston, were exceptional. No one could control Palmerston. In 1851, quite contrary to British policy, he made it known that he recognized the government in France which followed Louis Napoleon's coup d'état in December of that year. Queen Victoria was furious. There had already been a number of occasions on which Palmerston had conducted his own private foreign policy. The queen told Russell she would not tolerate this behaviour and Russell was forced to sack his Foreign Secretary.

Palmerston really did not mind. Against the background of all the excitement in France, Russell's government had introduced the Militia Bill, which brought the military under the Secretary of War. This would allow the government to raise volunteers to the militia in the event that some new French revolution should either spread to or be copied in England. The government even believed French revolutionaries might invade. That threat passed, but Palmerston, knowing what damage the Bill would do, moved an amendment which extended it. This gave the impression that the government still feared invasion – a nonsense which the Russell administration had to oppose. But Palmerston's amendment was carried. The government was defeated.

For nearly five years Russell had been Prime Minister, and now he had to step down. But he was not done with politics, nor they with him. The 1852 coalition of Whigs and Peelites was established with the unremarkable 4th Earl of Aberdeen, George Hamilton-Gordon, as Prime Minister. Having resigned in the 1846 debacle over the Corn Laws, he had succeeded Peel as the leader of that politician's followers. and would remain in the top job until his mismanagement of the Crimean War of 1854–6 forced him out of office. Briefly, Russell became the leader of the House of Commons. He tried to bring in a new Reform Bill, but had to accept that if he pushed it there would be so much opposition that the government would fall. Moreover, the war with Russia in the Crimea had begun, and the Cabinet was split into so many factions that it was inevitable that the criticism would claim its victims; Russell was one of them. He felt, in January 1855, that there had to be an inquiry into the way the government had managed the war. Aberdeen resigned. Victoria asked Lord Derby to form a government; he could not. She then asked Russell; nor could he.

Much to Victoria's disappointment, the person who could form an administration was Palmerston and he became Prime Minister. Russell at first did not want to be a minister, although he did accept the role of roving ambassador and in 1855 was Britain's representative at the Congress of Vienna, searching for a peace treaty to end the Crimean War. At the Congress, Russia opposed the terms and there was no support in London for Russell's view that England and France could act as guarantors. The concluding treaty was signed in Paris the following year. Russell decided to resign because he thought that he was right in his view that England, France and Austria could counterbalance any future ambitions of the Russians – and this was not really what Palmerston had in mind. It was not for another four years that Russell could return to government. He became Palmerston's Foreign Secretary – another irony, considering that Russell had sacked Palmerston from the same job. History had a good sense of timing for Russell. Being in power in 1860 was a moment when he could champion yet another cause, this time abroad. At that time, Italy was still a series of mini-states. There was a movement towards one nation under one king, and Russell was a great champion of this idea. He is credited with being an important influence in bringing about Italian unity, although Garibaldi may have had other views as to who was responsible.[13]

It was in July 1861 that the queen, who had long since warmed to Russell, a man who had stood by and supported the monarchy and the sensitive institutions which she so valued, raised him to an earldom: he became the 1st Earl Russell of Kingston Russell. But this was not to mark the end of his career. He became involved in the search for a solution to the cruel American Civil War. He (and Palmerston) failed to find a compromise that would have protected Denmark from the threats of a Prussian invasion of the Danish territory of Schleswig-Holstein. Schleswig-Holstein was so complicated an issue that, when Victoria asked Palmerston what it was about, he said: 'There are only three men who have ever understood it: one was Prince Albert, and he is dead; the second was a German professor who became mad; I am the third and I have forgotten all about it.'

In October 1865 Palmerston died and Russell, by now a Knight of the Garter, became Prime Minister once more – in the Lords, with Gladstone as his leader of the House of Commons. He survived for less than a year because the government was defeated over an intriguingly named issue, the Cave of Adullam. Adullam was the cave in which, in the Old Testament, David hid from Saul. In 1866 the political philosopher John Bright used this biblical reference, a common enough habit in Victorian times, to describe the way in which Whig radicals led by Robert Lowe[14] plotted against the government's plans for more votes for more people. Lowe and his fellow radicals did not believe the proposals were fair enough.[15] This opposition was the single act that, in 1866, brought about the collapse of Russell's government, and it virtually ended his career. Lord Derby became Prime Minister and his Tory administration brought in the 1867 Reform Act. The following year

Derby went and Disraeli succeeded him as Prime Minister, but by the end of 1868 Galdstone was back. He offered Russell a Cabinet post, but by now he was tired of that way of life. From the safety of the House of Lords Russell spoke with great passion of his long-time belief in reconciliation in Ireland, a notion that he had had as a small child.

He did one particular thing in the House of Lords that was not acted upon for nearly a century. In 1869, Russell suggested the introduction of life peerages. It was rejected, and never reappeared until the Life Peerages Act of 1958.

The last thirty years of his life were spent at Pembroke Lodge in Richmond Park, which belonged to Queen Victoria. He died there on 28 May 1878. Disraeli wanted him to have a state funeral and a tomb in Westminster Abbey. But Russell had never wanted such honours and he was laid to rest in the family vault at the family manor house at Chenies in Buckinghamshire. (The north chapel of the church, St Michael's, contains most of the monuments to the Russells.)

This small, fidgety man had a far-reaching effect on British political life and great influence on a monarch, though often reinforced by more famous characters. Yet he is often remembered only as the grandfather of a distinguished twentieth-century philosopher. Bertrand Russell was born in 1872. His father was Viscount Amberley, the eldest son of Lord John Russell; Bertrand's mother died of diphtheria when he was two years old and he lost his father when he was three. Before his parents died they had asked the great philosopher John Stuart Mill to be the boy's godfather, though this is perhaps not an accurate description since Mill, like themselves, was an atheist.

The future of the young Bertrand Russell was of great concern to the family, especially his paternal grandmother, who saw dark influences at work through those appointed as legal guardians of the child. His case went to the courts and his upbringing was given to his grandparents in whose care he remained until he was eighteen. After being widowed, his grandmother had remained at Pembroke Lodge, Victoria's grace and favour home, and it was here among the eccentric personalities of the Russell family that Bertrand grew up as a free and sometimes preoccupied thinker. Perhaps the greater influence of these formative years was not the unrelenting high-mindedness of Lord John Russell's widow, but the library left by that great man. Here was the uncluttered education he desired. It was from this rarefied atmosphere, perhaps curdled with late Victorian priggery, that Russell went up to Cambridge in 1890.

The career of Bertrand Russell and the influences exerted on him as a young man are recorded elsewhere. His brilliance first as a mathematician and then, so logically from that discipline, as a philosopher had in his twenties marked him out as one of the coming men of the twentieth century. His image and influence on those who never read a single word of his, who never heard him lecture nor wondered at his background and train of thought, were remarkable. His first months at Cambridge and his reflections on John Stuart Mill were turning points in his intellectual development.

Russell's first philosophical book, *An Essay on the Fundamentals of Geometry*, was written in 1897. Four years later he wrote *A Critical Exposition of the Philosophy of Leibniz*.[16] This work and, in 1900, his *Principles of Mathematics* (which was not widely published until 1930), gained Russell a reputation as a genius. In 1911 he became President of the Aristotelian Society.

At the outbreak of the First World War, Russell rebelled against the conflict and the notion of conscription and refused to volunteer. His Cambridge college, Trinity, did not renew his lectureship. When he tried to go to the United States in 1916, the Foreign Office refused to give him a passport and would not support his visa application. In 1918 he was imprisoned for sedition – he had suggested using American troops against British strikers.

In 1931, Russell inherited his title from his brother, Frank. Though Russell was not much welcomed by British academe, he was given a visiting professorship at UCLA (the University of California at Los Angeles) at the outbreak of the Second World War. However, he did not survive there long, soon falling out with the right-leaning UCLA President. As the war drew to a close, Russell, now in his seventies, gained wider public acknowledgement.

His influence on generations was triggered by the atomic bombing of Japan in 1945. Here were the beginnings of the peace movement and the anti-nuclear weapon campaign. His platforms were sturdy and many. It was Russell who gave the first Reith lectures on BBC Radio in 1949; this was the series that was eventually published as *Authority and the Individual*. That same year he was raised to the Order of Merit and the following year, 1950, he won the Nobel Prize for Literature. In 1954 Russell gave his famous broadcast on radio called 'Man's Peril'. The anti-nuclear campaign was on its way and in 1958 Russell became the first president of CND – the Campaign for Nuclear Disarmament.

This was not enough for the celebrated philosopher. In 1960 Russell, now eighty-eight, formed the extreme faction of CND – the Committee of 100. A mass rally in Whitehall in February 1961 resulted in Russell being sent to prison; he was quickly released, supposedly because of his age, but equally because he was too influential a figure to be detained long in case he died behind bars. None of this tempered his belief that the authorities were to be challenged at every step. He described Harold Macmillan, the British Prime Minister, and President Kennedy as being worse than Hitler.

It is said that old age does not come alone. Russell's particular weakness was that in his nineties he allowed himself to be used. The effective anti-American campaigner Ralph Schoeman persuaded Russell that the blame for almost every sadness in the world could rest in the White House. Schoeman's influence over Russell was so powerful that the great philosopher found letters published in the *Times* newspaper condemning the United States and signed in his name – but which he had not written. By the time of his death in 1970, the 3rd Earl Russell had become discredited in the public's mind. None of that should detract from his brilliance as a philosopher and the fact that this Russell was able to influence opinion, both popularly and politically, as much as earlier generations had by quite different means.

If, in modern memories, Bertrand Russell overshadowed his brother, John, that would not have been the case during the first half of the twentieth century. Bertrand became the 3rd Earl in 1931 on the death of that brother, who was no ordinary man himself. This Lord John Russell became a politician and a junior Labour transport minister in 1929 – the early days of the parliamentary party. But he was also known as a famous (perhaps infamous) bigamist. The London correspondent of the *International Herald Tribune* reported on 19 June 1901:

> Earl Russell is to be tried for bigamy. Society had almost forgotten the recent excitement caused by his second marriage in America with Mrs Somerville while the countess was still alive and making her living singing on the variety stage. It came therefore almost as a surprise when the afternoon papers came out with great headlines announcing the arrest of the earl. Bigamy being a felony, Lord Russell will be tried before his peers.

He went to prison for three months. The woman he had first married and who was referred to in the newspaper was Mabel, daughter of the baronet Sir Claude Scott. It was not a happy family. Mabel's mother, Maria, was sentenced in 1897 to eight months imprisonment for libelling her son-in-law. Russell's second, 1901 marriage ended in divorce in 1915, and he married for the third time the following year. His new wife was the writer Mary Annette, cousin of a more famous writer, Katherine Mansfield. The marriage did not last: they parted, although never divorced. The Russells had never been dull.

NOTES

1 John Stow (1525–1605), *Annals, or A General Chronicle of England*, 1580.

2 The skirmishes of the British and Spanish were in the context of the Revolt of the Netherlands (modern-day Belgium and Holland). The Revolt may be dated from 1566. The Spanish controlled part of the Netherlands and Philip II of Spain planned incursions into Netherlandish independence. The Calvinists, in particular, revolted. England's interest was primarily economic. When the northern provinces of the Netherlands declared independence in 1581, England became more involved and this, among other matters, led to the Spanish Armada of 1588.

3 At that time the charge of treason would have been laid under laws passed in the time of Edward III, and therefore it might have been argued that to plot was not an act of treason although to attempt to carry out the plot indeed was.

4 Edmund Burke (1729–97), Irish statesman and political philosopher. He became a Whig and fell out with Fox over his *Reflections on the French Revolution*. He was one of the most erudite political philosophers of the late eighteenth century, yet by all accounts an indifferent orator. Along with Disraeli, who rose to prominence more than half a century after Burke's death, he is sometimes spoken of as the father of twentieth-century Conservative ideology.

5 James Gillray (1757–1815), the famous late eighteenth-century engraver and caricaturist. He made his satirical observations of political and social stupidities without mercy.

6 The 'Ministry of all the Talents' was the government formed by Grenville in February 1806. Most of the people in it, including Russell, were really followers of Charles James Fox who died in September of that year. The government failed to manage the Napoleonic war, although it did help bring about one of the key pieces of legislation for the abolition of the slave trade. By March 1807 it had collapsed.

7 Charles X (1757–1836) took refuge in England and Scotland via St Petersburg at the start of the French Revolution in 1789. In 1795 he attempted to invade France, but failed and lived in England and Scotland until 1814. Eventually he became king, but tried to turn back the constitutional clock by restoring the absolute powers of the monarch. In 1830 he was thrown out by the July Revolution. Once more, Charles hurried to an exile in Scotland and later in Prague.

8 Russell, Sir James Graham, Lord Durham and Lord Duncannon.

9 Sir Llewellyn Woodward, *The Age of Reform, 1815–1870*, OUP, 1938.

10 Sydney Smith (1771–1845), moral philosopher, Canon of St Paul's.

11 Melbourne had never really wanted to go into politics. He had been inclined to become a poet, until his brother, Peniston, died and he succeeded to the family title, whereupon he was expected to enter the respectability of public life. He would become the mentor of the new queen, Victoria, for the first three years of her reign and, in spite of the big age difference, probably fell in love with her and she with him.

12 Duty on imported corn dated from the Middle Ages. In 1815 the Corn Law Act applied heavy custom duty to protect farmers who were facing reduced profits following the fall in the high price of corn after the Napoleonic Wars. The Anti-Corn Law League (1839) claimed the landowners were making excessive profits. Landowners (mainly Tories) claimed industrialists (the League's promoters) wanted cheap grain so they did not have to pay higher wages. The Tories were divided. Peel won the day in 1846, but the split ended his career.

13 Giuseppe Garibaldi (1807–82). In 1860 he led his private army of Red Shirts and conquered Sicily and Naples in an attempt to bring about Italian unity. The only part of Italy that successfully held out (until 1870) was Rome, although in 1862 and 1867 Garibaldi attempted to wrest it from the popes.

14 Later Viscount Sherbrooke, Lowe introduced the idea of pay-by-results for school teachers. Gladstone made him Chancellor of the Exchequer and he was instrumental in the disestablishment of the Irish Church.

15 Derby's 1867 Reform Act redistributed more than fifty seats. In theory, but not always in practice, skilled workers were enfranchised. It was not always simple to register for a vote and whatever reforms were claimed for the Act, no women were allowed to vote and only one third of the male population over twenty-one.

16 Gottfried Wilhelm Leibniz (1646–1716) was a rationalist philosopher who described the world as a composition of individually indivisible materials in a hierarchy with God at its summit.

FURTHER READING

AYLING, Stanley, *Fox*, John Murray, 1991.

BLAKISTON, Georgiana, *Lord William Russell and his Wife*, John Murray, 1972.

FRASER, Flora, *The Unruly Queen*, Macmillan, 1996.

CHAPTER THIRTEEN

THE NORFOLKS

There is a jewelled and silken-gartered image of an English aristocrat, unruffled in the gold lamé folds of privilege, which is familiar to many people. The setting is the supreme pageantry of the coronation in 1953 of Elizabeth II, its mastermind the Earl Marshal of All England, the Duke of Norfolk. The irony is that the young queen is the temporal head of the Church of England, and the Norfolks the temporal heads of the Church of Rome. For one moment the Protestant–Catholic divide that has caused such schism in these islands since the sixteenth century is healed.

For centuries the Norfolks have ruled over the regalia of successive English monarchs; inevitably, they came with the Normans. The first of the Norfolks was Hugh Bigod who, in the winter of 1136, became the Earl of Norfolk. The origin of the name 'Bigod' is obscure. It is quite possible that it was an often-used oath, 'bi got', and certainly for a couple of centuries afterwards it was a commonly used expression, frequently in satire. The first Bigod appears to have come from poor Norman stock – small landowners from Chanon in Normandy who were minor courtiers. He was part of the Conquest of England, but that does not mean that he fought at the Battle of Hastings; more likely he was one of those Normans much needed by William to settle the southern part of England in order to stake the king's claim over the people as well as the land.

In 1074 the then Earl of Norfolk was a man called Ralph de Guader. His estates were taken away, presumably by the king, and given to Roger Bigod, who certainly had them by 1079. He did not get the earldom of Norfolk with those estates. From *Domesday* we know that he held 117 manors in Suffolk and six in Essex: these were not, however, as grand as they seem and represented not much more than fortified villages, perhaps the equivalent of a modern rural parish. Nevertheless, with the Norfolk estates and those in Essex and Suffolk (although, in those days, Suffolk and Norfolk were considered as one) he was clearly a knight of some substance. The importance of the family might be reflected by the fact that he was steward to William Rufus and then to Henry I. It was from the latter that Roger Bigod was given the estate of Framlingham in Suffolk, which became the Bigod family seat. A further indication of his closeness to royalty was that his eldest son, William, was with Henry I's most treasured heir, also called William, in the famous White Ship disaster in November 1120. The ship sank off Barfleur on its way from France to England and both William Bigod and Prince William were drowned. The event led to one of the more cruel battles for the English throne after Henry I's death in 1135 (see Chapter 4).

Hugh Bigod, Roger's second son, therefore inherited his father's estates and became deeply and often treacherously involved in the succession struggle between King Stephen and Matilda. His treachery was not unusual, for few in those times and particularly in those circumstances did anything but protect their self-interest. It was Stephen who gave him the earldom of Norfolk; but, given what happened afterwards in the continuing battles for the crown, Hugh Bigod continued to change allegiances. Then in 1153, when the Angevin Henry landed in England to claim the throne as Henry II, Hugh Bigod once more abandoned Stephen. In 1169 the Archbishop of Canterbury, Thomas Becket, presumably under the king's eye, excommunicated him. His crime was that of holding on to lands that were owned by the monasteries. Bigod was a great feudalist, so it was not surprising that he was very much a leader of those barons determined to preserve their feudal authority over the ambitions of kings who wanted absolute power. He died in 1177, but not in the eastern counties, the scene of his triumphs, failures and about-faces; it is generally thought that he perished on pilgrimage to the Holy Land.

His son, Roger, did not become the 2nd Earl of Norfolk until 1189. Here again was a curious mixture of rebellion and feudalism: Roger had fought against his own father and for Henry II at the Battle of Fornham in 1173. But again, Roger's reputation for loyalty was as suspect as that of any other baron of the time. He had rebelled and was party to Magna Carta, and was considered important and powerful enough to be one of its guarantors – that is, making sure that King John kept to his side of the bargain. John did not much care for Bigod and took his estates away from him. But with the accession of Henry III the Bigods were once more in royal favour.

The 3rd Earl of Norfolk, Roger's son Hugh, had also been at Runnymede but did not long survive his father. It was at this stage of the family's history that a complex series of inheritances and marriages came together to begin a path that would make its way into the twenty-first century. Hugh Bigod died in or about 1225. He had been married to Maud, the eldest daughter of William Marshal, Earl of Pembroke. Marshal was a strong supporter of Henry II. Even though Richard the Lionheart fell out with him as a result, the two were reconciled sufficiently that in 1189 Richard allowed him to marry into the de Clare family, who held the earldom of Pembroke. On the death of Richard de Clare, William Marshal became Earl of Pembroke. It was shortly afterwards that Marshal became justiciar and then marshal of England. He fell out with King John, as most did; and was packed off to Ireland, as most without favour were. But John could not do without William for very long, and during the struggles with the barons he returned to become the king's chief adviser. When John died in 1216, Henry III ascended the throne. He was only nine years old and so William, as marshal of England, became his regent and thus ruled the kingdom.

It is in this context that we return to Norfolk, Bigod and the thirteenth century. Maud,[1] the widow of Hugh Bigod, 3rd Earl of Norfolk, now married the Earl of Surrey, William de Warenne. So three families have now joined together – Norfolk, Surrey and Marshal/Pembroke.[2] Bigod's son, Roger, became the 4th Earl. Here was a complicated case of inheritance and wardship. The boy was still a minor and his first guardian, appointed by the king, was the Earl of Salisbury. However, Roger Bigod then married Isabella, sister of Alexander, king of Scotland; thus the Scottish king became his guardian. In 1233 Henry III knighted Bigod, who was clearly the king's favourite. The castle at Framlingham was granted its own livery and in 1246 Roger Bigod became Earl Marshal of England through his mother (who was, remember, the eldest daughter of the Earl of Pembroke).

Although he was close to the king, it did not stop the two of them often falling out. Because of his seniority, Roger Bigod was going to be among those who made representations to the king to ease his powers if he expected to get the monies he was demanding from Parliament. In 1258 he was one of the twelve barons who tried to exact the constitutional reforms supposedly agreed with the king.

Another Bigod, Hugh, had been appointed justiciar and it was he who was responsible for the implementation of the government reform that was expected to give the king executive powers, but also to give Parliament more authority. For example, Parliament was to meet three times a year and be run by a kind of cabinet of powerful men. The basis for local government would be reviewed and some powers would be transferred from the monarch to the barons. These reforms, known as the Provisions of Oxford were no great success, but they do demonstrate that the early Norfolks were very much at the centre of English constitutional power.

The following year the barons, led by Simon de Montfort, were again unsettled and angry. Bigod declared for Henry III. The French king had been called upon to arbitrate and Bigod had gone to France to bring back the judgement. This was the beginning of the crumbling of the Provisions of Oxford and so Bigod, in the tradition of the family, changed sides. Following the important Battle of Lewes, Bigod is recorded as holding Oxford Castle against the king's men for de Montfort.

The next Earl of Norfolk, the fifth was another Roger Bigod, but not the son of the 4th Earl. He was a nephew, the son of Hugh Bigod the justiciar. Here is another example of the inability of any important noble of this period to avoid the terrible struggles for authority and even the crown.

This was the troubled reign of Edward I. The king's ideas for changing the way that England was governed had frightened the barons, who believed they would lose power. The terrible wars against the Welsh princes and the Scots and, seemingly inevitably, the French disrupted any plans to restructure the government. However, the barons saw saw this delay as nothing more than that and remained firmly committed to opposing the king's authority if it did not suit them. So, in February 1297, when Edward demanded that the barons give him money and men to invade France, they rebelled under Roger Bigod and the Earl of Hereford, Humphrey Bohun. Edward told the two barons that he wanted them to take the fight to Gascony while he, Edward, led forces in Flanders. Bigod said he could not do that. Was this not treason? Not according to Bigod who pointed out to the king that his honour allowed him to serve and fight outside England only at the side of the monarch. It is recorded that Edward told Bigod he would either do as he was told or be hanged, and that Bigod replied that he would neither do as he was told nor be hanged. As a result, Bigod and Bohun refused to serve in their official capacities – respectively Marshal of England and Constable of Hereford. The king had no choice but to take away these great offices from the rebellious earls. Edward I, not in a strong position, set sail for Flanders, leaving the young Prince Edward in charge. Bigod and Bohun set about their mischief. The prince, ill advised, agreed in the king's absence to their demands that the monarch should no longer have the right to exact taxes without the people's consent.

When Edward I returned to England in 1298, he was determined to invade Scotland. The king was now in a stronger position. Although the monarchy had (temporarily) agreed to limit its powers, Bigod's own authority was waning. Bohun had died that year, depriving him of his strongest ally and perhaps, in military terms, his senior partner. Edward now saw his chance to overcome Bigod. The latter was forced to surrender his estates and, by a quirk of late thirteenth- and early fourteenth-century procedure, declare the king to be his heir. Thus when Roger Bigod died in 1306, the monarch inherited his titles.

As we have seen, a title such as 'earl' may be created and, in modern times, inherited. However, this does not mean that the title will run for all time in the same family. It may become extinct because its last holder dies without heirs. Equally, in earlier times the king might confiscate the lands and the title. Therefore the period of a title is known as its 'creation'. So, for example, the 2nd Earl of Norfolk did not immediately follow his father, Hugh, as earl; he only became the Earl of Norfolk in 1189, so was known as the earl of the 1189 creation. Thus the present Earl of Norfolk is of the 1644 creation, even though the title has been passed – with intervals when it went elsewhere – to earlier members of his family.

If Roger Bigod had not surrendered his title and dignity to the king, the earldom would have been handed on to his brother. That brother continued the family line and so the earldom of Norfolk might easily have continued without a break into the present day. The debate about the circumstances of Roger Bigod's surrendering of the family title went on until the twentieth century. In 1906 the House of Lords declared that the action had been invalid. But whatever the rights and wrongs, the Bigod family would no longer be earls of Norfolk. (There is a further reminder, as a tailpiece to Bigod's life, of how the great families entwine. His first wife was the daughter of the chief justiciar of England, Philip Basset. She was, too, the widow of Hugh Despenser (see Chapter 3).

Edward I appears to have been set on reducing the powers of certain earldoms, and the opportunity of wresting the Norfolk title from the Bigods (never a family of lazy constitutional barons) would enable him to pull power back to the throne. The next earl of Norfolk, created in 1312, was Thomas of Brotherton who was a younger brother of Edward II. King Edward divided the Bigod estates between Thomas and another brother, Edmund. For good measure Thomas became Marshal of England, although when he died in 1338 without a son the marshalcy went to Margaret, his older daughter. It was this Margaret who became one of the earliest life peers – she was created Duchess of Norfolk, but only in her lifetime. The earldom carried on and was passed to her grandson, Thomas de Mowbray.

Today's Norfolk family are the Fitzalan Howards. The Howards first came to prominence in the thirteenth century when Sir William Howard, a lawyer and justice of assize for the northern counties, had the manor house at East Winch in Norfolk. He married Alice, daughter of the justiciar of Ireland, Sir Robert de Ufford, who took his name from a small village close to the Suffolk town of Woodbridge. A few years later Sir William married another Alice, daughter of Sir Edward Fitton of St. Germains; and later still he returned to Norfolk to marry a widow by the name of Joan whose husband, Baldwin, had died at Holkham in Norfolk.

By the early fourteenth century the family were established as warriors and courtiers. Sir John Howard was a gentleman of the bedchamber to Edward I. Another Sir John Howard was an admiral. Yet another Sir John was a sheriff. And in the fifteenth century Sir Robert Howard famously commanded the Channel fleet at the time of the Battle of Agincourt. It was this Howard who married Margaret de Mowbray, the eldest daughter of the 1st Duke of Norfolk (a title created in 1397 – see above). He then married Elizabeth FitzAlan: here was the original connection with the second FitzAlan lineage.

John Howard became the 1st Duke of Norfolk in the fifteenth century. He was particularly distinguished because Richard III gave him the title of Earl Marshal of England. John Howard therefore was the first Duke of Norfolk of the Howard family. His parents were Sir Robert Howard (he who commanded the Channel fleet) and his then wife, Margaret Mowbray, who was the daughter of Thomas Mowbray, who then held the dukedom of Norfolk. Margaret Mowbray was a cousin of John Mowbray, who inherited the title from his brother Thomas. It was Margaret who was one of the two heirs of John Mowbray.

In the Wars of the Roses John Howard was a Yorkist, and when Edward IV became king in 1461 he knighted Howard for his services and made him sheriff of Norfolk and Suffolk. In 1466 he became vice admiral for Norfolk and Suffolk and also treasurer of the king's household. Throughout all the political upheaval and the swapping of crowns between the Yorkist Edward IV and Henry VI of

Lancaster, Howard appears to have remained on Edward's side. Edward had fled the country but was back again in 1471, and Howard is recorded as declaring Edward king once again. His influence was undoubted. When in the summer of 1475 Edward invaded France, Howard was at the king's side. Again, his importance can be established from the fact that he was one of the envoys who arranged the truce between Edward and the French king at Amiens. As was the custom, a highly trusted member of either the king's family or his immediate circle had to remain behind as a sort of enforced house guest to guarantee the truce. Howard was that hostage, and his rewards were great estates in Suffolk and Cambridge.

In 1483 Edward died. The closeness of the two men was symbolized in Howard's carrying of the king's banner at his funeral. In that same year the new king, Richard III, gave Howard his highest honour, creating him Duke of Norfolk and Earl Marshal.[3] The king also ordered that the titles and dignities of Howard should pass down through the male members of the family, which is how John Howard became the first Duke of Norfolk of the Howard family. A possible darker side to him existed: it is said that it was John Howard who persuaded Edward IV's widow to allow her son, the young Duke of York, to be taken to the Tower with his brother.

When Richard III was crowned in July 1483, John Howard, Duke of Norfolk carried the crown and performed the duties of Earl Marshal of England. Howard had loyally served the royal cause of York and would die for it. In 1485, by then well into his fifties and against the wishes of many of his friends, he put on his armour in his determination not to abandon Richard III at the imminent great battle. On 22 August that year, on Bosworth Field, John Howard, Duke of Norfolk led the main body of the king's archers and was killed for his boldness.

Henry VII, who as Henry Tudor had overwhelmed Richard's forces at Bosworth, knew his politics: he married Elizabeth of York, but saw no advantage in continuing the succession of the powerful Howard family. In the first Parliament of his reign, the first Howard, Duke of Norfolk was deprived of his heritage by an Act of Attainder. This Attainder was eased in 1489, but only as far as the earldoms of the family were concerned (in 1483 the Howards had been created Earl of Surrey). Thomas Howard, John's son, having had part of the Attainder reversed, continued as a strong influence among the peers and within the court.

Henry VIII came to the throne in 1509, having become heir when his older brother, Prince Arthur, died seven years earlier. In 1510 the young Henry VIII executed Henry VII's tax collectors and then appointed Thomas Earl Marshal of England – though only in his lifetime. But Howard, like his father, was no simple courtier – there were very few in these times. In 1513 it was Howard who overcame the Scots at the Battle of Flodden in Northumberland. Its importance was that the Scots had invaded England while Henry VIII was fighting in France. Some twenty thousand Scots were met by a similar number of English commanded by Howard, who was then seventy years old. Half the Scottish force perished, including their king, James IV. Howard, still Earl of Surrey, trekked back to London a hero. The following year, Henry showed his pleasure and created the ageing aristocrat 2nd Duke of Norfolk, 'backdating' the title so that he would have all his father's estates and offices restored.

The Howards, when they were not being killed in battle or beheaded in spite, lived to good ages. Thomas, now Duke of Norfolk, lived on to 1524. His son, another Thomas, became the 3rd Duke. He too had distinguished himself at Flodden, and in 1533 he too became Earl Marshal of England. Most of them were good soldiers; some of them were also good politicians. Both Thomases now joined in the opposition to Henry's powerful Chancellor, Cardinal Wolsey. Perhaps the 2nd Duke mellowed, but his son did not and continued to stand against Wolsey. The young Thomas Howard's first wife was Anne, daughter of Edward IV. She died in 1513 and within a couple of months he had remarried. Here was a bringing together of two great families, even three. Thomas Howard's second bride was Elizabeth Stafford, the eldest daughter of the Duke of Buckingham and Elinor Percy, herself the daughter of the Earl of Northumberland. Bringing together the Buckinghams, the Northumberlands and the Norfolks produced a formidable powerbase against the movement that was trying to reduce the authority of the old families. But the ruthlessness of the court of this period was never to be underestimated, and Buckingham was executed for alleged treason. Curiously, at the moment of the purge of the old guard Howard was in that refuge of malcontents and less than prudent nobles – Ireland. Here was yet another peer who would find himself Lord Lieutenant of Ireland during interesting times. He stayed there until 1521, having not entirely succeeded in keeping order in Ireland with too few troops and even less money. It was a common enough tale.

He was then sent to worry the French coast. With a ragtag of ill-stored vessels Howard cut, thrust and savaged the French Channel coast. He is not remembered with any affection in Boulogne. To remove any risk of his boredom taking a grip of his political instincts, Howard was then sent north to do for the Scottish Borders what he had done for the French coastal towns. He appears to have been good at a form of pillage and plunder that would have excited Norse ancestors.

In 1524 this Thomas Howard inherited his father's title and became 3rd Duke of Norfolk. He did not, however have much time to settle at the family home, Kenning Hall in Norfolk, and seems to have been occupied with putting down the king's enemies in the Borders and even insurrections in his own counties. He did, however, find time to take the king's side against Wolsey. Norfolk was intent on destroying the man, plotted against him and is supposed to have put together the plan that poisoned Henry's mind and led to Wolsey's death on the road from York to London.

If Howard believed that he had the wisdom rather than simply the brutality to replace Wolsey as the eminent touchstone of Henry VIII's thinking, he was wrong. The matter of the day was, of course, Henry's divorce. It was Howard who, in 1529, threatened the pope that he would be disregarded in England unless he sanctioned Henry's divorce from Catherine of Aragon. So deeply would this

Howard be involved in the break with Rome that he would gather together much of the plunder from the monasteries. And although Henry's second wife, Anne Boleyn, was his niece, that would not not stop him, when Henry tired of her, from arranging her execution.

Howard's instruments of office were blunt. As we have seen, he was no Wolsey nor was he a Thomas Cromwell – Wolsey's protégé who replaced his master as the king's closest counsel. Cromwell became the king's Secretary and Master of the Rolls, in 1539 Lord Great Chamberlain of England and the following year Earl of Essex. It was he, and not Howard, who masterminded the annulment of the marriage of Henry and Catherine of Aragon in 1533. It was also Cromwell who drew up the arrangements to split England from the Church of Rome and to oversee the dissolution of the monasteries. Perhaps his biggest mistake was to persuade Henry that Anne of Cleves (whom the king had never met) was beautiful and that he should marry her. As the result of a conspiracy Cromwell was executed for treason in 1540.

Norfolk did not imagine Cromwell as a threat – he knew perfectly well that he was – so he needed no encouragement to join those who had set themselves against the king's adviser. In fact, many authorities believe that Norfolk was the ringleader of this opposition. It was Norfolk who, on 10 June 1540, arrested Cromwell on spurious treason charges. Once more it would seem that the Duke of Norfolk was the principal whisperer into the king's ear. Norfolk's style of influence and diplomacy had never been subtle: having disastrously married off Anne Boleyn to Henry VIII, Norfolk now produced yet another member of his family for the king's bed, Catherine Howard. Catherine, Henry's fifth wife, had been indulging in an affair with her music teacher, Henry Mannock – among others. In spite of the story-telling there is no real evidence that she continued her indiscretions once married to the king, and Howard might well have cemented the family to the monarchy for all time. Yet Catherine Howard was executed in 1542.

What was to be done with him? The king sent him to do what Howard did best – fight. In 1542 Howard resumed his particular form of barbarism on the Scottish Borders. The culmination of that venture came in November with the Battle of Solway Moss, when the English slaughtered the Scots and James V of Scotland is said to have dropped dead on hearing the news. In 1544, now in his seventies, Thomas Howard, 3rd Duke of Norfolk went off to war in France. It really was the end of his influence. The boring siege of Boulogne gained very little for his favour and, anyway, by then the Earl of Hertford was the new Cromwell in Henry's life. The family was falling out of favour: Hertford saw no good reason for any Howard to keep a good presence at court. Both Norfolk and his son Henry, the Earl of Surrey, were accused of treason. The family were not a loving group. Norfolk's wife had never forgiven him for taking what she saw as a rough washerwoman as a mistress; they had not lived together since 1533 and, as in many separations, the family took sides. So by 1546, when Norfolk was sent to the Tower accused of treason, very few credible character witnesses were on hand to help his case. There was nothing for it but to plead guilty and hope that the king, mindful of his sterling soldiery in the past, would pardon Norfolk. The 3rd Duke had never really understood diplomacy and politics. Once he had confessed, Norfolk's enemies introduced a Bill of Attainder against him. On 27 January 1547 the order was given for Norfolk to be executed the following day. Norfolk, still having learned nothing of politics, tried to obtain the king's favour – Henry was gravely ill anyway – by asking him if he would accept the Norfolk estates on behalf of Prince Edward. That did not do Norfolk any good either. On the morning of 28 January he was supposed to have his head cut off. But during the night, just hours before Norfolk's planned execution, Henry VIII died.

Perhaps wisely, the privy council – the lords who were ruling on behalf of the ill king and who would have to manage the transition to the new monarch – did not see any good reason to begin the new reign with the execution of such a prominent, albeit sometimes despicable, person, and Norfolk was left in the Tower. It was Mary, who succeeded to the throne on the death of Edward VI, who accepted his release on a point of law. In August 1553 Howard was restored as Duke of Norfolk; he was also made a member of the privy council and a Knight of the Garter. Two weeks later, as Lord High Steward, he sat at the trial of the Duke of Northumberland, an old enemy, and probably felt not a little enjoyment at sentencing the duke to death. In January 1554 Queen Mary once more needed the traditional services of Howard, by that time in his eighties. It was the time when rebels from Kent under Sir Thomas Wyatt, objecting to Mary's planned marriage to Philip II of Spain, were aiming to replace her on the throne with Princess Elizabeth. Howard marched into Kent to deal with Wyatt. He made a mess of it, and Wyatt, although he too would fail and be executed, marched on London. Norfolk now went home to Kenning Hall to die, which he did in the summer of that year.

Henry Howard, Thomas's son, had not escaped so easily as his father. and was executed in 1547. It was his son, another Thomas, who inherited the dukedom. When the 3rd Duke, his grandfather, had been restored to his titles, young Howard had received the title of Earl of Surrey. He was a courtier at Queen Mary's coronation and a gentleman of the bedchamber, a particularly important appointment coincidental with the arrival of Philip of Spain in England. In 1554, at the age of eighteen, he became 4th Duke of Norfolk (of the House of Howard) and Earl Marshal of England. Two years later he married Mary FitzAlan, the heiress of the 12th Earl of Arundel, but the following year the sixteen-year-old Mary died in childbirth. The son survived her death and so, through his mother, became the Earl of Arundel. His namesake, King Philip, became his godfather. Within a year he had a stepmother when his father, the young duke, married the heiress Margaret Audley.

Now came an interesting point in the Howards' history, traceable to the sometimes terrible figure of the 3rd Duke. It will be remembered that he had married off his niece, Anne Boleyn, to Henry VIII. In 1558, Anne Boleyn's daughter became Elizabeth I. Little wonder that the new queen called the young 4th Duke 'cousin'. He did not instinctively follow his grandfather's warlike profession. The queen sent him north to deal with the French troops who were in Scotland, but Norfolk had no stomach for it. He was far more inclined to the life of a courtier and, to some extent, to that of an academic. His father-in-law, Lord Audley, had founded Magdalen College, Cambridge; the building was still not completed, and it was the young duke who found the money to continue.

However benign a character Howard might be, he could not escape the intrigues of court. Inevitably he became one of those disturbed by the presumptions towards Elizabeth of the Earl of Leicester, Robert Dudley. His own private life was no less intriguing. When Margaret died, he married for the third time. Elizabeth, widow of Lord Dacre of Gilsland, herself died in 1567, when Norfolk thought it not a bad idea to marry off his children with the Dacre children and so expand the Norfolk estates. One of the Dacre uncles thought this quite wrong and took the matter to law. Normally it would have been heard in the court of the Marshal of England – but Norfolk held this appointment, and so a commission had to be set up to hear the case. The commission found for Norfolk.

The Duke of Norfolk, still in his thirties, was now the richest man in England. Yet he had no great power and felt that the Norfolks should have exactly that. He then hit on a scheme that would give him that power or, at least, standing. He thought he should marry Mary, Queen of Scots.

Elizabeth I had appointed a commission to try to decide what to do about Mary. Its three leading members were the Earl of Sussex, Sir Ralph Sadler and, inevitably, the Duke of Norfolk. There was a feeling that if Elizabeth refused to marry, then Mary's claim on the throne would win even more support. Hardly a month passed without some whisper of plot, counter-plot, rumour or, at the very least, suspicion. Norfolk appears to have thought Mary guilty, so a private plan was drawn up for him to marry her. That, so the hypothesis ran, would make Elizabeth happy, the stories of plotting would disappear and a reason would be found for Mary to be restored to her throne in Scotland (with Norfolk by her side). It would also allow Mary to be openly in line for the English throne, but not until the proper time came.

The whole affair was complicated by the political infighting at Court. Leicester had long tried to get rid of Cecil; now Leicester supported the idea of Norfolk's marriage to Mary, who apparently was not against it. Cecil, who had long observed Norfolk's plotting, now found himself being lobbied by Norfolk to promote the idea of the marriage with Elizabeth.

At a distance the whole context appears ridiculous; then, it appeared to many as alarming. Some nobles did not believe that Norfolk had the best interests of the queen as his motive; others thought him quite unable to cope with the Catholic pressures that would follow; yet others had not forgotten the way this richest man in the kingdom had contrived to gather the Dacre estates into the Norfolk holding. Nothing was or would be simple. Moreover, there was also a plan to rescue Mary from her house arrest in Fotheringhay Castle.[4] The curious part of this surely is that, considering how close Norfolk fancied himself to be to his 'cousin' Elizabeth I, there is no proper evidence that he ever disclosed the whole scheme to her; instead, he left it to others. At the very least, this would prove Norfolk ineffectual and something of a coward. At the worst, he would be seen as a traitor.

In the autumn of 1569, and in spite of Norfolk's humble professions of loyalty, Elizabeth could not set aside her suspicions and those who encouraged them. The queen was in a somewhat difficult position herself. The whole uncertainty that centred on Mary, Queen of Scots was too easily excited by claims of plots and treason; moreover, Norfolk was no minor peer. Yet in October he was sent to the Tower. He had no great support, especially when unrest in the north of England convinced Elizabeth that the plotting was all about her. Mary, Queen of Scots, having seen the uprisings put down, perhaps saw Norfolk as her only ticket to freedom. She wrote to him in the Tower saying that she would be faithful to him until death. It was not yet to come. He stayed in captivity until August 1570, by now having formally told Elizabeth that he had no intention whatsoever of marrying Mary.

Something in his character failed to tell him that he should give up the whole business while he remained credible: he has sometimes been described as a very vain man. However, this Duke of Norfolk was the wealthiest person in the land and considered the head of the English aristocracy. Moreover, there were still those who thought it possible that he could marry Mary after all, even though this would never happen without Elizabeth's agreement.

By now, Mary's followers had given up on easy, constitutional plans and were looking towards Spain for help. Stupidly, Norfolk now found himself doing the one thing he had always claimed he would not do and had probably never wanted to do: conspiring against the throne. It was Cecil, through his spies, who discovered that Norfolk had been in correspondence with Roberto Ridolfi, the go-between of the Spanish and Mary, Queen of Scots' party. As a merchant from Florence, Ridolfi had legitimate reason to be in England. He had Spanish support for the plot – for now it was exactly that – for the 4th Duke of Norfolk to marry Mary, Queen of Scots and, as Ridolfi saw it, to bring about the overthrow of Elizabeth. A letter was discovered, hidden in a pouch of gold, which showed Cecil that Norfolk had been writing to Mary and the Scottish plotters. Cecil interrogated Norfolk's staff, who told him about visits and conversations that were damning enough. Back to the Tower went Norfolk. In January 1572, he was tried for high treason.

No English monarch with any power has ever been entirely happy with the nobility. The earls who had swapped sides and plotted for and against the Saxon monarchs had set a precedent. The barons who had fought the powers of the monarchs from King John onwards were no different from the bankers and brokers who were to sit in city boardrooms in the twenty-first century.

So now, in the sixteenth century, Elizabeth, despite her 'mind of a man', felt little trust for her peerage. Norfolk, the most important peer in the realm, had to be made an example of. In June 1572, he was taken to Tower Hill and executed. He was never a bright man, and it was not necessary for him to have ended this way. Interestingly, for a family which would later be known as one of the leading Catholic houses of England, if not *the* leading house, Norfolk's most heartfelt protest was that he was 'never a papist since he knew what religion meant'.

The beheaded 4th Duke had a son called Thomas who went a long way to restoring the family's favour. In 1588 at the age of twenty-seven this Thomas Howard took part in the battle against the Spanish Armada, and put up such a good performance that he was knighted at sea on 25 June. He then commanded the English flotilla against the Spanish in the Azores, an engagement remembered because it was during this attack on the Spanish in March 1591 that Sir Richard Grenville was killed. The queen referred to him as 'good Thomas', and certainly his dashing exploits at sea against the Spanish appealed to her sense of gallantry. Closeness to the queen also meant being in the thick of the dangerous politics of the time, and Thomas Howard found himself commander of a force of soldiery that surrounded the house of the hapless Earl of Essex in February 1601. Essex was captured and sent to the Tower for his treasonable intentions; Thomas Howard sat as one of the judges at the earl's trial later that month. Considering the fate of his father, Thomas Howard might well have had mixed thoughts when the conclusion of the court was that Essex should be executed, even though his crime against the crown was more obvious.

When Elizabeth died in 1603 James I took well to Thomas Howard, creating him 1st Earl of Suffolk. Very grandly, as Earl Marshal of England he became joint commissioner (with the Lord Chamberlain) in charge of the Household and, less grandly, one of those appointed to deport, and worse, Jesuits in 1604.

So powerful was he that there is some evidence that the Spanish tried to recruit him as a spy against James I. There is no evidence that he accepted Spanish gold, but there is some to suggest that his second wife, Catherine, did supply the Spaniards with information about the court. She was the daughter of a Wiltshire knight, Sir Henry Knevet, and had already seen off one husband. There is little doubt that this Catherine Howard intended to exploit her husband's influences for her own good. She also used her considerable beauty to influence others to give her information and more. She might have continued to do so if it had not been for the smallpox epidemic of 1619 which left her alive but badly disfigured.

Although James I could not help but suspect almost every courtier of disloyalty, for the first decade or so Howard overcame the whispering of jealous rivals. After all, he was one of those who uncovered the infamous Gunpowder Plot in 1605. In the summer of 1614 Howard became the Lord High Treasurer of England – the official keeper and juggler of the kingdom's moneybags. But here lay political mantraps. In 1618 Howard was suspended from this post when it was found that too much money had been creamed off into too many influential hands. Howard was accused of embezzlement and of defrauding the king of jewels and money. His wife was also accused – probably correctly – of extortion. It was generally said that she was in the ancient business of demanding 'commission' from anyone doing business with or within the Treasury. In October 1619 the earl and countess were committed to the Star Chamber, found guilty and sent to the Tower. The general view is that Catherine was behind the embezzlement and misappropriation of the king's funds. They were kept in the Tower less than a fortnight, then fined heavily; their two sons lost their appointments as courtiers.

Thomas Howard should not be seen, as sometimes he is, as the dupe of his wife. He had been smart enough to put much of his estate, including his money, in the names of other members of the family before the officials demanded the return of all the embezzled money. He pleaded that if they looked at his books they would find he was a poor man. The king grew very angry and threatened to send him back to the Star Chamber; Howard realized that he might not get off so easily next time and promised to pay up. He drifted out of his dilemma and picked up a few dignities on the way, including the quite lucrative high stewardship of Exeter, but could never expect to be trusted again with such an important office as Treasurer. When he died in May 1626 he was more or less kindly remembered, but the stain of his wife's influence had long overlain the reputation of the dashing sailor who had fought so gallantly and successfully against the Armada and in the Azores and the waters off Cadiz.

A few years later, yet another Howard found himself in dire straits. In 1614 the then Earl of Arundel and his wife, Alathea Talbot (the daughter of the Earl of Shrewsbury), had a fifth son, William Howard. Brought up as a devout Roman Catholic, he was a favourite of Charles I and was knighted by him at his coronation in 1626. Eleven years later William Howard married Mary Stafford. For all sorts of heraldic reasons, not long after the death of Mary's father, Lord Stafford, William and she were created Baron and Baroness Stafford. Also for heraldic reasons (including a little jiggery-pokery) Howard became Viscount Stafford, took his seat in the House of Lords and with it acquired considerable influence.

In 1642 the Civil War began. Stafford and his wife went to live in Flanders, where he remained for at least five years. There is some documentation which suggests that Stafford attempted to return to England to restore his estates and those of his family. He may also have tried to act as a go-between in the cause of the exiled Charles II.

William Howard, or Viscount Stafford as he is more usually remembered, later rode an uneasy journey between his relief at being back in England under a restored monarchy and his disillusionment with the way in which he was treated. None of this should be surprising. Stafford seems to have believed that Charles II and those closest to him treated him with injustice. He did not always vote for the king in Parliament, which hardly helped his cause or the popular image of his personality and did little to suggest that he was not frequently on the fringes of some Catholic plot. This Howard, after all, was very much a Roman Catholic at a time when there was continuous paranoia over the possibility of Catholic plots against the throne and its authority.

Eventually, William Howard fell from grace over yet another popish plot – a victim of the perjury committed by the dreadful Titus Oates. Ironically, Oates had become a chaplain to the Protestants in the largely Catholic Norfolk household. Egged on by an equally scurrilous figure, Israel Tonge, Oates had ingratiated himself with Catholic families in search of a real or made-up plot against the throne – anything would do to denigrate the Catholics. Oates literally invented the so-called Popish Plot of 1678. He claimed that the Jesuits planned to kill Charles II and as many Protestants as possible and put the Duke of York, a Catholic convert, on the throne as James II. William Howard, Viscount Stafford, was implicated in this non-existent plot along with four other Catholic peers, Earl Powis and Lords Wardour, Petre and Belasis. Off they went to the Tower.

Stafford was the easiest to put on trial, probably because he was seen as a weak figure, and on 30 November 1680 he appeared at the beginning of his seven-day hearing. Oates claimed that Howard in his role as paymaster general of the army had received instructions from the pope to raise forces against the state. Two other so-called reliable witnesses claimed that Stafford had tried to hire them to murder the king. On 7 December he was found guilty by a majority decision and sentenced to hanging, drawing and quartering. Stafford had not had much support among the lords. He was never a popular member of the nobility and was not even much liked in his own family. It seems that the only person who spoke well for him was the future Duke of Norfolk, Lord Mowbray. Stafford continued to claim that he was innocent, and even went as far as trying to put the blame for the non-existent plot on to other peers. His fellow peers lost patience and on 29 December, after Charles II had agreed to commute the sentence to a less brutal form of execution, Stafford was beheaded at the Tower. It was not until 1824 that William Howard, the 1st Viscount Stafford, was recognized as having been the victim of the lies of Titus Oates, and received a posthumous pardon.

Lord Mowbray, who had spoken for Stafford, was the 7th Duke of Norfolk. He amassed authority and constitutional titles, such as Constable of Windsor Castle and warden of the forest and parks. These considerable honours (the previous warden had been Prince Rupert) show how close this Howard was to the power and decision-making of the very difficult period of the last few years of Charles II's reign – the time of the Rye House Plot to assassinate the king, and of Charles's rule without Parliament. When Charles died in 1685, Henry Howard, the 7th Duke of Norfolk, was one of those who put his signature to the proclamation of the new monarch, James II. This Howard was not a Roman Catholic but a committed Protestant, whilst the king was a convert to Catholicism. Being so close to the monarch, it was inevitable that Howard would find it difficult to reconcile constitutional and religious duties. There is a story that, when carrying the Sword of State before James II, Howard reached the door of the Roman Catholic chapel and refused to go any further; James told the duke that his father would have gone further; the duke is said to have replied that James's father would not have gone so far.

It is no surprise that the 7th Duke was among those who encouraged William of Orange to come to England. He raised a sufficiently strong army and the enthusiasm of the mayor and leading figures of Norwich and Norfolk to stand against popery and to hold the eastern counties for William. He was also in the front row of the peers, by choice even more than by rank, who voted for William to be joint monarch with the only rightful heir to the throne, Mary – James II's daughter.

Edward Howard, the 9th Duke of Norfolk, was also put on trial for high treason and that was because he took part in the Jacobite uprising in 1715. He was acquitted largely because the witnesses, almost miraculously for him, disappeared. Seven years later he was back in gaol because once again he had been implicated in Jacobite plots. Once again he got out. The 12th Duke, Bernard (1765–1842), is largely remembered for divorcing his wife because she was having an affair with the then Lord Lucan. The 13th Duke was something of a grand courtier as Treasurer of the Household, Captain of the Yeoman of the Guard and, more famously, a Protestant convert. This was in 1851, at the time of the illustrious Pope Pius IX. It was Pius, who published the papal bull *Ineffabilis Deus*, decreeing the Immaculate Conception. Equally sternly, he re-established the Roman Catholic hierarchy in England. It was this last point that made Henry Charles Howard, the 13th Duke, break with Rome. It is also said in the family that on his deathbed the duke sensed his conscience and took his final sacrament from a Catholic chaplain. From that period the Howards were recognized as the premier family of Roman Catholics in Britain – a sobriquet that understandably upsets more liberal Catholics.

Their home today remains one of the most famous buildings in England. Arundel Castle in Sussex is not dissimilar to Windsor Castle, although not so large. The building of the castle was started by Roger de Montgomery in 1067, the year after the Conquest. De Montgomery had not been one of William the Conqueror's knights but had had a far more responsible position: he had looked after Normandy while William was away fighting for England. Consequently, William rewarded him by giving him a third of Sussex and creating him Earl of Arundel – hence the castle. The castle was started in the eleventh century and has been in the ownership of the Howards since 1138. But the Howards did not really take a great interest in the place until the late eighteenth century when the 11th Duke began to restore it. Like all tenancies and dynasties, its story owes much to the ever-absentee land-lord. The long connection with the monarch, on whichever side, remains the fact that the Duke of Norfolk is Earl Marshal of All England. Perhaps the day is not far off when the utilitarian distinctions of modern government and its nervousness of historical precedent will remove that centuries-old dignity.

NOTES

1 Sometimes known as Matilda because the two names were at this time interchangeable. For example, the Empress Matilda was also known as the Empress Maud.

2 The present Duke of Norfolk, the seventeenth, is also Earl of Arundel, Earl of Surrey and Earl of Norfolk (as well as the Baron of Beaumont, FitzAlan, Maltravers and Howard of Glossop).

3 The appointment of Marshal in the Royal Household has its origins in the Holy Roman Empire and was adopted by the English court following France and Normandy. In England the Marshal was originally known as The Lord High Constable, a military figure rather than a steward or herald. By the fourteenth century, the Marshal had become a judge in the court of chivalry. In 1386 the then Earl of Norfolk became the first to hold the title Earl Marshal. In 1672, the Earl of Norwich (later Duke of Norfolk) was appointed the first hereditary Earl Marshal – by then, the duties were ceremonial, but powerful. Today the Earl Marshal presides over the college of arms and great state occasions with the Lord Great Chamberlain; the latter has precedence.

4 Fotheringhay Castle, Northampton. Mary, Queen of Scots, was held there in 1586 and executed there the following year.

FURTHER READING

HURSTFIELD, Joel, *Elizabeth I and the Unity of England*, English Universities Press, 1960.
WILLIAMS, Neville, *A Tudor Tragedy*, Barrie Books, 1964.

CHAPTER FOURTEEN

THE DALRYMPLES

In the eighteenth century, Sir John Dalrymple made an important discovery: how to make soap from herrings. He is not best known for this. John Dalrymple (1726–1810), later fourth baronet of Cranstoun, was one of the eighteenth century's distinguished Scottish historians. It was he who rummaged in the Jacobite papers, long hidden from most viewers, and from them claimed that Louis XIV of France was financing leading English Whig politicians, including Algernon Sidney and England's most famous general, the Duke of Marlborough, then plain John Churchill.[1] He is certainly known and remembered properly for his three volumes of British and Irish history.[2] But we need know nothing more of this John Dalrymple other than that he was a member of a Scottish family which produced some of the most famous legal minds and politicians of that land.

The Dalrymple titles certainly go back to the seventeenth century, when the first baronet of Stair was created in 1664. The family also keep the baronetcy of Killock, given in 1698. The first Viscount Stair appeared in 1690 and a Dalrymple became Earl of Stair in 1703. These are all Scottish titles.

The first Viscount Stair was Sir James Dalrymple, born in 1619. The family had always been deeply involved in Scottish affairs, particularly in Ayrshire. Dalrymple's father was the laird of Stair, an estate in Kyle in that county. Dalrymple's immediate ancestors had been persecuted by the infamous Scottish Archbishop Blackadder because the Dalrymples were followers of the ideas of the Reformist Church and its doctrine as defined by Wycliffe.

John Wycliffe, born in 1329, was one of the original opponents of papal doctrine and a champion of the idea that there should be secular authority over the clergy. Pope Gregory XI urged the bishops to put Wycliffe in prison. He undermined, so the bishops thought, the very constitution of the Church by preaching that it would be better off without a pope and certainly without bishops. Particularly important to his evangelism was the fact that he spoke to the people in English rather than the customary Latin. His own missionaries were known as 'poor priests', for they travelled the country as penniless itinerants spreading Wycliffe's word. This was a time when there was no English translation of the Bible, and therefore his interpretation and that of his followers was unusual: his own translation spread throughout the land. His supporters were known as Lollards, from a Dutch word meaning 'to mumble'.

The Lollards were active and established in Kyle, Dalrymple country. South-west Scotland, particularly Ayrshire, was the fertile territory in which the ideas of Wycliffe first grew north of the border. The Dalrymples embraced these views and were first chastised and then persecuted.

This did not mean that the Dalrymples were left in a wretched state. James graduated from Glasgow University in 1637 and then might have become a lawyer had it not been for the Civil War. He joined the Earl of Glencairn and commanded a troop of horse when the Scots defeated Charles I at the Battle of Duns Law.

Curiously, he then became an academic and taught logic and politics at Glasgow. By the autumn of 1647 James Dalrymple was a lawyer married to an heiress, Margaret Ross of Balneil, and living in Edinburgh where he became one of the small group who went to talk to the exiled Charles II to encourage him to return to Scotland. That he was a good lawyer, if not an immediately successful negotiator with Charles II, is beyond doubt. For Dalrymple, although closely connected with the events that led to the return of Charles II, is best remembered as the reformer of Scottish law. Cromwell had made him a judge even though Dalrymple had refused to swear an oath of allegiance to the Commonwealth. This refusal to take an oath which effectively would have meant the abandonment of the Scottish process of law proved a major constitutional defeat for Cromwell. The fact that he accepted Cromwell's invitation to be a judge was partly due to the personal pleadings of the royalist-turned-parliamentarian General Monck, although this did not save him from accusations that he was effectively treating with the enemy – Cromwell.

When Cromwell died in 1658, the courts were closed down anyway. But Monck still regarded him as the foremost advocate and constitutional adviser. It was Dalrymple who urged Monck to make sure that Parliament should be the people's seat of grievance as well as of power; this suggests that Dalrymple, although a monarchist, also held republican tendencies. At the time, most people still saw a black-and-white debate between absolutism (the concentration of power in the hands of the monarch) and utter rebellion (as with the Common-wealth). Dalrymple anticipated that the future of English constitutional law would be a monarch with limited powers, and advised Monck as much. If this seems obvious in the twenty-first century, it was not so in the seventeenth.

At first, Charles II was gracious in his appointments towards Dalrymple. He was made a judge at the court of sessions and was one of those given the powerful task of deciding what compensation, if any, might be given to those who had remained loyal to the concept of monarchy and had suffered financially through the rebellion. However, the existence of Charles II's court and the juggling for absolute power – if the king had no power, then nor did his courtiers – meant that people like the Duke of Lauderdale, who was Scottish Secretary when the monarchy was restored, were determined to maintain absolute power at the centre. His was the last initial that made up the Cabal which ruled on the king's behalf (see Chapter 12). Lauderdale was quite possibly motivated more by his need for uncomplicated order than by personal gain. Whatever the truth, and some of the judges could not so easily give way Dalrymple resigned. In the late summer of 1670 he was once again involved in the constitutional debate of who should sit in which Parliament. He and his Scottish colleagues wanted a union between Scotland and England. However, they insisted that the Scots should have the same numbers in the Westminster Parliament as in the Scottish Parliament, and there was no way that the English would ever agree to that. Once more, Dalrymple became leader of the Scottish judiciary. He was a judge, a legal reformer and one who had to fight the alien concept that, if the crown appointed a judge, that lawyer would be beholden to the monarch.

By the 1680s he had lost his foremost position on the bench. He was then able to get on with writing his much-admired work, *Institutions of the Law of Scotland*. Dalrymple's treatise covered Roman civil law and the laws of the Netherlands and France, together with Scottish civil and constitutional practice, and laid down the basic principles of modern Scottish jurisprudence which have become so greatly admired outside Scotland.

But Dalrymple could not be allowed to write quietly, for the religious animosities would not be still. The whole family, including his wife and indeed their servants, were persecuted and prosecuted. He fled to the Netherlands where he busied himself with writing philosophical dissertations on morality, theology and human knowledge. (Newton was writing at the same time, and his *Principia Mathematica* was published in 1687 while Dalrymple was working on his uncompleted *Ideas of Natural Theology*.) He must have been a very powerful figure, because various attempts were made to have him extradited from Leiden. He was even, in his absence, named as a conspirator in the Rye House Plot (see Chapter 10).

It is likely that the relief from persecution came about because his son had found favour with James II. It did not last long because, as with so many other advisers, Dalrymple's son soon fell foul of the king's temper. However, none of this was very important because the following year, 1688, was the year of the Glorious Revolution. Dalrymple was one of those who personally attended William of Orange when he sailed from Helvoetsluys for England; he was then seventy years old, and William was much taken with his wisdom and loyalty. William became a firm advocate of the Dalrymple family for the rest of his life and, even at his great age, Dalrymple himself was once more appointed senior judge in the court of sessions.

The Dalrymples needed royal patronage because their enemies would not let them be. The powerful Scottish political cabal known as the Club (see p. 229) continued to attack Dalrymple: it is said that there was hardly a crime in Scotland to which the Club did not attempt to link the Dalrymple name. So the controversy surrounding this family would continue, particularly with James's son who would always be linked with one of the most terrible moments in Scottish history.

That son was John Dalrymple, born in 1648. He was knighted by Charles II, although the reason is uncertain: one account suggests that the knighthood came because he was his father's son; another, because he helped to prevent the destruction of an English warship in the River Medway when the Dutch attacked in 1667. When he returned to Scotland he became a lawyer, by all reports one of the most eloquent of his day. When he went to the Scottish Parliament he was soon recognized as one of the most formidable orators of his generation.

Whatever his fluency, Dalrymple did not find himself on any silk road through politics. He was prosecuted for maladministration in the manner of collecting fines from the family's tenants. In September 1684 he was once again apprehended and examined for three months in prison. Here, then, was one of the most famous advocates and politicians of his day a prisoner of the state. His father, Sir James, was prosecuted for apparently helping the Earl of Argyll in his invasion of Scotland in support of the Monmouth Rebellion of 1685 (see Chapter 7). It was only a concoction of favour and political manoeuvring that saved the Dalrymples and their estates. Moreover, the religious problems were never far from this family. Towards the end of 1685, Dalrymple's fortunes seemed to revive and he certainly had the favour of the king. There was a suggestion that he was so influential that he might even be able to bring together the Scottish Presbyterian and Catholic parties; this was never likely.

Part of Dalrymple's task was to carry out the wishes of the monarchy in London. The Scottish connection with the English throne gave no comfort to the independently minded Scottish peers and Church. Dalrymple was instinctively drawn to the idea of William of Orange becoming protector of the Protestant faith and thus king of Great Britain – a title, incidentally, first claimed by James VI of Scotland as James I of England.

Since Dalrymple's father – he who had been prosecuted for his part in the Argyll invasion – was actually aboard William of Orange's ship when it sailed for England, it was no surprise that the son, Sir John, was among the first of the Scots to champion the case for William of Orange becoming joint monarch with Mary, his wife. In fact, it was as member of the Scottish Parliament for Stranraer that he moved the declaration that James Stuart no longer had a claim to the Scottish throne. Dalrymple then travelled to London as the third commissioner who would offer the Scottish throne to William and Mary.

William of Orange, when he became William III of England, relied almost entirely upon the Dalrymples to tell him the truth about who was for him and against him in Scotland and how he should best handle the politics of his northern kingdom.

William was at first confused by John Dalrymple's reputation; indeed, by that of the whole family. He had been told that the Dalrymples were thoroughly despised in Scotland; but how could this be if the young Dalrymple was trusted sufficiently to be one of the commissioners to offer William the Scottish throne? William was a practical soldier as well as a monarch; his sense of judgement and advantage was well tuned. Very simply, the Dalrymples were able to deliver their political promises. William also saw John Dalrymple as a unique window through which he could see the truth about Scottish management. No one questioned Dalrymple's patriotism as a Scot, but he was said to have the advocate's talent to lay before the king both the Scottish and the English viewpoints, and then to draw the balance of conclusions in the clearest manner to the ever-suspicious William.

Equally, the king could hardly dismiss from his mind the fact that Dalrymple had held office under the Catholic James II. It was certainly not a point lost on Dalrymple's Scottish enemies. For example, Sir James Montgomery – perhaps bitter because he had not gained high political office himself in Scotland – led the opposition to the increasing influence of the Dalrymples. This opposition, known as the Club, was successful for a considerable time and got a grip in the Scottish Parliament. The Club's members managed to push through an Act of the Scottish Parliament which forbade the king to appoint to public office anyone who had worked for James II. This was obviously aimed at clipping the wings of the Dalrymples. Montgomery also saw the opportunity, as well as the need, to use the Jacobites to help his cause. Yet, like so many political adventures in Scotland before and since, it achieved little lasting success. This was partly due to the Scottish habit of ignoring the long game of politics, of feeding on past – even clannish – animosities, and of seemingly being unable to avoid the constitutional as well as the political trap of jealousies.

In 1691 Dalrymple, by now holding the romantic family title Master of Stair, went with King William to Holland. It was here that he is said to have advised the king on how to go about the settlement of the Highlands. Against this background, in August 1691, Dalrymple produced for the king a proclamation that would declare an amnesty for all the Scottish clans who were against the monarchy. They were given until 1692 to declare their allegiance to the king. William needed this proclamation, but it is not certain whether Dalrymple really wanted it to work. He believed, it would seem, that it would be much better for the king if some of the clans ignored the offer of amnesty, that the king could take arms against them, teach them a lesson and thereby remind the whole of Scotland who indeed was king. The king's men prepared for war in the Highlands.

Dalrymple, as Secretary of State, had set his plan well. The oath of allegiance had a deadline that could not be ignored. Sir Thomas Livingstone was given the task of making sure that those who objected or did not comply were put to the sword.

The story of the Glencoe massacre of February 1692 is well told elsewhere. In simple terms, Maclan of the Macdonalds of Glencoe agreed to take the oath of allegiance. However, he did not do so until after the deadline, which was hardly his fault because apparently he turned up as instructed at Fort William on 31 December only to find the place empty. He therefore took the oath of allegiance late, on 6 January. Dalrymple and Livingstone were uncompromising. The Campbells, who were deadly rivals of the Macdonalds, were part of the arrangement for the attack on Glencoe. On 13 February 1692 at Ballachulish, Lochaber, thirty-eight of the Macdonalds were killed; others later died of their wounds; the women and children of the clan were turned out into the cold to freeze to death. At first, few people knew what had happened; it was not until April 1692 that details began to leak into the offices of the *Paris Gazette*.

Dalrymple certainly cannot be blamed for what happened at Glencoe; he might, however, be criticized for his failure to seek retribution. The massacre fell easily into his scheme of things. One difficulty with outright condemnation was that criticism of Dalrymple at the time would have been seen as criticism of the king. It was not until 1695, three years after the event, that a royal commission was established to find out what had happened at Glencoe. The commission's report criticized Dalrymple, accusing him of ordering the action.

Three hundred years on, the Glencoe massacre appears as a great tragedy and a terrible stain on Scottish history. At the time, however, the reaction to the event had far more to do with politics than with any sense of horror at the deaths of the Macdonalds. The clan were described variously as robbers and thieves, and there was no enormous sympathy for them. But to be able to bring about the downfall of Dalrymple, Master of Stair, was a heaven- (or perhaps hell-) sent opportunity. The criticism against him was that he had exceeded the brief approved by William III. We cannot know whether the king understood or had even read the plan Dalrymple had in mind. His general approval had to be interpreted by his lieutenants and again, given the time, the circumstances, the politics and the lack of communications, there is no way in which any letter of intent could be strictly observed, only its spirit.

What is important to our story is that William III was not swayed by Dalrymple's critics, most of whom clearly had motives far beyond any sense of justice. The king did not criticize him for what had happened. But Dalrymple saved William from any decision he might have contemplated, by resigning as Secretary of State. It was in that year, 1695, that Dalrymple's father died and he became Viscount Stair. Prudently, he did not take his seat in Parliament; It was not until February 1700 that he felt confident enough to enter the Lords. In 1703 he was clearly still in favour with the monarch – by then Queen Anne – for he was created 1st Earl of Stair. He kept out of office – or was kept out – but was the queen's principal adviser on Scottish matters, and once again a monarch was comforted by the fact that her adviser not only saw both sides of the Anglo-Scottish argument, but was able to present it in eloquent style.

This was a time when England and Scotland were moving towards the great Act of Union which took place in 1707. Dalrymple undoubtedly advised that, for the sake of both countries, union was necessary. Not surprisingly, there were those in Scotland who rushed to brand him traitor. Ironically, John Dalrymple, 1st Earl of Stair, died shortly after the final important article of the treaty was approved by Parliament: on 1 January 1707 he spoke long and wisely on the need for the joining together of the two constitutions, and succeeded in convincing the members. Afterwards, exhausted, he took to his bed, where he died seven days later.

The 1st Earl will always be remembered for Glencoe, which is a shame because his contribution to the political and constitutional life of Scotland was so much greater than some people imagine. Yet the Dalrymples were never far from political and military controversy.

His son John, the 2nd Earl, was brought up against the backdrop of these tragedies and even contributed to them when in 1682 (he would have been but eight years old) he shot dead his elder brother. It was an accident, yet his parents could no longer bear to have him near them. He went to live with his grandfather, Sir James Dalrymple, in the Netherlands. It will be remembered that Sir James was a confidant of William of Orange, and not surprisingly, young John came into William's court. William of Orange became his patron and his friend for life.

John Dalrymple, as might have been expected, became a soldier and, although there is no documentary evidence, probably served with William during his wars on the continent. In 1703 he became an aide-de camp to the Duke of Marlborough. He had very good wars and was celebrated for having saved the life of the future king of Sweden, the Prince of Hesse-Cassel. He probably served at the famous Battle of Blenheim, commanded a brigade at Ramillies and became colonel of the Scots Greys. At Oudenarde in 1708 he bravely drew fire when he found that, in the confusion of battle, two of his own battalions were shooting at each other. When they saw their commander, fire was ceased. He was once again commanding, by now as a major general, at the Battle of Malplaquet.

He battled through siege and counter-campaign, winning plaudits (including one from his future friend, Voltaire), the Order of the Thistle and his own medal, struck by the Elector of Saxony and King of Poland, Augustus, who much admired him.

Dalrymple had by now become a full general. But this was the early eighteenth century, and the ways of regiments were far different from those of today. There was no secure future waiting for him in the army. For family and financial reasons he was forced to sell his regiment to the Earl of Portmore. In Edinburgh, Dalrymple now took to politics, mindful of the fact that the Elector of Hanover would soon become George I of England, Scotland, Ireland and Wales. Yet there was more to Edinburgh than politics – a life which, incidentally, was proving difficult for him.

Dalrymple fell in love with Eleanor, the widow of Viscount Primrose. She is remembered as being beautiful, enormously strong-willed, wretchedly treated by her late husband, determined never to remarry and the subject of Sir Walter Scott's novel *My Aunt Margaret's Mirror*. Dalrymple pleaded for her hand, but Eleanor kept it firmly from his grasp. One who has been through the great campaigns, stirrup to stirrup, with the Duke of Marlborough is not easily deflected from his target. One night he climbed into her bedroom in the early hours and stood brazenly at her window. Eleanor, her reputation teetering, gave in and they were married.

Dalrymple found much favour with George I – they had known each other during Marlborough's continental campaigns – and became a lord of the bed-chamber. He was appointed envoy to Paris and, through some rigorous detective work, discovered the correspondence that resulted in the impeachment of Henry St John, 1st Viscount Bolingbroke. Bolingbroke had helped to plot the Jacobite rebellion of 1715 and after its failure had escaped to France, where he acted as private secretary to James Stuart, the Old Pretender.

Dalrymple's first task in Paris was to seek intelligence on the Jacobites and destabilize their relationship with the French court. In eighteenth-century Parisian society the best way to pick up the gossip was to provide a table upon which it could be laid out. Not surprisingly, therefore, Dalrymple quickly became known as one of the best party-givers in the capital.

Dalrymple, by 1719 a full ambassador and still entertaining on the most lavish of scales, had to find his own money to pay for it all. He failed. There were no great stock exchanges then on which he might dabble, and his best hopes lay in sinecures which paid pensions. He was saved from further expenditure in Paris when Robert Walpole became the first British Prime Minister and sent his brother, Horatio, to be ambassador at the French court.

Dalrymple returned to Scotland and his estates. In one part he is said to have planted trees to represent the battle positions at Blenheim, rather as Capability Brown did for Marlborough at Blenheim Palace. Dalrymple also restructured the family farm and was one of the first people to introduce large-scale growing of turnips – a vegetable that fascinated more than one British politician.[3]

Dalrymple messed in the politics of Scotland and failed, particularly in his opposition to Robert Walpole and to the Earl of Islay, who was Scottish Secretary. Consequently he lost one of his sinecures as vice-admiral of Scotland, together with his colonelcy of Inniskilling. He also lost his seat as a Scottish peer. Dalrymple then planned his campaign against Walpole with military precision, such as it was in the first half of the eighteenth century. He was quite successful, and when Walpole went out of office in 1742 Dalrymple became a field marshal. He was commander-in-chief of the army when England fell into the War of the Austrian Succession in support of Maria Theresa (see p. 181). In spite of remembering perfectly the lessons taught him by Marlborough, he was generally outfought by the French. At this stage, George II arrived in Germany to take command, and so Dalrymple found himself with his king at the famous Battle of Dettingen. In spite of his gallantry, but probably because of his short-sightedness, Dalrymple was captured; but after the battle he was released.

Dalrymple was not then trusted as a strategist by George II, who much preferred to stick to his Hanoverian advisers. Dalrymple tried to resign; George II tried to keep him. Dalrymple finally got his way, having given the king a lesson in European politics and his request that he should be allowed to return to his plough. In 1747, his regiments restored to him, including the Scots Greys, he died at Queensberry House in Edinburgh. He was remembered with affection and admiration as a soldier, a diplomat and a figure of romance.

The Dalrymples continued as one of those families that were always involved in the history of Scotland and England, although not necessarily as public figures.

For example, the 8th Earl of Stair was a celebrated soldier who publicly tried to rid the late eighteenth-century and early nineteenth-century army of corporal punishment. In 1832 he won the parliamentary seat of Midlothian for the Whigs. Modern political historians might note that Dalrymple's majority of sixty-nine in that election was considered at the time to be a warning that the Tories no longer had a right to rule in Scotland. Even today there are few lists of distinguished Scottish advocates and military men, particularly the navy, that do not include a Dalrymple.

NOTES

1 Sir John Dalrymple, *Memoirs of Great Britain and Ireland from the Dissolution of the Last Parliament until the Sea Battle of La Hogue*, 1790.

2 *Memoirs of Great Britain and Ireland from the Dissolution of the Last Parliament until the Sea Battle of La Hogue.*

3 Viscount Townshend, Walpole's brother-in-law and leader of the Whigs, retired from politics in 1730 and developed the family farms in Norfolk, especially the growing of turnips, and became known as Turnip Townshend.

FURTHER READING

CARLYLE, Alexander, *Memoirs of His Own Times*, 1860.

GRAHAM, J. Murray, *The Annals and Correspondence of the Viscount and the First and Second Earls of Stair*, 1875.

CHAPTER FIFTEEN

THE WALDEGRAVES

To modern readers, the name of Waldegrave is probably associated with William Waldegrave, who was a Cabinet minister in John Major's government. Yet he is just the most recent in a long line of the Chewton and Waldegrave family who have been active in British politics and warfare since the fourteenth century.

The first of the important politicians was a Suffolk MP in the 1370s, Sir Richard Wal de Grave. It was he who in 1381 became only the fifth Speaker of the House of Commons.[1] Not surprisingly, little is known of him except that he died in 1402. What is known is that the family took its name from Walgrave in Northamptonshire (the present William Waldegrave pronounces his name 'Walgrave'). A John de Walgrave was sheriff of London in 1205. One of his descendants, Richard, fought in France with Edward III in 1329 and became an MP for Lincolnshire in 1335; he was also recorded in 1343 as having been a friend of Humphrey de Bohun, the then Earl of Hereford (see Chapter 13). His son, again Richard, had a house in Suffolk and became a member of the 1376 Parliament for that county. He was also in Parliament at the time of Richard II, and it was he who in 1381 became Speaker of the House of Commons. It is recorded that he did not want to be Speaker, and asked Richard II to spare him the task, but the king would hear none of it. It was not a popular period in Parliamentary history, particularly as Speaker Wal de Grave was expected to preside over the revoking of so many of the concessions that Richard II had made towards the supporters of Wat Tyler's rebellion.

Sir Richard's son, yet another Richard, fought in the Hundred Years' War and led ten thousand Englishmen against the French. During the Wars of the Roses, Sir Thomas Wal de Grave distinguished himself at the Battle of Towton, in March 1461, a terrible affray fought during a snowstorm and in which the Lancastrians suffered enormously. The Yorkists, of whom Wal de Grave was one, were then led by Edward IV to York itself, and captured it. It was at this point that Henry VI escaped to Scotland. Thomas Wal de Grave was knighted for his bravery.

From about this point, the late fifteenth century, we find the name of the family written as one word rather than three. By now, the Waldegraves were well established at court. In the early sixteenth century John Waldegrave was the comptroller of Princess Mary's household. The connection between the Waldegraves and the Catholic Mary was a hazard of the time. John Waldegrave's second son, Edward born in 1517, took over the family estates at Borley in Essex (the oldest son had died) and, thanks to Edward VI, also had land in Northamptonshire. He became a courtier to the then Princess Mary, a Catholic. The privy council had decided that she should not be allowed to take part in the celebration of Mass. Religious fears and confrontations between Protestantism and Catholicism often led to the Tower of London: so it was with Sir Edward Waldegrave. He refused to bar the Princess from her devotions, and for his conscience was sent first to the Fleet prison and then to the Tower. He became dreadfully ill and was allowed out of the Tower, but remained under house arrest.

When Edward VI died and Mary became queen, she rewarded him for his suffering: he became a privy councillor and Master of the Great Wardrobe, and received two manors. One was Navestock in Essex and the other was the present seat of the Waldegrave family, Chewton Manor between Bath and Wells in Somerset. Such a relationship between courtier and monarch was usually fraught, and that between Mary and Waldegrave was no exception. He would allow her religion; what he could not easily do was agree to her plan to marry Philip of Spain.

Mary's hope had always been to reclaim England for Rome. She never understood the sense of fear and therefore hostility to the idea of her marrying her Spanish cousin, Philip. There were, as we have seen, revolts which she put down. Officially she joined England once more to Rome and while doing so earned herself the sobriquet 'Bloody Mary' which would be used by later commentators. Waldegrave found it very difficult to live with Mary's excesses; yet there is always a way with courtiers. He was given a considerable financial inducement and, instead of striding with constitutional placards against the Marian campaign, Waldegrave actually became one of the commissioners to hear the case for Mary's plan to re-enact the old heresy laws. Even with Mary's death in 1558, vexed religious prejudice followed him. Waldegrave was not admired by the new queen, Elizabeth I. When it was discovered that he was allowing Mass to be said in his own house, Waldegrave, his wife, their priest and even his small congregation were incarcerated. Edward Waldegrave died in the Tower of London on 1 September 1561 and was buried there.

The next Edward Waldegrave, who was the first baronet in that name, was an old man when the Civil War started. However, he was a royalist through and through and so, although in his seventies, he took command of royalist cavalry and fought energetically and certainly gallantly in Cornwall. It cost him and the family dearly: he lost a fortune and two sons. But he survived the war until the capture of his leader, Charles I, and died in bed in 1647.

The fourth baronet was Sir Henry Waldegrave, who became the first Baron Waldegrave of Chewton. The reason he was given the barony was that he gave the king a grandson. James II had a mistress, Arabella Churchill, with whom he had a daughter named Henrietta (see Chapter 7); she married Waldegrave. Their first son, named James, was born at the beginning of 1686. The king then gave the child's father his new title. In 1687, James II appointed Waldegrave Comptroller of the Royal Household and Lord Lieutenant of Somerset, but he did not enjoy his barony long and died in France in 1689. James Waldegrave now inherited his father's title, his mother's devotion and his king's patronage.

James was brought up a Catholic, like his father, and let us not forget that King James II was a Catholic convert. However, when his first wife Mary died, Lord James Waldegrave gave up his Catholic religion, declared himself a Protestant and took his seat in the House of Lords. This was a very grand statement. By now, James II had gone and the Glorious Revolution was long past, yet the conflict between the Catholic and Protestant persuasions had not settled. There was always a suspicion that the Jacobites would rise again – which they did, but unsuccessfully. James Waldegrave's position was no whimsy: here was a powerful young man whose family included even more powerful personalities. The Duke of Marlborough was the brother of Arabella Churchill, James's grandmother. James's uncle was the Duke of Berwick who was, in turn, the illegitimate son of James II and Arabella Churchill. Berwick was a staunch Catholic who had had to flee from England at the time of the Glorious Revolution and fought with his father's troops in an attempt to regain the throne. It was never to be, and Berwick escaped – even though he had taken a prominent part in the Battle of the Boyne in 1690. It was Berwick who helped Philip V defeat the English at Alamansta in 1707 during the War of the Spanish Succession; it was he who again led Spanish troops against the English and captured Barcelona in 1714. This was a prominent Catholic.

It is not surprising, then, that the Jacobite supporters thought they might have an ally. They did not. Robert Walpole, who became the first Prime Minister, took Waldegrave under his wing. In 1725, he was chosen as envoy to Paris to carry the good wishes and proclamations from George I to Louis XV upon the latter's marriage: a seemingly small if dignified mission, but one with obvious political undertones. Two years later he was appointed ambassador in Vienna, just as George II came to the throne. There is an indication here that, given the delicate diplomatic and military balance in Europe at the time, Britain had to have the supreme diplomat at the court of the Emperor. In 1729, James Waldegrave became Viscount Chewton and therefore Earl Waldegrave; then in 1730, he became Our Man in Paris. This was Walpole's personal and considered appointment, because James was replacing the first Prime Minister's own brother, Horatio. Nor should we forget his uncle: Berwick and the other Jacobites in exile lurked in the French capital. Yet again, the delicacy of his appointment should not be underestimated. After all, by his birth James Waldegrave was not so removed from the Jacobite inheritance. Spain was trying to detach the English, diplomatically, from the French. At the same time, there was a French movement to set the English at war with the Spanish. The opportunities for spying, scandal and intrigue were enormous, and they were fully exercised.

Throughout all this the position of England and Spain grew more difficult, and so therefore did Waldegrave's own position as ambassador. In October 1739 England and Spain declared war. A year later the Emperor, Charles VI, died and war across Europe appeared to be a question of time. Waldegrave was not a particularly well man and he died in April 1741.

His eldest son, also James Waldegrave, was born in 1715 and now became the 2nd Earl. He was the perfect courtier – even more successful at it than his father had been. This Waldegrave became George II's closest friend, and King George was not an easy man to get on with. Like his father, George I, he did not have an enormous regard for the English people he ruled, nor did he have much regard for his wife, the long-suffering Caroline of Ansbach who, apart from having to put up with his personality, had also to cope with his openly engaged infidelities. When younger, like all the Hanoverians he disliked his parents and had open political and family rows with George I. His father did not like him either. The family trait continued with George II at unambivalent odds with his son, Frederick, Prince of Wales. Politically, George II was in a dilemma. His son actually set up his own political opposition to his father, having moved out of the royal home and set himself up in Leicester House which became a meeting-place for radicals. The king would like to have got rid of his Prime Minister, Walpole, and it was only the intervention and guidance of Queen Caroline and his closest advisers that prevented him doing so. When she died in 1737, George II and Walpole were even further apart; the latter resigned in 1742, when Lord Carteret, who became Earl Granville, replaced Walpole as the king's political counsel. The double act of Carteret and George II led Britain by the nose into the silly War of the Austrian Succession between 1740 and 1748. Few thought that Britain's intervention would do any more than protect the interests of the Hanoverians – hence George II's determination to go to war. It was in this conflict, in 1743, that the king became the last British monarch to take part in a battle – Dettingen. Eventually, even George II could not protect Carteret and in 1746 he resigned and never again played much part in politics. Pelham, who had been prime minister since 1743 continued in office until his death in 1754.

Throughout all this, Waldegrave stood by the king. In 1743 he was appointed lord of the bedchamber – far more than the right to some ceremonial frippery. This was an appointment which gave him very close access to the king, and it suggested how much George II had come to rely on the young Waldegrave, not yet thirty. Partly because of his delight in the more social ways of the court, and also because he did not wish to involve himself in the desperate politics of the period, Waldegrave had a reputation for being not much more than a charming courtier. But that view does not make much sense, considering how often George II confided in him and sought his advice.

In 1752 he found himself involved in the less pleasant side of court life when the king persuaded him to become Keeper of the Privy Purse to the new Prince of Wales, Frederick's son, Frederick having died in 1751. This role was rather that of private secretary and adviser, and therefore Waldegrave had a considerable involvement in the education of the future George III – although it could hardly be said that Waldegrave himself was much of an academic.

The man who succeeded Waldegrave in 1756 was Lord Bute. This was the beginning of the saga that would lead to the bitter schism in British politics and the notorious political and legal combat between the Earl of Bute and John Wilkes and his publication the *North Briton* in the 1760s (see p. 140).

Be that as it may, Waldegrave now found himself involved in backstairs politics, starting rumours and inventing future scenarios, all designed to split the power of Pitt and Henry Fox. This was the period of the battle between the 1st Duke of Newcastle and his brother Henry Pelham on one side and Pitt and Fox on the other, although, as was the way of politics at this time, Newcastle would serve alongside Pitt in government until 1761. It was Pitt who recognized Waldegrave's power as a fixer and who tried to persuade him to tell the king that he, Pitt, should replace Newcastle as Prime Minister. It ended up with Waldegrave appearing as a cross between an arbitrator and a chief negotiator in some complex arrangement for the selection of a chief executive of Britain. On the face of it, the candidates were Devonshire, Pitt, Cumberland, Fox and even Newcastle. Waldegrave wanted the king to talk to each one, but he refused.

Everything pointed to Pitt becoming Prime Minister and, most importantly, First Lord of the Treasury, which was effectively the political leadership of the country.[2] Because George II disliked Pitt so much he actually ordered Waldegrave to become First Lord. So, much against his own wishes, James Waldegrave became Prime Minister; he lasted in office for five days in June 1757. The whole thing was a political farce. When he resigned – in no way could he withstand the political infighting and total lack of support from the big men of politics – Waldegrave told George II that being a Cabinet minister, never mind Prime Minister, was the biggest misfortune that could happen, certainly to him. It is true also that he very much cared for George II and their intimate relationship. Waldegrave probably understood that if he had attempted to remain in office he would inevitably have fallen out with his king.

A fortnight after Waldegrave's resignation, the king appointed him to the Order of the Garter. As a sign of George II's deep trust and affection, he installed Waldegrave himself; this was a rare occurrence.

George II died in 1760 and his grandson came to the throne, to rule as George III for sixty years. Here was the man so influenced by the Earl of Bute that he would be denounced by the political cabal that wished to rule in Parliament's name rather than Bute's. Waldegrave was then forty-five and might have been expected to have a reasonably long life and certainly to take a more active part at court. There was a reasonable expectation that Waldegrave could have become Prime Minister, but he truly did not have political ambition. He could probably have become ambassador to France or the king's Viceroy in Ireland, but his personality allowed him to be content at home, simply being the 2nd Earl Waldegrave and enjoying a sometimes charming life at court. He had married Robert Walpole's niece, Maria, and so his friendship with the first Prime Minister, by then an old man, was more than some political affair.

If Waldegrave had had a long life it is interesting to speculate where he would now sit in the political history of eighteenth-century England. He might even have become a Whig Prime Minister in more stable times. This was not to be. In 1763, at the age of forty-eight, he died of smallpox. He and Maria had no male heir to whom the earldom could be passed, and so his brother, a distinguished soldier, took the title. But he, John Waldegrave, also had an unexpected death. In 1784 he was travelling in his carriage, had a fit and succumbed.

The 4th Earl, George, was also a soldier and fought in the American War of Independence. He too, inevitably, was a courtier to George III and became Vice-Chamberlain of the Royal Household and Queen Charlotte's Master of Horse. He died in 1789, just forty-eight years old. The Waldegrave pattern of premature death continued with his son, the 5th Earl, who inherited the title at the age of five and was drowned in the Thames at the age of ten. The 6th Earl, another soldier, served with Wellington during the Peninsular War and later at Waterloo, but died, this time of natural causes, when he was fifty. The 7th Earl was distinguished for spending six months in gaol, having been found guilty on an assault charge. His wife Anne, the daughter of a doctor from Hastings in Sussex, moved in with her husband in the queen's bench prison. The 8th Earl Waldegrave, William, was born in 1788. Sent off to the navy, he stayed with that service for forty years when he retired as a proper rear admiral – not simply a courtesy title.

From then on, the Waldegraves were always somewhere, either at court, in politics or involved in the minor wars of the nineteenth century. One Viscount Chewton joined the navy, did not much care for it and went off to Canada to be a farmer. But he could not stay away from battles for long and so got involved in the French Canadian insurrections, then the Sikh wars in 1846 and, almost inevitably, the Crimea in 1854; he died from his wounds at the Battle of the Alma.

And so to the twentieth century. William Waldegrave is the son of the 12th Earl and was one of the youngest Fellows of All Souls, Oxford and a one-time Conservative Cabinet minister. He too became a peer – Baron Waldegrave. Here is yet another family which at first glance is barely known, but in truth, like all these dynasties, has always been close to the epicentre of influence in British life.

NOTES

1 The first person to preside over the House was Peter de Montfort in 1258. It was not until 1377 that Sir Thomas Hungerford was appointed with the title Speaker of the House of Commons. Given the difficult nature of the task and the exceptional behaviour of those who felt it was badly performed, in the fourteenth century it was a somewhat hazardous chair.

2 Modern prime ministers are still styled Prime Minister and First Lord of the Treasury, and the latter title is the only one shown on the door of No. 10 Downing Street.

CHAPTER SIXTEEN

THE CARRINGTONS

The story of the Carringtons is a perfect example of the contrast between the early British dynasties and those which appeared more or less from the eighteenth century. From the tenth to the end of the seventeenth century a powerful family would, more often than not, have to be prepared to fight physically to defend its influence and position as well as its estates. Leading families inevitably took sides or became associated with one party or another; thus they were permanently vulnerable to violent changes in the monarchy. By the eighteenth century the way of governance in England had become more civilized. Wars were still fought, and rebellions, particularly in Scotland, confronted. The growing of Empire distracted the magnates and, by the time of the Hanoverian governments of Robert Walpole, the English had long abandoned the sword as a means of changing the way the country was run and by whom it was administered.

So by the late 1700s the saga of which dynasties governed Britain had become a very dull affair for those seeking the pantomimicry of the bloody and bloodied ruling classes. The Carrington dynasty is a perfect example of a family which began to influence government as a late-comer to Whiggism. They assumed, rather than inherited, the divine right and duty to rule.

This family's interest for the modern reader is largely through just one member, the 6th Baron Carrington. Peter Carington (the family name has one 'r', the title has two) was Foreign Secretary in the Thatcher government and resigned over the Falklands affair in April 1982. However, the dynasty, which dates from the late eighteenth century, has been influential in British government and an extremely close friend of the royal family for nearly two hundred years.

One Carington was banker to Pitt the Younger. Another slipped an Irish actress into the bed of the unsuspecting (but not unwilling) Prince of Wales – the future Edward VII – and so began a series of events, which led to the death of Prince Albert; or so some in Victoria's court believed. Another was cold-shouldered by the rest of the family – not for anything disgraceful that he had done, but because they were jealous of his inheritance. The 6th Baron Carrington is a trusted and close friend of Elizabeth II and of Queen Elizabeth the Queen Mother.

The Carringtons took that name as the title for the barony. The family name was Carington with one 'r' and no one is quite certain why – not even the Carringtons. But we do know when this confusion first occurred: it was when the 1st Baron was looking for a name to call himself that was a bit smarter than Smith. For his surname was not Carrington at all – he was Robert Smith, a banker.

The Smith family can be traced back to the very early seventeenth century and it is known, for example, that on 1 November 1631 the vicar of Titheby in Nottingham baptized a baby called Thomas Smith. He went into the wool trade and became a stapler, which meant he spent most of his time controlling the sale of wool through its sorting, grading and pricing. As a respectable draper he was a rather superior shopkeeper, a tradesman of some standing in the local community, and his circle of friends certainly went beyond those he saw in the modest cottages of his everyday work. When still a young man Thomas Smith married Fortune, daughter of the master gunner of Nottingham Castle, Laurence Collin; they had a son and called him Abel.

The business profited from Smith's acute sense of when to use his money and when to use that of other people; he knew also when to lend and at what rate of interest. He understood drapery, wool and farming. He understood even better how to manipulate the monies of the people involved. He kept their accounts; soon he was keeping more than their accounts, he was managing their money. By his early fifties Thomas Smith had abandoned the wool house for the counting house and became a banker in Nottingham.

Thomas Smith died in 1699 and the small Smith Bank was taken over by his son Abel who increased the business and expanded his affairs after inheriting money from his mother's family. In 1717 Abel Smith had a son, also named Abel, and as a banker he very much lived up to his name. With a man called Payne, the grandson of Thomas Smith set up the private bank of Smith & Payne with branches in Lincoln, Hull, Nottingham and, most importantly, London.

The direct Carrington line, as it would become, was, however, through the sons of Abel Smith. His eldest son, George, changed his name to Bromley and became a baronet. The youngest son, yet another Abel, worked hard as a banker in London, as did his son Robert. Robert, born in 1752, was the first of the younger Smiths to be surrounded by politicians as well as financiers. His father Abel had become member of Parliament for Aldborough in 1774 and later for St Germains in Cornwall. Being an MP, even in the heady days when Parliament was establishing itself on more democratic lines, still enabled members to give most of their attention to other pursuits – Parliament was not an arduous task, although it was, for some, a consuming pastime. Robert, too, went into politics and, appropriately to his origins, between 1779 and 1796 was MP for Nottingham where the family had remained successful and respectable – the two not always coming together – country bankers. It was at this point that Robert Smith forged a close friendship that would initiate the Carrington political and court dynasty.

William Pitt the Younger had been elected to Parliament on his second attempt in 1781, at the age of twenty-two, for Appleby in Westmorland. He went to the Commons and sat on the opposition benches. In fact, much of the time he was on his feet, impressing as a gifted orator in a then often dull Commons. Rockingham offered him a junior ministry. Pitt turned it down, which indicated a sense of higher ambition and judgement, considering that many young men of his age would have been highly flattered. Moreover, it did not take a political genius to recognize that Rockingham's administration would not survive for many months. Pitt had everything to gain by waiting. He did not have to wait long. A year later, still just twenty-three, Pitt became Chancellor of the Exchequer. The then Prime Minister, Shelburne, was forced to resign that year and George III asked Pitt to take his place. Again, his astonishing self-control and judgement were apparent. He said no. The King then offered the job to the Duke of Portland, who from the outset did not have much chance of survival. Pitt had understood this perfectly. And so at the age of twenty-four, when the King asked again, Pitt said yes. He was mocked as being impossibly young to lead the country, particularly by the brilliant Charles James Fox who had wanted the job for himself. Pitt, in spite of all the predictions, remained Prime Minister for nearly twenty years. Into his close circle of friends and advisers he took the young Robert Smith, who now added political jealousies and backbitings to his profit-and-loss accounting. This was never more apparent than on the day he moved from the House of Commons to take his seat in another place.

One evening in 1796 Smith, who had by now become Pitt's banker as well as friend, was being driven in his carriage with the Prime Minister from Pall Mall back to Downing Street. The journey took them along the edge of St James's Park and into a loop around Westminster and Whitehall. The short cut, and the smart way to travel, would have been across Horse Guards Parade and beneath the archway. Yet only the privileged were allowed to take their carriages across that square. Robert Smith, understanding only too well the significance of this facility, asked Pitt there and then if he could arrange such a precious pass for him. Pitt shook his head. Certainly not. However, as some meagre form of compensation, he went on, he could arrange for his friend to become a baron. It would of course be an Irish barony, although, rather like the interregnum between deacon and priest, it would soon be a full English title.[1] That is how Robert Smith, banker, started the Carrington dynasty.

The mystery is why, with the considerable power achieved by being so close to one of the most remarkable prime ministers in British history, together with the family's undisputed wealth and prospects, Robert felt it necessary to bury the Smiths. Perhaps it was simple snobbery. Perhaps there was a real belief that the Smith family was related to some distant Carringtons. The Smiths came from Nottingham. In the next county, Leicestershire, there was a family called Smith-Carington. This was a very old and landed name; indeed, the original Caringtons were viscounts. Some of the Carrington records go so far as to suggest that, before their branch of the Smith family became drapers and bankers, earlier Smiths were in fact Caringtons. This seems unlikely. That the Carringtons came from that part of the world and were associated with the Smiths at some point is not disputed. It was certainly a very impressive pedigree. Hamo de Carington was probably around in the eleventh century and may have taken the name from Carenton in Normandy, thus fixing in the pedigree-seeking Smith mind that the ancestors of the drapers had come over with the Conqueror – even in the eighteenth century this would have had considerable social cachet. Hamo had the lordships of manors in Cheshire and was succeeded by a series of, then, quite famous de Caringtons, one of whom was a standard bearer to Richard the Lionheart during the third crusade. Did any of this matter? Clearly it did, because Smith the banker wished for more than respectability. He desired aristocracy.

So when Robert Smith was raised to the Irish peerage in 1796 and subsequently to the peerage of Great Britain in 1797, his letters patent gave him and his male heirs the title of Carrington. None of this explained why the surname Carington should be different from the baronial name Carrington. Most members of the family have assumed it was simply an heraldic spelling mistake which, once made, became official. It is far more likely that in Smith's search for family history, real or wished for, he decided upon the centuries-old Carington as a patronymic and chose the Cheshire village of Carrington (the lordship of which an eleventh-century ancestor he claimed had held) as the basis for the title.

Does any of this matter to our story of the saga of British dynasties? Most certainly it does. Centuries after the Godwines, the Despensers and the Mortimers, with whom this book began, cut and thrust their way to titles and livings, the English nomenklatura, that minority ruling class, craved the dignity which they believed titles and possessions brought to their natural instincts or desires to rule. It might be argued that here, on the eve of the nineteenth century, the British aristocracy was beginning its long decline. Even if that were so, the slope down which it would slip had titles and honours dug in a-plenty to which the new families would cling. Thus it was with the Smiths. Yet no barony could instantly create respectability on scarlet benches occupied in many cases by those who had no need to contrive family trees. Robert, the 1st Lord Carrington, understood this when he took his seat in the Lords. His fellow peers turned their backs on him. He was, despite all his efforts, in trade – a banker, a moneylender, therefore of no consequence and a man who should really have kept his place. Carrington was the first trader to sit in the House of Lords. Few of his ungracious fellows imagined that within a very few years the Carrington family would be one of the most influential at the court of Queen Victoria and among the friends of her heir, Bertie, the Prince of Wales.

The 1st Lord Carrington was, above all things, wealthy. He realized, too, that it was best that he got out of trade and into something vaguely respectable in the eyes of the aristocracy. He left banking to the Smiths and became a landowner, buying the considerable estates in Buckinghamshire and Lincolnshire which would remain in the family for the next one hundred years or so and some of them until the present day. One of the houses, Loakes Mansion House, became a national landmark which he renamed Wycombe Abbey. So this new landowner, with his interests in his tenant farmers, became a minister, President of the Board of Agriculture.

Until relatively recently most government ministries were not organized in the way we understand them today. They were, and were called, boards. Their chief executives were known as presidents and the name was used, for example, by the Department of Trade until the end of the twentieth century, even though its style lapsed on occasions – for example, when the Department of Trade and Industry was created. Therefore when the Conservative minister Michael Heseltine revived the styling 'President of the Board of Trade' he was maintaining a tradition in government which stretched back centuries.

In 1800 the 1st Lord Carrington took over the Board of Agriculture for three years. It was a ministry that was, at different times, run by members of his family until the 1950s. Carrington may have craved aristocracy and ministerial position, but he was no uncaring member of the new meritocracy. By all accounts he was a man of enormous compassion and his senses of reform extended from the need to promote concepts of universal suffrage, which could only be taken in short steps, to more fundamental expressions of his character including the need to make the lives of the less fortunate more bearable. The poet William Cowper in his 'Task Book' refers to the generous nature of this man:

Meanwhile ye shall not want
What conscious of your virtues we can spare,
I mean the man, who when the distant poor
Need help, denies them nothing but his name…

Carrington felt strongly that people should have proper government based on some form of voting that gave them the sense that they were being heard by those who did govern. However, he did not support what was then a revolutionary move towards what would become known as the Reform Act of 1832.

There were three Reform Acts in the nineteenth century and the Bill which preceded this, the first, was sent to the Commons in March 1831 against a background of open public dissent by people who felt they were, at the very least, under-represented. The Whigs were reformers, and it was Lord Grey's Whig administration which introduced the Bill. The Tories, not yet generally known as Conservatives, defeated the Bill within a month of its appearance. The government had no option but to call a general election on the principle of how Britain was governed. Perhaps the 6th Lord Carrington reflected on the irony of his family's role at this time, for he was an important member of the government of Edward Heath which 140 years later went to the country on the slogan: 'Not how is Britain governed, but *who* governs Britain'?

The Whigs redrafted the Reform Bill in June 1831, laid it before Parliament and once again it was rejected – this time by the House of Lords. The first Lord Carrington voted against it. His son Robert, however, was now a Whig MP: he voted against his father and for the Reform Bill.

This was no political quadrille. Vociferous reformers sensed their opportunities for better government and representation slipping. They took to the streets, and the government's militia, forerunner of the Territorials, was set upon them. At first sight this may seem a damning use of the army; but it should be remembered that, at this stage, 1831, there was no police force to act less spectacularly. Just before Christmas the Commons put its third Reform Bill before the House. Again Carrington's son voted for it and once more his father voted against it in the Lords. The militia was called out again. The government resigned.

This is the moment when the traditional ruling class of Britain, the peers, against whom successive monarchs since the beginning of our story had fought, were seen as the biggest single obstacle to what the people, the government and the still influential monarch believed was an affront to democracy. Not until 1911, and then again in the 1960s, 1930s and 1990s, would there be such direct conflict among those who concerned themselves deeply with the single question: 'What powers should the peers have in running an increasingly elected form of government?' The further importance to this account is that, on all four occasions from 1832 to 1998, a Carrington peer was actively involved in that debate. It was the 6th Lord Carrington who championed the concept of an elected Upper House. The 1st Lord Carrington most certainly did not believe that the Chamber should be reformed. But the king and the Whig government were determined that the peers would eventually have to give ground and allow the Reform Bill through.

From the tenth century onwards the barons, including those who drew up Magna Carta, had rarely had interests other than their own at heart. Generously, it might be said that through their powers they stopped bad monarchs from exploiting the country's coffers and prevented them corrupting the constitution of the kingdom; there is considerable argument for that case. But the right to rule and the assumed duty to do so was now facing its most fundamental test. The eighteenth-century development of prime ministerial and Cabinet governance had reached a stage where the party system was now presented as a reasonable form of democracy that went beyond the old notion of the barons versus the monarch and his or her supporters. It was against this background that Lord Grey went to the king, by now William IV, and told him that the only way to get through these reforms was for the monarch to create enough Whig peers to outvote the Tories. The peers backed down. The same argument was presented to the king when a similar confrontation occurred between the Lords and the Commons before the First World War. It was the threat used by the government of Tony Blair when he gained power in 1997 and embarked on yet another campaign for Lords reform.

Now, in 1832, Robert Smith (the family did not change their name to Carington until 1839) had triumphed over his father Lord Carrington's political convictions. Those convictions would seem, from the family history, to have come about from an understanding of the importance of commerce as the dominant factor in what was emerging as a British empire. Britain, even in 1832, did not have an empire as it was later understood. The effects of expansion and trade on the home estate were something which Carrington at least believed should be dominant in government thinking. He saw that, as a result of mercantile philosophy in politics, there had to be an opportunity to bring all like minds into political thought, but for those minds to be loyally set towards their ruling party. This, Carrington seemed to believe, had its basis in a strong family – both domestically and commercially – belief in holding together. Thus, if Carrington sat on the Tory benches, then unlike, say, Disraeli, he would offer total loyalty to the party ideology. Here was an expression of collective party and government responsibility. Carrington as a minister could not and, more importantly, would not ignore what he believed to be his duty to the government of which he was a member, which to him surmounted responsibility even to the party.

If this point seems laboured it is done to signpost much of the philosophy of the twentieth-century 6th Baron Carrington. Both men were often exasperated by, and even disliked, their party. Both the 1st and the 6th Lord Carringtons believed the duty of government to be higher than that of party dogma.

The first Carrington son, Robert, may have been a successful Whig MP, but he was not to be a distinguished politician; he was also the victim of considerable personal tragedy. The Smiths had done rather well on the social ladder in the late eighteenth and early nineteenth centuries. Young Robert Smith had married Elizabeth Forrester, the young and very beautiful sister of the Countess of Bradford, and the two attractive young people were very much part of the London social calendar. In 1832 Robert had rejoiced in the political revolution that brought about the Reform Act. He could not have imagined the terrible event that would swiftly follow that triumph. The previous year cholera had reached epidemic proportions in the Russian Baltic states, and ships from those parts brought it to the north-east of England. The lack of basic sanitation and medical knowledge meant that little could be done to stop its spread. On a Sunday morning in July 1832 the first Lord Carrington's daughter-in-law, Elizabeth, began to show symptoms of the disease; she died from it before midnight the same day. Although Smith would remarry, he became very gloomy and even more so four years later when his widowed father, the Baron, decided that he too would remarry. The new Lady Carrington was a widow with six children. This was hardly a time for open family rejoicing among those who would have preferred a less complicated arrangement with the Carrington family inheritance. There was nothing to be achieved by objecting – and there were vociferous objections from both family and friends – for Carrington had made up his mind. He married the widow and was dead in two years.

Now, in 1838, Robert Smith became the 2nd Lord Carrington. The following year the Smith name was dropped in favour of Carington[2] and in 1840 Robert remarried. The new Lady Carrington was the daughter of a somewhat more senior noble, the 21st Baron Willoughby de Eresby, a title that dated from the early fourteenth century. His daughter, Augusta Drummond-Willoughby, was a very clever woman who brought with her to the Carrington coat of arms a hundred quarterings.[3]

It was this marriage that began the almost two hundred-year history of the Carrington family as courtiers to successive British monarchs. Just as it was explained earlier that many appointments to the monarch became hereditary, so some would survive into the twenty-first century. One such appointment to the royal household was the office of Lord Great Chamberlain. Augusta Drummond-Willoughby came from the family which bore that hereditary title, and from the moment of their marriage the Carringtons would share this royal appointment. In practice this meant that one family would be Joint Hereditary Lord Great Chamberlain of England until the monarch died; then the other family would take up the appointment.[4]

The 2nd Lord Carrington was extremely wealthy thanks to the banking traditions in the family and, naturally, the way the estates had been developed. His father had built one of the finest houses in Whitehall, Carrington House,[5] which stood opposite Horse Guards Parade across which he was never allowed to travel even with his friend William Pitt. It was one of the first houses in London to have gas lighting, and into it came the glitterati of London's political as well as social society.

The time was one of great social unrest. The Chartist Movement, which came from the 1838 People's Charter, wanted six important changes to the democratic system: the Chartists appealed for equal votes for all men, the removal of property qualifications for members of Parliament, ballot voting, equal electoral districts, yearly parliaments and even professional MPs.[6] The movement was never as successful as sometimes suggested. Petitions might be signed by hundreds of thousands of people, but there was never a dreadful pressure on the governing parties to do anything more than take note.

As landowners the Carringtons were sympathetic to the ambitions of many of the agitators; as politicians they were not so easily moved. It is also true that they were hardly protected from the more physical moments of the Chartist protest. For example, in 1848 the government sent the cavalry to Westminster where the biggest demonstration in British history was planned. A small child, who would become Charles, the 3rd Lord Carrington, witnessed that demonstration as it passed along Whitehall. Later he wrote a memoir in which he remembered sitting at a window in Carrington House cheering on what his family – and certainly his governess – saw as a dangerous rabble. His ears were boxed for his pains.

> Gamekeepers sat in the hall [at Carrington House] with loaded guns between their knees. My father [the 2nd Lord Carrington] was on duty as a Special Constable in Whitehall and a troop of the Second Life Guards under Captain Mountjoy Martin were quartered on us.... Cannon was mounted at

Westminster Bridge, Buckingham Palace and at the Bank, with orders to fire if the Chartists advanced on London, given by the Duke of Wellington. ...Gaunt determined looking men marched through London with banners: this I vividly remember from the fact that I was well spanked for cheering them out of the nursery window...[7]

It was young Charles Carington, who in the twentieth century would be remembered as Uncle Charlie or Charlie Lincolnshire (he became the Marquess of Lincolnshire), who was now set to become the most colourful of all the barons over two centuries. In his early life there was clear indication of how far the once snubbed family had been accepted in higher and certainly more polite circles. For example, in the summer of 1854, when he was eleven years old, he was taken to Gloucester House in Piccadilly, the home of the Duke and Duchess of Gloucester, for a children's party. This was a very special occasion: Queen Victoria and Prince Albert were there with the young Bertie, the Prince of Wales and future King Edward VII. Charlie Carington was formally presented to the young prince, who was two years older. It seems that from that moment the young Carington and the young Prince of Wales became firm friends; it was a friendship that would last to the day of Edward's death fifty-six years later. The two friends quickly found they had one thing in common: they were both terrified of Prince Albert, and young Charlie talked about hiding from the Queen's consort in the bushes around Buckingham Palace. It is another indication of the close personal relationship between the Carington family and the monarch.

In 1856 he was packed off to Eton and then to Cambridge. His time at the university was rather like his time at Eton, where he had been taught, in his opinion, absolutely nothing other than 'to tell the truth and never to round on or betray a friend'.[8] Cambridge was a place to spend two years drinking bottles of claret without drawing a breath at gatherings of the exotic True Blue Club, winning the University's steeplechase or running the drag hunt with Nathaniel Rothschild – another family friendship that would endure to the present day. There were diversions, however, of a more serious nature; certainly there was one incident that would cement his most intimate relationship with the Prince of Wales and find him shouldering part of the blame for the death of that young man's father.

The influence of the young Charles Carington on the Prince of Wales and later, when both were mature men, should not be underestimated. The scandal of the actress slipped into the prince's bed while he was serving with his regiment in Ireland has rather overshadowed how the young lady got there in the first place. Charles Carington (not yet the 3rd Lord Carrington) put her there.

The Prince of Wales had long thought it a good idea to go into the army. The advisers to Victoria and Albert thought this an exceedingly bad idea, for they knew full well the ways of army officers. The prince was sent first to Edinburgh, then to Oxford and then to Trinity College, Cambridge. To make sure that an eye could be kept on the heir to the throne, and presumably to find something big enough for the entourage to attend him, Prince Albert rented Madingley Hall, just outside the city, for his son. Bertie pestered for the army. In 1861 it was agreed that he should be sent to the Curragh in Ireland and join, for a short break, the Grenadier Guards. However, the condition of the prince's attachment to this famous regiment was as demanding as could be contrived: he was to join in the most junior commissioned rank; he would then begin training to master every duty in that rank; then he would move to the next rank and do the same; this process would be repeated until he was able to command a brigade in the field. It was, of course, a nonsensical programme and the Prince of Wales failed. At the passing out parade, he was not a success. Now we come to that incident with the actress.

One night in the officers' mess there was a normally rowdy party. Among the prince's young officer friends was Charles Carington who had gone with him to Ireland. By this time Charles was a very junior cavalry officer, but his brother, Bill, had joined the Grenadier Guards, which was to become the family regiment. Bill Carington, too, was involved in the actress and the prince affair, as it was known. During the party it was arranged for Nellie Clifden to be tucked into the prince's empty bed, and when he returned to his quarters he was comforted by the actress. In fact, both Charles Carington and the prince shared the affections of young Nellie, not only at the Curragh but also in London when they returned. This was unfortunate for the prince, the Queen and Prince Albert, because the affair became very common knowledge and he was supposed to be getting married to Princess Alexandra of Denmark anyway.

But Nellie was already being joked about as Princess of Wales; moreover, there was a strong rumour that she was pregnant. How the scandal sheets of the day would have loved this if it had proved to be true. Prince Albert, already with a terrible cold, drove up to Madingley for earnest discussions with his very wayward son. It did Prince Albert no good at all: he was already ill, the stay at Maddingly made him worse and soon he was dying of typhoid fever. Victoria would find it difficult ever to forgive her son, or those who had led Bertie astray, for her husband's death. After his father's funeral, the Prince of Wales was sent abroad. Charles Carington continued to see Nellie Clifden and was good enough to write to the prince with news of the actress – some of it, anyway. The friendship between the prince and 'Uncle Charlie' was truly very close.

There was not a great deal for young Charlie to do after Cambridge and so his father wrote a cheque for £1200 which would buy him a commission in the cavalry. As soon as a position was available, Lord Carrington paid a further £600 so that his son could become a lieutenant. But Charlie Carington wanted to be more than a lieutenant; he wanted some sort of command, albeit a small one that was not too arduous. So the 2nd Lord Carrington wrote another cheque: this time, £3400 bought his son a small cavalry troop. With few exceptions, young cavalry officers were not really expected to be serious-minded career soldiers, and so Charlie Carington thought it a good idea to continue the family tradition in

Parliament. While his father was buying him a commission, at the same time Charlie was becoming Liberal MP for Wycombe in Buckinghamshire.

The 1860s and 1870s were not dull moments in British parliamentary history. This was the century of reform – industrially and commercially as well as politically. The 1st Lord Carrington and his son had fought passionately in the debate that led to the 1832 Reform Act. In February 1866 Gladstone's Reform Bill was on the floor of the House and the Carringtons once again joined in the debate. The young Carington was not entirely single-minded about the politics of reform, unlike his father who had by then become friends with the new generation of Tories, including Disraeli. The Prince of Wales, who had married Alexandra of Denmark in 1863, now regarded Charles Carington as one of his closest courtiers; when he and the Princess travelled to the German spas or, later, on a dull and gruelling tour of Egypt, Carington had to go with him.

His responsibilities took a different turn when, in 1868, the 2nd Lord Carrington died. Disraeli wrote to Charlie, now the 3rd Lord Carrington, that his father had been a man of tender affections and one possessed of a gushing heart. The bells of Wycombe church were muffled and tolled for a whole day. Almost all the influential aristocracy of England followed the funeral.

Similar respects were paid the following year when Eva, Charlie's sister, married the Earl of Harrington, Charles Petersham. The Archbishop of Armagh performed the service and the Earl of Rosebery[9] was best man. Disraeli was among the guests, as were the Percys of Northumberland and the Churchills. But not everyone had forgotten the family origins. Not long after the 2nd Lord Carrington's death, a very disagreeable article appeared in a journal called *The Queen's Messenger*. Its editor, Grenville Murray, questioned, in what would later have been called a very tabloid manner, the origins of the Carrington line into the aristocracy. There were those who still saw them as jumped up drapers in spite of their friendships with royalty. The journalistic abuse was too much for the 3rd Lord, who felt his beloved father as well as the family name had been desperately insulted.

In June 1869 Carrington decided he would seek his own form of justice. Having bought himself a rhinoceros hide whip he waited outside the Conservative Club and, when Grenville Murray appeared, whipped him. The scurrilous editor (and later in court he was indeed proved to be a scoundrel) ran into the Conservative Club, a common enough refuge for many whose reputation might be questioned. Carrington was not put off by the porter and followed Murray, gave him his name and address – which almost amounted to a challenge of honour – cracked the whip under his nose, then departed to his own club, Pratt's, took a drink and went happily to bed. The case that followed became notorious in its day.

Murray had apparently been at the Foreign Office but was expelled for dark circumstances surrounding some theft. The courtroom scenes were almost as farcical as that in the Conservative Club. What began as a heated debate turned into an attempt to steal documentary evidence; a scuffle to stop the public larceny quickly degenerated into fisticuffs. Carington, who as the defendant was presumably in police custody, vaulted from the dock and joined in the fracas to defend his stumbling and elderly solicitor, who was clutching the box to his breast. Murray, conforming to a picturesque stereotype, ran away and was never seen or heard of again in London society. Charlie Carington had most certainly established himself as a colourful character. His friend the Prince of Wales certainly thought so.

Although the prince and Charlie Carington had been friends since their teens and then through the hectic days at Cambridge, it was never to be forgotten that one was the heir to the throne while the other was heir to a minor barony. The 2nd Lord Carrington warned his son not to assume too much from the friendship and always to refer to the prince in the style 'Sir and Your Royal Highness, as royal people are touchy on such points'.[10] It is certainly true that people in very high places assume a great deal from friendships. Perhaps it is something to do with having a limited circle of friends, together with the experience that acquaintances rarely show displeasure towards them. Very soon the Prince of Wales came to rely heavily on his friendship with both young Caringtons, Charles and Bill. He certainly needed them when he became involved with Harriet Mordaunt and the subsequent divorce case.

Harriet was a pretty woman in her twenties whose husband, Sir Charles Mordaunt, rarely matched her vivaciousness and certainly not her eccentricities. She was an eager partygoer and had become the friend of the Prince of Wales, although not exclusively so. It is said that after the birth of their son, who was born blind, Harriet's eccentric nature became more apparent. She flung herself into difficult moods as well as, it seems, into the arms of amused suitors. She kept a diary in which she wrote about her affairs, though whether these jottings were fact or fiction is difficult to say. However, there were certainly a number of men in high society who had been pleased with her favours and her suffering husband most certainly believed her diary, which he had read after breaking into her writing table – in itself hardly an act above suspicion. Harriet, confronted with the diary, confessed all to Sir Charles, including, she said, that she had slept with the Prince of Wales. Her husband decided to divorce her.

The prince claimed he had never had an affair with Harriet and that it was all down to her imagination. A difficulty intended to contradict what the prince had said arose when Mordaunt produced letters written by Bertie to Harriet – yet these were hardly of a nature that would be tied in pink bows. Certainly the prince was not damned by them, but there was no stopping Mordaunt, and Bertie was told that he would have to appear in the divorce court. Princess Alexandra stood by her husband; so did his friend Charles, who had described Harriet as a 'nice woman; everyone had a good word for her'. This was not entirely true. At the beginning of 1870 the prince was due to be called to the witness box; at one stage he was to be cited as co-respondent. Society, however, has a way of dealing with these matters, and by the time of the hearing, the sad Harriet had been confined in a lunatic asylum. The prince, slightly relieved at his position, was called not to defend himself but as a character witness to defend Lady Mordaunt.

His performance was popularly received. Counsel asked solemnly, 'Has there ever been any improper familiarity or criminal act between yourself and Lady Mordaunt?' 'Never,' was the prince's response, and the court broke into impromptu applause. Carington did his popular best to make it clear that the prince had not been involved. There was sufficient precedent for heirs to the throne enjoying themselves, often to public acclaim, but in the 1870s, with an extremely disapproving mother and a sober sense of honour (not always remembered in the early hours of a partying morning), Carington and the prince put on a respectable face.

There may have been applause in court, but it was not universally endorsed. As one newspaper reported: 'even the staunchest supporters of monarchy shake their heads and express anxiety as to whether the Queen's successor will have the tact and talent to keep royalty upon its legs and out of the gutter'.[11] The concerns of the 3rd Lord Carrington not only for his friend, but also for the image of monarchy were not dissimilar to those of the 6th Lord Carrington during the difficulties of a later Prince of Wales in the 1990s. It is interesting to note also that the Victorian Prince of Wales, in spite of the efforts of that Carington, suffered public derision while the princess won the hearts of the nation. When she attended public functions, Alexandra was applauded and had people's sympathy as the wronged woman. For example, on one occasion, when the toastmaster called for the health of the Prince of Wales, the diners stood, raised their glasses and shouted, 'To the Princess!' The twentieth-century version was not, of course, so extreme, partly because a hundred years later the monarchy did not matter so much to the people.

It is well known that the prince felt no great need to mend his ways. It may be that Princess Alexandra was never able, as some have suggested, to express her love as fully as he did for her. Equally, no amount of analysis will get away from the simple fact that the Prince of Wales enjoyed himself and, however much he considered his solemn duties as heir and, later, as monarch, he would continue to do so in the most fundamental manner. Whatever the anxieties of the princess and the disapproval of the queen, Bertie could never resist a winning smile and a bare shoulder. Most ladies in society understood his nature, as did most gentlemen. The most famous of all his female companions appeared in his life in the spring of 1877.

It was in Greece, accompanied as usual by Carington, that the prince met Lillie Langtry. She was a parson's daughter who had married, at the age of twenty-one, Edward Langtry, a Belfast shipowner. Langtry had none of the social graces and, as it proved, little of the money demanded by London society. He took to drink and she to smart partying. It was Lord Randolph Churchill who described her as a most beautiful creature, but so poor that, it was said, she 'has but one black dress'. Bertie was besotted.

By the 1890s he had acquired, according to one of his relations, a habit of 'taking to young girls and discarding married women'. He also had an affair with

Daisy Brooke, the daughter of the Earl of Warwick. And even Lady Churchill was said to attract his attentions. The prince's love life was prolific and complex, especially when in 1898 he met the woman who was to be his mistress for the rest of his life, the famous Mrs Keppel, the admiral's daughter who married the Earl of Albemarle who, partly because of his own diversions, never objected to the affair. This was a somewhat heady world in which the 3rd Lord Carrington trod warily but humorously. It was he who coined the phrase that would be used for the rest of Edward's life – 'the Prince's other ladies'.

Carington may have been privy to the private life of the Prince of Wales, but he was more than an obliging courtier. He had, shortly after leaving Cambridge, become a Liberal MP and, although he left Parliament, continued to be on the fringe of politics and close to the most senior politicians. For example, Carington and Disraeli had become affectionate friends. During Disraeli's long illness leading to his death in 1881, Carington, a neighbour, would visit Hughenden, the former Prime Minister's house near Beaconsfield in Buckinghamshire, and read aloud to him. When the former Prime Minister died, for some reason the queen refused the Prince of Wales a row of carriages to attend the funeral; Carington invited the prince to travel by train to a nearby station, then to lunch at the Carington home, Wycombe Abbey, and finally to drive with the family to Hughenden for the funeral.

When he inherited his title Carington had given up his seat in the Commons and gone into the Lords. In 1881 he had become a privy councillor and became Leader of the House in Gladstone's administration. When the Liberals lost office in 1885, Carington began the family's long association with Australia. Appointed governor of New South Wales, he went out there with his beautiful wife, Lily, and his younger brother, Rupert Carington.

Of all the brothers of this generation, Rupert was the least distinguished. Charles was a celebrated courtier and later a famous minister. William, or Bill, was, like Charles, a very close friend of the Prince of Wales but was also much admired by Queen Victoria; he was a tall, elegant Grenadier who became the queen's equerry as well as Comptroller of the Household of the Prince of Wales and the Keeper of the Privy Purse. Rupert Carington, however, was not distinguished by much more than his consummate ability to spend money – often that of other people. In 1885 he was best described as having enormous taste but no funds. He had, for example, run up a bill with his shirtmaker for the equivalent of about £25,000 in today's prices. He probably had a lot of shirts. He certainly needed a lot of distance between himself and those to whom he owed money.

His spending did not stop when he got to Australia, and Charles Carington often had to pick up the bill(s) for his younger brother. There was therefore much relief when Rupert married Edith Horsfall, the eldest daughter of, until that point, a very prosperous sheep farmer. Rupert steadily worked his way through his wife's money. He eventually returned to his former occupation, soldiering, and much later fought in the Boer War with the South Wales Mounted Rifles and with a regiment that he had formed himself.

Rupert and Edith had a son, also named Rupert, who was to be the father of the 6th Baron, Margaret Thatcher's Foreign Secretary Peter Carington. Rupert also fathered two illegitimate children. One of them, a son, was sent into the Grenadier Guards. When the legitimate son tried to join the Grenadiers and fight in the First World War, he was told that he could not as it would be very bad taste for him to be in the same regiment, and certainly the same battalion, as his father's bastard. It was not until the illegitimate son was killed in action that the young Rupert was allowed to transfer to the Grenadiers.

Long before all this, in 1890, Charles Carington, the 3rd Baron, returned from Australia. He returned also to the company of the Prince of Wales. Three years later, not as a direct response to a steer from the prince but certainly not without his encouragement, Gladstone suggested to the queen that Lord Carrington should be sent to India as Viceroy. It would seem that the queen, although rather concerned that the Caringtons should not be sent to what she regarded as a hot and dirty place, agreed to the appointment. It might be noted that she rarely agreed with Gladstone, whom she much disliked. But Carington did not go to India. In the August of that year, 1893, he wrote in his diary that the Duchess of Connaught had told Gladstone that Queen Victoria wanted him to be Viceroy, but that the Prime Minister had been over-ruled by his Cabinet.[12] If that was the case (and Cabinet minutes were not kept in those days), the objection probably came from his Foreign Secretary and future Liberal imperialist Prime Minister Lord Rosebery. Rosebery wanted Lord Elgin to have the Indian appointment and he got his way. Elgin's credentials were perfectly reasonable: his father had been Governor General of India, Canada and Jamaica. More famously, his grandfather had given his name to the controversial marbles brought to England from the Parthenon in Athens.

There was, of course, no question of Carington slipping away into private life. He was by now Chamberlain to the queen and her household, and in 1895 he was elevated to the peerage to become Viscount Wendover of Chepping Wycombe in Buckinghamshire and the Earl Carrington. He would, some seventeen years later, rise even further in the noble hierarchy to become the Marquess of Lincolnshire.[13] After Victoria died in 1901, Lord Carrington carried St Edward's Staff at the coronation of her eldest son, his long-time friend.

In political terms Carrington is remembered for the work he did in government during the coming decade. In 1905, when Sir Henry Campbell-Bannerman became the Liberal Prime Minister, he asked Carrington to be President of the Board of Agriculture, a Cabinet appointment that had been held by the 1st Baron. The Board of Agriculture was a department of considerable importance. The nation had not been self-sufficient since the 1880s; there was, too, a considerable debate about the ways in which preference should be given to imports from the Empire. One side said there should be no preferences whatsoever; the other that Britain's responsibilities towards her Empire included a considerable debt for the way that some of the member states had selflessly fought alongside British forces in the largely pointless and unsatisfactory Boer War. Whatever the higher debate, in 1905 Carrington set about looking at reforms that would touch smaller landowners and farmers. Considering the Carrington holdings in Berkshire and Lincolnshire alone, he had first-hand knowledge of who wanted what and what would benefit those who needed rather than simply wanted. As *Vanity Fair* remarked, Carrington had 'excellent judgement and a good eye for opportunity'. It is tempting to observe that his sometimes hectic friendship with the man who was now Edward VII had well prepared him for this office and the need to exercise quietly his 'eye for opportunity'.

Carrington pushed through nine very difficult Bills, including the so-called Farmers' Charter, and did so by reconciling the considerable landowning differences in the Lords by good humour and not a little intellect. One of those nine Bills survived for the rest of the century. It was this legislation that established smallholdings. So convinced was he that people without money should have the chance of being tenant farmers on a small scale that he initiated the scheme by example, offering tenancies to would-be smallholders on his own estates. So enthusiastic was Lord Carrington for the idea of smallholdings, and so scrupulously fair was his legal draughtsmanship, that when the 6th Baron, Peter, attempted to restructure the family estates in Buckinghamshire after World War II he had the utmost difficulty in unravelling the 'good works' put in place by his celebrated ancestor.

In 1910 Carrington lost his dearest friend when Edward VII finally succumbed to the effects of a series of heart attacks shortly before midnight on 6 May. The only good news of the day was that his horse, Witch of the Air, had won the 4.15 at Kempton Park. 'I have heard of it. I am very glad' were apparently his last words. As a modern historian wrote: 'Lord Carrington was...shown into the darkened room; and as he looked down at the king's "beloved" face which appeared "quite happy and composed" above the collar of a pink shirt, he felt that he had lost the "truest friend" that he had ever had...'.[14] It had been a long, warm and eventful friendship, best marked, perhaps, by the fact that the Carringtons had named their son after their royal friend.

In 1912 Carrington retired from government, and it was at this time that he was created Marquess of Lincolnshire. Thereafter, he was always known in the family as Uncle Charlie or Charlie Lincolnshire. Then came the First World War. Uncle Charlie's son, Albert Edward, was just nineteen when the war started and joined his father's regiment, the Royal Horse Guards. In 1915 he was wounded and died shortly afterwards. Unlike the barony, which could pass to the nearest surviving male relative, the marquessate had to pass to a surviving son. Since Albert was Charlie and Lily's only son, there would be no new Marquess of Lincolnshire nor a Viscount Wendover.

Charlie Lincolnshire lived on until 1928. He was a celebrated figure, continually seen in royal circles and much concerned with the family estates which stretched from a castle in Wales – once the haunt of the bloodthirsty Mortimers –

to the more peaceful rolling hills of Buckinghamshire and the blander holdings of Lincolnshire. When he died, the barony passed to his youngest brother, Rupert. It might have gone to Bill Carington, who would have been a baron with more distinguished credentials. He had followed Charlie as MP for the 'family seat' at Wycombe (the 1832 Reform Bill which was supposed to have removed rotten boroughs, was not entirely effective). Bill Carington had joined the Grenadiers and had served effortlessly in Egypt where he was decorated and, even more easily, on public duties in London where he was not. A great favourite of both Queen Victoria and Edward VII, he was an elegant and blameless courtier. Yet he died, childless, in 1914.

Step forward, his creditors never far distant, Rupert Carington. He may have been the surviving Carington, but he did not survive for long. He was dead the following year, 1929. His legitimate son, another Rupert, was a difficult man and, within the family, in a somewhat difficult position. Rupert Carington, the 5th Baron, was brought up in Australia, and perhaps if the First World War had never taken place he would have stayed there. But the death of Charlie Lincolnshire's son in 1915 and the age of his own father made it very clear to the young Rupert that he would inherit the title as long as he too did not perish in the war. He survived the fighting, but not the wrath of the Carington women who frankly resented the fact that this outsider would one day become the 5th Baron.

Rupert Carington was, however, looked after by the Colville family. The Colvilles of Culross have a long and noble line: the title goes back to 1604 in Scotland, and in 1902 the then Lord Colville was created a viscount. It was during Victorian times that the Colvilles and Caringtons became family friends. When the new heir to the Carrington barony arrived in London to join the Fifth Dragoon Guards at the start of the First World War, he was certainly not befriended by his own family and was therefore 'taken in' by the Colvilles. In 1916 he married Lord Colville's daughter, Sibyl. Like all the Caringtons, the young Rupert had served at the front line, and he was wounded twice. He left the army in 1924 and bought a house on the edge of Dartmoor – as far away from the rest of the family as was feasible. It was there that he lived until his death in 1938, leaving no great mark and making no apparent outpourings of affection. His son, Peter Carington, found him a distant figure, which was not so unusual for the times.

When his father died, Peter Carington was already in the army. At Eton he had had a modest career. When the time came for him to go, it would seem that he had the choice of the army, the City or farming. Neither his housemaster nor his father expected much of him. From Sandhurst he joined the family regiment, the Second Battalion Grenadiers and won the Military Cross in the Second World War during the capture of the bridge at Nijmegen.

After the war Peter Carrington decided that he should take his seat in the House of Lords and, in some ways following in the steps of Uncle Charlie, have a political career as well as being a courtier. Even in 1945 the Carringtons were still very close to the royal family, and this 6th Baron would become as trusted as had been Uncle Charlie and Bill Carington. The first six years in the Lords were spent in opposition. When Churchill was finally returned as Prime Minister, Carrington was given a job as junior agriculture minister as had been the 1st and the 3rd Barons. He then served, with not a few political hiccups, until 1982 in every Conservative administration.

Three times he had to offer his resignation: the first as junior agriculture minister over the infamous Crichel Down affair;[15] then as navy minister over the Vassall spy case;[16] and finally in 1982 when, as Foreign Secretary, he had failed to persuade the Prime Minister to take early action in the dispute between the Argentine government and the Falklands. Furthermore, Carrington had not made sure that the Foreign and Commonwealth Office had sufficiently understood what was happening in the South Atlantic before the invasion of the islands. This may be a harsh judgement on his part in those events, for there were complex political confusions in the Thatcher government. There was a complete failure by the Joint Intelligence Committee in London to understand what was happening in the months preceding the invasion. There was, too, a failure by the British Embassy in Buenos Aires to warn London sufficiently of the Argentine intentions. Carrington could not be expected to have control over those circumstances and events. Yet he insisted on resigning because he felt it the honourable thing to do; and his resignation was accepted because it made political sense.

Thus ended the political career of the Carrington dynasty, which had lasted almost two hundred years. It was a dynasty that had risen from country banker via royal confidant to national figure. Most of all, it had represented the end of the British historical concept of a ruling dynasty that was often more influential than the monarchs its members served. It was, in simple terms, the end of a dynastic system that assumed not only the right to rule, but also the duty to do so.

NOTES

1 Baron Carrington of Bulcot Lodge (Ireland) and the following year, 1797, Baron Carrington of Upton, Nottinghamshire.
2 However, the surname Carington was not finally confirmed by Royal Licence until 1880.
3 Quarterings are the coats of arms which show the marriages into a family of an heiress.
4 The 7th Marquess of Cholmondeley is the present holder of the office. Whoever is Lord Carrington when a new monarch takes the throne will become Lord Great Chamberlain. This presents an interesting constitutional point in the twenty-first century. Since the House of Lords has been reformed to exclude all but carefully selected hereditary peers, the successor to Peter Carington, the 6th Baron Carrington, would have no seat in the Upper House. However, at this time the 7th Baron might well be entitled to a seat because of his office in the royal household.
5 Now the Old War Office.
6 MPs were not paid until the twentieth century.
7 The 3rd Lord Carrington (1843–1928), private papers, Bledlow.
8 Carrington private papers.

9 Prime Minister 1894–5.

10 Carrington private papers, Bledlow.

11 *Reynolds' News*, February 1870.

12 The Duchess of Connaught was Princess Louise Margaret of Prussia, the wife of the Duke of Connaught who was Prince Albert, Queen Victoria's third son.

13 These hereditary titles lapsed at his death in 1928 because his only son had been killed in 1915.

14 Christopher Hibbert, *Edward VII*, J. P. Lippincott Company, New York, 1976.

15 In 1938 the government made a compulsory purchase of 725 acres at Crichel Down in Dorset. After World War II, the Agricultural Ministry (in which Carrington was a junior minister) refused to let the owners buy back the property. A public inquiry in 1954 forced the Ministry to back down. Sir Thomas Dugdale, Carrington's boss, resigned. Churchill refused Carrington's resignation.

16 William Vassall was an Admiralty clerk convicted of spying in 1962.

FURTHER READING

BLAKE, Robert, *The Conservative Party*, Heinemann, 1970 (revised 1997).

CARRINGTON, Lord, *Reflect on Things Past*, Collins, 1988.

WOODWARD, Llewellyn, *The Age of Reform*, OUP, 1962.

CHAPTER SEVENTEEN

THE NEW DYNASTIES

The intriguing questions of the new millennium are these. Who are the powerful dynasties of modern times? Which families continue the tradition of dynastical power at the highest levels? Indeed, what do we now understand by 'power'?

It is right to point to the Cecils and see, for example, the influence of certainly two marquesses of Salisbury during the twentieth century. At its outset the 3rd Marquess, Robert Arthur Talbot Gascoyne-Cecil, was still Prime Minister; he was the last statesman to hold that office and govern from the House of Lords. Immediately after the Second World War the 5th Marquess, 'Bobbity' Salisbury, was leader of the opposition in the Lords, commonly a not very stimulating appointment. But it was this Cecil who devised the so-called Salisbury Convention which declared that an opposition in the Lords should not block legislation which had been heralded in a government's election manifesto. It was perhaps the most constructive contribution to the constitutional power of the second chamber that century. At the end of the century it was the youngest of the Cecil parliamentarians, Robert Cranborne, who worked in the shadows of the Lords' reform debate and, until the new Conservative leader William Hague clipped his political wings, formed a reasonable and to most peers acceptable arrangement for the future of that place.

There are others, for example the Boyd-Carpenters, whom we find dotted about the senior echelons of Whitehall and the military. Sir Archibald Boyd-Carpenter was an MP; so was his son, John, who became Conservative Chief Secretary to the Treasury and Paymaster General before being given a life peerage in 1972. His daughter, Sarah, married into the celebrated family of Lord Hailsham. Her husband was Douglas Hogg, sometime Minister of Agriculture, and as Sarah Hogg she was an influential Downing Street adviser and respected economics journalist. In 1995 she too went to the House of Lords as a life baroness. The Jays and their extended family are connected through the media and politics, though not always on the same side. Baroness Jay is the daughter of a former Prime Minister, James Callaghan. Her ex-husband, Peter Jay, was ambassador to Washington and economics editor of the BBC. His father was Lord (Douglas) Jay, the sometime Labour minister. Indirectly they are related to the Bottomleys: both Virginia and her husband, Peter, have been Conservative ministers.

Clearly there are many examples of mini-dynasties in the late twentieth and early twenty-first centuries. Yet there is no sense that they will survive as great influencers as did, for example, the Cecils. Perhaps, wrongly, the temptation to look for spectacular schemers is too great. This story has been full of people who could truly change the course of British history; some lost their way, others their heads, none our interest. Perhaps the greater truth is that the power of the dynasties, with a couple of exceptions, had faded by the end of the eighteenth century. It is hardly a new notion that the influence of the British aristocracy had become diluted by that period.

Until the 1700s, the nobility had by and large ruled England: most monarchs had survived courtesy of the barons, earls and dukes. It is clear that, even when factions of peers squabbled, it was for influence over the governance of these islands. However much a monarch might exploit his or her right and belief in absolutism, in the concept that the king or queen should have absolute power, the reality was that the long-term power lay in the hands of the barons. The success of a ruler would in retrospect be judged by the way in which that monarch had exploited, controlled and, in some cases, usurped the power of the aristocracy.

Until the late seventeenth century, Parliament only assembled when the monarch called it together – the period of the Commonwealth was the obvious exception. The monarch usually called Parliament because he wanted money, either to support a lifestyle or to wage war. The erosion of this right was the barons' doing, not that of the people. For much of the time, the barons attempted to establish parliamentary rule as opposed to absolutism on behalf of themselves; most certainly not for the good of the people.

From this concept we can see that, as Parliament removed power from the monarch to its own Houses, the Commons and the Lords, it was also beginning a second transition, that of removing power from the aristocracy to the House of Commons. Thus the gathering of parliamentary authority following, as just one example, the establishment of a first minister – later, in the early eighteenth century, to be known as a prime minister – reinforced the authority of Parliament. The emergence of proper Cabinet government, even though it tended to be aristocratically based, enhanced this authority. As slowly universal franchise and suffrage succeeded the system of patronage, so the holders of office gradually became more accountable not to the aristocracy and the great dynasties, but to the so-called people. With the erosion of the monarch's power came the realization that the great families' inherited authority was also disappearing.

Furthermore, the expansion of industry and commerce, the diversification of resources and the expansion of empire in the nineteenth century distracted many members of dynasties. There was simply more for people to do, wider horizons across which power could be exercised. It is true that colonial exploitation and exploration had been part of the great English adventure since the sixteenth century. But it was the phenomenal imperial expansion, together with the industrial and financial revolution of the late eighteenth and the whole of the nineteenth centuries that diverted families which in past times had plotted and plundered in the corridors of Whitehall and royal palaces.

Moreover, by the late nineteenth century a new aristocracy was emerging. The middle classes who had blossomed and made good in the industrial revolution, had a peculiarly British attitude to success. German engineers and industrialists, for example, made their fortunes and then sent their sons into the workshops and on to the shop floors to learn the skills of their fathers, so that they could become even richer and more successful; but their British counterparts had a different ambition for their sons. They saw their accumulated wealth as an opportunity to scale the British class system and so, instead of sending their sons into the factories, they sent them to the public schools (which is why so many were founded in the second half of the nineteenth century), then to the universities, then to the boardrooms. Here, perhaps, was a reflection of the fact that the British – partly because of the country's class system – never exploited the industrial genius of the nineteenth century.

By the twentieth century there were plenty of aristocrats – more than ever before – but the power of the aristocracy was no more. The individual would always succeed on the principle of 'It's not who you know, but who knows you.' Where, then, were the new power brokers? Most obviously they were to be found among the ranks of the most influential area of twentieth-century history, the media.

Max Aitken was born in 1879 in Maple, Ontario. He came from no powerful family – his father was a minister in the Presbyterian Church; yet by the time he was thirty, Aitken was a millionaire. The money did not come from newspapers, although the way he made it certainly got on to the Canadian front pages. By the turn of the century Aitken had become a stockbroker and then very wisely engineered a deal in an ostensibly boring industry – cement. In 1910 he contrived the amalgamation of some Canadian cement mills and made a fortune. He then emigrated to Britain. As a citizen of a dominion he was able to stand for Parliament, and in 1911 became an MP. Immediately he was appointed private secretary to Andrew Bonar Law, who had that year become the Conservative opposition leader and would go on to be Colonial Secretary in the first part of the Great War coalition government. In 1916 Lloyd George formed his War Cabinet, and Bonar Law became Chancellor of the Exchequer. In 1922 and 1923 Bonar Law was Prime Minister, albeit one of the less notable holders of that office. Nevertheless, Max Aitken had taken political tuition from a sound practitioner. Towards the end of the First World War Lloyd George made Aitken Minister for Information. By then, Aitken had been created Baron Beaverbrook.

The following year, Beaverbrook started to reshape popular daily journalism in the British Isles. He bought the *Daily Express*. Here was a vehicle for his immense belief that what mattered in British life, and should matter in the thinking of the British political mind, was the greatness of the Empire. Beaverbrook, a son of that imperial history, was not simply full of nostalgia but saw the Empire as an enormous source of world influence, which then it was: it could still account for much of the world's trade, natural resources and commerce.

At the beginning of the century, when Beaverbrook was making his money in North America, he could see a Britain which accounted for some 30 per cent of world trade. Perhaps half of the global fleet in which trade was carried was registered in Britain, and the majority of insurances and reinsurances went through the City of London. Beaverbrook lobbied government and industry in a vain hope that these figures would not slide towards the increasingly successful and, from Beaverbrook's point of view, intrusive emerging nations of Germany, Japan and America; thus he needed the biggest platform he could find. The *Daily Express*, which had first been published in 1900, and the *Sunday Express*, which he founded in 1921, were to become a gigantic soapbox for Beaverbrook's views. Together, these newspapers would have the largest circulation of any in the world at that time. In 1929 Beaverbrook added to the stable by buying the *London Evening Standard*. From this time, with the symbol of the crusader at its masthead, the Beaverbrook propaganda machine relentlessly campaigned for its owner's utter belief that the success of Britain would rely entirely on a government policy of what was called Empire Free Trade. And until the 1960s, the Beaverbrook press was second to none.

Churchill took to Beaverbrook and his ideas. Most of all, he took to the Canadian's personality and determination that made things happen. So, when Churchill became wartime Prime Minister, he made Beaverbrook his Minister of Supply. The task was straightforward: Britain needed aircraft, and Beaverbrook was to make sure that they were built. It is debatable whether the newspaperman was the enormous success people sometimes imagine him to have been, yet no one has ever doubted his reputation as one of the great newspaper barons of the century, and certainly as one of the most influential figures.

For example, during the Abdication Crisis of 1936 and 1937 it was Beaverbrook, along with the other press magnate of the day, Alfred Harmsworth, who gathered together the editors of national and important regional newspapers and ordered them to tell no more than was absolutely necessary about the affair of Edward VIII and Mrs Simpson. Remember, everyone but the British public knew what was going on between the couple. Those who read overseas newspapers would have had a fair idea, but there was a general agreement in the British press that it was not in the public interest to print the story for as long as it could reasonably be suppressed. The newspaper editors met at Warwick House in St James's, where Beaverbrook and Harmsworth took charge and told them to print only the bare details. This was a degree of self-regulation that could never be hoped for today. The Duke of Windsor, writing in *A King's Story* a decade later, has this to say about that Warwick House meeting: 'With the cooperation of Harmsworth & several others he [Beaverbrook] achieved the miracle I desired – a "gentlemen's agreement" among newspaper editors to report the case without sensation. The British Press kept its word & for that I shall always be grateful....'

Beaverbrook never expected anything but obedience to his wishes, and those who worked for him perfectly understood this. Most of them thoroughly enjoyed the feudal concept of journalism. A newspaper is vulnerable to wishy-washy editorial policy; strong, but equally good, leadership breeds success in any industry, particularly the newspaper business where it properly inspires its journalism. The synergy of Beaverbrook's personality and the times during which he owned the *Daily Express* and *Sunday Express*, produced one of the most remarkable platforms of influence witnessed in the twentieth century. Beaverbrook was ever present in the minds of his reporters, editors and readers. A telephone call at two in the morning to a backbench editor would revamp a whole leader column or front page. 'This is what you've gotta write' became a familiar phrase in the black smoked glass building in Fleet Street. Wherever in the world there was a story, Beaverbrook's editors would send not just one person but a whole team of reporters and photographers to cover it. The papers' writers and editors became legends.

When Beaverbrook died in 1964 (the year before Churchill), the decline of his empire began. His son, the young Max Aitken, refused to take his father's title. In the Second World War he had been an admired fighter pilot; his friends were faster than his father would have encouraged, his life altogether more glamorous. His personality could never match that of his father, and his influence on the papers could never be as strong.

His leadership also coincided with a great change in the British newspaper industry: the challenge of television was perhaps exaggerated; the economics of newspaper printing were not. In the 1970s the *Express*'s great rival, the *Daily Mail*, was revitalized. The *Mail* had two enormous assets. First, it had a new editor, the young David English (recently poached from the *Daily Express*), who was to become one of the toughest editors seen in Fleet Street during the second half of the twentieth century. He combined that discipline with a genius for journalism. The second part of the *Daily Mail* formula was that English had at his shoulder one of the last of the great newspaper barons, Vere Harmsworth. It was a formidable combination which would gradually eat into the old Beaverbrook empire until the latter became a less than significant player in the uncompromising war that left Fleet Street a thoroughfare of journalistic ghosts.

The Harmsworths (who became the Rothermeres and the Northcliffes) made up one twentieth-century dynasty. The 1st Viscount Northcliffe was born Alfred Charles William Harmsworth in 1865 in Chapelizod, Dublin. The family soon moved to London, where Harmsworth took to journalism even before he had left school. During his holidays he got a job reporting for the local newspaper – his sense of style might have been remarked on because he wrote the gossip column for the school magazine.

In the 1880s George Newnes, the founder of another famous publishing house, started a magazine called *Titbits*; it was, and would remain for more than a century, one of the most popular magazines in Britain. In 1888, in an attempt to imitate *Titbits*, Harmsworth and his brother Harold started their own magazine, *Answers to Correspondents.* It was not an enormous success. However, Harmsworth was not discouraged. He spotted a new market and in 1890 began to publish a children's paper called *Comic Cuts.* Showing a sense of business acumen that would remain with the family, Harmsworth realized that a rival could easily come along and start something similar. So Harmsworth did exactly that: he set up his own rival comic, called *Chips.* He always believed that if there was going to be any competition it was going to come from himself, and he would leave the rest to the accountants. Two years later, in 1896, Harmsworth, having looked at the American newspaper market, started another paper in London; this was the *Daily Mail.* Showing once again how they understood markets as well as journalism, the two brothers decided that there was room for a paper that would look at the world from a woman's points of view. So in 1903 they launched the first daily newspaper in Britain aimed at the female market, the *Daily Mirror.*

Alfred Harmsworth demonstrated that the family had wise commercial instincts as well as journalistic ones when he began to buy enormous tracts of timber in Canada. Very soon the family had its own forest to provide the pulp to produce newsprint at the cheapest possible price. In 1908 Harmsworth, by now Viscount Northcliffe, bought what was to be, for the moment at least, his flagship. Much to the surprise of the newspaper world as well as the City, he bought the *Times* and decided to use it as a platform for his own political ambitions. Using a newspaper in this way would never work for Beaverbrook, and it did not for Northcliffe.

The other Harmsworth, Northcliffe's slightly younger brother Harold, became the 1st Viscount Rothermere. He went in a different direction from his brother, both journalistically and politically. Northcliffe had been a bitter enemy of Lloyd George; Rothermere was not. Rothermere fell out with his brother and put most of his efforts into building the circulation of the *Daily Mirror* and launching yet another paper, the *Sunday Pictorial.* When Northcliffe died in 1921 Rothermere got his hands on the *Daily Mail;* it was a formidable newspaper empire.

They were by no means the only family of press barons to emerge in the same period. For example, the Berrys were also a product of late Victorian enterprise. James Gomer Berry was born in 1883 in Merthyr Tydfil and was a newspaper proprietor. He became the 1st Viscount Kemsley and in the 1930s took control of the *Sunday Times.* That too seemed a powerful position from which to influence the political and social thought of the nation.

Another of the magnates, Roy Thomson, a Canadian like Beaverbrook, later bought that same *Sunday Times.* Thomson made his money in the 1930s in the early days of broadcasting. He saw the weakness of the new industry as its lack of sufficiently powerful transmitters and relay stations; sensibly, he built his own transmitter and set up a broadcast station which would one day be the world-famous NBC. By the 1950s, Roy Thomson owned more than thirty Canadian and American newspapers. In 1953 he based himself in Edinburgh and bought *The Scotsman.* By the end of that decade he had truly become a press baron and a television station owner − which he likened to a licence to print money. He bought out the Kemsleys (which is when he got the *Sunday Times*) and then passed on his empire to his son Kenneth. A new dynasty was born.

The lesson of the four newspaper baronies – the Rothermeres, the Northcliffes, the Kemsleys and the Thomsons – is that, powerful as they were, these dynasties could not stand alongside the great families we have seen so far. It is true that they could wield great influence because every day of the year and, with the arrival of broadcasting, every hour of every day, they could reach the masses who voted governments in and out. Yet too often the power of the written press has been exaggerated. Certainly in the eighteenth century, with the example of Wilkes's *North Briton*, there was no doubting the constant drip of vitriol. In equal measure it annoyed those whom it was intended to annoy and encouraged those for whom it fought. When the *Spectator* in the early nineteenth century lampooned the monarch's concern for his pet giraffe, everyone (with the exception of some serious authors) understood that the journal was attacking one of King George's lady friends. Newspapers – or, in some cases, the lack of them – have most certainly been fundamental to the sensitivities of social and political life in all countries. In 1903, the would-be Russian revolutionaries started *Iskra*, which in 1912 became the Bolshevik newspaper, *Pravda* ('truth'). In 1917, Stalin and Molotov joined the board and tried to ban Lenin's writing – they thought it too wild. To tell the people of twentieth-century Britain the truth seemed a fundamental obligation that society had to support. Therefore, the newspaper dynasties perhaps became the closest imitators of the power brokers we have followed from the tenth to the nineteenth centuries.

Today, perhaps the most powerful newspapers are the financial journals. The pink analysis of corporate affairs at international level will easily reflect the true state of a nation and influence its future. The white pages act at best as a barometer, but rarely as the epicentre of the political and social weather front. So where now lies the power that past dynasties manipulated?

What distinguished the twentieth century from those before is a sense that power is less obviously wielded. Universal suffrage suggests that the power of the modern state is held by the people. Yet, more accurately, we might think that the people have power within their grasp – nothing more. The power of earlier dynasties was great enough to change the course of British history. No dynasty has that today. People can change the smallest footnote by their demonstration of unease or anger, but just as Wat Tyler did not change much, nor did, for example, the protesters of the Campaign for Nuclear Disarmament. Indeed CND demonstrated the scale of the difference between the way of past influence and that of today. Events which conspire to drag a nation to war, or a government to political disunity, or even a decade to economic decline – and then the next to social and economic recovery – are, on deeper analysis, often beyond the power of the individuals who govern.

The monarchy no longer has any powers other than to inspire tepid debate about its future. Government has power to vary the taxes we pay; MPs no longer have effective power to quiz the executive on its performance and the way in which it spends our money. The people certainly have the power to vote governments in and out; yet a sitting tenant of Downing Street loses an election. An opposition no longer has such a radical programme that it demands to be elected. Those who would contend that the election of the Labour Party in 1997 contradicts this view might remember that most of its policies were also those of the existing Conservative government. The question was this: who was better able to manage those policies?

Given the influence of European legislation, the function of a British government is more to manage the estate as if it were some medieval earldom. In the Middle Ages, every so often the monarch would summon his barons to demand changes in the way the shires were administered, to trade favours and ultimately to bargain for more money to carry out his greater ambitions. For medieval monarch, read Brussels; so, the twenty-first-century earldorman is there to protect his fiefdom against the interests of absolutism. We rely almost solely on the media to bring us some details of this affair. Yet the daily barkings of our national watchdogs reflect rather than determine power.

The great dynasties have at various times emerged to exercise their sometimes radical influence. The Cecils and the Waldegraves are ready examples. Others not mentioned have been in and out of modest office for centuries. There is a small group of dynasties who have sat in Parliament since its early forms without ever coming to public notice – whatever that should mean. The Edgcumbes, for instance have been fighting military and political battles since the 1400s.

An Edgcumbe became the MP for Plymouth in 1447, and from that century, there was an Edgcumbe in Parliament for thirteen generations. They represented Devon and Cornwall constituencies as MPs, and then sat and spoke in the House of Lords. The first Edgcumbe MP was William; the last Edgcumbe was also a William, the member for Plymouth between 1859 and 1861. He then went to the Lords as the 4th Earl of Edgcumbe. The last Edgcumbe to sit in Parliament was the 6th Earl of Mount Edgcumbe, who left the House of Lords in 1945 – all but five hundred years after the first member of the family had taken his seat.

The family had never been far from the centre of power, even though their influence was mainly unremarked. Sir Richard, who was MP for Tavistock and died in 1489, fought at the Battle of Bosworth Field in 1485 on the side of the Earl of Richmond, Henry Tudor, against Richard III and was knighted for his valour. His grandson, also Richard, built the family house, Mount Edgcumbe in Plymouth, which was, according to the actor David Garrick, the haunt of the muses. Later, the barony and earldoms would be styled 'Edgcumbe of Mount Edgcumbe'. The 1st Baron, created in 1742, was a Whig MP in Cornwall and Chancellor of the Duchy of Lancaster. The 2nd Baron was comptroller of the Royal Household. The 1st Earl of Mount Edgcumbe, created in 1781, was an admiral, Whig MP and Treasurer of the Royal Household. The 3rd Earl was a courtier to both William IV and Queen Victoria and the 4th Earl was Lord

Chamberlain. And so continued the high and sometimes discreet offices of the Edgcumbe family; like so many of the dynasties always ready with a cupped hand at the elbow of the English monarchy and the power of government.

In truth, fewer than three thousand families appear to have governed these islands during the past thousand years. Most of them have, outside their immediate circles, been quite unknown to the people they governed. Moreover, the majority of those families have never held great office and yet have been about seats of government either nationally or locally when their vote or their alliance was called on.

Interestingly, none of the families we have looked at in the preceding chapters are new members of the aristocracy. The Carringtons just sneak into this category of old families, but only just. The American historian, Ellis Wasson, has observed that seven out of ten of the grandee families between 1660 and the outbreak of World War I in 1914 got their titles in medieval times. Only twelve 'new' families emerged in the 1600s and only half that number during the following hundred years.[1]

Most of these families fall into the category of those who have exercised quiet influence, with occasional interludes of political and military rowdyism. They are members of the small band of rarely noticed political activists who have been in and out of the governance of Britain for centuries without making many headlines, yet have always been worthy footnotes in that history.

For centuries in these islands the nomenklatura has made up something less than two per cent of the population. When that population was smaller than a couple of million it was so; centuries on, when the population had risen to more than 56 million, it was still governed by fewer than two per cent of the nation. From reeve to monarch and in more modern times from parish councillor to prime minister, the pattern of power has not much altered. Even in small villages, the dynasties have ruled. They may have had little grandness and simple tombstones, but in some sense the yeoman dynasties have been as powerful in their own domains as the Mortimers and the Howards – and they have kept their heads.

NOTES
1 Ellis Wasson, *Born to Rule*, Sutton, 2000.

FURTHER READING
CLARKE, Peter, *Hope and Glory*, Penguin, 1996.
LEE, Christopher, *This Sceptred Isle – Twentieth Century*, BBC/Penguin, 2001.

THE BRITISH MONARCHY

Monarch	Born	Acceded	Died
SAXON AND DANISH			
Egbert		827	839
Aethelwulf		839	858
Aethelbald		858	860
Aethelbert		858	865
Aethelred		865	871
Alfred the Great	849	871	899
Edward the Elder	870	899	924
Aethelstan	895	924	939
Edmund	921	939	946
Eadred		946	955
Eadwig	before 943	955	959
Edgar	943	959	975
Edward the Martyr	c.962	975	978
Aethelred II ('the Unready')	c.968–9	978	1016
Edmund Ironside	before 993	1016	1016
Cnut	c.995	1017	1035
Harold I (Harefoot)	c.1016–17	1035	1040
Harthacnut	c.1018	1040	1042
Edward the Confessor	c.1002–5	1042	1066
Harold II (Godwineson)	c.1020	1066	1066
NORMAN			
William I ('the Conqueror')	c.1027–8	1066	1087
William II	c.1056–60	1087	1100
Henry I	1068	1100	1135
Stephen	by 1100	1135	1154

Monarch	Born	Acceded	Died
ANGEVIN			
Henry II	1133	1154	1189
Richard I	1157	1189	1199
John	1167	1199	1216
PLANTAGENET			
Henry III	1207	1216	1272
Edward I	1239	1272	1307
Edward II	1284	1307	*dep.* Jan 1327
			died Sept 1327
Edward III	1312	1327	1377
Richard II	1367	1377	*dep.* Sept 1399
			died Feb 1400
Henry IV	1366	1399	1413
Henry V	1387	1413	1422
Henry VI	1421	1422	*dep.* March 1461
		restored Oct 1470	*dep.* April 1471
			died May 1471
Edward IV	1442	1461	*dep.* Oct 1470
		restored April 1471	*died* April 1483
Edward V	1470	1483	1483
Richard III	1452	1483	1485
TUDOR			
Henry VII	1457	1485	1509
Henry VIII	1491	1509	1547
Edward VI	1537	1547	1553
Jane	1537	1553	1554
Mary I	1516	1553	1558
Elizabeth I	1533	1558	1603
STUART			
James I (VI of Scotland)	1566	1603	1625
Charles I	1600	1625	*beheaded* 1649
COMMONWEALTH (DECLARED 19 MAY 1649)			
Oliver Cromwell, Lord Protector		1653–8	—
Richard Cromwell, Lord Protector		1658–9	—

Monarch	Born	Acceded	Died
STUART (RESTORATION)			
Charles II	1630	*restored* 1660	1685
James II (VII of Scotland)	1633	1685	*dep.* Dec 1688
			died Sept 1701
Interregnum 11 December 1688 to 13 February 1689			
William II	1650	1689	1702
and Mary II	1662	1689	1694
Anne	1665	1702	1714
HANOVER			
George I	1660	1714	1727
George II	1683	1727	1760
George III	1738	1760	1820
George IV★	1762	1820	1830
William IV	1765	1830	1837
Victoria	1819	1837	1901
SAXE-COBURG			
Edward VII	1841	1901	1910
WINDSOR			
George V	1865	1910	1936
Edward VIII	1894	Jan 1936	*abdicated* Dec 1936
			died 1972
George VI	1895	1936	1952
Elizabeth II	1926	1952	

★*George IV was declared Regent on 5 February 1811*

INDEX